Critical Heidegger

The eleven essays in *Critical Heidegger* first appeared in the much admired, four volume set, *Martin Heidegger: Critical Assessments*, also edited by Christopher Macann. *Critical Heidegger* brings together in a more accessible form a selection of the best work on Martin Heidegger from a number of key commentators working in Europe. Many of the essays are translated from German and French originals – not previously available in the English language – and are an essential guide to the current European reception of Heidegger. The work presented in *Critical Heidegger* represents the future of Heidegger studies and will have a considerable impact on English-language Heidegger studies.

Essays in this collection include:

- *Marlène Zarader*, 'The mirror with the triple reflection';
- *Franco Volpi*, 'Dasein and *praxis*: Aristotle';
- *Jean-Luc Marion*, 'Heidegger on Descartes';
- *Christopher Macann*, 'Heidegger's Kant interpretation';
- *Michael Haar*, 'Critical remarks on the Heideggerian reading of Nietzsche';
- *Maria Villela-Petit*, 'Heidegger's conception of space';
- *Françoise Dastur*, 'The ekstatico-horizonal constitution of temporality';
- *F-W von Herrmann*, 'Way and method in philosophy';
- *Samuel IJsseling*, 'The end of philosophy as the commencement of thinking';
- *Otto Pöggeler*, 'Does the saving power also grow? Heidegger's last paths';
- *Ernst Tugendhat*, 'Heidegger's idea of truth';
- *Karl-Otto Apel*, 'Wittgenstein and Heidegger'.

Christopher Macann is Professor of Philosophy at Regent's College, London. He undertook his doctoral work under Paul Ricoeur in Paris, since which much of his professional career has been spent in America. He is the author of *Kant and the Foundations of Metaphysics* (1981) and *Presence and Coincidence* (1990), as well as *Four Phenomenological Philosophers: Husserl, Heidegger, Sartre, Merleau-Ponty* (1993). He also edited *Martin Heidegger: Critical Assessments* (1992). *Four Phenomenological Philosophers* and the four volume Heidegger collection were both published by Routledge.

Critical Heidegger

Edited by Christopher Macann

London and New York

First published 1996
by Routledge
11 New Fetter Lane, London EC4P 4EE

Simultaneously published in the USA and Canada
by Routledge
29 West 35th Street, New York, NY 10001

Phototypeset in Times by Intype, London
Printed and bound in Great Britain by TJ Press (Padstow) Ltd,
Padstow, Cornwall

British Library Cataloguing in Publication Data
A catalogue record for this book is available from the British Library

Library of Congress Cataloguing in Publication Data
A catalogue record for this book has been requested

ISBN 0–415–12949–4 (hbk)
ISBN 0–415–12950–8 (pbk)

Contents

Acknowledgements

Karl-Otto Apel 'Wittgenstein and Heidegger: language games and life forms'. Originally published in *Philosophisches Jarhbuch* (Freiburg), vol. 75, 1, Halbband (1967), then reprinted in *Heidegger* by Otto Pöggeler (ed.), Berlin (1969). Translated from the German by Christopher Macann and reprinted by kind permission of the author.

Françoise Dastur 'The ekstatico-horizonal constitution of temporality'. First published in *Heidegger Studies*, vol. 2 as 'La constitution ekstatique-horizontale de la temporalité' and rewritten by the author for this collection.

Michael Haar 'Critical remarks on the Heideggerian reading of Nietzsche'. Original piece written for this collection and published by kind permission of the author.

Samuel IJsseling 'The end of philosophy as the commencement of thinking'. First published as 'Das Ende der Philosophie als Anfang des Denkens' in *Heidegger et l'Idée de la Phénoménologie* by F. Volpi (ed.), Kluwer Academic (1988) and translated by Christopher Macann. Reproduced here by kind permission of the author and editor.

Christopher Macann 'Heidegger's Kant interpretation'. Original piece written for the collection.

Jean-Luc Marion 'Heidegger and Descartes'. First published in the *Revue de Métaphysique et de Morale* (1987) as 'Heidegger et Descartes'. Translated by Christopher Macann and reproduced here by kind permission of the author and editor.

Otto Pöggeler 'Does the saving power also grow? Heidegger's last paths'. Translated from the German by Henry Pickford and reprinted by kind permission of the author and translator.

Ernst Tugendhat 'Heidegger's idea of truth'. Originally published as 'Heideggers Idee von Wahrheit' in *Heidegger* by Otto Pöggeler (ed.),

Berlin (1969). Translated from the German by Christopher Macann and published by kind permission of the author.

Maria Villela-Petit 'Heidegger's conception of space'. First published as 'L'espace chez Heidegger. Quelques repères' in *Etudes Philosophiques* and extensively rewritten by the author for this collection.

Franco Volpi 'Dasein as *praxis*: the Heideggerian assimilation and the radicalization of the practical philosophy of Aristotle'. First published as 'Dasein comme praxis' in *Heidegger et l'Idée de la Phénoménologie* by F. Volpi (ed.), Kluwer Academic (1988) and translated by Christopher Macann. Reprinted by kind permission of the author and editor.

Friedrich-Wilhelm von Herrmann 'Way and method: hermeneutic phenomenology in the thinking of the history of being'. First published as 'Weg und Methode: zur hermeneutischen Phänomenologie des seinsgeschichtlichen Denkens' by Vittorio Klostermann, Frankfurt a/m (1990) and translated by Parvis Emad. Reproduced here by kind permission of the author, the translator and the publisher.

Marlène Zarader 'The Mirror with the triple reflection'. First published in the *Revue de Philosophie Ancienne* no. 1 (1986) as 'Le mirroir aux trois reflets' and translated by Cozette Griffin-Kremer. Reproduced here by kind permission of the author.

Introduction

Christopher Macann

In the four volume collection of articles on Martin Heidegger published in Routledge's *Critical Assessments* series, I apparently exceeded my brief. Instead of simply reprinting the best material on Heidegger which had already appeared in English, I allowed myself the liberty of translating a great deal of excellent work from the French and the German and, furthermore, of commissioning a number of original pieces. The result: more than half of the material in the hardback edition cannot be found anywhere else in English. It is this 'misunderstanding' which explains the present paperback edition.

Although all the pieces reprinted in this edition either started life in the four volume collection or began a new life in English in that collection, there was still so much material to choose from that, inevitably, some hard decisions had to be made. Not surprisingly, most of the pieces in this reprint are drawn from volumes I and II, the volumes devoted to Heidegger's philosophy and to his interpretation of historical philosophers.

As we approach the end of the century, it is inevitable that philosophers should ask themselves the question: what next? For a century that opened in a blaze of intellectual glory, it appears to be closing not with a bang but a whimper. To take only philosophy: the century opened, on the continental side, with the dual triumph of Husserl's phenomenology and Bergson's vitalism. On the Anglo-Saxon side, Russell's transformation of logic led to an analytical tradition fortified by the resources of a powerful symbolic methodology while, across the ocean, American pragmatism was still producing some of its most impressive writings.

While phenomenology moved from strength to strength – not only through the various phases of Husserl's own development, but also through the work of such original successors as Scheler, Heidegger, Sartre and Merleau-Ponty – analytical philosophy also demonstrated a fertility and versatility of its own. Moore's common sense realism contrasts radically with the logical positivism of Russell, early Wittgenstein and then later on, Ayer or Quine, while Wittgenstein's later work led in the direction of a 'linguistic revolution' which, at the hands of Austin, Strawson,

Hampshire, Ryle and then later on, Anscombe and Searle, temporarily appeared to have transformed the entire conception of the discipline. By this time the divergence between the Anglo-Saxon and the continental tradition had grown so great that communication had become virtually impossible. This communicative *impasse* seemed only to confirm the conviction, held on both sides, that each tradition held the key to the truth or to some fairly conclusive method for the resolution of outstanding philosophical questions and problems.

Things then began to fall apart. On the analytic side, the transformation of the question 'What is *x*?' into the alternative question 'How is the concept of *x* employed in everyday discourse?' appeared to be leading in the direction of ever more vacuous and trivial semantic pursuits. The development of the science of logic proceeded unabated, but in so technical a manner as to cut this remarkable development off, ever more, from the traditional concerns of philosophy. On the continental side, the first break with the substantive enquiries of phenomenology (both transcendental and existential) and neo-Hegelianism came with structuralism, which then yielded pride of place to deconstructivism and then, later on still, to relativism and pluralism.

Two central considerations can be seen to have guided this 'destructive' development. First, the *medium* of philosophy has become its *topic*, and this in two essentially different ways. Ordinary language philosophy took discourse, the *spoken language*, as its theme while deconstructivism focused upon the text, i.e. *written language*. The shift in emphasis from what is expressed to an examination of the medium through which it is expressed finds its parallel in the art where, in music, sounds themselves, and in painting, colours themselves, have come to be the central concern of their respective arts – to the point where three minutes of silence or a blank canvas can actually figure as a work of art!

Second, features of the general philosophical enterprise which have always been regarded as a part of the *secondary* task of critical assessment have now been promoted to the status of a *primary* task, indeed as the only legitimate task remaining to philosophy today. That philosophers should be careful in the use of terms (since language is the medium of philosophy), particularly in the selection of those central terms which have often been designated as fundamental categories, is something which has never been in dispute. But never before has the *whole* task of philosophy been regarded as reducible to conceptual analysis – as it is with 'linguistic philosophy'. That the task of the philosophical critic consists, in part, of the identification of inconsistencies and contradictions in the works of those figures whose thinking is under investigation has never been in dispute. But never before has the *whole* task of philosophy been conceived as the identification of just such inconsistencies and contradictions, indeed as the identification of such crucial contradictions as can be said to underlie, and therefore to justify, a wholesale dismissal of the entire tradition of Western philosophy – as it is with 'deconstructivism'. That the task of the historian of philosophy consists, in part, of situating the thinking of a given philosopher in the social and intellectual context out of which his thinking emerged has never been in dispute. But never before has the *whole* task of philosophy been conceived as the establishment of the contextual character of philosophical thinking – as it is with 'relativism'. That at any given time a multiplicity of different positions will be assumed by philosophers of differing persuasion has never been in dispute. But never before has the *whole* task of philosophy been conceived as the justification of just such a plurality – as it is with 'pluralism'.

The legitimacy of a shift in the focus of philosophical attention from the substantive issues with which philosophers have grappled through the centuries to linguistic or meta-theoretical investigations appears to draw some justification from the intellectual sophistication with which these new investigations have been conducted. However, even here signs of deterioration are evident. On the analytical side, intellectual sophistication often assumes the form of 'technical' sophistry. Formal logic often features as the instrumental *modus operandi* and the indisputable success of contemporary technology is taken as confirmation of the legitimacy of this approach. On the continental side, intellectual sophistication has often come to assume the form of 'rhetorical' refinement. Word plays of excruciating nicety and aesthetically pleasing linguistic flourishes often take the place of substantive enquiries.

An intellectually sophisticated, but philosophically uninformed, observer of these developments would be forgiven for supposing that a part of the reason for this redirection of philosophical attention might have to do with the absence today of any distinctively human themes which press, urgently and unavoidably, upon those of us whose very disciplinary nomenclature calls us to be 'lovers of wisdom'. In order to assess this claim, an interesting parallel may be drawn with the situation at the end of the last century.

Almost exactly one hundred years ago, Hegelianism, neo-Hegelianism and even Marxism had already lost their authoritative impact. J.S. Mill was already dead and the speculations of Bradley and McTaggart could easily be dismissed as the pale and empirically unwarranted imitation of an already out-dated Hegelianism. It might have seemed at that time as though the great days of philosophy were over, as though philosophy had run its course, to be replaced by the very disciplines to which it had given rise – physics, psychology, sociology, anthropology, mythology, logic, linguistics. A certain *fin de siècle* insouciance prevailed, upheld by the relatively long period of peace and prosperity which the advance of science and technology seemed destined to prolong indefinitely.

Alas! There followed the shattering impact of the wars and revolutions of the first half of the twentieth century, events of such appalling and irrational ferocity as to cancel, at one stroke, the Victorian 'faith' in human progress.

The events of the past fifty years might have given us similar grounds for self-congratulation, especially here in the West. We have enjoyed an extended period of peace and prosperity, albeit, lived out under the ever present threat of the Cold War. The collapse of communism now seems to have brought even that threat to an end. Once again, there seems to be some grounds for indulging in a certain *fin de siécle* insouciance. However, what I would like to suggest is that the carefully researched, sophisticated, often elegant, but also frequently 'irrelevant' philosophical enquiries which hold sway in academia today are taking place at a time when the human species faces a crucial test of its wisdom, perhaps the most critical test with which it has ever been confronted in its entire history.

To quote from my introduction to the first volume in the *Critical Assessments* collection:

> Momentarily, we are congratulating ourselves on the suspension of the Cold War. But this suspension can always itself be suspended. More realistically, the proliferation of nuclear weapons throughout the Third World makes it likely that a nuclear confrontation of some kind is going to take place before very long. In the meantime, the apparent withdrawal of the threat of world war is matched by an equally apparent advance in the scope and scale of local wars, wars whose barbarism surpasses that of the world wars themselves. Countries which, like Peru or Mexico, were historically (the Inca and Aztec empires) always able to feed their people adequately are now unable to provide for a rapidly increasing population despite the resources of agricultural technology (or perhaps because of them). Famine on a scale never before known faces Africa, and epidemics on a scale rarely seen before now confront not only the undeveloped world but its fully industrialized leaders. And even if all these dangers are overcome, or circumvented, by the intelligent use of technology, this very technology threatens to bring with it an environmental destruction for which there exists no parallel in past history.[1]

To these dangers might be added the very evident deterioration of the social contract which upholds the kind of liberal democracy upon which we, in the West, have placed our trust. The breakdown of the family, soaring crime rates, the ever increasing incidence of pathological obsessions and addictions, encouraged and reinforced by a media which has become ever more irresponsible in its quest for higher visibility and audience ratings, are beginning to cast so ominous a shadow over the tone and quality of everyday life that our Western societies are presently turning out, in ever greater abundance, *children* who vandalize, murder and rape.

As we approach not merely the end of the century but the end of a millenium, it must surely be apparent that we are living in times of crisis. In this respect, Heidegger plays a pivotal role – enigmatic and ambiguous as both his life and his later reflections might have been. He lived through the worst, learned from the tragedy in which he himself participated and, in his later work, strove to develop a new kind of 'thinking' which would be more responsive to the spiritual aspirations of humanity. His master, Edmund Husserl (like Jaspers later), was even more personally embroiled in the ideological catastrophe of the 1930s and 1940s and gave to his last great work a title which reflected the depths of his philosophical despair: *Krisis*.

In times of crisis, Nietzsche insisted, philosophers are needed. But surely not to debate the question of the 'end' or the 'closure' of philosophy or to indulge in meta-theoretical assessments of the present philosophical situation; still less to fall back upon a scholarly examination or critical deconstruction of the texts which go to make up what has come to be known as the history of philosophy. If the nation state is no longer a viable social organization, it is surely time to think the overcoming of national divisions. If our technological progress is coming to represent more of a threat than a solution, it is surely time to think the integration of the scientific revolution within a broader frame of reference that acknowledges the more manifold aspirations of human kind. If the materialism characteristic of the 'spirit' of technology is fast undermining the traditional moral restraints, it is surely time to resurrect the spiritual wisdom inherent in the cultural products of a by-gone age. In reaction to the meta-theoretical investigations which preoccupy philosophers today, is this not the moment to revive the time-honoured, phenomenological slogan 'To the things themselves!'?

Yes; but what are the things which should properly engage the attention of philosophers today? In this introduction I can only offer a few proposals.

If science and technology remain the dominant mode of thought, then a philosophy which does not give these things their due is surely doomed to failure. What might broadly be called 'analytic' philosophy has always taken scientific method as its paradigm. And so a philosophical thinking which failed to come to terms with the methods and the goals of analytic philosophy would seem to run the risk of not engaging those very things which presently determine the course and character of human affairs – for better or for worse.

On the other hand, the ontological philosophy of this century was originally conceived as an attempt to get to grips with things themselves in the concrete context of actual life and *against* both the *superficiality* of that instrumental thinking about being to which technology gives rise and the *abstractness* of transcendental phenomenology. But, as I have often tried to point out, transcendental philosophy is also needed both to explain the origin, and indeed the very possibility, of the 'ontological revolution' inaugurated with Heidegger's *Being and Time* and, moreover, to serve as an essential corrective against the 'direct', all too direct, route opened up by what might be called Heidegger's 'ontological regression'.

To put it in other, and more metaphorical, terms; in its laudable effort to react against both the taken for granted superficiality and the technical complexity of what Husserl called the 'natural attitude' and what Heidegger termed the realm of the 'ontic', phenomenological philosophy needs to retain both the depths and the heights. For the higher the heights which are scaled, the deeper the depths which can be plumbed. And the deeper the philosophical foundations are laid, the higher the edifice that can be constructed on that ground. Furthermore, if the (transcendental) heights to be scaled are to stand for something more than just an epistemological exercise, a meta-theoretical reflection upon the unreflected character of our habitual theory and praxis, a new 'spiritual' interpretation of transcendental consciousness is called for, one in the context of which these so-called 'heights' can also attest to a radical transformation in the very being of human being.

There are many signs that such a 'synthetic' vision is on the way, is fighting its way back up against the prevailing currents of technical specialization and life-remoteness. There are so many that it would be impossible to do justice to them in an introduction of this kind. Instead, I would simply like to note that it is in the spirit of conjectures such as these that I have spent the last fifteen years working towards a new contribution to ontological phenomenology. *Being and Becoming* seeks to integrate transcendental and ontological phenomenology on the one side, with phenomenological and analytic philosophy on the other, while at the same time bringing back into philosophy some of the traditional, spiritual questions which preoccupied philosophy for so long but which have temporarily been relegated to the dispensable sphere of 'windy' esotericism or 'logic-chopping' scholaticism.

Such is the secularity of contemporary philosophy that readers might even find these references to 'spirituality', to 'wisdom', to a 'higher' consciousness embarrassing, if not positively offensive. It behoves us to remember that this century has been the most brutal and barbaric century in all recorded history and that the means of destruction presently at our disposal already indicate that without some conception of the possibility, and indeed the necessity, of a profound *spiritual* transformation we are, as a species, doomed. In Heidegger's own words: 'Only a God can save us!'.

Note

1 Macann, C. (1992) 'Introduction' in *Martin Heidegger: Critical Assessments* by C. Macann (ed.), London, Routledge: 14.

1

The mirror with the triple reflection

Marlène Zarader

> . . . Die
> Sternblume, ungeknickt, ging
> zwischen Heimat und Abgrund durch
> dein Gedächtnis.
>
> Paul Celan

These pages have a double objective. In the first place, to show that the way in which Heidegger interprets the pre-Socratics – in consequence, the way in which he understands their relation to later thinking, whether it is a matter of later Greek thinking or of that which stems from the latter – attests to a notable evolution in the course of the work, an evolution in which it is possible to distinguish three distinct periods, each irreducible to the other. In the second place, to show that, no matter what the period in question, the status accorded to the early Greeks carries with it the main lines of Heidegger's thinking at that time, thereby making possible a division of his entire work. These main lines of thought are to be found variously sketched in each of the periods in question; on the one hand, a certain conception of history as well as the manner in which Heidegger himself stands in relation to this history, on the other, a certain conception of being (more exactly, of the question of being), as well as the way in which Heidegger defines the task of thinking with regard to this question.

This double project implies that I stick to the main lines (my objective being precisely to set them out here), letting go of the more detailed analyses – to which I have devoted a more extensive study elsewhere.[1]

I

The first period was that of Marburg. The master work obviously remains *Sein und Zeit*, but the context in which it was developed can now be brought to light more clearly since we are now in possession of several lectures given by Heidegger during the years 1923–8.[2]

What is the status he attaches to the earliest Greek thinkers? The first point to note is that, in Heidegger's view, no break can be made between the pre-Socratics and Plato. Thought through in a fundamental continuity, they are for the most part characterized by an undifferentiated plural: 'The Greeks'. This is because, at this time, Heidegger was most concerned with what separated 'the Greeks' from the rest; though even here it is not possible to talk of a break, in the strict sense of that word. What is regarded as distinguishing the former from the latter is something in the order of a covering over. The questions which were still 'alive' with Plato and Aristotle have lost their appeal, as well as their urgency, in the 'hardening'[3] inaugurated by the tradition. If in this epoch thinkers still play a model role, it is the Greeks', and if it is possible to attribute a leading role to certain figures it is to Plato and Aristotle,[4] through whom a 'battle of giants over being' makes itself known.[5]

Moreover, this battle will have to be resumed in order to carry it further still than Plato and Aristotle succeeded in doing. The latter are therefore the object of a double critique. On the one hand, they proved incapable of carrying their investigations through to the end, and of bringing them to full clarity and this because they failed to get as far as the crucial question concerning the 'meaning' of being. This is why their investigations have to be prolonged. On the other hand, and more seriously, they already began to formulate an answer by understanding being within the field of *Vorhandenheit*. In this respect they still belong themselves to the very tradition which it is necessary to 'de-construct'.

The task entered into during the Marburg period is therefore characterized by a double movement of 'return to the origin'. On the one hand, a movement backwards, in the order of the historical luminaries, back toward the origin of the entire Western tradition. This movement assumes the form of a return to Greek ontology and by way primarily of the Aristotelian problematic. On the other hand, a movement in depth, in the order of the conditions of the possibility, back towards the Aristotelian problematic, which now finds itself subjected to a new phenomenological inquiry.[6]

It might well appear as though this double move were something like the first attempt – still incomplete, since not pushed back to the pre-Socratics – at that movement towards the origin which characterizes the later works. This is not however the case, and I would like to indicate quickly the structural differences which make up the specificity of this period.

In the first place, if Heidegger is guided by the double concern of 'climbing higher' (in history) and of 'digging deeper' (in the process of questioning), these two concerns do not, nevertheless, coincide. By that I mean that the phenomenologically inspired movement in the direction of the foundations of Platonico-Aristotelian conceptuality make no claim to rejoining, or recovering, a more original *moment*. The destruction of the tradition certainly brings with it a 'remembrance' (*Erinnerung*) of the inaugural texts (Plato–Aristotle), but the critical work accomplished on these texts does not in any way imply the 'commemoration' (*Andenken*) of another text which would precede it. In climbing upwards into the transcendental field no *trace* is encountered in history.

In the second place, if Heidegger's research aims at a deepening of the process of questioning it does not, for all that, attempt to disengage another question. To be sure, Heidegger makes it clear that the Platonic question has not been posed in a sufficiently radical way, but it is nevertheless this question which remains, in his view, what is 'worthy of being questioned'.[7]

Hence the paradoxical character of this first position adopted by Heidegger *vis-à-vis* ontology. While, in a certain respect, being more critical than it will be later, it is, in the final analysis, much less critical. It is more so, first because it adopts the radical language of 'destruction' (instead of the more prudent language of *Verwindung*), and then because it remains caught in a perspective of denunciation (an unavoidable perspective, once the covering over has been charged to the account of the thinking, without yet having been attributed to being itself). But at the same time it is much less so to the extent that the critical accent bears much more upon the issue of transmission (where the question is no longer posed and therefore implicitly finds itself resolved) than on that of inauguration (where this question, even though inadequately clarified, at least has the merit of being posed). But, as we shall see later, as soon as another 'inaugural injunction' has been issued, it will prove necessary to go back beyond Plato towards another question. It will be this latter question which will then have to be worked out and not the Platonic question.

To put it more broadly, in spite of the renewal inaugurated in the process of ontological questioning, the general configuration within which such a process is inscribed remains unchanged. Throughout these years there is only one beginning for Heidegger (even though the latter is still not considered from the double standpoint: manifest/latent); from which there consequently follows only one single history which is indissolubly linked with that of being and of ontology (in accordance with the requirements of ontology itself, which claims that being is certainly its question).

As a result, Heidegger cannot situate himself other than in the perspective of a continuation of this same history (which has to be brought to its truth). Furthermore, the task of thinking is defined as the 'accomplishment' of metaphysics, and the question of being is reduced to the explicit elucidation of its 'meaning'.

To conclude: the status of the Greeks, in the course of these years at Marburg, is ambiguous. But it is the Greeks, *as a whole*, who are both solicited and criticized at one and the same time. So far from it being the case that remembrance and critique are distributed about distinct figures (the pre-Socratics/Plato), in two distinct moments of history (original/derived), divided into two questions (fundamental/directive) and into two registers (un-thought/thought), none of these splits are operative – in any case, they are not operative *as such*.

I do not want to spend any more time on these early years. A recent article, devoted to Heidegger's relation to the Greeks through the Marburg period,[8] succeeds in bringing out very well the specificity of this first epoch. For my part, I would simply like to pursue the movement on further and bring it to a conclusion, by showing the nature of Heidegger's relation to the Greeks through the remainder of his itinerary.

II

The second period is far better known.[9] It begins with the 'turn' (i.e. towards the beginning of the 1930s) and continues throughout most of Heidegger's works. What occurs to Heidegger at this time is that forgetfulness of being, formerly attributed to thought, must be turned back onto being itself: it is being which 'makes itself' forgotten, precisely because the act of drawing back belongs to its development as such, or rather, constitutes the sole means of this development. This entails an immediate consequence. Although it is necessary to distinguish two planes – one in which being develops, and whence it can thus be reached (the Dasein), and one in which it is forgotten (history) – the thinker searching for being is henceforward concerned only with one plane: that of history, where being develops specifically *as* forgotten. It is thus within this plane, and to the extent that it is absent, that being might be reached.

Does this mean that the difference between the giving of being and its conjuring away has disappeared from the Heideggerian problematic? Not at all. This difference is shifted within the only plane that subsists, and it is within this plane alone that the double figure now develops. History is in fact not only the site of forgetfulness/withdrawal (the one being identified with the other). It is the site of withdrawal and of forgetfulness: the place where the withdrawal of being takes place (which is inherent to being itself) *and* the forgetfulness of this withdrawal (which, all the while being founded on the former, none the less remains within the realm of thought). That is to say that it is the realm of a *double* concealment.

What is to be the position of the thinker with regard to history understood thus? Since there is a doubling of concealment, the task will necessarily be one of duplication. On the one hand, there is no question of tearing it away from its withdrawal, but on the contrary, of retaining it more firmly than ever, that is, of recognizing it as this withdrawal itself. But, on the other hand, how would it be possible to recognize the withdrawal, if not by tearing it away from the forgetfulness in which it was held captive throughout our long history? Thus appears the necessity of a sharing out: the taking over by thought of the first plane of concealment (withdrawal) implies going beyond the second (forgetfulness).

However, if *forgetfulness* can be undone, it can only be so for Heidegger by rediscovering *memory* (I shall come back immediately to this link, which is as rich in consequences as in presuppositions). And whence would the thinker rediscover memory, if not from this inaugural time in which being, while *already* happening in its withdrawal, had not *yet* taken on the veil of forgetfulness? This is the privilege of the 'Greek morning'; it does not consist at all in being not having withdrawn there yet, but rather in its dispensing itself as what it is in reality, that is, as withdrawing – a withdrawing which was lost as such in later history, that is, forgotten and ever more decisively covered over.

Thus we see something like a genesis of prevalence granted to the pre-Socratics taking shape. It is in order to carry out the separation of the two registers of concealment that Heidegger is led to the split in the Greek world.[10] And it is precisely the link established from the one to the other (a link between a separation in the order of meaning and a split in the historical order – or, if one prefers, a link between forgetfulness, which must be undone, and memory, which must be rediscovered) which constitutes the specificity, as well as the limits, of this second period.

It all happens in fact as if Heidegger, committed since the turn to a thinking which attempts to break with the categories of presence (and which does in fact break off by affirming that being dispenses itself enigmatically as withdrawal), does not manage to go to the limits of his own audacity. Being is certainly understood as withdrawing, thus as forgotten, but *it is necessary* (Heidegger seems to think) that it was not always forgotten, thus that the concealment which constitutes it was not concealed from the start: it is necessary that it be, for an instant at least, revealed outright as the withdrawal it is and that, for this reason, the decisive act through which it *escapes* should none the less have been *given*. In other words, it is necessary that the truth of being *should have taken place* – be it only for the time of a flash of lightning.

It is this flash of lightning – or, to put it more rigorously, the idea of its dazzling light which went out as quickly as it came[11] – which disappears, as we shall see, from the very first texts. It was only when Heidegger had finished the long turn-around outlined in the beginning of the 1930s that he broke the last ties with the former conceptuality. To remain subject to these ties, in fact, was not only to think being as a presence. It was also to think that the absence, that absence which constituted the true character of being, had given itself at one time to the present, thus marking out a privileged instant in history. When being had become an absence never given as such, an absence understood as having always/already made itself absent, the movement was finished. But, at the same time, the 'Greek morning' had lost its privileged position.

Before going on, I would like to make a point clear that might lead to misinterpretation. Heidegger never stated that the first Greeks had *thought* being or truth better than their successors. Consequently, he never envisioned or encouraged any sort of *return* to the pre-Socratics. On the contrary, he unceasingly insisted on the fact that what he is commemorating, on the basis of a renewed meditation on the Greek language, had never been thought – and not even in the beginning. None the less, in his eyes, there is still a difference between the pre-Socratic beginning and what follows it. What does it consist of, then? This is a question too rarely asked and to which the texts offer only one answer in the final analysis: this difference consists of a greater or lesser *nearness* to the unthought, a nearness that finds its meaning completely in the *category* (which one can judge to be risky) of *experience*. What is not thought can in fact be experienced, thus constituting a sort of space where thought moves: this is the case of the first Greeks, and their privilege. It can thus no longer be the object of any experience, that is, it cannot only remain unthought, but even find itself, as such, covered over. It is this covering over which constitutes the long history of metaphysics.

Thus, Heidegger's interest, beyond Platonic ontology, for what he calls the 'Greek morning' is not to be interpreted in the naive perspective of a return. It remains true that throughout most of his work, Heidegger divides up the Greek landscape, formerly seen as unitary, according to a cleavage based on the Platonic idea. Just as we have noted for the first period a (relative) privileging 'of the Greeks' – who are supposed to have thought what the later tradition forgot – so what stands out in the second period is a (far more radical) privileging of the 'first Greeks' – who *experimented* with what no one had thought, but what the later tradition, inaugurated by Plato, was not even to experience. Here we see how Heidegger distances himself from the first period (since he recognizes that no one, not even the first Greeks, thought the truth of being), as well as how he remains removed in relation to the third (since he none the less affirms that this truth did have its witnesses in history).

What are the consequences for the ensemble of the second Heidegger's thought of this fundamental position he adopted toward the Greeks? The first, consisting of a new conception of the beginning, immediately entails a second, i.e. a radically new reading of history. That is, by granting the status of 'initial thinkers' to those who were formerly only 'pre-Socratics', Heidegger makes two distinct shifts possible. (1) The departure point is duplicated. It can no longer be reduced to the manifest beginning, which opens up with Plato, but includes a completely different one – hidden, covered over, unrecognized – which appeared with the very first Greeks. (2) At the same time, history is dissociated – it is no longer something which manifests itself on the basis of the Platonic question, but which assumes the form of another question, a hidden question, which emerges with the first Greeks. Thus to affirm, as did the metaphysical tradition, the inaugural character of Socratic–Platonic conceptions is not only to misunderstand the genuine beginning. It is, far more essentially, not to take into account a whole side of history – i.e., to condemn oneself to misunderstanding its essential doubleness.

We must now consider each of these shifts more closely. First, the duality of departure points. What is the precise status of each of them? Two elements deserve to be emphasized. Initially, both of them have a function of inauguration. One the one hand, the Greek morning sets in motion a particular question which, from Plato on, will be forgotten. However, on the other hand, the Platonic act not only stands in relation (misrepresentation) to what goes before it. To the extent that what precedes it was never thought, this act too has an inaugural status. We thus find ourselves in the presence, not of one initial time and of a simply derived stage, but of two initial times. Second – and paradoxically – the one (Platonic ontology) is closely dependent upon the other (the initial setting in motion), since it is only constituted by the recuperation, in the mode of a recovering, of the former time. In this sense, it has a secondary or derived position in relation to the other.

How can we reconcile these two aspects? In other words, how can we explain the fact that Platonic ontology is secondary, while being, in a certain sense, primary? How can we claim that one time is derived from the other without falling back upon the linear illusion, the metaphor of the line (which would eliminate the inaugural duality)? There is only one solution and it is the one Heidegger adopts: he affirms that there are two departure points, but they do not have the same status. The one has an original status, the other only a derived status. The one inaugurates our destiny, though we still cannot define it as the beginning of thought (since it does not belong to its order), while the other inaugurates the history of thought, without being the source of what is destined to be part of it.

Hence, what we see becoming clearer, in what at first appeared to be a simple doubling of the departure point, is a gap between an unthought origin and a thought beginning, a gap that does have a hierarchy, since the one finds its truth in the other. It is in the light of this doubling and this gap that we can consider the second consequence, i.e. the dissociation of history.

First, the doubling. If, from Heraclitus to Plato, we find not so much a debate about the same question as rather the setting up of two distinct registers of questioning, we are dealing with a double derivation. On the one hand, that of manifest history, that of the directing question (*Leitfrage*): it begins with Plato, and is brought to a high point in the work of Nietzsche, is called metaphysics and is interpreted, in its truth, as the history of the beingness of being. On the other hand, there is a secret history, that of the fundamental question (*Grundfrage*): it begins with the first Greeks, escapes from thought in the very act of its first emergence and is only recollected with Heidegger. It is called the history of being and is interpreted, in its finally unbound truth, as the history of a withdrawal.[12]

Second, the gap. All that has been said up to this point only makes up a first presentation, necessarily temporary. For, in reality, the history of metaphysics is itself, throughout its long development, the history of being. In these conditions, is it possible to sustain the argument that we are dealing with two derivations? Yes and no. No, in the sense that there is in fact only one line. Yes, however, in the sense that this line, in its own particularity, is a Fold, and that it more than allows, namely actually requires, two registers of decoding: our history can be considered in the light of the thought (history of metaphysics) or of the unthought (history of being). Why can we not dispense with this folding? Because it is only by a folding that the line, in its unity, finally becomes thinkable: our history can only be explained in the order of the thought on condition that it is returned to the order of the unthought.

Between these two registers, where does Heidegger stand? At the very heart of their conflictual unity. He is in fact the one who, because he knows how to distinguish, can articulate. In Heideggerian terms: the one who, because he can recognize Difference, can think it as unity.[13] This leads us to a third consequence, parallel to that noted during analysis of the first period. The question was the following: how does Heidegger define his own position in relation to history? In order to measure the course thus far, let us recall the answer that was given at that time. History still being conceived of in a unequivocal manner, Heidegger located himself then in continuity with it, i.e. within the direct line of ontological questioning. However, in order to pursue the same question further, he had, on the one hand, to return to his point of departure (the 'reminiscing' about what had formerly been considered as the beginning, i.e. Plato/Aristotle), while, on the other hand, he had to examine the latter 'in depth' and in a line of thinking inspired by Husserl's phenomenology.

In relation to this first picture, the second period carries out a triple shift. First, the critical work done on Platonico-Aristotelian conceptuality can no longer be termed 'examination in depth', because it requires a leap, a passage to another register. Second, this 'leap beyond' does not touch a more fundamental stratum in the order of meaning, but a more original inscription in the order of history: it takes us back toward the other departure point and this is why it is called the *Schritt zurück*. Third, and finally, since this other departure point never belonged to the order of thought, it can no longer be a question of 'reminiscing' about a 'beginning' (even if earlier than the Platonico-Aristotelian beginning aimed at during the first period), but rather of the 'commemoration' of an 'other beginning' (*Anfang*, and no longer *Beginn*). Briefly: what was formerly conceived of as a movement back to the foundations of Platonico-Aristotelian conceptuality now becomes a step back in the direction of the origin.[14]

A certain number of other consequences follow from this, consequences which it is best to interpret in the light of those already brought out in the analysis of the first period. First of all, the task of thought. In line with the movement of examination in depth (of the Aristotelian scheme), it was formerly defined as 'realization' (of metaphysics). In line with the movement of the *Schritt zurück* (in the direction of the Greek morning), it is now defined as *Andenken*. It is no longer the conclusion of a question already asked at the beginning, but rather the recollection of another question, unthought from the origin. This definition of thought as memory signals in two directions at the same time. First, while the idea of a culmination indicated that it was a matter of taking a question asked (if insufficiently elaborated in the beginning) further still, the idea of a recollection indicates that it is necessary to return to a question that was never asked as such, even if it came from even further back. This first connotation of the term recollection would thus respond to the question: what must one think? However, on the other hand, the idea of a culmination also indicates that this insufficiently elaborated question allows for a more satisfactory examination, that it could (and must) be brought to the clarity of a concept, i.e. be made the object of what *Sein und Zeit* termed an 'explicit elucidation'.[15] The idea of recollection indicates that this unthought origin toward which one must return can never be grasped, discovered or uncovered, with regard to what it 'is': one can only remember it, or better still, commemorate it, within a 'faithful thought'. This second connotation of the term recollection would thus respond to the question: how must one think?

These two connotations are obviously not unconnected. If what one must meditate upon is a trace which thought never conjugated in the present, then this can only be meditated upon in the future perfect. The word 'recollection' says both: it says that what we are to be faithful to lies far behind, at the origins of our history, as something always/already withdrawn, and it says that, in order to be faithful to it, thought must transform itself: it must no longer be the grasping of a substance, not even the elucidation of a meaning, but the recollection of a difference.

There is finally a last consequence – which is also, by right, the very first, and which will enable us to close the circle. The question of being transforms itself. It is no longer a question of bringing to light a unity of meaning given at the same time as 'being'; it is a question of directing oneself toward the darkness wherein it takes shelter, i.e. of remembering that which withdraws. What then does withdraw throughout the long, supposedly unequivocal, history of metaphysics? It is precisely this doubleness and its enigmatic unity. That is, being as Difference.

The end of our analysis thus offers the key to all that precedes it. If the entire second period of Heidegger's itinerary can be characterized by a series of cleavages – and cleavages formerly poorly understood, which Heidegger had to construct patiently – it is because being 'is' Difference – and a difference withdrawn from the start, which encourages its own misunderstanding, thus the obliteration of the cleavages.

III

Is there a third period? That is obviously the question which this new treatment of the subject will arouse. Taking the *Kehre* into account and utilizing it to better bring out the fundamental positions adopted in the course of a life's work, both these processes are based upon an interpretation which is largely underwritten by Heidegger himself. However, to affirm that at the end of his development he would have committed himself to another turning point in which positions adopted during the previous decades would have been placed in doubt or seen as out-dated is certainly running a risk: that of proposing a division which, even if it does run through his work, is never made the explicit theme of it.

I do think, none the less that we cannot pass over this new division and that the outlining of a 'third period' is necessary for several reasons. Necessary, first of all, because of the theme we have developed here. The privilege granted to the Greek morning is often projected upon the ensemble of Heidegger's thought, as if, by making the one coincide with the other, the former could be used to define the latter. We have however

seen that *it had not been clearly outlined* at the beginning of his development and we shall also see that *it had already been set aside* by the end
of it. A subtle setting-aside that was not always clearly marked out but
for which the main evidence is provided to us by Heidegger himself when
he *renounces*, on a decisive point, the interpretation which dominates his
work. Of course, he utilized this dominant interpretation for some thirty
years in any number of texts. The renunciation comes at the very end
and in a few pages. Unless we decide (and according to what criteria?)
that certain texts will be taken as determinative for the understanding
of a thinker while others will be ascribed to accident or a break in the
train of thought, it remains difficult for us to take for granted an interpretation which Heidegger himself did not recognize as his own.

Second, if his view of the Greeks cannot be dissociated from a particular way of locating the beginning, defining history and thinking the
question of being (as I have attempted to show for the two preceding
periods), then we may presume that such a noticeable change in his
understanding of the first Greeks must imply – or indicate – an equally
significant modification in the ensemble of his thought. Do the later texts
(those of the 1960s) indicate such a modification? It is only by being
attentive to the difficulties and discordances which characterize these
later texts that we have any chance of resolving the question of this third
period. Do these discordances, once clearly set apart, agree with one
another? Do they make up a relatively homogeneous setting? And, if
this is the case, how can this unity of the later texts be structured in
accordance with the other 'periods' in Heidegger's development? It seems
to me that one of the tasks of contemporary criticism is perhaps to
respond to these questions.

We must not forget that, if Heidegger did not really outline this
ultimate unity in its specificity and its difference from the other periods,
he did nevertheless grant it a place and a name. Its place is in the
collection *Zur Sache des Denkens*, which contains the three most significant texts on the new positions: 'Das Ende der Philosophie und die
Aufgabe des Denkens' (1964), which corrects and modifies the former
interpretation of the 'Greek morning', 'Zeit und Sein', and the 'Seminar'
devoted to it (1962), which presents the double question of being and
history in a new and quite troubling light.[16] The name which delimits a
space for a thinking which is still unexplored and with regard to which
it is a question, says Heidegger, of 'committing oneself', is *Ereignis*.[17]

Let us take up again, point by point, each of the shifts carried out in
the course of these last years. The gesture which will mark our point of
departure is the re-establishment of the previously interrupted continuity
between the pre-Socratics and Plato. It was assumed until then that Plato
had initiated a change in the essence of truth, making it move from an
uncovering (ἀλήθεια) to rectitude (ὁμοίωσις).[18] More generally, it was

assumed that the 'Greek morning' constituted a privileged time in history when something of being stood out in its own truth and was, at least within the register of experience, perceived as such. But here is what Heidegger writes about ἀλήθεια and the 'change of essence' in truth which was thought to have taken place in Plato:

> We must recognize that ἀλήθεια, the uncovering in the sense of the lighting up of presence, is henceforth and exclusively [*sogleich und nur*] to be experienced [*erfahren*] as the rectitude [*Richtigkeit*] of representation and statement. But then, even the affirmation of the mutation of the essence of truth [*von einem Wesenswandel der Wahrheit*] which would have led from uncovering to rectitude, is no longer tenable. Instead of this, we must say: ἀλήθεια, as the lighting up of presence and presentification [*als Lichtung von Anwesenheit und Gegenwärtigung*] in thought and word, happens henceforth [*sogleich*] in the perspective of ὁμοίωσις and adequatio, that is, in the perspective of a conformity [*Angleichung*] in the sense of a correspondence [*Ubereinstimmung*] between representation and what is present.[19]

This text is rich in information. The dividing line between the initial 'experience' and later philosophy is considerably clouded over. Metaphysics, of course, retains its status as a derived construction which cannot be understood in itself. But Heidegger formerly believed one could discover, in the Greek morning, the 'original' figure. He now recognizes that this figure, in its first blossoming and its very first giving, was already derived, that it was *derived from the beginning*, that there was no original nor any covering over. It is this reunifying of the Greek scene which seems to constitute the basic shift. For the moment, we need to examine the various consequences, as we did for the preceding periods.

The first is that it is no longer necessary to retain the principle of a double *beginning*, one more original than the other. Of course, we must look at something which, in some of its features, still resembles an 'origin'. But no one in history, and no time in history, was close to it. What underwrote and legitimized the distinction of the beginnings was precisely this subtle hierarchy of closeness. Once this has been broken down, it is no longer necessary to retain two points of departure: one having opened in the split second of a lightning stroke, without being recognized or thought, and the other, which took place in the decline of this split second, and which was alone to have a posterity in the order of thought. No longer having the room to develop *in* history itself (even on the threshold of this history), the inaugural bolt of lightning was never really able to *take place*.

If thus 'the Greeks' are again thought of as a unity, if what happens with Heraclitus is only and immediately (*nur und sogleich*) what will be made thematic by Plato and will continue until Nietzsche, then the initial complication, belonging to the second period, can be abandoned: occidental thought begins with the very first Greeks; Plato limits himself to continuing them; ontology does not begin anything (not anything, in any case, which is of the order of a break); there is only one beginning and it is an errant beginning.

The second consequence: this reunified beginning results in a *history* which is itself simplified. It is best however to be quite precise here. To speak of simplification does not in any way mean affirming that the Fold would disappear. But what is new is that the hidden side is, to a certain extent, let loose: not having ever reached land, even in the beginning, *it loses its anchor point in history*. Of course, as early as the second period, the unthought was recognized as having always been unthought. But, precisely, it did 'reach land', in such a way that the history of thought was not to be assimilated simply to history as such. Beyond the strict register of thought, there were those of experience (*Erfahren*), of premonition (*Ahnen*), still others perhaps – registers which rightfully belonged to occidental history, which were even dominant in its beginnings (the whole meaning of 'morning') and which allowed the unthought to insert itself, even obliquely, *in* this history. While now occidental history, since its very first opening and in all its dimensions, is played out entirely on *one* of its sides. As for the other side, it remains what must be aimed at or thought, but it no longer overlaps anything which takes place; it does not rejoin any historical trace; it has had no witness – *and thus no guarantor* – in history.

The third consequence: how did Heidegger see himself in relation to history thus understood? As long as the unthought retained its anchor point in history, Heidegger had no need to depart from this history in order to think it. He did indeed need to make a 'leap', but it was an intra-historical one, since he made it by moving back from the derived to the original, i.e. from one beginning to another. The movement played itself out less *in* history than *in relation* to it. It is less a 'step back' than a 'step to the side'. History being entirely grasped as a unity, the person who attempts to think it, i.e. to send it back to its unthought truth, can no longer place himself *in* it. There is simply no room left for him in this history, because there is no trace he can insert himself into.

The fourth consequence: the task of thought, the leitmotif of the lecture of this title[20] is that it is now a question of thinking 'the lighting up of presence' (*die Lichtung von Anwesenheit*). Is this a shift in relation to the task defined previously? Indubitably. But this shift cannot be accomplished unless we distinguish the different occurrences of the word *Lichtung* in Heidegger's work. *Lichtung* has only one meaning, clearly defined: it names the unapparent opening whence comes that which is given. But by 'what is given', Heidegger sometimes means the present or being – and in this case, the unapparent opening from which it comes is presence itself. Taken in this context, *Lichtung* denotes being. In the text we are dealing with, by 'what is given', Heidegger means presence or being – and in this case, the unapparent opening from which it comes is an even more initial land. In this context, *Lichtung* no longer denotes being, but the whole possibility of its being given – that is, it exactly matches the semantic field of the word *Ereignis*. To sum up, the word *Lichtung*, which indicates a formal movement of withdrawal of giving, receives a different 'value' according to the quality of what is given (and thus of what withdraws): *Lichtung von Anwesenheit* is not synonymous with *Lichtung als Anwesenheit*.[21]

Once this confusion has been cleared up, the task of thought as it is defined in the 1964 text ('Das Ende der Philosophie') is no longer distinguishable from the one presented two years earlier in 'Zeit und Sein'. In both cases, the task no longer consists in thinking being (in order to recognize it as difference) or in illuminating history (as the history of being). It consists in thinking their common origin. Their origin, i.e. *that whence* they were dispensed from being as time, thus *that whence* our history could be what it was. But moving back to this land of giving also makes possible a double gesture, for which it is important to evaluate the link.

(1) The claim that this history, as such, is *terminated*. And this, to the precise extent to which it was carried back to that which granted it. If the history of being is, as Heidegger always said, the history of the withdrawal of presence in its different historical periods, it cannot be sent back to that which formulated this withdrawal without coming simultaneously to its closing. It is thus revealed that the history of being only perpetuated itself through the unthought which it enfolded (and not in spite of it) and that, once 'illuminated' it lost at one and the same time its secret and its very drive. Thus the first 'disturbing' theme of the 'Seminar' is legitimized: that of an end to history.[22]

(2) The claim that this history (precisely because it was taken back to its provenance and found its conclusion there) can be *abandoned*. It is in this sense once again that the ultimate 'step back' becomes the very first 'step aside'. Having projected ourselves into the land of the *es gibt*, this makes everything which is derived therefrom thinkable, everything which came under the heading of presence and history of being. But this also allows us to see the broader realm of what is not derived, which remains unknown for us, as well as unnamed. This means that it opens onto the possibility of another thought and perhaps of another future which would no longer be a history. Thus the second disturbing theme of the 'Seminar' falls into place: our history no longer constitutes what is to be thought.[23]

It is in this context that we may best insert the fifth consequence, i.e., the last position adopted by Heidegger in relation to the *question of being*. In fact, it is only the translation of the preceding double statement. Committing oneself to the land of the *Ereignis* is in effect reaching the 'essential provenance' of being, thus taking it back to its 'ownness' – and it is at one and the same time a way of having done with it. The work of explanation being complete, it no longer has a claim upon us. Hence the third disturbing theme of the 'Seminar': that of a 'taking-leave' of the question of being.[24]

These two statements (the history of being is finished/it can be abandoned) are not only linked together. They are also articulated most closely with the whole series of 'consequences' which I brought out as characteristic features of the last period. The fact of thinking the *end* of history and jointly its *abandonment* (fourth consequence) has the condition of its possibility in the leap Heidegger made in locating himself *outside* this history (third consequence), a leap having its own condition of possibility in the act through which history, formerly split, was *reunified*, this reunification being entailed by the fact that truth – or its trace – was no longer to be inserted *in* it (second consequence).[25]

What did these last analyses tend toward? Toward showing, first, that a number of disconcerting statements by the later Heidegger have a unity (i.e. are concordant among themselves) in their reference to *Ereignis*, understood as the realm of donation. Second, that this realm proposes answers – *new answers* – to the ensemble of those questions (the beginning, history, the task of thought and the question of being) which formerly allowed us to recognize different 'periods' in Heidegger's itinerary. Third and most important of all, it is in the light of the differentiation between *Ereignis* and the question of being that it is possible to understand the relation of necessity which unites the third period to the two before it. What is more, the status granted to the Greeks enjoys the status of a *privileged sign* even if it does not possess that of a driving force. It only remains to elaborate upon these last two points.

In the second part, we saw that the division of the Greek landscape went hand in hand with a whole series of splits, themselves contemporary with the central attempt: thinking being as difference. What stands out in the third part is that the reunification of the Greek landscape (taken as the point of departure for the analysis) cannot itself be dissociated from a withdrawal from the ensemble of divisions, itself contemporaneous with a new attempt: 'diverting the focus of being'[26] (therefore of the difference).

The passage from one period to another thus appears in its necessity. What happens at the end of his work and explains all the shifts we have followed is that the question – i.e., also the task – is henceforth elsewhere. What was divided can be withdrawn under the heading of unity, because what is to be thought now is the *relation* between this re-established unity and its possible *outside*. In clear terms: what is to be thought is no longer the difference between being and beingness, but the relation between being (which *is* only through its difference to being-ness – though it is no longer this which is being insisted upon) and its giving; no longer the difference between metaphysics and the thought of being but the relation between the thought of being (which alone can elucidate metaphysics – though this is no longer what is being insisted upon) and another thought. What is the condition for such a change? I shall propose – with caution – that it consists in the fact that Heidegger, no longer seeing any privileged time in history, can henceforth distance himself from it and consider it as an ensemble.[27] And what is its conse-quence? It is that the relation between this ensemble and its other, that is, between a unity and the outside from which it comes (and to which it can be led back), can become a question. It is indeed this question which moves to the very centre (under the auspices of the term 'giving') when thought 'commits itself to *Ereignis*'. That is, *Ereignis* elucidates not only the internal coherence of the third period but also its insertion into the ensemble of Heidegger's itinerary.

In these pages, I have attempted to outline a double curve of develop-ment. Along the first, we find the little history of the Greek morning with its triple status: first understood as the beginning (hesitant) of what Plato and Aristotle will raise to full conceptuality, then as a starting signal (decisive) for a question that ontology will condemn to forgetful-ness, finally as the beginning (henceforth without glory) of this forgetful-ness itself. The history of the Greeks in Heidegger's works is thus that of a unity broken and then re-established, but re-established after an overthrow: if Plato appears in the beginning as a continuation or realiz-ation of the pre-Socratics (in the register of truth), at the end, it is the pre-Socratics who appear as a prefiguration of Plato (in the register of misunderstanding).

On the second curve, we find the great history, History itself as it can be grasped through Heidegger's triple project: first to continue it by delving into it, then to elucidate it by recollecting it, finally to abandon it, by taking leave of it. For me, the principal interest in the outlining of these two curves lies in their articulation: because the one closely adheres to the other, follows it in each of its movements, we are able to bring this movement to light.

However, this revealing is not without danger. By elucidating – in a light which we can justly call relatively stark – Heidegger's positions, I have partially altered their nature. Left on their own within the text where they had their being, their outlines were not so keen nor their contrast so marked. By emphasizing, as I have done, the breaks in the itinerary, I have betrayed the continuity. For there is indeed a continuity. Heidegger always moves along the same path, a path one can (and must)ⁱ grasp as a unity. It is none the less true that this unity is not simple, that it has 'stations' – stations which one can (and must) bring to light as well. This obligation is all the more impelling in that Heidegger, at the end of his life, made an attempt at an auto-interpretation under the heading of unity: emphasizing the continuity of that preoccupation which led him from Brentano to Trakl, or the persistence of the question leading from *Sein und Zeit* to 'Zeit und Sein'. This is a possible (and accurate) light to see it in, but it is not the only one possible, nor the only one that is accurate. For Heidegger's itinerary is at once continuous *and* discontinuous. By insisting as he does on the unitary aspect, Heidegger left us to come to terms with the differences, without himself carrying out the work of differentiation. It is up to us to take this on, that is to outline the limits that were not immediately evident. As my objective was to make them intelligible, I was forced to *exaggerate* them.

This objective having been at least partially achieved, it remains for me to undo what I have been doing throughout these pages – to recall that the duality of the question was already sketched out as early as *Sein und Zeit*, that the going beyond presence, accomplished in *Ereignis*, was already played out in the very thought of presence as it was developed in the heart of his works; that, in one or other of its dimensions, *Ereignis* is the *accomplishment* of the question of the truth of being which is itself closely contiguous with the question of the 'meaning' of being, etc. Thus, Heidegger's itinerary does not strictly include – except for purely occasional questions – *changes in course*. It does however include, in the strict sense, *turning points*, places where the path curves inward, where the direction is modified and refined, without truly recanting – but in finding its end elsewhere and otherwise. The Greek morning which the prophetic Heidegger neglected at first and which he later sought out and recognized as blind, formed here the site of a *topography of turning points*.

Translated by Cozette Griffin-Kremer

Notes

1 Cf. *Heidegger et les paroles de l'origine* (Paris: Vrin, 1986).

2 The volumes presently available are volumes 20, 21, 24, 25 and 26 of the *Gesamtausgabe* (*GA*).

3 *Sein und Zeit* (*SZ*) (*GA* 2), §6, p. 22.

4 Cf. *Die Grundprobleme der Phänomenologie*, *GA* 24, p. 453 (French tr., p. 382). Heidegger confirms here that 'at the beginning of ancient philosophy',

being is still taken as beings, that is, 'explained with the help of ontic determinations'. And he adds: 'This way of interpreting being will remain current for a long time in Greek philosophy, even after the decisive progress brought about by Plato and Aristotle in the posing of the problem'.

5 *SZ*, §1, p. 2.

6 For this double movement the *Logik* (*GA* 21) should be consulted. Also, *Die Frage nach der Wahrheit* (*GA* 21) and *Die Grundprobleme der Phänomenologie*.

7 A claim which obviously has to be qualified. If a question is posed in another manner (in a more radical manner etc.), is it still the same question? Without pretending to be able to resolve this question here, I would like nevertheless to propose several components of a reply. (1) It is indubitable that the question of the 'meaning of being', posed in *Sein und Zeit*, is *already more* than that characteristic of ontology, namely, of the 'being of beings' (even if the latter is envisaged from the standpoint of a unity of signification). (2) It could be however that is *not yet* that of the 'truth of being', characteristic of the later texts. (3) Between this 'already more' and this 'not yet' there reigns a difference of *radicality*. It has to do with the fact that in the movement of the 'already more', the word 'being' keeps its earlier meaning – which it loses, by contrast, in the execution of the 'no longer'. What I mean is that what is decisive in the transition from the problematic of 'meaning' to that of 'truth', is that 'being' no longer says the same thing in the one expression as in the other. When Heidegger was pursuing the meaning of being, it was a matter of that being furnished by ontology, even if its meaning, as well as the horizon of this being, was not made explicit by it. When he starts to pursue the truth of being, it is a matter of that being which reveals itself to ontology, and of which it has never spoken, which it never even succeeded in envisaging – the history of thinking then being recognized as envisaging, under the name of being, a different question altogether, namely, that of the beingness of beings.

If these distinctions can today be drawn more finely, it is evidently on account of the publication of the lectures. Previously we were obliged to read the first eight paragraphs of *Sein und Zeit* in the light of writings subsequent to 1930. So naturally we were inclined to project upon it distinctions which, while being certainly pre-figured by it, were however not operative in it. The interest of a text like *Grundprobleme der Phänomenologie* is precisely that of having permitted this to appear in another light.

8 J. Taminiaux, 'Heidegger et les Grecs à l'époque de l'ontologie fondamentale', *Etudes phénoménologiques*, No. 1, ed. Ousia, 1985.

9 We may note that publication of the Marburg courses is quite recent – and still unfinished – and that the texts from the later years, perhaps due to insufficient distance, have remained fairly little analysed by current criticism.

10 Naturally, it is also because he reads the pre-Socratics, and so on. I do not claim to propose a universal key, but am trying simply to bring out *one* dimension of explanation by putting this split back into the horizon of necessity which can, at least partially, give some account of it.

11 Cf. for example *Vorträge und Aufsätze* (Pfullingen: Neske, 1978), p. 221: 'Once, however, in the beginning of Occidental thought, the essence of language burst forth [*aufblitzte*] like a flash of lightning in the light of being. . . . But the flash of lightning went out suddenly.' And, a few pages later (ibid., p. 237), Heidegger takes it up again: 'This first lighting up of the essence of language disappeared immediately, it was covered over.' Taking only the example of the word *logos*, it would be easy to show that, for Heidegger, *all* the 'fundamental

words' (*physis, alétheia, eon*, etc.) also burst forth in light only to go out immediately.

12 For the distinction *Grundfrage/Leitfrage*, cf. particularly *Einführung in die Metaphysik* (1935, *GA* 40), as well as *Vom Wesen der menschlichen Freiheit. Einleitung in die Philosophie, GA* 31.

13 i.e. think it, not as a simple *Unterscheidung*, but as an *Austrag*, a term for which Heidegger asks us to understand both the differend and its conciliation. For the development of this terminology (and this thought), see particularly: *Identität und Differenz* (Pfullingen: Neske, 1957), p. 63 and *Unterwegs zur Sprache* (Pfullingen: Neske, 1975), p. 25.

14 Of course, it is understood that the origin in question here is not only in history: it stems from the scheme (transformed, for that matter) of the 'foundation'. In exactly the same way, the *Schritt zurück*, mentioned above, is not only a step backwards in history: it also stems from the scheme (transformed) of 'examination in depth'. I am not affirming at all that we move here from one order (of meaning) to another (of history). I am saying that henceforth the two move together and that it is precisely this conjunction which was absent in the first period.

15 *SZ*, §2, p. 6.

16 *Zur Sache des Denkens* (Tübingen: Niemeyer, 1960). The collection also contains the short text entitled 'Mein Weg in die Phänomenologie', 1963. It is understood that the later period is not limited to the texts cited. However, if it is brought out in a number of other texts, it is in these that it is most clearly made into a theme.

17 I have shown elsewhere, in a comparative chart of different occurrences of the theme (*Heidegger et les paroles de l'origine*), that *Ereignis* is certainly *named* in earlier texts, but that is only *properly thought out* during the decade 1950–60, and is only fully *explicated* at the end of the decade and the beginning of the next.

18 'Platons Lehre von der Wahrheit', *Wegmarken* (Frankfurt am Main: Klostermann, 1967), pp. 135–9 (*Qu. II*, pp. 152–5).

19 'Das Ende der Philosophie und die Aufgabe des Denkens', in *Zur Sache des Denkens*, p. 78 (*Qu. IV*, pp. 135–6).

20 'Das Ende der Philosophie und die Aufgabe des Denkens'.

21 This structure is developed by Heidegger himself, but in another text and with regard to another term: that of 'letting'. There he distinguishes the two acts of 'letting the present happen' (to the presence) and 'letting presence happen' itself. The distinction is clearer in German, where one can follow the passage from the pair *Anwesende/Anwesen* (characteristic of his 'mature' works) from the pair *Anwesen/Anwesenlassen* (characteristic of later texts). Cf. 'Zeit und Sein', in *Zur Sache des Denkens*, p. 5 (*Qu. IV*, pp. 18–19), as well as the corresponding commentary in the Seminar, *Qu. IV*, pp. 39–40 (69–70).

22 'Seminar über den Vortrag Zeit und Sein', in *Zur Sache des Denkens*, pp. 44–5 (*Qu. IV*, p. 75). For the analogy on this point with Hegel, cf. ibid., p. 53 (87).

23 ibid.

24 ibid., p. 58 (93).

25 That is, the very last hypotheses of Heidegger would simply be impossible – even impossible to envisage – within the scope of the second period alone to which the ensemble of Heidegger's itinerary is often reduced. One does not abandon that which one holds oneself within; one can only elucidate it differently on the basis of a new perspective made possible by the place occupied in the

space of the within. However, if one is outside, it is the whole of the territory which may be neglected at the same time that it is circumscribed. To sum up, if Heidegger was able to envision the exploration of an 'elsewhere' at the end of his work, it is because he was already there.

26 'Zeit und Sein', in *Zur Sache des Denkens*, pp. 5–6 (*Qu. IV*, p. 19).

27 But have we here really the condition or simply one of the dimensions of the change? I admit I do not see this very clearly.

2

Dasein as *praxis*: the Heideggerian assimilation and the radicalization of the practical philosophy of Aristotle[1]

Franco Volpi

1 Introductory considerations: the presence of Aristotle in the work of Heidegger

There has never been any doubt as to the importance of Aristotle for Heidegger's thinking. Even at those moments which were least favourable for a comprehension of the meaning and the constant presence of Aristotle in the work of Heidegger, it would have been difficult to ignore the significance Heidegger accords to certain central themes belonging to the thinking of Aristotle, such as the problem of being or the problem of the *physis*, problems which, in Heidegger's speculations, also become dense thematic points which are continually recovered in the course of his development. Besides, Heidegger himself frequently underlined the importance that Aristotle has assumed in the formation and the development of his philosophical perspective.[2] And if, in addition, one considers how many important studies on Aristotle have been motivated or inspired by Heidegger,[3] one has at one's disposal reasons for supposing that the Heideggerian reading of Aristotle has penetrated much deeper than the published texts would, up to a few years ago, have allowed one to conclude. In any case, even if one limits oneself to the former, it is possible to trace the influence of Aristotle on Heidegger throughout the entire extent of his thinking, reaching from the youthful reading of the dissertation of Franz Brentano *Von der mannigfachen Bedeutung des Seienden nach Aristoteles* right up to the interpretation of being and the concept of *physis* in the essay written in 1939 and published in 1958.[4]

However, hitherto it has not been possible to reconstruct the continuous line of Aristotle's influence across the totality of Heidegger's work. It is only today, thanks to the publication of the university lectures, that one is in a position to get a more exact idea of the intensity of Heidegger's confrontation with Aristotle and to try and reconstruct it in its essentials. One can also say the same for Heidegger's confrontation with other great founding moments in metaphysical thinking, such as the works of Descartes, Leibniz, Kant, Hegel and Husserl.

In particular, the publication of the lectures for the Winter term 1925/6: *Logik: Die Frage nach der Wahrheit*,[5] and of that of the Summer term 1927: *Die Grundprobleme der Phänomenologie*,[6] has contributed documents of the first importance for the reconstruction of, and the confrontation with Aristotle. The same thing holds, one might say, of the lectures given in the Summer term 1931: *Aristoteles, Metaphysik IX, 1–3: Vom Wesen und Wirklichkeit der Kraft*[7] and of certain parts of the lectures from the Winter term 1929/30: *Die Grundbegriffe der Metaphysik: Welt–Endlichkeit–Einsamkeit*.[8] Numerous elucidations are also to be found in the publication of the lectures from the Summer term 1924 on *Rhetoric*,[9] in that of the following term 1924/5 on Plato's *Sophist*[10] (which, in its first part, carries a detailed interpretation of book VI of the *Nichomachean Ethics*) and finally in the lectures from the Summer term 1926: *Grundbegriffe der antiken Philosophie*,[11] in which Heidegger handles the history of Greek philosophy from Thales to Aristotle and the final part of which is devoted to an interpretation of the totality of the Aristotelian philosophy. We will also find a number of fundamental indications, with regard to the beginning and to the first decisive development of the Heideggerian interpretation of Aristotle, in the lecture course from his first teaching assignment at Freiburg. Today, we are in a position to confirm this from the first of these lecture courses (which have just been published), that from the Winter term 1921/2: *Phänomenologische Interpretation zu Aristoteles: Einführung in die phänomenologische Forschung*;[12] and in such a way that one can only hope that the other lecture courses from the first Freiburg teaching period, lectures which have not yet been included in the anticipated publication programme (on the grounds that one is not in possession of the original manuscript) might one day be published. By the same token, one has to hope that the celebrated interpretation of Aristotle, which Heidegger sent to Natorp and a résumé of which he even considered publishing in Husserl's *Jahrbuch für Philosophie und phänomenologische Forschung*, will also be published.[13]

2 The confrontation with Aristotle during the ten-year period of silence which precedes *Sein und Zeit*

In what follows, I will try to bring to light a speculative core whose impact upon the confrontation of Heidegger with Aristotle was, in my opinion, considerable at a particular moment, that is, during the ten-year period of silence which precedes the publication of *Sein und Zeit* and which coincides with the years of the first teaching at Freiburg (from 1919) and with those of the teaching at Marburg. The main reason for this limitation is that, both from the thematic point of view and from that which concerns the intensity of the confrontation, this period is without doubt the most interesting and, at the same time, the least investigated of Heidegger's extended engagement with Aristotle. In fact, I think – something that would have appeared strange only a few years ago – that this phase of Heidegger's thinking can be characterized in a definitive fashion by a radical appropriation and a voracious assimilation of Aristotle's ontology and of practical philosophy and this, more specifically, not only where Heidegger mentions Aristotle and interprets him explicitly but also and more especially, where he doesn't talk about him and seems to concentrate upon the speculative elaboration of the problems which converge later in *Sein und Zeit*. It's for this reason that, in order to grasp the full meaning of the confrontation of Heidegger with Aristotle, one has to take care not to be misled either by a zealous determination to verify the philosophical exactitude and extent of the Heideggerian reading or by too exclusive a concentration upon what Heidegger says about Aristotle explicitly. It is more important to adopt a perspective suitable to grasping and understanding how Heidegger takes up, assimilates, transforms and realizes certain of Aristotle's problems and determinations by rethinking them in relation with the fundamental questions which he confronts within his speculative horizon.

A few preliminary remarks are necessary in order to sketch out, at least in its main lines, the general horizon within which I see the confrontation of Heidegger with Aristotle taking place in this period. In my opinion, this confrontation is characterized (1) by the fact that it is to be situated in the framework of a radical resumption of fundamental themes which the Greeks thought out for the first time in a manner which has become decisive for the history of Western philosophy, themes which, since Hegel and Nietzsche, nobody has been able to take up as radically as Heidegger. (2) It is also characterized by a specific methodological disposition which can be designated, very generally, as a placing in question of the Western metaphysical tradition, a questioning which becomes more and more radical, to the point of ending up with a demand for an overcoming (*Uberwindung*, *Verwindung*) of this tradition. In the period under consideration, this calling in question is defined by Heidegger himself as 'destruction', and more precisely as phenomenological destruction (which, together with reduction and construction make up the triple articulation of the phenomenological method).[14] (3) Finally, from a thematic point of view, the confrontation with Aristotle up to *Sein und Zeit* is characterized by the fact that it bears fundamentally upon three main problems which are also the main problems of *Sein und Zeit*, namely the problem of truth, the problem of the ontological constitution of human life and the problem of time; the general horizon within which Heidegger confronts all these problems is certainly one which is marked by the question of being.

Of these three main problems, I will in particular consider the one which is central for the comparison I propose to make between Dasein and *praxis*, namely, the problem of the ontological constitution of, and of the fundamental and unitary modality of being which belongs to, human life. First of all one has to ask how Heidegger comes to identify and to treat this problem within the horizon of that question of being which he begins to raise, as he says himself, as early as his reading of Brentano's dissertation.

3 The problem of the unity of being *qua pollachos legomenon* as the guiding principle of Heidegger's research

There are undoubtedly many elements and speculative suggestions which have played a role in the formation of the Heideggerian problematic and which it would be worth our while to examine in detail. In the framework of an analysis of the relation with Aristotle, allow me to limit my task here to the elucidation of the only function, in the genesis of the three problems indicated, played by the question of being *qua pollachos legomenon*, a question which Heidegger takes notice of mostly by way of Brentano's dissertation.

According to the autobiographical testimony which he himself volunteered in *Mein Weg in die Phänomenologie*, his attention was from the very beginning captured by the problem of the plurivocity of being and, in consequence, by the question of understanding and of determining the fundamental and unitary sense, if there is one, which upholds the plurality of the others. In other words, if Being is to be expressed in multiple and diverse modalities and significations, what is its fundamentally unitary meaning, what does Being itself mean?[15] As is well known, in his dissertation, Brentano examined the four fundamental significations of being (the *pollachos* can consequently be considered as a *tetrachos*) which Aristotle catalogues and examines, especially in the *Metaphysics*, to wit: (1) the meaning of being according to the categorial figures (*to on kata ta schemata ton kategorion*), (2) the meaning of being in as much as it is true (*to on hos alethes*), (3) the meaning of being according to the power or the act (*to on dynamei e energeiai*), (4) the meaning of being in itself or incidentally (*to on kath'hauto kai kata symbebekos*). Faithful to the Aristotelian–Thomist tradition, Brentano did not however limit himself solely to describing the doctrine of the four fundamental significations but also tried to grasp their unitary connection in terms of the analogical unity of being. More precisely, in his attempt at a solution,

he placed especial emphasis upon the fundamental character of the categorial signification and considered substance (*qua* primary category) as
the unitary term to which all the other significations were related. So
Brentano conceived ontology as ousiology, by interpreting being in a
categorical horizon – to the point that he went so far as to attempt a
sort of deduction of the categories on the basis of the general concept
of being.[16]

When, therefore, in *Mein Weg in die Phänomenologie* Heidegger
declares that from the time of this reading of Brentano the problem of
Being and of its unitary meaning did not cease to bother him,[17] I think
we have to take this testimony seriously, not as if it were an idealizing
stylization of his philosophical formation aiming to display a constant
attention for the question of being, even at the beginning but, on the
contrary, as a credible document attesting to the effective genesis, in his
youthful reflections, of the problem which was to remain central throughout his entire thinking. If one takes the autobiographical testimony of
Heidegger seriously one can even take matters further than he was willing
to explicitly acknowledge on this issue and recover the traces of an
intensive reflection on the four meanings of being not only in the first
writings – especially in the doctoral thesis on Duns Scotus[18] which deals
with the categorial signification of being – but also in the later speculation
from the 1920s to *Sein und Zeit*, which, on the surface, no longer has
anything to do with the problem of being *qua pollachos legomenon*.

The hypothesis which I wish to advance is that the fundamental direction of Heidegger's philosophical research in the course of the 1920s
consists in a research into that unitary and fundamental sense which
upholds the plurivocity of being. In particular, I want to suggest that,
with this end in view, Heidegger at this time probes the four meanings,
one after the one, to verify which among them can be considered as the
fundamental and unitary meaning. Soon left unsatisfied by the ousiolog-
ical and analogical solution sustained by Brentano,[19] Heidegger, in the
1920s, concentrates his in-depth examination upon the meaning of being
qua true. Behind this examination there clearly emerges the intention of
determining whether this signification can assume the role of the fundamental meaning. Amongst the texts presently published, the lecture
course from the Winter term 1925/6 (*Logik: Die Frage nach der
Wahrheit*), but also the conclusive part of that from the Winter term 1929/
30 (*Die Grundbegriffe der Metaphysik: Welt–Endlichkeit–Einsamkeit*) and
the first part of that of the following term (*Vom Wesen der menschlichen
Freiheit: Einleitung in die Philosophie*) attest to the central character of
the equation of Being and truth for the Heideggerian comprehension of
Being – all of which points out the value of the phenomenological reading
of Aristotle. And in my opinion it is also necessary to concede that, with
the same aim in view, Heidegger goes on as well to examine the signifi-

cation of being from the standpoint of actuality and potentiality, as is attested by the lecture course from the Summer term 1931 (*Aristoteles, Metaphysik θ, 1–3: Vom Wesen und Wirklichkeit der Kraft*), again with a view to determining whether it can hold up as the fundamental signification.

In this context I would also like to suggest the hypothesis that, later on, Heidegger sees in the three significations of being assembled by Aristotle a fundamental point of departure, within the metaphysical domain, for recovering, by digging down beneath it, a more originary and primary pre-metaphysical determination of Being. I conclude that it is by questioning the four fundamental significations of being according to Aristotle that Heidegger comes to finalize these characteristics which more and more he will attribute to Being itself in so far as it is thought out of an originary experience. In attempting to go back beyond the determination of the *on hos alethes*, Heidegger comes to attribute to Being the character of *aletheia* and that, by the same token, it is by questioning the determination of the *on dynamei kai energeiai* that he comes to attribute to Being, thought in a more originary manner, the character of *Physis*.

I would now like to show how, on the basis of his prevailing interest in the problematic of the plurivocity of being and the unitary meaning which upholds it, Heidegger arrives at a recuperation of Aristotle's practical philosophy (and principally of the thematic of the 6th book of the *Nichomachean Ethics*), when, in the course of the 1920s, he concentrates upon the signification of being as true.

4 The central character of the signification of being *qua* true and the topology of the loci of the truth

A preliminary remark is called for concerning the phenomenological character of the attitude with which Heidegger prepares the confrontation with Aristotle and carries it through. This character concerns the methodological attitude just as much as the thematic horizon of the confrontation. Moreover, one should not believe that, in announcing the phenomenological inspiration of his reading of Aristotle, Heidegger simply wanted to pay a tribute of gratitude to his master Husserl or, worse still, cover and conceal from him his detachment from phenomenological orthodoxy by using a purely nominal title. In effect, the methodological attitude which in *Sein und Zeit* is characterized by 'destruction' and which, let us say up to the *Kehre*, embodies the spirit in which Heidegger confronts the tradition, undoubtedly owes its origin to a variation and an integration of the phenomenological method theorized by Husserl. Just as for Husserl the philosophical attitude of the reduction which stands opposed to the natural and naive attitude of common sense places the former between brackets, so with Heidegger, an analogous critique has to be exercised, even when facing the evidence of the history of thinking, that is to say, when faced with the philosophical positions assumed and accepted by the tradition. And just as with Husserl the reduction was connected to phenomenological constitution, so, with Heidegger, destruction is a function of ontological foundation and construction. As Heidegger himself makes known, reduction, destruction and construction constitute the three essential and equally original elements in the phenomenological method.

> The conceptual interpretation of being and its structures, that is, the reductive construction of being, necessarily implies a destruction, or, in other words, a critical *de-construction* [*Abbau*] of the received concepts which are at first necessarily operative in order to go back to the source from which they were drawn. . . . The three fundamental elements of the phenomenological method: reduction, construction, destruction are intrinsically dependent upon one another and have to be founded in their mutual belonging together. Philosophical construction is necessarily destruction, that is to say, de-construction, brought about by way of a historical return to the tradition, to what has been transmitted; this does not in any way mean a negation of the tradition nor a condemnation obliterating the latter but, on the contrary, a positive appropriation of this tradition.[20]

But in what concerns the phenomenological configuration of the thematic horizon within which Heidegger approaches Aristotle and, in particular, his practical philosophy, one has to bear in mind that this approach was adopted in the context of a concentration upon the problematic of being *qua* true and that the circumstance which was certainly determinative in this analysis is that Heidegger arrived at it on the basis of an in-depth study of Husserl's *Logical Investigations* (the traces of which can now be seen in the first part of the lecture course of the Summer term 1925 published under the title *Prolegomena zur Geschichte des Zeitbegriffs*.[21] In the course of reflecting upon the comprehension of the truth proposed by Husserl, Heidegger systematically develops a conviction which had already taken root in Husserl's work, to wit, the conviction that judgment, assertion, understood as a synthesis or dihairesis of representations, does not constitute the original locus of the manifestation of truth but a dimension which has undergone a restriction with regard to the ontological depth and the originary extent of the phenomenon. Developing this conviction in a systematic way, Heidegger finishes up questioning three traditional theses on the truth, to wit: (1) the thesis that the truth consists in an *adequatio intellectus et rei*, (2) the thesis that the originary locus of its manifestation is the judgment, in as much as it is the connection or division of representations and of concepts, (3) the thesis that the authorship of these two theorems has to be attributed to Aristotle.[22]

In fact, with his thesis that not only acts of synthesis but also monothetic acts of simple apprehension can have a truth-character, Husserl had already called in question the traditional theory of truth as adequation. With this end in view he had also introduced a decisive distinction, namely the distinction between the truth of the proposition or of the judgment (*Satzwahrheit*) and the truth of intuition (*Anschauungswahrheit*), the latter is considered the more originary truth and therefore represents the foundation of the former. In addition, Husserl had introduced a fundamental innovation, recognized by Heidegger, which consists in the distinction and the theorization of categorial intuition. Conceived on the analogy of sensible intuition, it enabled Husserl to explain that modality of the apprehension of the elements of judgment whose identification (*Ausweisung*) goes beyond the sensible intuition, elements which, in the traditional theory of truth, had been understood as belonging to the domain of the categorial.[23]

Deepening the direction in which these Husserlian theses proceeded, Heidegger theorizes a fundamental distinction between the purely logico-categorial meaning of being-true (*Wahrsein*), which belongs to the proposition, and the ontological meaning of truth (*Wahrheit*), which belongs to the phenomenon of truth in its originary scope. In Heidegger's eyes, it is precisely this originary ontological depth of the phenomenon of truth which Aristotle takes account of as the decisive dimension, even if, clearly, he also recognizes the restricted signification of that being-true which is referred to the proposition. In consequence, Heidegger seeks to restore to those Aristotelian texts which bear upon the truth their originary scope, by freeing them from the fixed prejudices of a certain interpretative tradition which had prevailed hitherto and which can, according to Heidegger, even be found in a reading of Aristotle like that of Jaeger, which is innovative in other respects. Thus, the Heideggerian calling-in-question of the traditional theory of truth, initiated by the Husserlian phenomenological approach, goes along with a highly ontological reading of certain basic texts of Aristotle, such as *De interpretatione* I, *Metaphysics* IX, 10, *Nichomachean Ethics* VI.

Heidegger proceeds toward an uncovering of the more profound ontological meaning of the phenomenon of truth by way of a kind of triple argumentative progression:

(1) First of all, he distinguishes the semantic aspect of the *logos*, that is to say, the property of having a signification, an aspect which belongs to every form of the *logos*, and the apophantic character which is not

present in every form but only in that form *par excellence* of the *logos* which is the *apophansis*, predication or assertion. The specificity of this particular form of the *logos* consists in the fact that it is a synthesis or a dihairesis of concepts and in the fact that, as such, it possesses the character of being-true or being-false, more precisely, of being-able-to-be-true or being-able-to-be-false.

(2) Then Heidegger inquires into the ontological foundation of predicative discourse, of the *logos apophantikos*, with a view to identifying the ontological condition of the possibility of its being-true or being-false. And he finds it in the ontological constitution of human life itself, in Dasein, which contains in itself the intrinsic possibility of assuming; even better, of being itself an uncovering attitude, that is to say, of opening, and of opening itself in relation to, being.

(3) Finally, deepening his calling-in-question, Heidegger inquires into the ultimate ontological foundation of the uncovering of being by Dasein. And he arrives at the conclusion that this foundation is to be sought in the fact that being itself has the ontological constitution of something which gives itself, which is accessible to and perhaps grasped by the particular being which bears within itself the uncovering attitude, that is to say, Dasein. With reference to the latter, being is potentially *manifestativum sui*. It is evident, manifest, disclosed, *un-verborgen*, *a-lethes*. The truth conceived as *a-letheia*, as *Un-verborgenheit*, is therefore an ontologically constitutive character of being itself. It is an ante-predicative determination with reference to which the being-true or being-false of predication is a derived and restricted property.[24]

Following this argumentative progression, Heidegger arrives at a sort of topology or hierarchy of the loci of truth which he develops by assimilating certain Aristotelian theses in a radicalizing elaboration. In a somewhat expeditious but adequately synoptic fashion one can sum up the framework of this topology of truth as follows:

(1) The true is above all being itself in as much as it possesses the character of being manifest, disclosed. With this thesis Heidegger revives the ontological potency of the Aristotelian understanding of the truth which can be expressed in the equation: *on hos alethes*.

(2) The true is secondly Dasein itself, human life, in the sense that it is uncovering and that it develops this characteristic in its fundamentally uncovering attitudes. Behind this thesis it is not difficult to see the recovery of an Aristotelian idea, to wit, the idea of the Aristotelian determination of the human soul (psyche) as being-in-the-truth (*aletheuein*). In Aristotle, in fact, and especially in Book VI of the *Nichomachean Ethics*, Heidegger sees an analysis of the different ways in which the soul uncovers being, is in the truth, an analysis which has not yet been obscured by modern theoretical prejudices. And he therefore sees in

this analysis the first complete phenomenology of the fundamentally uncovering attitudes of human life, of Dasein.

(2.1) First of all, there is the specific modality of uncovering proper to the human soul and which distinguishes it both from the Gods and from the other animals: it is made manifest by way of the *logos*, which insti- . tutes the links and precisely under the five modes of being-in-the-truth, proper to the soul: *episteme, techne, phronesis, nous, sophia*;[25]

(2.2) but this modality of uncovering, determined by the *logos*, is founded in a direct and immediate manner of acceding to being and of uncovering it, which latter takes place either in the *aisthesis*, about which Aristotle says that it is always true (*aei alethes*),[26] or in the *noesis*, which apprehends its object through a direct contact by, so to speak, touching it and which, for this reason, and because it neither effects a synthesis nor a diaresis, cannot be false but can simply not take place (in the *agnoein*).[27]

(3) The true is finally the form *par excellence* of the *logos*, to wit, the *logos apophantikos* or *apophansis*, that is to say, predication or assertion in its affirmative (*kataphasis*) or its negative (*apophasis*) form. And this holds either in the sense that the *logos* is an *aletheuin qua legein*, or in the sense that the *logos* is *alethes qua legomenon*.[28]

It will now be necessary to undertake a deeper examination of the way in which Heidegger, having detached the comprehension of the phenomenon of truth from this latter dimension, that is, from the derivative and restrictive structure of predication, finishes up by radicalizing his inquiry into the traditional metaphysical conception of the truth. If, indeed, and thanks to his appropriation of Aristotle, Heidegger gains an ontological outlook which permits him to take the problem up again in a radical manner, there still remains open the question of the non-explicit presuppositions upon which even the Aristotelian conception of the phenomenon of truth is founded, and founded as a character of being *qua* manifest. The question Heidegger poses is the following:

What does Being have to mean if being-uncovering is to become comprehensible as a character of Being and even as the most authentic of all? If, in consequence, beings have in the end to be interpreted relative to their Being on the basis of being-uncovered?[29]

Even at this time, towards the middle of the 1920s, the vision of the problem which characterizes and will characterize Heidegger's thinking more and more is being clearly formed. Here already Heidegger thinks it possible to claim that the unquestioned foundation of the Aristotelian equation of Being and truth consists in the presupposition of a well-defined relation between Being and time and therefore in the

presupposition of a certain comprehension of Being and of time themselves. Why? Because, in order that the truth, in the sense of being-
uncovering, of being-disclosed (*a-letheia*), can be characterized as an
ontological characteristic of entities, the being of entities must first be
implicitly understood as presence (*Anwesen*), for only what has previously been understood as present can later be determined as discovered, as disclosed, that is to say, as true (*a-lethes*) in the sense
suggested by the Heideggerian etymology of the Greek word. But the
interpretation of Being as presence has its implicit foundation in the
presupposition of an unquestioned connection of Being with time, in the
context of which the dimension of the present is taken to be the determinative dimension of time. In other words, with regard to an understanding of time which privileges the dimension of the present, there corresponds an interpretation of Being in which the primacy is consequently
accorded to presence.

In this way Heidegger clears and, at the same time, prepares the
ground for his interpretation of the history of metaphysics. Indeed, he
arrives at the conviction – confirmed a little later by the celebrated
interpretation of the Platonic myth of the cave – that metaphysical thinking is structured and takes form as the thinking of presence, that is to
say, as a thinking which does not pose, in a sufficiently radical fashion,
the question of the relation between Being and time in all its articu-
lations. Heidegger arrives at this conclusion by way of his interpretation
of the problem of truth in Aristotle from the time of the lecture course
of the Winter term 1925/6. In a passage from this course which is very
significant in this regard, he says:

> The pure being-uncovering of beings, as Aristotle conceives it with
> reference to the simple, this pure being-uncovering signifies nothing
> other than the pure present, non-displaced and immovable, of what
> is present. Being-uncovering [*Entdecktheit*], that is to say in this case
> the pure present is, as present [*Gegenwart*], the supreme mode of
> presence [*Anwesenheit*]. But presence is the fundamental determin-
> ation of Being. So, being-uncovering, as the supreme mode of pres-
> ence, that is as present, is a mode of being and precisely the most
> authentic mode of being of all, presence itself which is
> present. . . . That is to say: since Being is understood as presence and
> being-uncovering as present, and since presence [*Anwesenheit*] and the
> present [*Gegenwart*] are present, Being as presence can and even must
> be determined by the truth as present, and in such a way that the
> present is the supreme mode of presence. Plato already designated
> Being as present. And the term *ousia* which, in the history of philo-
> sophy, is peddled in a completely senseless fashion as substance, means
> nothing other than presence in a well-determined sense. One has to

emphasize that the Greeks, Plato and Aristotle, did in fact determine Being as presence. But they were very far from understanding what that really means when they determined Being as presence and as present. . . . Once one has understood this problematic of the intimate connection of the understanding of Being on the basis of time, one is then certainly in possession of a clue with which to return to an elucidation of the history of the problem of Being and of the history of philosophy in general.[30]

Following which, Heidegger, from this moment on, tries to get back either beyond the ultimate presupposition on which the ontological understanding of the phenomenon of the truth is based or beyond the unquestioned presuppositions of Western thought which, from Plato to Husserl, take on for him the form of a metaphysics of presence.

If however the progressive radicalization of the calling-in-question of the comprehension of truth certainly already indicates the final direction in which Heidegger will deepen his confrontation with metaphysics, and if it exhibits several aspects which make it interesting and which provide a motive for further examination, nevertheless it seems to me that it is still not carried through in the spirit and with the intentions which will later characterize his proposal with regard to the overcoming of metaphysics. Or better: if Heidegger already envisages here the possibility and the necessity of calling-in-question the fixed philosophical themes of the tradition, this calling-in-question still does not aspire to overcome, and so to abandon, metaphysical thinking with a view to moving off in another direction. Rather, it is a matter of a calling-in-question which proceeds from the conviction that metaphysics is not built on a sufficiently radical basis and which does not therefore envisage an overcoming of metaphysics in the sense of *Uberwindung* or of *Verwindung* but rather of a foundation which is more truly original. In fact, at this time Heidegger still thinks that it is possible to achieve a radical foundation for ontology by way of a Dasein's analytic and, in consequence, right up to the Kant book of 1929, he calls his programme 'fundamental ontology' or 'metaphysics of Dasein', thereby attributing to the terms 'ontology' and 'metaphysics' a meaning which is entirely positive. It is precisely with a view to a radically founded construction that Heidegger assumes the methodological attitude of the 'destruction', an attitude which allows him to clear the way.

In what concerns the foundational attitude of this programme, I don't think it is an accident if, up to the *Kehre*, Heidegger pays special attention to Aristotle, Descartes, Leibniz, Kant, Husserl; and if, after the *Kehre*, on the contrary, with the progressive radicalization of his critique and with the circumventing of metaphysics, he abandons any foundational intention. And it is also significant that this progressive radicalization ripens within a horizon which is marked by the confrontation with Nietzsche, that is to say, with the densest and most advanced point in the corrosive critique of Western philosophy, a horizon which is marked at the same time by an assiduous restitution of pre-Socratic thinking, that is to say, a thinking which precedes the metaphysical decision of the West, a horizon which is marked finally by an affinity for, and a proximity to, the twilight theophany of Hölderlin which, with reference to the destiny of metaphysics, represents the alternative, and the possibility of the new God to come.

5 The uncovering structure of Dasein and the focalization of the horizon of *praxis*

To return to the question of the role of the problematic of the plurivocity of being and, in particular, of the signification of being as true, one might say that it is while analysing this last signification in the horizon of the founding intentions mentioned above that, in the course of the 1920s, Heidegger comes to place at the centre of his speculative efforts the problem of the apprehension and determination of the fundamental ontological structure of human life, of the psyche, of Dasein, more exactly, of the latter in its specific character as being-uncovering, in its being an *aletheuein*. So it is within the typically phenomenological horizon of the problem of the constitutive structure of the 'subject' that Heidegger interprets the Aristotelian determination of the psyche as *aletheuein*, and it is by way of this juncture of a phenomenological approach with Aristotelian elements that he paves the way for his analysis of existence.

But why is *praxis* central, and where does it get this characteristic? From what is the importance of the *Nichomachean Ethics* (an importance announced in my title) derived? There are many indications which, in my opinion, speak in favour of the hypothesis that Heidegger arrived at an Aristotelian determination of *praxis* while trying to solve the problems that Husserlian phenomenology had raised but which, in his view, the Husserlian understanding of subjectivity had left open rather than resolved.

In Heidegger's view, Husserlian phenomenology got stuck in a fundamental aporie, to wit, the aporie of the belonging of the subject to the world and of the simultaneous constitution of the world by the subject. Heidegger did not find satisfying the solution proposed by Husserl, a solution which consisted in distinguishing the psychological subject which participates in the world and the transcendental subject which constitutes the world, and which distinguishes the reality of the former from the ideality of the latter. Certainly, Heidegger shares with Husserl the conviction that the constitution of the experience of the world cannot be explained by retreating to a being which has the same modality of being, the same ontological constitution as the world. Heidegger, however, distances himself from Husserl because the Husserlian determination of transcendental subjectivity seems to him to have been won, predominantly and unilaterally, on the basis of a theoretical consideration of the acts of the life of consciousness.[31]

Why this impression? Because, by way of his analysis of the phenomenon of truth and by way of the topology of the loci of its manifestation, Heidegger comes to be convinced that *theoria* is only one of the different possibilities and modalities of the uncovering attitude through which man accedes to being. Alongside *theoria* and before *theoria* there is, for example, the uncovering attitude of *poiesis* or that of *praxis* by means of which too man is related to being and apprehends it. Heidegger takes his bearings from Aristotle precisely because Aristotle still retains the plurality of the uncovering attitudes of human life and, in the 6th book of the *Nichomachean Ethics*, offers the first systematic analysis differentiating the three fundamental uncovering attitudes of the soul, to wit, *theoria*, *poiesis* and *praxis*, together with the specific forms of knowledge which go along with them, namely, *sophia*, *techne* and *phronesis*.

In consequence, I think that one's chances of coming to terms with the speculative labour of Heidegger during the 1920s are improved if one rereads the analysis of Dasein, developed in the fundamental ontology, in the light of the phenomenological reading of Aristotle, in particular, the *Nichomachean Ethics*, and if one pays attention to the fact that the results of this voracious assimilation of Aristotle are often deposited in passages and in argumentative connections where Heidegger does not speak about Aristotle explicitly.

6 Aristotle's practical philosophy as the background to the analysis of existence: correspondences, transformations, differences

It is precisely the Aristotelian horizon of certain fundamental determinations developed by Heidegger in his analysis of existence which I want to bring out by identifying the correspondences by means of which one can see how Heidegger takes up again and reformulates the substantive meaning of equivalent concepts from the practical philosophy of Aristotle in a few fundamental terms of his own analysis.

The first correspondence, a correspondence which is so obvious that it stands in no need of a special proof, is the correspondence between the three fundamental modalities of being, namely, Dasein, *Zuhandenheit* and *Vorhandenheit*, modalities distinguished and determined in the lectures from the 1920s, as also in *Sein und Zeit*, and the three Aristotelian determinations of *praxis*, *poiesis* and *theoria*. (1) *Theoria* is the uncovering attitude which has both a descriptive and a veritative character, for it is directed toward the simple affirmation of the way in which things behave, the apprehension of the truth of beings; the knowledge which belongs to it is *sophia.* According to Heidegger, when human life assumes this uncovering attitude, being presents itself in a modality he calls *Vorhandenheit.*[32] (2) *Poiesis* is the productive, manipulative, uncovering attitude, in which one finds oneself when one handles entities and this attitude aims at the production of works. *Techne* is that kind of knowledge which guides the latter towards its objective. When one assumes this attitude, beings present themselves to us in that modality of being which Heidegger calls *Zuhandenheit.* (3) *Praxis* is the uncovering attitude which is realized in this form of action, whose goal is contained in itself (*hou heneka*), that is to say, in its success as action and not in something external to it (*heneka tinos*). *Phronesis,* or prudence, is the kind of knowledge which belongs to the latter and which gives it its orientation. My hypothesis is that the uncovering attitude of *praxis* is the attitude on which Heidegger bases his analyses, with a view to attaining the fundamental thematic determinations with which he designates the ontological structure of human existence, of Dasein.

This last correspondence, which certainly appears as the most problematic and the most disputable, but which, in my view, is for all that the most significant and the most central, has to be developed in greater detail. But first, it would be suitable to make a brief remark about the nature of the Heideggerian recovery of the fundamental meaning of the three determinations of *praxis, poiesis* and *theoria.* It is obvious in fact that Heidegger does not commit himself to a simple recovery of these determinations but that, in taking them up, he profoundly modifies the structure, the character and the connection of these determinations. The most perceptive transformation seems to me to be the accentuation, better the absolutization, of the ontological character which, to a certain extent, they also possess with Aristotle, but which, with him, is not the only character, not even always the determinative character. Let me explain: Heidegger explains the Aristotelian determinations of *praxis, poiesis* and *theoria* as if they were only modalities of being, thereby rigorously excluding any understanding of their ontic significance. Clearly, what interests Heidegger, from the standpoint of a determination of the fundamental ontological structure of Dasein, are not particular *praxeis, poieseis* and *theoriai* but only the ontological power of these concepts. To be sure, in Aristotle's text he finds indications which can sustain his highly ontological reading: if, for example, one considers the distinction between *praxis* and *poiesis* brought to light in the *Nichomachean Ethics* VI, in connection with *Metaphysics* IX, 6, one can see quite clearly that even with Aristotle it is not a question of a purely ontic distinction, that is to say, that it does not refer exclusively to particular actions amongst which certain would be *praxeis* and others *poieseis*. It is a distinction which also has a philosophical and ontological meaning to the extent that it points out a modality of being. With the result that it is capable of referring to the same ontic class of actions while introducing an ontological distinction: making a speech, for example, can be either a *poiesis*, a production of *logoi*, or a *praxis*, the exercise of an activity which is its own goal; the distinctive character of this activity, its distinctive modality of being, which arises out of the intention and out of the goal with regard to which it is executed, does not become apparent at the ontic level but only upon the ontological plane. It is the ontological quintessence of the Aristotelian concepts of *praxis*, of *poiesis* and of *theoria* that Heidegger underlines in his interpretation and which he extracts and absolutizes through his recuperation of these concepts in the determinations of Dasein, of *Zuhandenheit* and of *Vorhandenheit*.

One other determinative transformation is the change of order in the hierarchy of the three attitudes. It is not *theoria* which is considered to be the supreme attitude, as the highest and preferred activity for man. Rather, in the ontological context established by Heidegger, it is the attitude of *praxis*, linked to a whole series of other determinations implied by it, which becomes the central connotation, to the extent that it is conceived as the fundamental modality of being and as the ontological structure of Dasein. Together with this reversal, there goes a change in the relation with the other determinations: *Zuhandenheit* (which recovers the determination of *theoria*) and *Vorhandenheit* (which corresponds to the determination of *theoria*) are connected and tied to Dasein (for which, ontologically speaking, *praxis* is the modality of being). They indicate, respectively, the ways of being in which, correlatively, beings are bound up depending on whether Dasein, the 'originary *praxis*', is articulated together with beings in the constative and observational attitude or in the manipulative and productive. *Poiesis* and *theoria*, together, are both modalities of the unitary attitude of Dasein which Heidegger names *Besorgen*. In this way, by tracing *poiesis* and *theoria* back to a deeper common dimension, Heidegger obtains two further results: he shows the connection between *Zuhandenheit* and *Vorhandenheit*, between *poiesis* and *theoria* and between the latter and Dasein, the originary *praxis*. In addition, and against the traditional conception, he succeeds in showing that *theoria* is not an originary attitude but that it is derived from a modification of the poietic attitude (in consequence, as is well known, from the phenomena of *Auffälligkeit*, of *Aufdringlichkeit* and *Aufsässigkeit*[33]).

Ontological interpretation, hierarchic displacement and unitary structuration are the determinative transformations to which Heidegger subjects the Aristotelian concepts of *praxis*, *poiesis* and *theoria* in the recovery of their substantive meaning. But what is the rationale for

these transformations? In view of the impossibility of offering a detailed
analysis, I will limit myself here to what seems to me to be the basic
reason. This consists, in my opinion, in the fact that Heidegger moves
progressively towards the conviction that the Aristotelian determinations
in question, as they are presented in the *Nichomachean Ethics*, are in
fact indicative of the three fundamental uncovering attitudes of human
life, the three forms in which the soul is in the truth, and that they
therefore constitute the first completely phenomenological analysis of
Dasein, but that Aristotle does not succeed in posing explicitly, and in
a sufficiently radical manner, the problem of the unity which lies at the
bottom of these three determinations and which sustains them. In other
words, Aristotle did not succeed in grasping the fundamental ontological
constitution of human life. According to Heidegger, as is well known,
this omission is due to the fact that, by remaining within the horizon
of a metaphysics of presence, Aristotle remains tied to a naturalistic
understanding of time which prevents him from seeing that the unitary
structure of human life is originary temporality.

**7 Dasein as the 'ontologizing' of *praxis*: the practical origin of the
determinations of existence (*Zu-sein, Sorge, Jemeinigkeit, Worumwillen,
Befindlichkeit* and *Verstehen, Gewissen, Entschlossenheit*) and the
consequences**

But why then, and in spite of this critique, does one have to insist on
the fact that the understanding of the modality of the being of Dasein
is drawn from an ontologized concept of *praxis*? Because it seems to me
that several indications speak in favour of this thesis, which tells us
in an undeniable fashion that the characterization of Dasein and the
determination of its fundamental structures are accomplished within an
eminently 'practical' horizon (in the Aristotelian sense of *praxis*). By
interpreting the structures of Dasein across the filigree of the Aristotelian
understanding of *praxis* and of its sustaining categories, I will then try
to bring to light the structural, conceptual and even sometimes terminological correspondences between Heidegger's and Aristotle's vision of
the problem, without thereby ignoring or denying the differences. In as
much as the points taken into consideration previously prepare the way,
the legitimacy of this reconciliation of determinations which, on the
surface, are so divergent will appear self-evident, both in and of itself,
and in the context of the concepts and terms which this reconciliation
makes possible. Besides, one can count upon the confirmation deriving
from the fact that Heidegger himself, in his interpretations of Aristotle,
and notably of the *Nichomachean Ethics* from the 1920s, explicitly under-

stands the *episteme praktike* as an ontology of human life, of Dasein, and also suggests the equation of Dasein and *praxis*.[34]

7.1 Having-to-be (Zu-sein) as a practical determination

To begin with, in my opinion, one has to read the characterization of Dasein as having-to-be (*Zu-sein*) in an eminently practical sense. Having-to-be is introduced by Heidegger in paragraphs 4 to 9 of *Sein und Zeit*. With this characterization, indicative of the modality in which Dasein is and relates itself to its being, Heidegger wants to stress that this relation of Dasein to its being is not carried through in an attitude of observation and assertion, in a sort of turning back upon itself, in a theoretical and reflective introspection, but rather in a typically practico-moral attitude in which what is at stake is the very being of Dasein and in which one has to come to a decision about this being and uphold, whether one wants to or not, the weight of this decision. In other words, Heidegger wants to point out that Dasein does not in the first instance stand in relation to its being with a view to asserting and describing its significance and essence, to saying, for example, that it is *animal rationale*, but to decide what to do with this being, to choose, amongst different possibilities, the one which he will assume as his own and realize.[35]

To be sure, one cannot ignore the fact that Heidegger only retains the practical connotation of the ontological structure of Dasein as having-to-be as long as he pursues the project of apprehending and of determining the structure of Dasein in its specificity on the basis of Dasein itself in its purity. One knows that, later, when Dasein is no longer understood in itself but out of the horizon in which it is always already constituted, Heidegger will systematically eliminate all trace of this practical connotation and will determine the 'open' character of existence no longer as having-to-be, but as ek-sistence in the opening of being.[36] But precisely the very insistence with which Heidegger retracts the practical characterization of Dasein leads one to believe that it is the right way to recuperate the first Heideggerian understanding of the ontological modality of existence.

7.2 Care (Sorge) as the root of the practical structure of Dasein

It is only on the basis of the practical comprehension of the auto-referential structure of Dasein that it becomes possible to grasp, in its structural unity, the other existential connotations that Heidegger proposes. It becomes understandable, for example, why Heidegger designates the fundamental modality of *Erschlossenheit*, the open character of Dasein and the unity of the existential determinations by means of a concept which, from the thematic point of view, comes from practical philosophy, namely, the concept of care (*Sorge*). The determination of *Sorge* through which Heidegger takes up again and points out the phenomenon which Husserl designated as intentionality is, in my opinion, drawn from an ontological interpretation of the character of human life, designated by Aristotle through the term *orexis*. The proof? It is enough to collate the passage from Aristotle's text in which the term *orexis*, or the corresponding verb *oregomai*, appears and to see how Heidegger translates them. One discovers that he always makes use of his term *Sorge*. The most notable passage comes from the beginning of the *Metaphysics* where the initial proposition '*pantes anthropoi tou eidenai oregontai physei*' is translated by Heidegger as 'Im Sein des Menschen liegt wesenhaft die Sorge des Sehens', whereby it is important to stress not only the correspondence between *oregontai* and *Sorge* but also the ontological interpretation of *pantes anthropoi* by 'Im Sein des Menschen'.[37]

Within the same practical horizon one also comes to understand better why Heidegger designates as *Besorgen* (at the root of which lies the productive-manipulative disposition of *poiesis* rather than the constative-descriptive disposition of *theoria*) the modality within which Dasein lays itself open to and relates itself to things, and as *Fürsorge* the modality of being through which Dasein is in relation with others. One understands better because these determinations have their common unitary root precisely in the practical character of *Sorge*, and that indicates, again, that the entire structure of Dasein is practical in nature.

It isn't necessary to recall here how Heidegger directs his analysis toward an investigation of the unitary foundation which sustains the auto-referential practical structure of Dasein, indicated by *Zu-sein*. As is well known, Heidegger finds this foundation in the idea, thematized and conceptualized by him, according to which Dasein is not something that is realized and fulfilled in the momentary actuality of a pure activity but is structurally a *capacity* (*Seinkönnen*) which surpasses and reaches beyond the confines of presence in order to be exposed to the temporal ecstasis of the future, in which the projection of its possibilities is unfolded, and the past, which is always the horizon and the inevitable context for projection. So, for Heidegger, *capacity* is a modality of being characterized by a fundamental ontological and temporal suspension proper to Dasein in as much as the latter is originally open and free-for; and since this liberty is not something that Dasein chooses but which belongs to its very ontological constitution, it follows that Dasein perceives it as something which it cannot get rid of, as a weight, the weight of the unbearable lightness of its being which makes itself known in the *Grundstimmung* of anxiety.

Heidegger draws certain fundamental conclusions from the ontological interpretation of the practical structure of Dasein.

(1) Against the metaphysical priority of the present and of presence, he upholds the primacy of the future. Precisely because Dasein is related

to its being in a relation of a practical kind, when deciding about its being the being which represents what is at stake in this decision is always a future being, for – as Aristotle frequently underlines – deliberation (*bouleusis*) and decision (*prohairesis*)[38] bear upon the future.

(2) The being toward which Dasein stands in relation in the practical auto-reference is always the very being of Dasein itself, and it's for this reason that Heidegger attributes to it the character of *Jemeinigkeit*, being in every instance mine. I surmise that with this determination Heidegger is rethinking, and giving an ontological interpretation of the meaning of, a characteristic which belongs to the knowing of *phronesis* and which Aristotle formulates when he says that *phronesis* is a *hautoi eidenai*.[39]

(3) In view of all these elements Heidegger upholds a radical distinction between the ontological constitution of Dasein and that of beings different from Dasein, by basing it on the consideration that Dasein is the only being ontologically constituted as a *Zu-sein*. Upon this distinction Heidegger also founds the ontic and ontological priority of Dasein, and he criticizes the inadequate radicality of the metaphysical differentiation of man and nature, subject and object, consciousness and world, precisely because they are not rooted in a true apprehension of the fundamentally unitary structure of human life.

(4) The practical determination of the being of Dasein finally implies the rejection of the traditional theory of self-consciousness, conceived as a knowledge of self of a reflexive and informative kind and obtained by way of an *inspectio sui*, by way of a sort of turning back of consciousness, or of the subject, upon itself. The identity of Dasein is constituted practically to the extent that the latter refers, according to its own nature, to its *Zu-sein*, by assuming the latter or by not assuming it. In addition, this self-reference is not developed exclusively by means of transparent acts of the understanding but also depends upon 'inferior acts', on moods, on the sensible and passive components of human life. In this way Heidegger puts a double distance between himself and the metaphysical tradition where the specificity of the being of human life is re-duced and restrained within the objectifying categories of pure observation and within a theoretical horizon dominated by doctrines of presence and of consciousness.

The practical structure which designates and determines the ontological constitution of Dasein is the result – and this is still my contention – of a kind of speculative sedimentation (in Heidegger's thinking and even in the terminology of this period) of the essential meaning of the determinations of being and of the moral life of man presented by Aristotle in the *Nichomachean Ethics*. We are talking here of a sedimentation produced in the form of an ontological interpretation and whose intention is to validate and to realize the ideas which it takes up again. To be sure, by linking the Heideggerian analysis of existence so closely to Aristotle, doubts inevitably arise, doubts which can moreover be based, at least apparently, on Heidegger's own text. In fact, in his presentation of the programme of an existential analytic, Heidegger quite explicitly distances himself from Aristotle: he criticizes, for example, the Aristotelian thesis in accordance with which the primacy of man is founded on the fact that the soul, in as much as it knows, is a kind of reflection of all beings, or this other thesis according to which the essence of man consists in his *anima rationalis*. Nevertheless, one should note that Heidegger did not fail to acknowledge, on several occasions, his indebtedness vis-à-vis Aristotle. This even happens in the course of his existential analyses where, ordinarily, Heidegger covers up and effaces the traces of his productive assimilation.[40] Let us therefore consider which are the relevant determinations of Aristotle's practical philosophy taken up in Heidegger's existential analysis. To do this, and so to verify our thesis, it will be necessary to reread the critical passages from the existential analysis in a spirit which I would call a deciphering rather than interpreting, a spirit which is however well supported by the Marburg texts and which, in addition, finds ample support in *Sein und Zeit*.

What is taken up first of all is the general framework of the problem which engages Aristotle's attention. In fact, one can say that in the horizon established by the consideration of *episteme pratike* – a term, I want to emphasize, translated by Heidegger as *Ontologie des menschlichen Lebens* – Aristotle considers human life in totality as a *praxis* and not as a *poiesis*;[41] and *praxis* is considered as the specific *kinesis* of human life, which is not simply oriented toward the conservation of life itself, towards living pure and simple (*zen*), but which is *bios*, the project of life which, once vital conservation is assured, comes to terms with itself in the space which opens up before it in relation to the problem of how to live, that is, to the choice of the preferable form of life for man, to the problem of living well (*eu zen*) and to the means suited to realizing this goal. This means that man, *qua* political animal endowed with *logos*, carries the weight of the responsibility of deliberating (*bouleusis*), of choosing and of deciding (*prohairesis*) about the modalities and the forms of his life by turning toward that which he takes to be the best. As we know, it is the wise man, the prudent man (*phronimos*), who succeeds in deliberating well, in choosing and deciding well and who realizes right action (*eu prattein*), the good life (*eu zen*) and therefore happiness (*eudaimonia*).

This fundamental intuition of Aristotle's is taken up again in my sense by Heidegger and reformulated by means of a transformation which ontologizes and radicalizes it while accentuating its substantial significance. In fact, for Heidegger Dasein too is that particular being whose being is always in question and this most especially in that eminently practical sense in which Dasein has to decide about the forms and modalities of its own self-realization, even in those limiting cases where this decision is a matter of not deciding or abstaining from making a decision. As Aristotle would have it, Dasein is the being who must decide, *ta hautoi agatha kai sympheronta*.[42] And just as with Aristotle, one's success in life is determined by following the *phronesis*, with Heidegger too it's only when Dasein is attentive to the call of conscience and recognizes this 'having to decide' as its task and as its very being, that is, when it recognizes itself in its practical character by assuming the latter in the projection of its own possibilities, in the realization of its *praxis*, it is only then when Dasein takes responsibility for its being that it realizes itself as authentic (*phronimos*).

It is also possible to maintain that, in the 1920s, Heidegger is concerned to identify and determine the *Grundbewegtheit*, the fundamental characteristic of mobility proper to the being of human life in the practical self-reference by which it is determined. In the Aristotelian thesis in accordance with which *praxis* is *kinesis tou biou*, the movement specific to human life,[43] Heidegger sees decisive support for, and substantial confirmation of, the direction of his research, which leads him to distance himself from Husserl in order to come nearer to Aristotle and, at the same time, to filter his reading of Aristotle through the problems which he inherited from Husserl. In this way a highly productive interaction ensues between the demand for a speculative enrichment, which makes use of Aristotle, and a reading of Aristotle which is fertilized by a speculative orientation which determines in advance the problems to be tackled.

It is not possible to offer here an analysis of Aristotle's understanding of *praxis* and it is still not possible to pursue in detail the interpretation offered by Heidegger of Book VI of the *Nichomachean Ethics* due to the absence of certain texts like the Winter 1924/5 lectures on Plato's *Sophist*, the introductory part of which contains a detailed reading of Book VI, or the Summer 1926 lectures, the last part of which is entirely devoted to a general interpretation of Aristotle's ontology, including what Heidegger calls the ontology of human life, that is, the *episteme praktike*. But the evidence in our possession does nevertheless suffice, in my opinion, to indicate at least the basic direction of Heidegger's thinking.

In what concerns the central concept of *praxis*, Heidegger thinks he detects in Aristotle, as we have seen, a dual employment of the concept: an ontic employment in which the term indicates particular *praxeis* and in accordance with which these *praxeis* are certainly distinguished but at the same level as the *poieseis* and the particular *theoriai*: this is how it is used for example at the beginning of the *Nichomachean Ethics*; and a philosophical and ontological use in which *praxis* does not indicate particular actions but a modality of being. In this latter sense, *praxis* is the concept employed to determine the modality of being proper to human life, its specific *kinesis.* It is this use of the term one finds, for example, in *Nichomachean Ethics* VI, 5, or in *Metaphysics* IX, 6. The fundamental structure of this *kinesis* is *orexis* in its two consecutive moments of *dioxis* and *phyge*, and what characterizes human life more exactly is an *orexis* closely bound to *nous praktikos* and susceptible of being oriented by the *dianoeisthai* of the *logos*, in the case of *phronimos*, by an *orthos logos. Praxis* arises out of the juncture of these two moments, *orexis* and *nous*, by way of the process of deliberation (*bouleusis*) which ends up in choice and in the decision to act (*prohairesis*). If the *orexis* is right and the *logos* true, there results not only good deliberation (*euboulia*) but also the success of the *praxis*, *eupraxia*.

Reflecting in depth upon the Aristotelian structure of *praxis* and upon the determinations which it contains, Heidegger draws therefrom, I think, so many fundamental determinations which he no longer considers as particular moments of action but, due to his having 'ontologized' the concept of *praxis*, as ontological characteristics of human life. It follows that in his existential analysis one finds, hidden and disguised in an ontological envelope, an entire series of conceptual and terminological correspondences with the Aristotelian conception of *praxis*. But before examining them, it is necessary to insist again upon the nature of the transformation that Heidegger accomplishes in taking up the Aristotelian understanding of *praxis*.

It has already been pointed out how Heidegger, both with and against Husserl, appropriates the Aristotelian characterization of the three fundamentally uncovering attitudes (*praxis, poiesis, theoria*) and it has already been emphasized that with this appropriation he criticizes the lack of an explicit position on the problem of the fundamentally unitary determination which upholds all the others, and traces this lack back to the metaphysical horizon of presence and to that naturalistic understanding of time which prevents Aristotle from grasping the fact that the unitary structure of human life is originary temporality. Taking up again Aristotle's fundamental indications but freeing them at the same time from the metaphysical hypotheses by which they are conditioned, Heidegger thinks that it is important to reformulate these practical determinations as ontological designations, as modalities of being: this is where one finds the origin of their ontologizing interpretation. In other words: against the theoretical and objectifying unilaterality of modern metaphysics, Heidegger finds it worthwhile to take up again the fundamental intuitions of Aristotle's practical philosophy, intuitions which lie outside such a unilaterality. However, it is still necessary to purify them of the metaphysico-anthropological slag in which they are embedded. From an inadequately pure ontological point of view, the Aristotelian understanding of *praxis* is situated in the general framework of a prior conception of man as *animal rationale* and remains bound to the latter. It depends upon and falls with such a conception. According to Heidegger, on the contrary, since the validity of my metaphysical and anthropological framework is in doubt, the practical understanding of human life no longer refers to anything which can be relied upon. Every substantive support which was operative in the tradition is now considered derivative and defective with regard to an originary action, to that *praxis* which constitutes the being of Dasein and which must be understood in and for itself regardless of any pre-determination and pre-constitution. In the absence of any region in which it can be constituted, *praxis* has to be self-constituting; and in this way it becomes the originary ontological determination, self-sufficient, its own objective. It becomes *ou heneka, Worumwillen.*

Here we come across a fundamental difference. With Aristotle, the practical issue represents a particular way of viewing human life, precisely in as much as the latter is capable of action and in as much as it is itself action. It is therefore just one particular issue among others, alongside, for example, the physical, biological or psychological issue. In addition, it is not a privileged issue but, by virtue of the lesser degree of precision (*akribeia*) to which it lends itself, it has been considered a sort of *philosophia minor*. In any case, it does not exhaust the understanding of human life. With Heidegger, on the other hand, practical determinations are not determinations which exist alongside other possible determinations but represent the ontological constitution of Dasein itself. This means that as constitutive, their content is not something that Dasein can freely choose to have or not to have but is something from which it cannot be abstracted. Decision, for example, or *praxis* itself, are not conceived as possibilities which Dasein can realize or not, but become ontological predicates which characterize its being before, and therefore independent of, its will, its choice, its decision.

This brings with it another displacement in the characterization of *praxis*. There, where it is conceived as a possibility which one can grasp or not, *praxis* takes on a, so to speak, positive connotation. It is a possible way of realizing the being of man but not necessarily the only way. But if it becomes the very ontological structure of Dasein it is its inevitable character, the impossibility of avoiding it which is then underlined and accentuated. Hence, *praxis* is not only in question in the execution of determinate actions or in the pursuit of particular goals, it precedes each execution and each pursuit. And it is precisely this characteristic of inevitability, arising from the 'ontologization' of *praxis* as a structure of Dasein which confers upon the being of Dasein the characteristic of weight, which conveys the impression that the lightness of this being is unbearable.

The 'ontologization' of *praxis* then provokes a last transfiguration. It results, so to speak, in the evaporation of its specific weight as an activity and in the loss of certain characteristics which, with Aristotle, belong to it constitutively; above all, its inter-personality and its rootedness in a *koinonia*. With Heidegger, 'ontologization' drives *praxis* into a sort of heroic solipsism which deforms its very appearance.

So it appears undeniable that the Heideggerian 'ontologization' of the Aristotelian concept of *praxis* provokes some fundamental transformations and displacements. But in spite of these transformations and displacements, the prevailing correspondences will still have to be examined by considering how the Heideggerian determination of the 'open' structure of Dasein takes up again the decisive moments of the Aristotelian understanding of the moral being of man.

7.3 The articulation of Sorge in the complementary determinations of Befindlichkeit and Verstehen

It is well known that Heidegger establishes the openness of the being of Dasein, its *Erschlossenheit*, by affirming the originary unity of Dasein and world. The unitary sense of *Erschlossenheit* and of its *Existenzialien*, is care (*Sorge*), its three structural moments are *Befindlichkeit*, *Verstehen* and *Rede*.[44] However, the simple translation of these terms, almost impossible in any case, does little to help one grasp the meaning which Heidegger confers upon them. Rather, it tends to conceal this meaning. It might be helpful to consider that, with these concepts, Heidegger takes up again, rethinks and elevates to ontological rank so many transitional determinations of the being of man as 'subject' of action, by transforming them and inserting them into the ontologically more profound and more radical context established by his metaphysics of Dasein. In *Befindlichkeit*, he elevates to ontological rank and leads back to its unitary root, the determinations of the acting subject which had traditionally been thought within the framework of the doctrine of the passions, that is to say, as moments of passivity, of receptivity and finitude.[45] Similarly, in *Verstehen*, I believe that Heidegger ontologizes the active moment of projection and of spontaneity. The two moments are, in addition, co-originary with regard to the third moment, *Rede*, which will be left here in parentheses, but about which one can say that it designates the ontological foundation of the rational and discursive character of Dasein. What has to be underlined is the correspondence of these moments to two central determinations of the Aristotelian theory of action. Let us see how.

Befindlichkeit[46] represents the ontologization of ontic moods in as much as it is the ontological foundation of their possibility. In *Befindlichkeit*, which is rooted in *Sorge*, Dasein is open to its having-to-be. It is confronted with the nudity of its 'daß es ist und zu sein hat', more precisely, in such a way that its 'whence' (*Woher*) and its 'whither' (*Wohin*) are hidden from it. This is its *Geworfenheit*. What Heidegger wants to point out with this determination is that there belongs to the constitution of Dasein not simply elements which are pure, transparent, suited to spontaneity and rationality but also moments which are troubled and opaque, the condition of the possibility of which he tries to determine through the concept of *Befindlichkeit*. For Heidegger, in other words, human life constitutes both itself and its own identity by taking account not only of its transparence, its self-determination and its spontaneity but also in assuming as its own, the opacity of its *Stimmungen*, which latter follows precisely from the fact that it is, in its fundamental structure, *Sorge*. The constitutive function of *Stimmungen* is valid even for the purest attitudes of human life, that is to say, for *theoria*, about which Aristotle says, as Heidegger reminds us, that it can only take place in the calm of *rhastone* and of *diagoge*.[47]

In order to bring out the relation to Aristotle what is important here is that Heidegger, in the very paragraph in which he deals with *Befindlichkeit* (§29) explicitly cites Aristotle, more exactly, the doctrine of the passions (*pathe*), especially as presented in book II of the *Rhetoric*. While disengaging this doctrine from the context in which Aristotle situated it, Heidegger maintains that it has to be interpreted as 'the first systematic hermeneutics of the everydayness of being-with-one-another' (*die erste systematische Hermeneutik der Alltäglichkeit des Miteinanderseins*), and he also notes that since Aristotle hardly any progress has been made in the understanding of the passions, at least until phenomenology. In addition, we also know that Heidegger devoted the lectures of the Summer term 1924 to this ontological reading of the Aristotelian doctrine of the passions. Even if, in order to offer a more precise evaluation, we should wait until this text has been published, one can already affirm without hesitation that this retrieval of the Aristotelian doctrine of the passions plays an important role in the Heideggerian project of a complete and radical comprehension of the structure of human life, comprehension of such a kind that it cannot be reduced exclusively to an analysis of cognitive acts, still less to scientific cognition.

In what concerns the complementary determination with regard to *Befindlichkeit*, that is, *Verstehen*,[48] one can say very generally that it represents the ontological condition of the possibility of active and spontaneous determinations, of the auto-transparence of Dasein. It is the determination which reflects the productivity of capacity (*Seinkönnen*). In spite of the meaning suggested by the German term and even more, by the Latin translations, *Verstehen* indicates the ontological status of Dasein in as much as it is activity, in as much as it has the character of *Entwurf*, in as much as it projects its being by relating itself to itself in the practical attitude referred to above. Without entering into the details of the analysis of this determination, it is enough to take up again the synthetic definition which Heidegger gives of it: *Verstehen* is 'the existential being of Dasein's own potentiality-for-being; and it is so in such a way that this being discloses in itself what its being is capable of'.[49]

The fact that Heidegger considers *Verstehen* as an ontological modality of *Seinkönnen*, that he attributes to it the structure of the project, and that he associates its signification with the ontic signification of 'knowing how to do something' certainly places this determination within the horizon of practical comprehension. To be sure, *qua* ontological, strictly speaking, it precedes any distinction between theory and *praxis*. But that doesn't prevent its thematic connotation, arising from the field of *praxis* and the fundamental features of the phenomenon of acting from which it proceeds, being filtered through the ontological network. If, for example, one takes the retrieval of the treatment of *Verstehen* conducted in the lecture course of the Summer term 1927: *Die Grundprobleme der Phänomenologie*, where the filter for excluding every ontic determination is not so tight as in *Sein und Zeit*, one finds the claim (highly significant for my thesis) that *Verstehen* is 'the true sense of action' (*der eigentliche Sinn des Handelns*).[50] Heidegger's determination to refuse any interpretation of *Verstehen* in the sense of a cognitive operation opposed to *Erklären* is also, and evidently, directed toward defending the practical conception of *Verstehen*.

But the practical horizon for the Heideggerian comprehension of *Verstehen* also becomes apparent in the function which the latter fulfils in the constitution of the identity of Dasein. The structure of the project proper to *Verstehen* also implies a knowledge, a sight (*Sicht*), which accompanies and orients the projecting. It is the self-knowledge through which Dasein achieves transparence, *Durchsichtigkeit*. This last term is the one Heidegger employs, as he points out himself, to avoid the identity of Dasein being conceived in the horizon of *Warhnehmen*, of *Vernehmen*, of *Beschauen* and of *Anschauen*, that is to say, in the horizon of acts of apprehension of a theoretical kind, acts upon which the traditional understanding of self-consciousness depended. The Heideggerian effort to be rid of the theoretical horizon of presence therefore gets deposited in the determination of *Verstehen* and of *Durchsichtigkeit*; on the other hand, the effort to reach a more originary comprehension of the being of Dasein also gets deposited therein. However, as the terms chosen by Heidegger and the explanations which he gives demonstrate, it seems to me evident that this more radical originality is attained through the ontological exploitation of the thematic field of *praxis*, even if the ontological elimination of every ontic element aims at placing the originary comprehension of the being of Dasein at a more profound level than that of *praxis*, ontologically conceived.

The hypothesis I am going to risk is that through *Verstehen* (and in spite of all the transformations which are produced and which I do not wish to deny) Heidegger rethinks and reformulates the substantive meaning of the function which, in the Aristotelian theory of action, is filled by the *nous praktikos*. Just as the latter is the complement of *praxis*, so *Verstehen* represents the determination corresponding to *Befindlichkeit*. To be sure, *Verstehen* is not confined within the limits of a theory of action but concerns the totality of *Dasein*: as such it is to be explained with reference to things like *Besorgen* (implying *poietic* and theoretical attitudes), with reference to other things like *Fürsorge*, and with reference to itself as *Worumwillen*. And it has its roots, just like *Befindlichkeit*, in the unitary structure of *Sorge*. And so it obviously finds its place elsewhere than in the *nous praktikos* of the Aristotelian comprehension of action. But in spite of this displacement, in conceiving of the being of Dasein as *Sorge*, as complementary to and co-originary with *Befindlichkeit* and *Verstehen*, of *Geworfenheit* and *Entwurf*, of *Reluzenz* and of *Praestruktion*, that is to say, as the unity of passivity and activity, of receptivity and spontaneity, of horizon and constitution, one can say that Heidegger takes up again and reformulates, in an ontologically radicalized framework the same problem as Aristotle grasped and confronted in Book VI of the *Nichomachean Ethics* where he says that man is the *arche* which is at the same time *orexis dianoetike* and *nous orektikos*.[51] And just as with Aristotle the connection of *orexis* and of *nous* always takes place across the *logos*, in an analogous fashion Heidegger theorizes the co-originality of *Befindlichkeit* and *Verstehen* with *Rede*.

To be sure, Heidegger insists upon the differences. He tells us that

> care, as an originary totality, 'precedes' in an apriori-existential fashion, any 'behaviour' and 'situation' of *Dasein*: which means that it too is always already to be found therein. It follows that this phenomenon does not in any way express a primacy of the practical attitude over the theoretical attitude. The purely intuitive determination of something present is no less characterized by care than is a 'political action' or calm resignation. 'Theory' and 'praxis' are possibilities of being of a being whose being has to be determined as care.[52]

This passage, which appears opposed to my thesis, in fact confirms it. For, on the one hand, Heidegger can obviously and with reason proclaim the differences to the extent that he interprets *Sorge* not as a determinate comportment of Dasein, whether theoretical, practical or poietic, but as the unitary ontological foundation which renders possible all the different comportments. But, on the other hand, in order to specify the essential characteristics of this unitary foundation he has recourse to determinations and to concepts which he borrows from Aristotle's practical philosophy. The very fact that on several occasions he experiences the need to distract us from an interpretation of *Sorge* in this sense, rather than allaying our suspicions only confirms that it is precisely in this direction that the source of his determination has to be sought.

Similarly when, immediately afterwards, Heidegger says that 'the phenomenon of care in its totality is essentially something that cannot be torn asunder; so any attempts to trace it back to special acts or drives like willing and wishing or urge [*Drang*] and addiction [*Hang*], or to construct it out of these will be unsuccessful'; and when he adds: 'willing and wishing are rooted with ontological necessity in *Dasein*'s care; they are not just ontologically undifferentiated experiences occurring in a "stream" which is completely indefinite with regard to the meaning of its being'. This is no less the case with urge and addiction which too are grounded in care in so far as they can be exhibited in Dasein at all. In affirming all this Heidegger obviously wants to underline the extreme radicality of his comprehension of the being of Dasein as *Sorge* and so to confirm the ontological precedence of *Sorge* with regard to the traditional practical determinations which he mentions. But the necessity of drawing a line between the ontological level of *Sorge* and that of the other determinations depends precisely upon the fact that, outside of all that, and from the thematic point of view, *Sorge* is homogeneous with them. Besides, it is precisely this very homogeneity which allows *Sorge* to be the unitary ontological foundation. Because it is only between homogeneous elements that a relation of foundation can be established.

This homogeneity between care and the other traditional practical determinations of *orexis* and *appetitus*, of inclination and addiction, becomes even clearer and more undeniable in the treatment of the phenomenon which Heidegger handles in the lectures of the Summer term 1925. In this course, Heidegger presents the phenomenon of *Sorge* in a closer relation with the moments of drive (*Drang*) and addiction (*Hang*) which he seems to consider as the explanation for the structure of *Sorge* itself. In spite of the fact that Heidegger never ceases to underline the difference in ontological depth between the traditional determinations and his own, the appearance of *Sorge* in the two moments of *Drang* and *Hang* confirms its correspondence with *orexis* and its two moments of *dioxis* and *phyge*.[53]

7.4 Gewissen *as the 'ontologization' of phronesis*

In the light of these considerations, one also understands why, as Gadamer recalls, confronted with the difficulty of translating the term *phronesis*, Heidegger could exclaim: 'Das ist das Gewissen!'[54] Evidently, he was thinking of his determination of conscience (*Gewissen*) as the locus where potentiality for being, the fundamental practical determination of Dasein, becomes manifest to itself. In *Sein und Zeit* (§§54–60), it is indeed the case that conscience is characterized as the locus for the 'attestation by *Dasein* of its authentic potentiality-for-being' (*dase-insmäßige Bezeugung eines eigentlichen Seinkönnens*); there, where Dasein is ready to listen to the appeal of conscience in the attitude of wanting-to-have-a-conscience (*Gewissen-haben-wollen*) and of resoluteness (*Entschlossenheit*), it is able to attain the authentic realization of existence.[55] In an analogous fashion, with Aristotle, *phronesis* is the knowledge which constitutes the horizon in which *praxis* can succeed as *eupraxia* and human living, which is, in sum, a *praxis*, can be realized as living well (*eu zen*). And just as with Aristotle, *phronesis* always implies knowledge of *kairos*[56] so conscience, with Heidegger, is always referred to the *Augenblick*.[57]

So Heidegger certainly had his reason for translating *phronesis* by *Gewissen*; and, for my part, I think I have reason for thinking that *Gewissen* is the ontologization of *phronesis*. The passage from the *Nichomachean Ethics* which arouses the Heideggerian exclamation to the effect that *phronesis* is *Gewissen* furnishes, in my opinion, both the occasion and the motive for an ontologizing operation. Consider the end of chapter 5 from Book VI where Aristotle, after having given a definition of *phronesis* as *hexis elethes meta logou pratike peri ta anthropoi agatha kai kaka*, admits that even this definition does not suffice to entirely exhaust its essence. For it is something more than a *hexis*. Curiously enough, Aristotle does not succeed in saying what it is, but limits himself to developing a proof which confirms his claim: any *hexis* can be forgotten but *phronesis* cannot be forgotten.[58] I suppose that in reflecting upon this question: in what is phronesis 'more'? Heidegger must have arrived at the conclusion that, if it is more than a *hexis* and if, therefore, it cannot be overlooked, it must be a characteristic of the soul itself. It therefore has to be ontologized. But the ontologization of *phronesis* yields as a result *Gewissen*.

7.5 Entschlossenheit *as the 'ontologization' of* prohairesis *and the other possible correspondences*

One could continue this catalogue of correspondences and indicate how the same ontologization is accomplished by Heidegger in the case of other determinations of Aristotle's practical philosophy. I am going to limit myself here to an inventory. With the term *Jemeinigkeit*,[59] as I have already indicated, Heidegger ontologizes the determination by means of which Aristotle designates a characteristic which belongs to *phronesis*, the fact that it is a 'knowledge concerning the self' (*to hautoi eidenai*). And again: the designation of Dasein as *Worumwillen*[60] is the ontologization of the determination of *praxis* as *hou heneka*. In fact, since the distinctive characteristic of *praxis* is the fact that it is not with reference to anything else (*heneka tinos*) like *poiesis*, but that it contains in itself its own goal (*hou heneka*) and since Dasein is pre-eminently an ontologized *praxis*, the latter must possess, *par excellence*, the characteristic of *hou heneka*. This is the characteristic that Heidegger attributes to it with the designation *Worumwillen*.

Finally, the determination of *Entschlossenheit*[61] is, in my opinion, the ontologization of *prohairesis*, with this difference, that the latter is situated as a special moment within the Aristotelian theory of action, while *Entschlossenheit* is a characteristic of the being of Dasein. An indisputable confirmation of this latter correspondence comes from the fact that, in translating Aristotle, Heidegger renders *prohairesis* by *Entschlossenheit*. Among the passages which attest to this, the one which seems to be particularly significant occurs in the lecture course of Summer 1926, on the *Grundbegriffe der antiken Philosophie*. Heidegger interprets the passage from Book IV, 2 of the *Metaphysics*, where Aristotle differentiates philosophers into dialecticians and sophists, and translates:

> Dialektik und Sophistik haben gewissermaßen dasselbe Gewand angezogen wie die Philosophie, aber sie sind es im Grunde nicht; die Sophistik sieht nur so aus. Die Dialektiker zwar nehmen ihre Aufgabe ernst und positiv, sie handeln vom *koinon*, aber es fehlt ihnen die Orientierung an der Idee des Seins. Beide bewegten sich um dasselbe Gebiet wie die Philosophie. Die Dialektik unterscheidet sich durch die Art der Möglichkeiten: sie hat nur begrenzte Möglichkeiten, sie kann nur versuchen; die Philosophie dagegen gibt zu verstehen. Die Sophisten unterscheiden sich durch die Art der Entschlossenheit zur wissenschaflichen Forshung: sie sind unernst.

What has to be underlined is that Heidegger translates here with *Entschlossenheit zur wissenschaflichen Forschung* what, in the original Greek, stands as: *prohairesis tou biou*.

8 Conclusive considerations: from Heidegger to Aristotle and from Aristotle to us

I hope that the correspondences I have pointed out will, if not prove, at least render plausible, the general thesis with regard to a retrieval by Heidegger of the framework for the problems posed by Aristotle's practical philosophy, and to a general correspondence between the practico-moral understanding of human life with Aristotle and the Heideggerian existential analysis. With this in mind, I would like to finish up by citing a passage which shows very clearly, and yet again, how Heidegger struggles to get close to Aristotle or, if you prefer, to bring Aristotle close to himself. Towards the end of the lecture on the 'Grundbegriffe der antiken Philosophie', having dealt with the five modalities of the *aletheuein* of the *psyche* and the movements which correspond to them, Heidegger poses the problem of the unitary structure of the *psyche*, of the being of human life, and he replies by giving, with Aristotle, the following definition of man: '*anthropos* ist *zoion*, dem die *praxis* zukommt, ferner *logos*. Diese drei Bestimmungen zusammengezogen: *zoe pratike tou logon echontos* ist das Wesen des Menschen. Der Mensch is das Lebewesen, das gemäß seiner Seinsart die Möglichkeit hat, zu handeln.'[62]

To be sure, one must also add that in taking up again the Aristotelian determinations of *praxis*, Heidegger 'ontologizes' them and that this ontologization is the equivalent for him of a radicalization. For it permits him to grasp the fundamental unitary connection which upholds these determinations and which is, notoriously, temporality conceived in an originary way (*Zeitlichkeit*). At the end of all this, and once he has carried through his 'ontologization', Heidegger takes up a distance with regard to Aristotle. Aristotle was not able to see originary temporality as the unitary ontological foundation of the determinations of human life which, nevertheless, he grasped and described, because he remains within the horizon of a naturalistic, chronological and non-chairological understanding of time. Even the celebrated aporie of the relation between the *psyche* and *chronos* explicitly raised by Aristotle (*Physik* IV, 14, 223 to 21, 29) which is handled in a magisterial manner by Heidegger in his commentary on the Aristotelian treatment of time,[63] seems to be insufficient, in Heidegger's eyes, to extract Aristotle from the horizon of the naturalistic understanding of time.

And yet: Aristotle does anticipate correctly, even if only at the ontic level, the intuition which Heidegger raises to the ontological power with the equation of Dasein and *Zeitlichkeit*. This is a conjecture which can be based upon a passage from *De anima* III, 10, where it seems as though Aristotle attributes to man, as a specific characteristic distinguishing him from animals, the perception of time (*chronou aisthesis*).[64] The attribution is, to tell the truth, controversial; but the fact that Heidegger, who shows that he knows the passage very well, nevertheless interprets it without hesitation in this sense, and the fact that, in addition, he links the perception of time with the capacity for action in order to define the specific character of human life, lends unquestionable credence to this conjecture. To explain the difference between the *orexis* of animals and that reasonable action proper to human life, he refers to the passage mentioned at *De anima* III, 10, and he translates:

Der Gegensatz von Trieb und eigentlich entschlossener, vernünftiger Handlung ist eine Möglichkeit nur bei lebendigen Wesen die Möglichkeit haben, Zeit zu verstehen. Sofern das Lebendige dem Trieb überlassen ist, ist es bezogen auf das, was gerade da ist und reizt, *to ede hedy*: darauf strebt der Trieb hemmungslos, auf das Gegenwärtige, Verfügbare. Aber dadurch, daß im Menschen die *aisthesis chronou* liegt, hat der Mensch die Möglichkeit, sich *to mellon* zu vergegenwärtigen als das Mögliche, um des willen er handelt.

Can one still remain in doubt about the deep furrow that the voracious interpretation and assimilation of Aristotle has dug in Heidegger's speculative path? Obviously, I think not; but I also think that it is no longer possible to doubt that Heidegger's thinking succeeds in reactivating and reformulating the substantive meaning of certain fundamental problems posed by Aristotle with a radicality of which no one else seems capable today. In this sense, and especially for the phases on which I have concentrated my analysis, this thinking represents one of the most dense and significant moments in the presence of Aristotle in our century. By means of it we are referred back to Aristotle and from Aristotle to us. With a view to gaining an awareness of the problems of the contemporary world, of nihilism and technology, Heidegger has taught us that it is necessary to immerse oneself in the Aristotelian bath – and this before any speculative utopianism, before every form of rebellion or dadaist thinking in which most of those who have wanted to take up his challenge and try to think the problems which we inherited from him, have fallen.

I know that the Heideggerians are going to say: you have completely reduced Heidegger to Aristotle, to the point of finding in Aristotle a correspondence and even an anticipation of the fundamental discovery made by Heidegger at Marburg, the specification of the unitary ontological structure of Dasein in originary temporality. The non-Heideggerians, on the contrary, will protest as follows: what you have tried to pass off as Aristotelian doesn't have much to do with Aristotle and looks more like a philosophical pastiche produced by a fascination with Aristotle.

My response: I know that one has to be on one's guard against this danger but one has to risk it. If I gave the impression of levelling Heidegger down to Aristotle, the optic distortion is inevitable and I apologize for it. I simply wanted to show – against the old existentialist interpretation, and against more recent interpretations which only see in Heideggerian thinking (much too expeditiously and much too rapidly), the overcoming of the tradition – how Heidegger spanned this tradition and entered in depth into a confrontation with its dominant founding moments by reinstating the substantive sense of the confrontation with Greek culture. I am aware that I adopted only one among other possible routes and that I threw light upon only one of the numerous facets of Heidegger's work. I am also aware that what I have done is only a first step on the way to understanding the meaning of Heidegger's speculative path, a step which necessarily has to leave aside other possible readings without moreover trying to compete with them. Finally, I am particularly aware that the interpretation I have proposed still has to face the explicit retractions undertaken by the second and last Heidegger. But if it is objected that my reading gets under way by neglecting the interpretation Heidegger himself has given to his thinking, I have to reply: if that is a sin, it is a sin I have committed voluntarily. Moreover, I have no intention of repenting.

Translated by Christopher Macann

Notes

1 For the citation of writings by Heidegger published in the *Gesamtausgabe* (Frankfurt: Klostermann, 1975ss.) we will use the sign *GA* followed by Arabic numerals to indicate the volume.

2 Especially with regard to autobiographical considerations contained in the letter to W. J. Richardson from the beginning of the month of April 1962 and published as the preface to the study by the latter entitled *Heidegger: Through Phenomenology to Thought*, Phaenomenologica 13 (La Haye: Nijhoff, 1963), pp. vii–xxiii, and in 'Mein Weg in die Phänomenologie' (1963) reproduced in M. Heidegger, *Zur Sache des Denkens* (Tübingen: Niemeyer, 1969), pp. 81–90; cf. also the preface to the first edition (1972) of the *Frühe Schriften*, reproduced in *GA* 1, pp. 55–7.

3 I am thinking here, in the first place, of that interpretation and reproduction of Aristotle's practical philosophy proposed by Hans-Georg Gadamer in the celebrated chapter on the contemporary interpretation of Aristotle's Ethics from *Wahrheit und Methode* (Tübingen: Mohr, 1960), of certain interpretations of Eugen Fink (*Metaphysik der Erziehung im Weltverständnis von Platon und Aristoteles* (Frankfurt: Klostermann, 1970), but also of numerous monographs such as: Walter Bröcker, *Aristoteles* (Frankfurt: Klostermann, 1935); Helen Weiß, *Kausalität und Zufall in der Philosophie des Aristoteles* (Bale: Haus zum Falken, 1942); reprinted (Darmstadt: Wissenschaftliche Buchgesellschaft, 1967); Wilhelm Szilasi, *Macht und Ohnmacht des Geistes* (Berne: Francke, 1946) (in particular the second part which contains the interpretations of the *Nichomachean Ethics* VI, *Metaphysics* IX and XII and *De anima* II); Karl Ulmer, *Wahrheit, Kunst und Natur bei Aristoteles. Ein Beitrag zur Aufklärung der metaphysischen Herkunft der modernen Technik* (Tübingen: Niemeyer, 1953); Alfredo Guzzoni, *Die Einkeit des on pollachos legomenon bei Aristoteles* (Freiburg University, Ph.D. thesis, 1957); Ernst Tugendhat, *Ti kata tinos. Eine Untersuchung zu Struktur und Ursprung aristotelischer Grundbegriffe* (Freiburg-München: Alber, 1958); R. Boehm, *Das Grundlegende und das Wesentliche. Zu Aristoteles' Abhandlung 'über das Sein und das Seiende (Metaphysik Z)'* (La Haye: Nijhoff, 1965); Ernst Vollrath, *Studien zur Kategorienlehre des Aristoteles* (Ratingen: Henn, 1969), and *Die These der Metaphysik. Zur Gestalt der Metaphysik bei Aristoteles, Kant and Hegel* (Ratingen: Henn, 1969), pp. 15–92; Fridolin Wiplinger, *Physis und Logos. Zum Körperphänomen in seiner Bedeutung für den Ursprung der Metaphysik bei Aristoteles* (Freiburg-München: Alber, 1971); Ute Guzzoni, *Grund und Allgemeinheit. Untersuchung zum aristotelischen Verständnis der ontologischen Gründe* (Meisenheim: Hain, 1975); Karl-Heinz Volkmann-Schluck, *Die Metaphysik des Aristoteles* (Frankfurt: Klostermann, 1979); Ingeborg Schüßler, *Aristoteles,*

Philosophie und Wissenschaft. Das Problem der Verselbständigung der Wissenschaften (Frankfurt: Klostermann, 1982).

4 M. Heidegger, *Vom Wesen und Begriff der Physis, Aristoteles, Physik B, I,* reproduced in *GA* 9, pp. 239–301.

5 In 1976 in *GA* 21 (text established by Walter Biemel).

6 In 1975 in *GA* 24 (text established by Friedrich-Wilhelm von Herrmann).

7 In 1981 in *GA* 33 (text established by Heinrich Hüni).

8 In 1983 in *GA* 29–30 (text established by Friedrich-Wilhelm von Herrmann).

9 *GA* 18.

10 *GA* 19.

11 *GA* 22.

12 Appeared in 1985 in *GA* (text established by Walter Bröcker and Käte Bröcker-Oltmanns).

13 Cf. E. Husserl, *Briefe an Roman Ingarden,* Phaenomenologica 25 (La Haye: Nijhoff, 1968), pp. 25–7. In a letter addressed to Gadamer (from the year 1922) Heidegger sets out in detail the contents of this interpretation: 'First part (ap. 15 sheets) deals with *Nich. Eth. Z, Met.* A, 1–2, *Phys.* A. 8; the second (same length) *Met.* ZHQ, *De motu an., De anima.* The third part appears later. Since the Jahrbuch will be published later I can offer you a separate copy.' The letter is quoted in G.-G. Gadamer, *Heideggers Wege* (Tübingen: Mohr, 1983), p. 118. (Gadamer lost the copy of the manuscript Heidegger had sent him during the bombing of Leipzig, but another copy of the manuscript has since been found and published in *Dilthey-Jahrbuch,* 6 (1989), pp. 228–69.

14 Notoriously, Heidegger clarifies the meaning of the 'phenomenological destruction' of the history of ontology in *Sein und Zeit* (*GA* 2), §6. Further valuable information is to be found in the lectures of Summer 1927, *Die Grundprobleme der Phänomenologie,* where one learns how Heidegger is able to get the idea of a destruction from an extension of the Husserlian method of reduction and how, as a result, he conceives the triple articulation of the phenomenological method of reduction, destruction and construction (cf. *GA* 24, §5).

15 Cf. Heidegger, *Zur Sache des Denkens,* p. 81.

16 Cf. F. Brentano, *Von der mannigfachen Bedeutung des Seienden nach Aristoteles* (Freiburg: Herder, 1862; reprinted Hildesheim: Olms, 1960).

17 In addition to Brentano's dissertation, Heidegger also mentions the treatise by Carl Braig, *Vom Sein, Abriß der Ontologie* (Freiburg: Herder, 1896); for the analysis of the contents of this last work, in connection with the genesis of the problem of Being in the young Heidegger, I refer the reader to my monograph *Heidegger e Aristotele* (Padova: Daphne, 1984), pp. 52–64.

18 M. Heidegger, *Die Kategorien- und Bedeutungslehre des Duns Scotus* (1915), reprinted in *GA* 1, pp. 189–411.

19 In a later but nevertheless very interesting statement which is to be found in the lecture course of Summer 1931, Heidegger says:

Since medieval times, the first proposition of Met. IX, 1, had served as the basis for the conclusion that the fundamental meaning of being in general – even for the four meanings together, not just for one (the categorial meaning) and its multiplicity – was ousia, which it was customary to translate as 'substance'. In the 19th century this tendency became even more pronounced (especially with Brentano) because, in between, being-possible and being-real had been recognized as categories. This is the reason why it has become a received opinion that the Aristotelian doctrine of being was a 'doctrine of substance'. This is a mistake, issuing in part from an inadequate interpretation of pollachos; more precisely, it was not understood that what was being opened up here was simply a question. (Even W. Jaeger's reconstruction of Aristotle was based upon this error.)

(*GA* 33, pp. 45–6)

20 *GA* 24, p. 31. In the same context of the Heideggerian development of the phenomenological method one finds illuminating indications in the ontological orientation which Heidegger provokes in the self-understanding of phenomenology. The latter is not a redirection of the natural attitude towards a philosophical disposition which opens up a perspective on the constitutive operations of subjectivity but it brings about a transition for any ontic consideration of being to its ontological consideration, that is, to a consideration which bears upon the modalities of being and, therefore, upon the being of beings. But listen to Heidegger:

> Being must be grasped and thematized. . . . The apprehension of being, that is, phenomenological research, is directed necessarily and in the first instance at beings, but only in order to be definitively re-directed from beings and led back to their being. The fundamental element in the phenomenological method, in the sense of a leading back of the questioning from beings naively apprehended to being, we designate by the expression *phenomenological reduction*. Therewith we make use of a central term of Husserl's phenomenology, though only in a nominal and not in a real way. *For Husserl*, the phenomenological reduction, which he first worked out expressly in *Ideas*, is a method for reading back the phenomenological viewpoint from the natural attitude of humans living with each other in a world of things, to the life of transcendental consciousness and its noetic-noematic lived experiences in which objects are constituted as correlates of consciousness. *For us*, the phenomenological reduction means the leading back of the phenomenological viewpoint from an apprehension of beings (however determined) to an understanding of their being.

(*GA* 24, pp. 28–9)

Here, as also in the objections advanced on the occasion of the drafting of the *Encyclopedia Britannica* article, the Heideggerian critique of Husserlian phenomenology seems not to be an immanent critique which moves back within the Husserlian position to its specific presuppositions. In my opinion, it assumes the form of a sort of ontological torsion which gets away from the Husserlian position right away and, so to speak, attacks it from the rear. And it has to be added that Heidegger introduces, with reference to Husserl, a decisive change not only in the attempt to understand the philosophical approach in an ontological and non-transcendental sense but also in the attempt to understand the motives which provoke the redirection of the natural attitude towards the philosophical. The redirection does not consist in a fictive operation which takes place in the head of the professional philosopher but lies rooted in a fundamental *Stimmung*, that is in an anxiety in which the conversion from inauthenticity to authenticity is prefigured and in which, consequently, there takes place that assumption of the existential disposition which is the philosophical disposition *par excellence*.

21 *GA* 20, pp. 13–182. The original subtitle of the lecture 'Prolegomena zu einer Phänomenologie von Geschichte und Natur' very clearly announces Heidegger's intention to keep close to Husserlian phenomenology, at least with respect to its terminology.

22 Cf. M. Heidegger, *Sein und Zeit*, §44, and *GA* 21, p. 129.

23 These positions are presented in the *6th Logical Investigation* (sect. II, chap. VI: 'Sinnlichkeit und Verstand') which is the Husserlian text to which Heidegger prefers to refer. With regard to the confrontation between Heidegger and Husserl, I refer the reader to what I have written in 'Heidegger in Marburg: Die Auseinandersetzung mit Husserl', *Philosophischer Literaturanzeiger*, 37 (1984), pp. 48–69, and in 'La trasformazione della fenomenologia da Husserl a Heidegger', *Teoria*, 4(i) (1984), pp. 125–62.

24 One can find this argumentative progression in the lecture from the Winter term 1925/6 (cf. *GA* 21, p. 1, Hauptstück). It can also be found in that of the Winter term 1929/30 (*GA* 29/30, §72–3), where the quest for the ontological foundation of the phenomenon of truth takes a significant turn. The emphasis is no longer on the uncovering attitude of *Dasein*, but rather on its being-free (*Freisein*), that is, no longer on the spontaneity and the productivity of *Dasein*, but on the ontological character (being-free) of the horizon constitutive of its condition. Finally, it can be found in the lectures from the Summer term 1930 (*GA* 31, §9), where, in interpreting *Metaphysics* IX, 10, Heidegger concentrates on the *on hos alethes*.

25 Cf. Aristotle, *Nichomachean Ethics* VI, 3, 11139 b 15–17.

26 Cf. Aristotle, *De anima* III, 3, 427 b 12; 428a 11, 428 b 18.

27 Cf. Aristotle, *Metaphysics* IX, 10. Heidegger, at least twice, spends a considerable time on the interpretation of this critical chapter of the *Metaphysics*, in the lectures from 1925/6 (*GA* 21, pp. 170–82) and in that of 1930 (*GA* 31, pp. 73–109).

28 Heidegger insists upon this differentiation in the introduction to the lectures from the Winter term 1924/5, to wit: (1) *to pragma esti alethes*, (2) *he psyche aletheuei*, (3) *ho logos hos legein aletheuei*, (4) *ho logos hos legomenon esti alethes*. Obvious traces of this topology of the loci of truth are to be found in *Sein und Zeit*, §§7B and 44.

29 *GA* 21, p. 190.

30 *GA* 21, pp. 193–4.

31 As is well known, the Heideggerian critique of Husserl's understanding of consciousness makes itself known on the occasion of their unsuccessful collaboration on the drafting of the article on phenomenology for the *Encyclopedia Britannica*. The different drafts of this article and Heidegger's critical remarks have been published in *E. Husserl, Phänomenologische Psychologie, Vorlesung Sommersemester 1925*, ed. W. Biemel, Husserliana IX (La Haye: Nijhoff, 1962). Cf. in addition the article by W. Biemel, 'Husserl's Encyclopaedia-Britannica-Artikel und Heideggers Anmerkungen dazu', *Tijdschrift voor Filosofie*, 12 (1950), pp. 246–80. Today, it is also necessary to take into account the detailed articulation of the Heideggerian critique in the university lectures: cf. *GA* 20, §§4–13; 21, §§6–10; §§4–5. A confrontation with Husserl (more exactly with the article 'Philosophie als strenge Wissenschaft') is also to be found in the first Marburg lectures (*Der Beginn der neuzeitlichen Philosophie*, 1923–4, *GA* 17).

32 Confirmation of this correspondence comes from the suggestive conjunction that by *Vorhandenheit* Heidegger translates (and, I would add, 'ontologizes') the Aristotelian idea of wonder (*thaumazein*), in which the desire for knowledge is rooted: '*dia gar thaumazein hoi anthropoi kai nun kai to proton erxanto philosophein, ex arches men ta procheira ton atopon thaumasantes*' (Aristotle, *Metaphysics* I, 2, 982b 12–13).

33 Cf. M. Heidegger, *Sein und Zeit*, §16 and also 69b.

34 Traces of this understanding and of this suggestion can be found first in

texts from this period published by Heidegger himself: from the *Anmerkungen zu Karl Jaspers' 'Psychologie der Weltanschauungen'* (1919/21; *GA* 9) to the book on *Kant und das Problem der Metaphysik* (1929; *GA* 3). For example, in the lecture 'Phänomenologie und Theologie' (1927) one finds the statement: 'Existieren [ist] Handeln, *praxis*' (*GA* 9, p. 58). But they are to be found explicitly elsewhere, especially in university lectures, notably in the introductory part of the lecture from the Summer term 1924/5 on the *Sophist* and in the concluding part of the latter from the Summer term 1926 on the 'Grundbegriffe der antiken Philosophie'. While waiting for these texts to be published, one can draw valuable hints from the book by H. Weiß, *Kausalität und Zufall in der Philosophie des Aristoteles*; H. Weiß, who attended the lectures given by Heidegger, makes a fairly circumstantial summary of the Heideggerian interpretation of Aristotle's practical philosophy in chap. 3 of his book, by entitling it significantly: 'Menschliches Dasein – praxis' (pp. 99–153).

35 The practical structure of the reference of Dasein to its being has been well analysed by E. Tugendhat, *Selbstbewußtsein und Selbsbestimmung. Sprachanalytische Interpretationen* (Frankfurt: Suhrkamp, 1979), pp. 164–244.

36 The withdrawal of the emphasis placed upon the practical connotation of Dasein as having-to-be and the substitution for the former of a thematization of its ontological horizon as ek-sistence is to be found in numerous writings, for example, in the last part of *Was ist Metaphysik?* (1929), in *Vom Wesen der Wahrheit* (1930, 1943), especially in §4, in *Einleitung in die Metaphysik* (1935), in the *Brief über den Humanismus* (1946), in the *Einleitung* to the 5th edition (1949), of *Was ist Metaphysik?*, and besides in marginal notes from the 'Hütten-exemplar' of *Sein und Zeit*, published in the *GA* 2. In what concerns the emphasis accorded to Aristotle, I find it very significant that the conversion from one perspective to the other should be clearly announced in the reproduction of the interpretation of the phenomenon of truth with Aristotle, previously handled in the lectures of 1925/6 and in the lectures of 1929/30 in an interpretative direction that Heidegger himself declares to have been altered (cf. *GA* 29/30, §72–3).

37 Cf. *GA* 20, p. 380. Previously, in place of *Sorge* Heidegger had employed the term *Selbsbekümmerung* (corresponding to the Greek *epimeleia*), a use which one finds, for example, in the review of Jasper's *Psychologie der Weltanschauung* (cf. *GA* 9, pp. 1–44, in particular pp. 30–5), and in the lecture course of the Summer term 1920/1 *Einleitung in die Phänomenologie der Religion*.

38 Cf. for example Aristotle, *Nichomachean Ethics* VI, 2, 1139b 7–11, and III, 5.

39 ibid., VI, 1141b 34.0.

40 In a revealing note from *Sein und Zeit*, §42, for example, Heidegger says that if he

came to accord a dominant role to that 'care' which governs the previous analytic of *Dasein*, it is in the context of his attempts to interpret the Augustinian anthropology – that is the Greco-Christian – with reference to the foundations established in the Aristotelian ontology.

The fact that Heidegger here talks only of the Aristotelian ontology and does not mention the practical philosophy should not deceive us for, according to him, the latter is also an ontology and, more specifically, an ontology of human life.

41 '*Ho de bios praxis, ou poiesis estin*' (Aristot. *Politics* I, 4, 125a 7).

42 Aristotle, *Nichomachean Ethics* VI, 5, 1040a 26.

43 Cf. Aristotle, *Eudemian Ethics* II, 3, 1220b 27 and 6, 1222b 19.

44 Cf. Heidegger, *Sein und Zeit*, §§39–45.

45 The fact that Heidegger translates the Augustinian term affection with *Befindlichkeit* brings an important counter-proof against this association. It is to be found in the lecture *Der Begriff der Zeit* (1924), where Heidegger quotes Augustin *Lecture* XIII, 27:

in te anime meus, tempora metior, noli mihi obstrepere quod est. Noli tibi obstrepere turba affectionum tuarum. In te, inquam, tempora metior. Affectionem, quam res praetereuntes in te faciunt, et, cum illae praeterient, manet, ipsam metior praesentem. Non eas, quae praeterierunt, ut fieret: ipsam metior cum tempora metior.

Heidegger paraphrases:

In Dir, mein Geist, messe ich die Zeiten. Dich messe ich, so ich die Zeit messe. Komme mir nicht mit der Frage in die Quere: Wie denn das? Verleite mich nicht dazu, von dir wegzusehen durch eine falsche Frage. Komme dir selbst nich in den Weg durch die Verwirrung dessen, was dich selbst angehen mag. In dir, sage ich immer wieder, messe ich die Zeit; die vorübergehend begegnenden Dinge bringen dich in eine Befindlichkeit; die bleibt, während jene verschwinden. Die Befindlichkeit messe ich in dem gegenwärtigen Dasein, nicht die Dinge, welche vorübergehen, daß sei erst entstände. Mein Michbefinden selbst, ich wiederhole es, messe ich, wenn ich die Zeit messe.

(M. Heidegger, *Der Begriff der Zeit*, ed. H. Tietjen (Tübingen: Niemeyer, 1989), pp. 10–11.

46 Cf. Heidegger, *Sein und Zeit*, §29.

47 Cf. Aristotle, *Metaphysics* I, 2, 982b 22, quoted by Heidegger, *Sein und Zeit*, §29.

48 Cf. Heidegger, *Sein und Zeit*, §31.

49 'Das existenziale Sein des eigenen Seinkönnens das Dasein selbst, so zwar, daß dieses Sein an ihm selbst das Woran des mit ihm selbst Seins erschließt' (Heidegger, *Sein und Zeit*, §31).

50 *GA* 29, p. 393.

51 Aristotle, *Nichomachean Ethics* VI, 2, 1139b 4–5. Cf. the treatment of *orexis* in Heidegger, *Nietzsche*, vol. I (Pfullingen: Neske, 1961), pp. 66–8.

52 Heidegger, *Sein und Zeit*, §41.

53 Cf. Aristotle, *Nichomachean Ethics* VI, 2, 1139a 21–3. The correspondence between *Sorge* and *orexis* is all the more interesting in that Heidegger goes out of his way to find a determination corresponding to *Sorge* not only in Aristotle but also in Kant. He thinks he can find it in the *Gefühl der Achtung*, which is at the bottom of *personalitas moralis* (cf. *GA* 24, pp. 185–99). Heidegger emphasizes explicitly that the Kantian concept of *Gefühl der Achtung*, conceived on the analogy of such opposed determinations as *Neigung* (which arises in the course of the self-elevation of practical reason) and *Furcht* (which arises in the course of the submission of the law) would correspond to the Aristotelian concept of *orexis* with its two moments of *dioxis* and *phyge* (cf. *GA* 24, pp. 192–3).

54 Cf. H.-G. Gadamer, *Martin Heidegger und die Marburger Theologie* (1954), reproduced in the already cited collection by the same author, *Heideggers Wege*, pp. 29–40, in particular pp. 31–2. But cf. also the slightly different version of

the same episode in H.-G. Gadamer, 'Erinnerung an Heideggers Anfänge', *Itinerari*, 25 (1–2) (1986) (dedicated to Heidegger), pp. 5–16, esp. p. 10.

55 The importance of conscience for Heidegger can be measured by the fact that in 'Anmerkung zu Karl Jaspers' *Psychologie der Weltanschauung*' Heidegger has already made known the need to analyse this concept and its history in connection with the problematic of existence, and not simply as if it were a matter of a task of scholarship (cf. *GA* 9, p. 33).

56 Cf. for example, Aristotle's *Nichomachean Ethics* I, 4, 1096a 26, 32 (where *kairos* is defined as *to agathon en chronoi*) or III, 1, 1110a 14 (where Aristotle says that the *telos tes praxeos* is *kata ton kairon*).

57 Cf. Heidegger, *Sein und Zeit*, §68.

58 '*Lethe tes men toiautes hexeos estin, phroneseos de ouk estin*' (Aristotle, *Nichomachean Ethics* VI, 5, 1140b 29).

59 Cf. Heidegger, *Sein und Zeit*, §9.

60 Cf. Heidegger, *Sein und Zeit*, §§18, 26, 41, 69c.

61 Cf. Heidegger, *Sein und Zeit*, §§60, 62.

62 The end of this passage is also important: 'Derselbe Mensch taucht dann wieder bei Kant auf: der Mensch der reden, d.h. begründend handeln kann.' It is not necessary to note that it is a question of the same man that one finds in Heidegger.

63 Cf. *GA* 24, §19a.

64 Cf. Aristotle, *De anima* III, 10, 453b 5–8.

3

Heidegger and Descartes

Jean-Luc Marion

1 The continuing presence of Descartes in the development of Heidegger's thinking

Although it is more or less taken for granted that Heidegger never ceased to be concerned with Nietzsche or Aristotle, his relation to Descartes can very easily appear to be secondary. Neither those who comment on Heidegger nor those who examine Descartes have much to say on the relation of the former to the latter, indeed both are quite likely to ignore it altogether. Whatever the reasons might be for this oversight they cannot diminish the significance of one solid fact: even if one only considers the matter chronologically, Descartes appears at the very outset of Heidegger's career and preoccupies him right up to the very end. To take account solely of the texts which have already been made available through the publication of the *Gesamtausgabe* (in 1985), evidence of an intense debate with Descartes is to be found from 1921 right up to 1974.

In a course of lectures, given as a *Privatdozent* at Freiburg during the Winter term 1921/2, under the title *Phänomenologische Interpretationen zu Aristoteles: Einführung in die Forschung*, the only course of lectures prior to the Marburg period which is still available, Heidegger does not so much deal with Aristotle as sketch out an introduction to phenomenology; however, this introduction opens up a philosophy. Instead of Aristotle it is Descartes who is in question. First taking account of the *Ich-Metaphysik* in its Kantian and phenomenological moments he ends up with Descartes, whose limitations are already clearly marked out. The '*sum*' is certainly supposed to be as primary for Descartes but it is precisely at this point that the difficulties emerge. For instead of sticking to the '*sum*' he already opens up a pre-conception of the meaning of being in the mode of a simple affirmation (*Feststellung*) and moreover an affirmation of the indubitable character of being (*Unbezweifelbaren*).

The fact that Descartes was able to deviate in the direction of a posing of the epistemological question and even, from the standpoint of the history of ideas (*geistigesgeschichtlich*), managed to inaugurate such a question only gives expression to the fact that the '*sum*', its being and its categorial structure, did not present a problem for him. Rather the meaning of the word '*sum*' was for him understood in an indifferent sense (*indifferenten . . . Sinn*), absolutely unrelated to the ego, formally objectified (*formal gegenständlich*), uncritically assumed and therefore not elucidated.[1] From the time of this sketch of an interpretation, Descartes appears as having accentuated the certainty of the *ego* and having simply assumed the *sum* in an uncritical fashion. In other words, the mode of being exemplified by the *sum* is taken in its supposedly most obvious sense, as indisputable and common to all and therefore is in fact thought on the basis of an acceptance of the mode of being which pertains to objects. Descartes emphasizes the question of the *ego* (hence the inauguration of a theory of knowledge) and overlooks the question of the *sum* (hence an objectifying interpretation of every *esse*). Paradoxically, in the eyes of the young Heidegger, Descartes already poses the question of the mode of being of the *sum*, precisely in overlooking it in favour of a question about the status and the power of the *ego*. This confrontation with Descartes, sketched out so early, is more amply developed from the time of Heidegger's residence at Marburg. In fact, this period opens and closes with a course of lectures explicitly devoted to Descartes. In his first winter term (WS 1923/4), Heidegger undertakes an *Introduction to Modern Philosophy* (*Der Beginn der neuzeitlichen Philosophie*); it was supposed to appeal to the figure of Descartes, at least if you are ready to believe the testimony of the last course of lectures given at Marburg in the summer of 1928. 'This course, given in the Summer term of 1928, attempted to come to terms with Leibniz. . . . In my first term at Marburg, 1923/24, I sought to adopt a corresponding position with regard to Descartes, which latter was then incorporated into *Sein und Zeit* (§19–21)' (*Wegmarken*, *GA* 9, p. 79). It should be emphasized that this last course of lectures not only confirms that the earlier course was devoted to the study of Descartes and, moreover, that it consequently anticipated what was said in *Sein und Zeit* §19–21 but also that it dealt with Descartes in so far as the latter was continued in Leibniz who,

> like Descartes, sees in the I, in the *ego cogito*, the source from which all metaphysical concepts have to be drawn. However, with Leibniz as well as with his predecessor (Descartes) and his successors, this return to the I remains ambiguous because the I is not grasped in its essential structure and in its specific mode of being.
>
> (*GA* 9, pp. 89–90)

From these texts drawn from his period at Marburg, but also from the preceding period one has to conclude – all the more because others will undoubtedly confirm this clear preoccupation – that Heidegger, from the very beginning of his 'path of thought' appreciates the importance of Descartes; but he does not attribute it to what, according to the tradition, his contemporaries saw it as consisting in, namely, the establishment of the *ego* upon the plane of a transcendental (or quasi-transcendental) principle. He locates it on the contrary in what Descartes himself conceals behind the evidence and the dignity of the *ego cogito* – in the indeterminateness of the mode of being of this *ego*, whose *sum* remains indeed so indeterminate that it falls under the sway of the mode of being of objects. So Heidegger does not question the *ego cogito* with regard to the primacy of its cognitive origin but rather the ontological indeterminateness of the *esse*, that which it conceals from view rather than that which it proclaims. Thus the encounter with Descartes marks Heidegger's point of departure more clearly than his other confrontations.

But this stand is also characteristic of his later texts. To limit oneself to one strictly chronological criterion, it should be emphasized that Descartes remains an essential preoccupation right up to the end. (1) In 1969, the second 'Thor Seminar' recalls Descartes' historical position: 'What happened between Hegel and the Greeks? The thinking of Descartes'; or 'With Fichte one finds the absolutization of the Cartesian *cogito* (which is only a *cogito* to the extent that it is a *cogito me cogitare*) into an absolute knowledge' (*Questions IV*, pp. 263 and 282).[2] (2) In 1973, the 'Zähringen Seminar' carries the interpretation of the Cartesian *cogito* to its height on the basis of the question of being:

> subjectivity is not itself called in question with regard to its being; since Descartes, in fact, it is the *fundamentum inconcussum*. Throughout the entirety of modern thought, proceeding from Descartes, subjectivity consequently constitutes the obstacle standing in the way of the question concerning being.
>
> (*Questions IV*, pp. 319–20)

(3) In 1974, one of the very last texts, 'Der Fehl heiliger Namen' ('The lack of sacred names'), once more points to this obstacle by taking up again the theme of the first course of lectures at Marburg: 'At the beginning of modern thought we find/In an orderly manner and before any elucidation of the matter of/the thinking of the *Treatise on Method*:/ Descartes' *Discourse on Method* and the/*Regulae ad directionem Ingenii*' (*GA* 13, p. 233). Even from a chronological standpoint, Heidegger's thinking constantly comes to terms with that of Descartes, and in a confrontation which is just as constant as that which links him to Nietzsche or Aristotle. This textual fact which confirms the frequency with

which Descartes is cited in the works of his maturity does not neverthe-less suffice to elucidate Heidegger's encounter with Descartes. Rather, the very existence of such a confrontation demands to be understood. The abundance and the persistence of Cartesian references only itself becomes intelligible with reference to the concepts which both motivate and justify it. What identifiable conceptual reason leads and constrains Heidegger, from the beginning to the end of his itinerary, to discuss Descartes?

2 The phenomenological motive for the originary confrontation with Descartes

At the very moment when Heidegger was expounding and critiquing Descartes at Marburg, Husserl was expounding and approving Descartes at Freiburg in a course of lectures given in the winter term 1923/4, from which the work *First Philosophy* was drawn. In fact Husserl did not wait as long as this (nor, a fortiori) until the *Paris Lectures* of 1929 to place Descartes at the centre of his reflections; well before *Ideas*, his lectures at Göttingen had already undertaken this task in 1907, as also in other texts.[3] Phenomenology, at least in its Husserlian form, had, well before Heidegger, already linked its destiny with the interpretation of Descartes. Nothing of any phenomenological significance could be decided, at least in principle, without a discussion about Descartes. The Descartes that Heidegger encounters enjoys the status of being phenomenologically motivated if not that of being a phenomenologist. At first Descartes appeared for Heidegger in a positively phenomenological light through the intermediary of Husserl. In other words, Husserl's authority, especially after the turn of 1907, had invested Descartes with a phenom-enological dignity such that all discussion about Descartes reverts to a discussion with Husserl. More precisely, any discussion of those Cartesian themes which Husserl had sanctified was equivalent to a theoretical discussion with Husserl himself. The equivalence between Descartes and (Husserlian) phenomenology can be deployed in two directions; either Descartes is a phenomenologist because he anticipates Husserl; or Hus-serlian phenomenology is not fully phenomenological, because it remains trapped in Cartesian positions which have not been criticized, or even recognized. Very early on, Heidegger decides to take the second direc-tion. The distance that he takes up with regard to the Husserlian interpre-tation of phenomenology will be carried through by way of a critique of the Cartesian presuppositions which lurk in the latter. Descartes will undergo a critique, but a critique which is at first addressed just as much against Husserl who is now regarded as being less of a phenomenologist in virtue of his Cartesian heritage. So Descartes appears as Husserl's non-phenomenological motif.

Thus, in the course of lectures given in the summer of 1925 and entitled *Prolegomena zur Geschichte des Zeitbegriffs*, Heidegger attempts in §11 an 'immanent critique of phenomenological research', by examining how the latter manages to determine pure consciousness. In other words,

> For us, [i.e., Heidegger] the question remains: does the elaboration of the thematic field of the phenomenology of intentionality [i.e., that of Husserl] bear upon the question concerning the *being of this region*, upon the *being of consciousness*; that is, what does being in general mean here when one says that the sphere of consciousness is a sphere and a region of *absolute* being? What does *absolute being* mean here? What does being mean when it is used of the being of the transcendent world, the reality of things? . . . Has phenomenology in general been able to establish the methodological basis to render intelligible this question concerning the *meaning of being*, a question which ought to have been raised first of all and which nevertheless remains unasked? . . . Has the region of consciousness – pure consciousness – been determined in its being as the fundamental field of intentionality, and if so how?!
>
> (*GA* 20, pp. 140–1)

It should be noted that here, in 1925, Heidegger puts to Husserl and to the region of consciousness the same question and the same critique which he had been putting to Descartes and his *ego cogito* since 1921. Establishing the epistemological priority of the ego and of consciousness constitutes an advance but it does not dispense with the need to determine the mode of being of this first term. Descartes is repeated with Husserl, not only positively, with the bringing to light of the condition of all certainty in knowledge, but also negatively, with the evasive forgetfulness of the mode of being proper to originary certainty. Husserl must certainly have encountered and noted 'an unsurpassable difference of essence' (ein unüberbrückbarer Wesensunterscheid; *Ideen I*, §43/Husserliana III, p. 99), 'a genuine abyss of meaning' (*ein wahrer Abgrund des Sinnes*; *Ideen I*, §49/Husserliana III, p. 117) between consciousness and the reality of the world. For all that, is it possible to see this gap as one with 'a necessary and absolute being' (*ein notwendiges und absolutes Sein*; ibid.)? In short, is it possible to think an epistemological gap by naming an ontico-ontological gap, as if 'the most radical difference in principle between modes of being in general, that between consciousness and reality' (*die prinzipielle Unterschiedenheit des Seinsweisen, die kardinalste die es überhaupt gibt, die zwischen Bewusstsein und Realität*; *Ideen*

I, §42/Husserliana III, p. 96) followed from the very fact of the irreducibility of consciousness to what it constitutes? It would have been better if Husserl had not limited himself to repeating the epistemic terms of the opposition – an absolutely certain because knowing consciousness and a reality which is contingent and relative, because known – and undertook instead to work out the respective modes of being of the two terms; for the reasoning he employs to sketch out these two modes of being arises out of a duality – certainty, contingency – which wholly belongs to the mode of being of that very worldly reality and therefore arises out of being being understood as subsisting permanently in the present. Like Descartes, Husserl takes up residence in that sphere of being proper to consciousness, with the result that he evades the supposedly fundamental question of its mode of being. Thus consciousness pays the price, so to speak, of its epistemic priority, with an implicit, but unqualified, submission to that mode of being which belongs to the world. Husserl carries through his abandonment of the question of the being of consciousness by relying implicitly upon Descartes. In fact, he quotes Descartes both to define and to obscure the mode of being of consciousness: 'L'être immanent est aussi indubitablement au sens de l'être absolu en ce que principiellement *nulla "re" indiget ad existendum*' ('Das immanente Sein is zweifellos in dem Sinne absolutes Sein, dass es prinzipiell *nulla "re" indiget ad existendum*'; *Ideen I*, §49/Husserliana III, p. 115).

Several comments are called for here. (1) Husserl certainly thinks he has defined the mode of *being* of consciousness since he deduces absolute-being from immanental-being. (2) To tie things up, he cites the authority of Descartes, *Principia Philosophia*, *I*, §51: '*Per substantiam nihil aliud intelligere possumus, quam rem quae ita existit, ut nulla alia re indigeat ad existendum.*' The encounter between these two thinkers certainly cannot be put down to chance since, in addition to their agreement over the epistemic primacy of the *ego*, they also concur in defining the mode of being of the latter by way of substantiality. (3) Husserl, however, modifies Descartes' formula: he omits the *alia* in 'alia re', and only accepts *res* in inverted commas: '. . . nulla "re" . . .' Why? Obviously because *alia* (*res*) would imply that consciousness was itself, and first of all, a *res*; but Husserl precisely intended here to oppose consciousness to *realitas*; he therefore has to contravene accepted philosophical procedure and modify that part of Descartes' formula which would have implicitly extended *realitas* to *res cogitans* to retain only the application of substantiality to the ego. (4) This arrangement, and the difficulty which makes it necessary, proves already that Husserl is, in connection with Descartes, employing an insufficient and unadapted determination. For Descartes, in fact, substantiality covers not only the *res cogitans*, but also (though not without difficulty) the whole of *res extensa*, and so contradicts – rather than confirms – the Husserlian privilege accorded to consciousness: '*substantia corporea et mens sive substantia cogitans*' (*Principia Philosophia, I*, §52). A second contradiction may be added to the first. For Descartes, finite substance, thinking as well as extended, attests to a radical deficiency *vis-à-vis* God, and in such a way that the substantiality which the ego has to share with extension (first disagreement with Husserl), is only valid relative to God and is in no way absolute (second disagreement with Husserl). (5) These differences do not cast doubt on Husserl's intimate familiarity with Descartes; they prove, on the contrary, that his dependence was much more powerful than any divergence in matters of detail.[4]

An encounter as exemplary as this – Husserl citing Descartes to attempt a determination of the mode of being of consciousness – could not have escaped the attention of Heidegger. In fact, the same lecture course of 1925 takes note of Husserl's formula and identifies it, with precision, as a recuperation of Descartes. He is therefore able to cast suspicion upon its ontological inadequacy. Immanence, indubitability and absoluteness do not in any way make it possible to think the *being* of consciousness.

> This third determination – absolute being – is not, in its turn, to be regarded as determining beings themselves in their being, but as grasping the region of consciousness itself from within the order of constitution and attributing to it, and from within this order, a being which is formally anterior to any objectivity.
>
> (*GA* 20, p. 145)

The Cartesian distinction does not make it possible to found the difference between the regions – which is itself ontological. Heidegger reduces to nothing both the endeavour and the textual adaptation Husserl imposes upon Descartes' formula. In this case it is Heidegger who defends the orthodoxy of the Cartesian text and precisely because he stands opposed conceptually to Husserl. There is more, Heidegger continues. Not only does Husserl go astray by taking up again and forcing upon Descartes an inappropriate response, not only does he conceal the authentic determination of the mode of being of consciousness by thinking that a simple recuperation of Cartesian certainty will suffice, but he gets things even more radically wrong by assuming a Cartesian question which has no phenomenological legitimacy.

> The first question for Husserl is certainly not that of the character of being of consciousness [*nach dem Seinscharakter des Bewußtseins*], what prompts him is rather the following consideration: *How can consciousness in general become the possible object of an absolute*

science? What motivates him most fundamentally is the *idea of an absolute science*. But this idea that *consciousness has to be the region for an absolute science* is not one which he himself simply discovered but is the idea which had occupied *modern* philosophy since *Descartes*. The working out of pure consciousness as the thematic field for a phenomenology is not arrived at *phenomenologically by a return to things themselves* but by a return to a traditional conception of philosophy [*nicht phänomenologisch im Rückgang auf die Sachen selbst gewonnen, sondern im Rückgang auf eine traditionelle Idee der Philosophie*].

(*GA* 20, p. 147)

Let us assess the extent and the precision of Heidegger's critique of Husserl. (1) The question of the mode of being of consciousness receives no response because Husserl remains dependent upon Descartes. (2) Husserl, in sketching out the authentically phenomenological difficulty of the being of consciousness, emphasizes the non-phenomenological ideal of a certain science of consciousness. We are at this point not very far away from the patricidal declaration launched in this same course of lectures. 'Phenomenology is then, with regard to the duty of determining its own proper field, non-phenomenological!' (*GA* 20, p. 178).[5] (3) If Husserl deviates from phenomenology, he does so because of the persistence in him of the Cartesian ideal of a *Mathesis universalis et universalis (sima) sapientia*, so defined in the *Regulae*. From Heidegger's point of view, Descartes therefore plays the unworthy role of obstructing Husserl's path toward phenomenology. Between Husserl and a true phenomenology, therefore between Husserl and Heidegger, Descartes arises as a unique obstacle. The 'affinity' which unites Husserl and Descartes[6] therefore designates a unique phenomenological obstacle which phenomenology will have to overcome if it wishes to be what it is. Henceforward, to make progress along the phenomenological path which Husserl has abandoned, Heidegger will not merely have to abandon Husserl but 'destroy' what held him to Husserl – Descartes himself.

In this way it becomes possible to understand why Descartes was so important for Heidegger. The chronological importance of the debate which he arouses follows from the phenomenological radicality of the question he poses – precisely by not posing it. To think about Descartes certainly does not mean, for Heidegger, to repeat the *instantiation* of the *ego* as others, like Hegel, Schelling and Husserl, have tried to do in their own way, nor yet to turn it on its head, like Nietzsche, but to destroy it with a view to bringing to light, as the phenomenon which was hidden by it up until then, the mode of being of the *ego* (or of what was supposed to take its place), and in such a way that it can be distinguished from the mode of being of intra-mundane entities. Destroying the *ego* does not come down to abolishing it ontically but rather undertaking to bring out its ontological dignity – in short, destroying the *ego* opens the way to *Dasein*. In this sense, the importance of Descartes in Heidegger's thinking comes down to his constituting the obstacle *par excellence* standing in the way of the ontological fulfilment of phenomenology. In as much as he stands in the way of the ontological fulfilment of phenomenology with his conception of the *ego*, Descartes makes it difficult for us to appreciate the significance of *Dasein*.

3 The first omission: the indeterminateness of the 'ego sum'

In 1927, and in accordance with what had been sketched out since 1921, Descartes appears, in *Sein und Zeit*, as 'an extreme counter-example' (*Sein und Zeit*, §18/88, 37). By featuring as the extreme counter-example of the ontological problematic of mundanity Descartes pushes phenomenology to its last extremity by misunderstanding the mode of being of worldly beings; but by doing this he calls in question – as we shall see – the mode of being of all beings, beginning with *Dasein*. In fact, 'the interpretation of the world begins in the first instance with some entity within-the-world; so we shall accordingly try to clarify this approach ontologically by considering what is perhaps the most extreme form in which it has been carried out [in seiner vielleicht extremesten Durchführung]' (p. 89, lns 5–7), namely, the Cartesian ontology of the world. In this extremity it is moreover a question of the 'phenomenological destruction of the "*cogito sum*" ' (p. 89, ln. 27) which is announced by Heidegger as the third part of his debate with Descartes after §§19–20, sketched out in §21 and referred to the unpublished 'Part Two, Division 2' (p. 89, ln. 28). The objection brought against Descartes applies to two deficiencies, that *vis-à-vis* the world and that *vis-à-vis* the ego, both of whose modes of being fall short, though in a different way. It should also be noted that the objection brought against Descartes precedes the celebrated analysis of the *res extensa* of §§18–21,[7] where it only finds a first confirmation though it appears initially with reference to the *cogito sum* and right from the Introduction to *Sein und Zeit*. This is valid, let us remember, for the entire plan announced in §8 and therefore for the part which remained unpublished. The principle which introduces subjectivity into the whole of modern philosophy has two characteristics: it claims to bring about an absolutely certain beginning and, at the same time, thinking about being is not to be found there in as much as the *esse* is masked by the *sum* and so remains unthought in the shadow cast by the *ego*, the only thought in evidence.

Since, in the course of this history certain distinctive domains of

Being have come into view and have served as the primary guides for subsequent problematics (Descartes' *ego cogito*, the subject, the 'I', reason, spirit, the person), these regions, in conformity with the thoroughgoing way in which the question of Being has been neglected, remain unquestioned as to their being and the structure of their being.

(§6/H. 22, lns 13–18)

Or again:

In taking over Descartes' ontological position Kant made an essential omission [*ein wesentliches Versäumnis*]: he failed to provide an ontology of *Dasein*. This omission was a decisive one in the spirit of Descartes' ownmost tendencies. With the '*cogito sum*' Descartes had claimed that he was putting philosophy on a new and firm footing. But what he left undetermined [*unbestimmt*] when he began in this 'radical' way was the kind of Being which belongs to the *res cogitans*, or – more precisely – the meaning of the Being of the '*sum*'. By working out the unexpressed ontological foundations of the '*cogito sum*', we shall complete our sojourn at the second station along the path of our destructive retrospect of the history of ontology. Our interpretation will not only prove that Descartes had to neglect [*versäumen*] the question of Being altogether; it will also show why he came to suppose that the absolute 'Being-certain' of the *cogito* exempted him from raising the question of the meaning of the Being which this entity possesses.

(§6/H. 24, lns 16–29)

A number of remarks should be made at this point. (1) §6 of *Sein und Zeit* calls Descartes in question firstly, and before all else, on the grounds of the meaning of the being of the *sum*; or rather, the Cartesian omission of the meaning of being in general is noticeable first and foremost with regard to the *ego cogito*; only the order in which the first part is arranged and the absence of the second part can convey to the reader the feeling that Heidegger emphasizes the doctrine of *res extensa* in his debate with Descartes. (2) However, the *ego cogito* and the *res extensa* furnish the phenomenological destruction undertaken by *Sein und Zeit* with two comparable 'omissions': Descartes misconstrues the mode of being of the *ego*, because he holds to the certainty of its existence without distinguishing such an epistemic category from an ontologically determinative existential; if he holds here to the idea of certainty, it is because he is going to transpose it over to the *ego* on the basis of that domain where it has first been demonstrated as an object of a methodical science, namely, extension; for if, epistemically speaking, the object depends upon the *ego*, at least with regard to this tacit and indecisive (let us call it nebulous) ontology, the *ego* borrows its own interpretation as certain from the *res extensa*. In any case, the two 'omissions' go together and display the same inadequacy: the indeterminateness of the meaning of being. (3) The two dimensions of this peculiar inadequacy exactly anticipate the two regions distinguished by Husserl: the absolute region of consciousness, the relative region of the things of the world. And, just as Descartes fails to think them as such, Husserl also fails to think their respective ontological meanings. It is therefore quite in order to treat and spell out these two deficiencies brought by *Sein und Zeit* against Descartes as two integral parts of the 'destruction' of the history of ontology; so, positively speaking, as a breakthrough beyond the phenomenological obstacle presented by Descartes.

Usually presented as the thinker of the *cogito sum*, Descartes could more properly be seen as incapable of thinking this same *cogito sum*, or at least of thinking the *sum* on the basis of the *esse*; for Descartes reduces the *sum* to the *cogito* and the *cogito* to the *ego*. The *ego* itself can only be characterized by an epistemic determination – that of a first and absolutely certain principle which renders possible any knowledge of other beings. Proceeding from beings which are known to the knower, the extension of this certainty is only able to satisfy the requirements of a method through a procedure of generalization by leaving indeterminate and in the shade the question of the meaning of being for the *ego*. This indeterminateness marks Descartes' first and most radical omission: 'a total ontological indeterminateness with regard to the *res cogitans sive mens sive animus*' (§6, pp. 24, 31); or again:

> Descartes, to whom one attributes the discovery of the *cogito sum*, as the point of departure for all modern philosophical questioning, examined – within certain limits – the *cogitare* of the *ego*. By contrast, he leaves the *sum* completely unclarified [*unerörtet*], even if he can be regarded as having posed the *sum* on as original a plane as the *cogito*.
>
> (§10/455, 39–46, 4)

In condemning such a lack of determinateness, Heidegger is not contesting the certainty of the knowledge of the *cogito qua cogito*; it is even very remarkable that he does not get involved in the fashionable, though idle and facile, debate about the legitimacy of the reasons which led to a demonstration of the original, absolutely indubitable and necessary, existence of the ego *qua cogito*. Heidegger's critique bears on another point altogether: does the epistemic certainty which offers the *ego* as the first certain object for a knowledge of what in fact it is itself suffice for an ontological determination of its own proper mode of being? By his very silence on this point Descartes lays claim to the univocal character of certainty (which keeps the same meaning and validity when it is transferred from known objects to the knowing subject). But this univocality is only founded (moreover as the medieval *univocatio entis*) upon an entrenched indeterminateness; better: this certainty remains not merely ontologically indeterminate but entirely indifferent to the question of the various modes of being of the meaning of being. Descartes assumes first of all that this certainty applies in the same way to the entire (though heterogeneous) series *cogitatum–cogitato–ego*. But he simply assumes that, just as the *cogitatum* is, in the light of the nebulous ontology of the *Regulae*, supposed to find the concrete determination of its mode of being in certainty, the *ego* too requires no other determination of its meaning of being than this same certainty, purely and simply. The certainty of the *ego cogito* does not therefore do away with the indeterminateness of the *sum* nor of the *esse* but simply reinforces it. This evident certainty allows Descartes to abandon any interrogation on the mode of being implied by this very certainty and results in its meaning of being being regarded as obvious, self-evident. '*Nota est omnibus essentiae ab existentia distinctio*' (Adam and Tannery (AT), VII, 194, 12), was his response to Hobbes. Descartes not only misses the question of the meaning of being, he masks this very omission by remaining blind to the epistemic evidence of the *cogito*. Descartes' first omission consists in his having left himself out of account.

This failure to come to terms with an omission finishes up however by deciding the mode of being of the *ego*: if Descartes fails to think his *sum* as such he still does think it implicitly on the model of intra-mundane being and in accordance with a reflective (*Rückstrahlung*) comprehension of the world on the basis of the explication of *Dasein* (§5/16, 1), for '*Dasein* is inclined to fall [*verfallen*] into the world in which he finds himself and to interpret himself reflectively [*reluzent*] on its basis' (§6/ 21, 11–12).[8] By virtue of the failure of any approach to the meaning of the being of the *ego*, the mode of being of intra-mundane beings becomes the attractive and interpretive pole of the mode of being of non-intra-mundane beings. The Cartesian *ego* (as also its substitutes and derivatives throughout the entire metaphysical tradition right up to its Husserlian avatar) differs essentially from *Dasein* in this: it is not seen to exist and therefore is not thought in accordance with its own proper mode of being but is always, and from the first, distorted by those intra-mundane beings from which it quite improperly borrows its own mode of being.

4 The second omission: the permanence of intra-mundane beings

But the impropriety has now been reduplicated. For, just as the Cartesian interpretation of the *ego* fails to take account of its manner of being and also fails to understand this omission, so the absence of this interpretation condemns the *ego* to being swallowed up in the mode of being of intra-mundane beings to which moreover it does not belong in principle, with the result that the interpretation of the manner of being of intra-mundane beings fails, with Descartes, to take account of the phenomenon of the world by replacing the latter with the univocal and minimum subsistence of what lies at hand (*Vorhandenheit*). In accordance with an analysis as celebrated as it is ambiguous and ephemeral,[9] the mundanity of the world is manifest less by the subsistence of being at hand (*vorhanden*) than by their interplay as instruments, handy and ready-to-hand (*zuhanden*); in this interplay, a being is defined by what it is used for (*um . . . Zu*), and with regard to an end which, under the diverse aspects served by interests, utility, function, organization, etc., etc., ultimately depends upon that 'to which it returns' (*Bewandnis*), therefore, to *Dasein* itself, which, in this way, opens the way to the world in its mundanity. The subsistence. of the present-at-hand (*Vorhandenheit*) only follows from *Zuhandenheit* by way of a deficiency and impoverishment of the ready-to-hand and in response to theoretical demands alone. The object required by the theoretical attitude can only remain isolated as an atom of evidence persisting in its perfect subsistence, neutralizing all finality in its pure objectivity. The object of the theoretical attitude is obtained through just such a methodological reduction and abstraction. It does not precede what is utilizable and ready-to-hand but follows it through an impoverishment and elimination. This operation which inverts the phenomenological pre-eminence of the *Zuhandenheit* over the *Vorhandenheit* comes from Descartes. The privilege which this method accords to mathematical knowledge does not rest, for him, upon the intrinsic excellence of this science but upon its ability to attain the certainty and the permanent subsistence of an object. The primacy accorded to mathematics follows, according to Descartes, from the privilege accorded from the first to the permanent subsistence of an objectivity whose certainty is the very meaning of the being of intra-mundane beings.

> If anything measures up in its own kind of Being to the Being that is accessible in mathematical knowledge, then it *is* in the authentic sense. Such entities are those which always are what they are. Accordingly, that which can be shown to have the character of something that constantly remains (as *remanens capax mutationum*), makes up the real Being of those entities of the world which get experienced. . . . The kind of Being which belongs to entities within-the-world is something which they themselves might have been permitted to present; but Descartes does not let them do so. Instead, he prescribes for the world its 'real' Being, as it were, on the basis of an idea of Being whose source had not been unveiled and which had not been

demonstrated in its own right – an idea in which Being is equated with constant presence-at-hand.

(§21/95, 36–96, 12)

'The constant presence-at-hand of things' (*ständige Dingvorhandenheit*; 99, 15) is only able to fix the meaning of the being of intra-mundane beings by degrading it to something which is susceptible to certainty and this at the expense of the phenomenality of the world. The interpretation of being in general as the permanent subsistence of the present-at-hand not only misses the meaning of the being of the *ego* by leaving its *sum* undetermined as such; it also, and before all else, misses the meaning of the being of those intra-mundane beings with regard to which, nevertheless, it claims to provide the perfect knowledge. These two limitations meet in a common and more original inability to think the being of beings in general.

What assessment could the historian of philosophy – if perchance he were able to detach himself from the philosopher – give to such an analysis and 'destruction' of Descartes? Without anticipating a more extensive discussion which would have to be conducted in another context, we will stick here to three remarks.

(1) Heidegger confirms that *ständige Vorhandenheit* obscures and monopolizes the meaning of being by relying on the Cartesian interpretation of *res extensa* as *substantia*, itself reduced to what *remanet* (= *verbleibt*) in every reduction (according to AT, VII, 30, 19 and on and *Principia Philosophiae, II*, §4, cited in *Sein und Zeit*, §§19 and 21). This reference is obviously very correct. However it hides another reference which attributes permanence (*remanet*) first to the *ego* and before the *res extensa* itself. For before asking '*Remanetne adhuc eadem cera?*' and replying '*Remanere fatendum est*' (*Meditatio II*, AT, VII, 30, 19–20), therefore before encountering the *res extensa* (which, it should be said, does not yet appear in the analysis of the piece of wax), Descartes had already reduced the *ego* to the *cogito* '*ut ita tandem praecise remaneat illud tantum quod certum est et inconcussum*' (AT, VII, 25, 22–4). If permanence characterizes certainty as a (failed) manner of being, it should have been introduced with the first certainty and it is therefore with regard to the *ego cogito* that the diagnosis of permanent subsistence should have been conducted. Each time that it thinks, the *ego* remains. Such an omission of a Cartesian reference is surprising when it comes from so precise a connoisseur of Descartes as Heidegger, and all the more so since this first 'remaining' confirms, rather than the reverse, the general thesis advanced by *Sein und Zeit*. *Vorhandenheit* not only determines intra-mundane being but, through a species of reflection (*Rückstrahlung*), flows back upon the *ego* itself and closes it off from all access to its true being. It could be objected,

and quite rightly, that since §§19–21 only deal with the kind of mundanity that is missing in Descartes, they are not required to mention a text dealing with the *Vorhandenheit* of the *ego*. If this reply is admitted however, another question arises. Did Heidegger not make use of the 'remaining' of the *ego*, established in AT, VII, 25, 22–3 in the second part, section 2, devoted to the 'ontological foundations of the *"cogito sum"* ' (§8/40, 4)? But this hypothesis would imply that he took advantage of a text which supported it at the very moment when he ignored it!

(2) The omission of the meaning of being in general is marked, in Cartesian texts, by the inadequacy of the doctrine of substance. Heidegger pertinently points out that substance is not supposed to affect us directly: '*non potest substantia primum animadvertit ex hoc solo, quod sit res existents, quia hoc solum per se nos non afficit*' (*Principi Philosophia, I*, §52, cited §20/94, 4–6). Thus, the inquiry into the nature of substance is, from the first, diverted into an inquiry into its principal attribute, which itself remains unknown in principle. There follows a radical 'equivocation' about the term (§20/94, 27; §19/20, 2), in the course of which its ontological is confused with its ontic meaning, with a view to circumventing the former that much more easily and taking refuge in the treatment of the latter.

The debate about the distinction between finite and infinite substance, a debate to which Descartes accords a primary importance, only succeeds in reinforcing this basic orientation towards the ontic meaning of the term *substance*. The Cartesian treatise on substance in *Principia I*, §§51–4 totally ignores Aristotle's discussion about the ουσια, which is at least ontological in intent. For the most part this reproach, brought by Heidegger against Descartes, seems justified.[10] The debate is deepened with a second, less visible but more important criticism. In bringing what is ontological in *substantia* under the ontic, Descartes necessarily confuses the ontological difference:

> Because something ontical is made to underlie the ontological, the expression 'substantia' functions sometimes with a signification which is ontological, sometimes with one that is ontical, but mostly with one that is hazily ontico-ontological. Behind this slight difference [*Unterschied*] of signification however, there lies hidden a failure to master the basic problem of Being.
>
> (§20/94, 29–33)

To this *grundsätzlichen Seinsproblem*, Heidegger adds, in a note to his personal copy, a simple formula: *ontologische Differenz* (ibid.). A decisive addition! For it shows that by obscuring the ontological in *substantia*, Descartes prompted the very apriori in which Husserl remains trapped in as much as he thinks it possible to distinguish substances (or 'regions') solely on the basis of ontic criteria, that is, without undertaking to distinguish (ontologically) their respective modes of being. Finally, he shows that Descartes failed to confront the difference between being and beings, the only difference which would have made it possible for him to fix ontologically the distinction between beings and substances. The convergence between these two shortcomings – the meaning of the being of the *ego* and the meaning of the being of intra-mundane beings – results from the original evasion of the ontological difference. The reintegration of Descartes in the history of metaphysics by way of what in *Sein und Zeit* is still only called a 'destruction of the history of ontology' (§6), is supposed to bring to light in him the essential feature of metaphysical thinking: that it fails to come to terms with the difference between being and beings. Since, in *Sein und Zeit*, this difference still remains implicit, even though it is effectively operative, it only represents an objection to Descartes under the form of the two omissions with regard to the meaning of the being of beings. This does however suffice to trace the phenomenological inadequacies of Husserl back to their geneological source in the Cartesian ontology – something that had to be demonstrated.

(3) Could one not, nevertheless, bring against the analysis of *Sein und Zeit*, the objection that Descartes did indeed work out a theory of the world? Surely the mundanity of the world first becomes an explicit problem when the *ego* asks itself whether it is not alone in the world, '*me solum esse in mundo*' (AT, VII, 42, 22), and then again when he undertakes to prove its existence in *Meditatio VI*? These two references only however suffice to draw an argument in favour of the thesis upheld by *Sein und Zeit*. In the first case, the *ego* only eventually accedes to other beings on the basis of itself, that is to say, on the basis of the ideas which it is capable of entertaining with regard to those beings. Thus they are represented as determined in advance *qua* certain objects, therefore in accord with subsisting persistence (*Vorhandenheit*). God does not constitute an exception to this determination and, symptomatically, there is no place for the other to be found therein.[11] In the second case, the very fact that the 'existence of the external world' has to be proved constitutes – more the absence of a convincing proof of which Kant complained in taking up the Cartesian theme (§43/204, 9 and 25) – the true phenomenological 'scandal'. For the world can only owe its existence to such a proof in as much as it is first reduced to the status of a presentation standing in need of realization, that is, of *Vorhandenheit*. Proving (or not) the existence of the world presupposes that one had already missed the mundanity of the world – i.e., its appearance within the phenomenological horizon.

These two Cartesian omissions therefore really come down to one – that of having grasped 'the being of "*Dasein*" solely in the mode of the being of the *res extensa*, as substance' (§21/98, 7–10). And it is from this standpoint that he addresses Kant.

> The 'consciousness of my *Dasein*' means for Kant: consciousness of being being present-at-hand [*Vorhandenheit*] in Descartes' sense. The term '*Dasein*' therefore designates just as well the being present-at-hand of consciousness as it does that of things [*sowohl das Vorhandenheit des Bewußtseins wie das Vorhandenheit der Dinge*].
>
> (§43/203, 25–8)[12]

5 *Dasein* as the 'destruction' of the *ego cogito*

Descartes' two omissions with regard to the thinking about being can be traced back in the end to one unique incapacity to think the being of beings outside the context of *Vorhandenheit* which, in turn, results from a misunderstanding of the ontological difference – at least in so far as it is taken in accordance with its negative formulation: 'Being can never be explained in terms of beings' (§43/203, 3–4).[13] The *ego* is set up by Descartes, and after him by Kant no less than by Hegel, as a privileged being with a view to rendering other beings intelligible and to taking account of the meaning of being to be found in them, in short, to furnishing them with an ontic guarantee and an ontological legitimacy. But at the same time, and to an ever increasing extent, the meaning of that being which belongs to it remains completely undetermined. The indeterminateness of the mode of being of the *ego cogito* invades every other being and takes away from them their ontological solidity – 'the absence of any ontological ground [*ontologische Bodenlosigkeit*] for the problematic of the self [*Selbst*] from the time of Descartes' *res cogitans* to Hegel's concept of spirit' (§64, n. 1/320). In other words,

> 'if idealism' signifies tracing back every entity to a subject or consciousness whose sole distinguishing features are that it remains *indefinite* in its Being and is best characterized negatively as 'un-Thing-like', then this idealism is no less naive in its method than the most grossly militant realism.
>
> (§43/208, 6–11)

In consequence, what separates Descartes (and those he made possible) from the question about the meaning of being is what separates the *ego cogito* from *Dasein*. *Dasein* recovers in it an echo of what the *ego* (*cogito*) already exhibits. *Da-*, there, this unique spot where everything else can consequently take place; but with the *ego cogito* the everything else only has the status of *cogitatum* because I am limited, *qua ego*, to the *cogitare*.

By contrast, on the basis of *Dasein*, the *Da* imparts upon everything else nothing less than *Sein*, being. There where the *ego* invites thought or rather lets itself be thought (even to turn itself into a simple thought) without ever giving rise to being in any determined or determining sense, *Dasein* gives being by determining the manner of being of other beings, since in advance, and by right, it determines itself to be according to its own proper manner. The *ego* certainly *is* but it is without thinking about itself since it only thinks of thinking the thinkable whose respective manner of being is no more fixed than its own. By thinking about itself as only being through and for the exercise of the *cogitatio*, it masks the complete absence of any decision with regard to the being of beings (reduced to the status of pure and simple *cogitata*) first by way of the epistemic evidence of its ontologically mobile existence and then by way of the certainty of the other truths. *Ego cogito*, not *ego sum* still less *Dasein* – the very formula betrays the indeterminateness which both disqualifies Descartes ontologically and accounts for the two omissions for which he is responsible. Henceforward, any interpretation of Descartes to be found in *Sein und Zeit* will have to be thematized solely in line with this opposition between the *ego cogito* and *Dasein* and in conformity with the declaration in principle that 'the *res cogitans* is neither ontically nor ontologically equivalent to *Dasein*' (§14/66, 27–8).

It only remains to develop these oppositions. With regard to the first, the *res cogitans* is not ontically equivalent to *Dasein* since the *res cogitans* possesses only an ontic awareness of itself and since *Dasein* does not think of itself (from the point of view of the *res cogitans*) as being itself another *res cogitans*. Although this opposition is never explicitly developed by Heidegger, it can easily be reconstituted in at least three steps. (1) The *ego* is a thing which shares the *realitas* of intra-mundane beings whether ready-to-hand or present-at-hand; by contrast, 'the being of *Dasein* has at the same time been distinguished from [*abgegrenzt gegen*] the modes of being (ready-to-hand, present-at-hand, reality, *Zuhandenheit, Vorhandenheit, Realität*) which characterize entities with a character other than *Dasein* (§44/230, 18–20). The *res* of the *ego* leads to the Husserlian difficulty of effectively distinguishing the region of consciousness from the region of the world. *Dasein* cannot be counted among the number of real things nor does it admit reality into itself since it precedes and renders possible the very mode of being of reality. (2) The *ego* can be defined in terms of the absolute primacy in it of the theoretical attitude. It is born out of doubt, but this doubt does not itself become applicable until every immediate relation (whether pressing, useful or necessary) has disappeared: 'no conversation . . . no care nor passion' (AT, VI, 11, 8, 9–10), '*curis omnibus exsolvi*' (AT, VII, 17, 13–18, 1). By contrast, 'scientific research is not the only nor even the most proximate mode of being of this entity (sic Dasein)' (§4/11, 35–6).

In fact, *Dasein*'s relation to the world is based upon concern, a concern which manipulates and utilizes beings as ready-to-hand, therefore without the least trace of disinterest. *Dasein* arrives at a theoretical attitude only later and by a procedure of subtraction. 'If knowing [*Erkennen*] is to be possible as a way of determining the nature of the present-at-hand by observing it, then there must first be a *deficiency* in our having-to-do with the world concernfully' (§13/61, 26–8). *Dasein* is not limited to adopting the theoretical attitude by challenging the so-called 'natural' attitude (in fact, concernful utilization of being as ready-to-hand), but both establishes and surpasses the one and the other because, more radically still, it makes them possible. (3) Finally, the *res cogitans* is confined to the domain of the *cogitatio* and devolves upon the other *res* that of *extensio*, this in accordance with an almost irremediable split. As a result, the *res cogitans* slips out of space – which also slips away from it. Because *Dasein*, on the contrary, is not defined from the first by the representation of what is present-at-hand (*vorhanden*) it does not exclude the disclosure of a fundamental spatiality. The 'spatiality of *Dasein*' (§23/104, 33) is based upon the de-severing (*Entfernung*) by means of which it abolishes the distance between an entity and itself. This same abolition of the distance, or deseverance, qualifies the original ekstasy of *Dasein*, its being-in-the-world. By contrast with the subject of idealism, based upon the *ego cogito*, 'the ontological "subject" properly so called, namely *Dasein* . . . is spatial' (§24/111, 33–4). *Dasein* is neither non-extended in the manner of the *ego cogito* nor extended: it is spatial, not non-extended. Thus, by refusing to take over the common title of *res*, *Dasein* is not constrained *vis-à-vis* the *res cogitans* but, on the contrary, surpasses it by not allowing itself to be limited either by the theoretical attitude or by the non-extended. This merely confirms that, taken as an entity, *Dasein* does not coincide with the *res cogitans*.

But since the 'ontic characteristic of *Dasein* consists in this, that it *is* ontological' (§4/12, 11–12), its ontic opposition to the *res cogitans* can only prepare the way for the ontological opposition which distinguishes it from its opposite (this time on the basis of itself and not its opposite). Undoubtedly the *res cogitans* can lay claim to a multiple 'primacy' but not to just such an 'ontological primacy'. On three points at least the opposition between them becomes irreducible.

(1) With regard to *Dasein*, its being is at issue; this being has to decide about its very own being and, in this decision, not merely its own (mode of) being is at issue but being pure and simple, therefore the mode of being of other entities which, for their part, are incapable of deciding either about themselves or about anything else (§4/12, 4–12; §9/41, 28–42, 2, etc.). *Dasein* enters into a surprisingly uncertain relation with itself. So very far from being reassured about itself by coming to know itself

as such, it only knows itself by coming to terms with the game that is being played with regard to itself – the game of its being that being whose being is at stake and which always has to decide with regard to this privileged being. *Dasein* only knows itself authentically when it recognizes that its being is in question, undecided and all the more uncertain for being placed beyond the possibility of certainty. *Dasein* is at stake. And such a stake is, in the end, beyond both uncertainty and certainty and definitely sets *Dasein* in opposition to the *ego cogito*. Undoubtedly, Heidegger is wrong textually to characterize it as a *fundamentum inconcussum* (§6/24, 34–5); however, Descartes does indeed see in it a '*fundamentum, cui omnis certitudo niti posse*' (AT, VII, 144, 24–5), 'quite firm foundations' (AT, VI, 31, 18–19); and Descartes certainly wants to see it as unshakeable: '*minimum quid . . . certum et inconcussum*' (AT, VII, 17, 7). More, the *ego* itself immediately takes on the figure of a foundation, better of an autarchic and self-sufficient foundation: 'a foundation which is entirely my own' (AT, VI, 15, 6). In thinking itself, the *ego* takes hold of itself and makes itself its own; not only is all uncertainty thereby surpassed but the certainty of the foundation, which is henceforward definitive, extends to every other *cogitatum* to come. The *ego* certainly decides about itself but only to abolish any play in this its own self-certainty. And if the *ego* decides, in the future, about other entities, it will only be to reduce them, as so many *cogitata*, to its own certainty. Thus *Dasein* does indeed inaugurate a game, that of the being of other entities through its own, there where the *ego* closes off all uncertainty, first of all in itself, then in the *cogitata*.

(2) *Dasein* exists, but existence is defined as possibility: '*Dasein* always comports itself on the basis of its existence, of a possibility of itself to be itself or not to be itself' (§4/12, 25–6). Existence signifies: being outside oneself, and in such a way as only to be in the mode of a possibility of being and in accordance with the stake which brings this entity into a play with its being, therefore with being itself; existence implies the ekstasy of a *Dasein* thrown out of itself in the play of being, with regard to which it is up to him to decide. When the *res cogitans* takes hold of itself with certainty by saying '*ego sum, ego existo*' (AT, VII, 25, 12–27, 28),[14] it immediately interprets its *sum*, therefore its being, as an existence. Could this be the kind of existence which characterizes *Dasein*? On the contrary, Heidegger insists:

> when we choose to designate the Being of this entity (sic *Dasein*) as 'existence' this term does not and can not have the ontological signification of the traditional term '*existentia*'; ontologically, *existentia* is tantamount to Being-present-at-hand, a kind of Being which is essentially inappropriate to entities of *Dasein*'s character.
>
> (§9/42, 8–12)

Does one have to prove that Descartes, in fact, means by *existentia* the counterpart of a simple essential possibility, which is abolished by certain and unequivocal permanence? He himself does not even bother to define existence considering, as he does, that it is self-evident. '*Neminem enim unquam extitisse tam stupidum crediderim, qui prius quid sit existentia edocendus fuerit, antequam se esse concludere potuerit atque affirmare*' (AT, X, 524, 10–13). For the *ego cogito*, *existentia* implies the inauguration of the *Vorhandenheit*; for *Dasein*, existence signifies the abandonment of self and a surpassing of *Vorhandenheit* with a view to entering into that possibility which it is definitively.

(3) Finally, 'to *Dasein* there belongs essentially being-in-the-world' (§4/ 13, 12–13). Contrary to the Husserlian limitation, intentionality is not confined to the theoretical attitude because the relation to the world does not concern, first and foremost, the constitution of things. Intentionality is enlarged and radicalized to the point at which, in advance and out of itself, it opens up the 'I' upon something like a world. This is the only way in which it is possible to move from one entity to the being of all the others. This critique of Husserl which plays an important part in the composition of *Sein und Zeit* and which is to be found throughout the text is also valid of Descartes, on account of the 'affinity' which unites them. Descartes in fact reaches the *ego cogito* on the basis of a hypothesis with regard to his independence *vis-à-vis* the entire possible world. The *ego* appears in fact when, and only on condition that, worldly beings disappear under the sway of hyperbolic doubt. The *ego* is defined as follows: 'a substance whose entire essence or nature consists solely in thinking, which is not located anywhere and which does not depend upon any other material thing' (AT, VI, 33, 4–7). Heidegger is perfectly justified with reference to Husserl and to Kant (and therefore also Descartes) in talking of a 'worldless "I" ', '*weltlose Ich*' (§63/316, 1), of a 'worldless subject', '*weltlose Subjekt*' (§75/388, 23). The classical difficulties of an opening on the world from a Cartesian standpoint do not have to be recalled here. They simply confirm the diagnosis made by Heidegger. Thus *Dasein* is certainly not to be found in the *res cogitans* since the *ego* can be defined as the very opposite of *Dasein*, an entity whose being is not in question. Reciprocally, *Dasein* can be defined as the very opposite of the *ego cogito*: that entity which is *not* in so far as it thinks. With regard to the *ego cogito*, *Dasein* therefore undertakes a relation of 'destruction'.

6 *Dasein* as the 'confirmation of the *ego cogito*'

Such a relation of destruction would however be pointless if an ontology could not be found in the *ego*, limited as it is to thinking. For the 'destruction' always bears upon the 'history of ontology'. So some kind of metaphysical situation has to be imputed to the ego, a situation which inserts it into the history of a misunderstood ontological difference. The reappraisal of the *ego cogito* follows therefrom since it still exhibits a figure of the being of beings, even though only in an obscure and forgetful manner. But this historical (historicist rather) imputation would not enjoy any legitimacy if the *ego cogito* could not justify its ontological pertinence even inauthentically and obscurely, not just in the course of the history of ontology but in the 'new commencement'. Even if only to retain its hermeneutical role in metaphysics, the *ego* has to hold on to and reserve for itself a potentiality for being. We shall therefore have to examine *Sein und Zeit* to see if it does justice to these two postulates concerning the *ego cogito*.

From the – dominant – point of view of his 'shortcoming', the Cartesian *ego* finds itself unable to manifest the meaning of being, a property which characterizes *Dasein* alone. The ontico-ontological antagonism between the *ego cogito* and *Dasein* appears sufficient (§5) to permit us to balance it out (without either insisting upon it or weakening it) by taking note of another relation between these same antagonists. To be sure, the *ego cogito* is presented as the most extreme adversary of *Dasein*. However, *Dasein* would not be engaged in so urgent a task of destruction if certain of its very own characteristics could not be found therein. It is in fact impossible for *Dasein* not to recognize itself in at least four characteristics of the *ego cogito*, and this in accordance with a spirit of rivalry which is all the more disturbing for being aggravated by these very similarities:

(1) *Dasein* 'does not come to an end [*Ende*] when it simply ceases, but it exists in a finite manner [*existiert endlich*]' (§65/3209, 37–8); finitude cannot be added as something extrinsic to an existence which, for this reason, would not enjoy an infinite (*endlose*) duration; it provides an essential determination for a *Dasein* which exists only for a term, for a death which comes to it out of the future; in as much as it marks the being-toward-death of *Dasein*, finitude opens the way to its own ekstatic temporality through the primacy of the figure which stands opposed to that temporality of *Vorhandenheit* which accords the primacy to the present as enduring. But the *ego cogito* is also characterized by finitude: '*cum sim finitus*' (AT, VII, 45, 21): this latter finitude does not simply possess an anthropological function (the *ego* must die, it is lacking in perfections, etc.), but quasi-ontological, for it is in fact this finitude which provokes doubt, therefore brings out the *cogitatio* which, in turn, institutes the beings of the world as so many *cogitata* to be constituted; for this reason, the finitude of the *ego* determines the meaning of the being of beings other than the *ego*. The relevance of this connection certainly remains hidden to and by Heidegger since he only envisages

the finitude of the *ego* in the horizon of a 'Classical-Christian anthropology' (§10/48, 27)[15] and so reduces the relation between finite and infinite substance to an efficient production, with a view to refusing all originary validity to Cartesian finitude. It still holds however that the *ego* can only establish the beings of the world as *cogitata* (either on the basis of itself *qua cogito* or indissolubly), because it exists in accordance with an essential finitude. Furthermore, the later mediation developed by Heidegger on the *cogitatio* – Representation, *Vorstellung* – will continue to develop this implication. So *Dasein* confirms the *ego* from the standpoint of finitude.

(2) *Dasein* is the being whose being is in question only on condition that this being is its own, in person: 'its essence consists much rather in this that each time it has its being to be as its own [*es je sein Sein als seiniges zu sein hat*]' (§4/12, 22–3); or again:

> That Being which is in issue for this entity in its very Being is in each case mine. . . . Because *Dasein* has *in each case mineness*, one must always use a *personal* pronoun when one addresses it: 'I am', 'you are'.
>
> (§9/42, 23–9)

Dasein could not be itself, that is, be that very own being whose being is in question, save in a personal way. Nobody can take the place of *Dasein*; *Dasein* cannot stand in for anyone else; even if it's you who are *Dasein*, this *you* will have to say 'I' of itself, just like myself; even and even especially if the role of *Dasein* is played by someone else, this role must be played in the first person because it has to be played *in person*. Thus, even if *Dasein* does not call itself an *ego cogito* at first, it can only say, -*sein* by saying '*Ich bin*', therefore '*ego sum*'. Thus *Dasein* inevitably talks of itself, at least in the first instance, as an *ego cogito*: '*ego sum*' (AT, VII, 25, 12 = 27, 9), '*je suis*' (AT, VI, 32, 19 = AT, II, 38, 9–10 = AT, III, 247, 2, etc.). This comparison seems absolutely decisive. In fact, Descartes did not simply inaugurate the liaison between the *cogitatio* and existence in a 'subject'; he linked them in a 'subject' which is itself always interpreted (in the theatrical sense of that term) in the first person, or better, in a personage (*persona*, in the theatrical sense) which has to be played in person (again theatrical in that it assumes the function of an 'I' – by saying 'I', *hoc pronuntiatum, Ego* (AT, VII, 25, 11–12). Descartes' successors will tend, on the contrary, to eliminate this engagement *of* and *to* the ego; or rather, to replace the first formula with another which nobody has to perform in person: '*sum cogitans*'; or again, they will abolish it altogether either by the way of subtraction (Malebranche), or by that of generalization (Leibniz). What distinguishes Descartes is therefore not simply the necessary liaison he establishes between two simple natures (*cogitatio* and *existentia*) but, more particularly, the performance of this necessary link between them by the non-substitutable *ego*. In this respect he exactly reproduces the non-substitutability which characterizes *Dasein*. So *Dasein* confirms the *ego* from the standpoint of mineness (*Jemeinigkeit*).[16]

(3) The finitude and non-substitutability of *Dasein* comes to it from the fact that it is in such a way that its being is an issue for it; this manner of being belongs to it in virtue of its being-toward-death, for death is the ownmost, the most absolute and the least surpassable possibility. In fact, 'death is the possibility of the pure and simple impossibility of *Dasein*' (§50/250, 39–40). Faced with death, *Dasein* finds itself exposed to its own, last impossibility, partly because death is inconceivable to us ontically (unimaginable), partly because death brings to an end that very possibility which *Dasein* is (more even than the possibility of its doing this or that). But the *ego cogito* knows a similar paradox, not with regard to its death but with regard to its liberty. For possibility arises in Cartesian terms with absolute freedom, the only infinity formally located in the finite *res cogitans*. The impossibility of this absolute freedom becomes apparent when it confronts divine omniscience and omnipotence, which latter destroy the very notion of the possible. In such an encounter the *ego cogito* not only confronts the impossibility of that possibility (liberty) which the theory requires of it; it also confronts the possibility of impossibility since, in the practical order, it decides to act as if it could act freely even though it is incapable of comprehending such a possibility. In each action, the *ego cogito* acts as if it were free and as if the impossible (an event not necessarily pre-determined by God) became once again open to possibility.[17] The possibility of the impossible applies therefore to liberty just as it does to being-toward-death. Thus, once again, *Dasein* confirms the *ego* as the possibility of impossibility.

Even if one concedes the textual basis of these comparisons, they will appear superficial and even pointless considering the gulf (both ontological and ontic) which Heidegger never ceases to place between the antagonists. How can one avoid disqualifying these fragile similarities when one bears in mind the indeterminateness which afflicts the *ego cogito* (§6/24, 21 and 31; 25, 11; §10/49, 28, etc.)?

(4) But precisely this indeterminateness itself remains undetermined and in such a way that it can be employed to bring the *ego cogito* and *Dasein* together as much as it separates them. Notice that for a long time *Dasein* itself, under the auspices of the 'I', itself remains 'undetermined' (§25/116, 6); up to the analysis of anxiety, its being (and not simply that of the ego) remains 'ontologically undetermined' (§39/183, 21–2). In other words, getting rid of indeterminateness presents a difficulty even for *Dasein*, to the point that the final §83 leaves one with the impression that it still has not been resolved. There is more. The charge of

indeterminateness, brought first against the *cogito* and then again against *Dasein* reaches a positive and legitimate phenomenological determination in the most decisive moments of *Sein und Zeit*. Three instances at least attest to this. First, that anxiety where *Dasein* opens itself to anxiety in a totally undetermined way (*völlig unbestimmt* §40/186, 18–19, in the same terms as 24, 31); *Dasein* does not open itself to anxiety in the face of a determinate being because it is precisely affected by the impossibility of finding such an entity, an entity from which it can flee or which it can repel; thus 'the specific indeterminateness of that in the face of which *Dasein* finds itself in anxiety makes itself apparent: the nothing and the nowhere (*das Nichts und Nirgends*)' (§40/188, 28–30). In short, it is through indeterminateness that *Dasein* arrives at that determinateness which belongs to it in accordance with care (*Sorge*), at anxiety. It is this indeterminateness which makes it possible for *Dasein* to transcend being with a view to a nothingness which will come back again later to being. Indeterminateness is in this instance ontologically determinative. Second, because being-toward-death represents a possible way of being for *Dasein* it brings with it the indeterminateness of the moment of death. 'With the certainty of death there goes the indeterminateness (*Unbestimmtheit*) of its 'when' (§52/258, 23–4; see also §53/265, 22, etc.). The indeterminateness of the moment of death holds *Dasein* open in the possible which, in its turn, brings to light a temporalization through the future; so in this instance, indeterminateness determines temporally. Third and last, that resoluteness through which *Dasein* decides (possibility) about itself in its very being (anxiety) bears the character of 'positive' indeterminateness (§57/275, 3):

> To resoluteness, the *indefiniteness* characteristic of every potentiality-for-Being into which *Dasein* has been factically thrown, is something that necessarily *belongs*. Only in a resolution is resoluteness sure of itself. The *existentiell indefiniteness* of resoluteness never makes itself definite except in a resolution; yet it has, all the same, its *existential definiteness*.
>
> (§60/298, 30–5)[18]

The ontic indeterminateness (indefiniteness) of *Dasein* guarantees its existential (therefore ontological) indeterminateness. In fact, this indeterminateness indicates that *Dasein* is not interested in any determinate entity but engages itself in the horizonal projection of all beings in general, therefore, in the end, transcends beings in general toward their very being. From our point of view, it is worth emphasizing here that indeterminateness can assume an eminently positive meaning, on condition that it frees *Dasein* from any determinate being and frees it for being in general. Where are we to draw the line between the indeterminateness of the *ego cogito* and the indeterminateness of *Dasein*? It certainly cannot be drawn on the basis of a distinction between determinateness and indeterminateness but between two modes of indeterminateness – ontic, on the one hand, ontological, on the other. The *ego cogito*, ontically determined as a particular real being among others, remains ontologically indeterminate. Ontologically determined (as the sole being whose being is in question), *Dasein* remains, as such, ontically indeterminate in the face of determinate beings. The *ego cogito* and *Dasein* share a certain indeterminateness but they manifest it differently – in accordance with an ontological difference. Subject to this indispensable qualification, one may conclude that *Dasein* confirms the indeterminateness of the *ego* – to the point of almost being the very opposite of the latter.

7 The recuperation of a Cartesian horizon in *Sein und Zeit*

What conclusions can be drawn from these conditional confirmations? Unquestionably, the 'destruction' of the *res cogitans* would not have been so urgent at the time of writing the Introduction to *Sein und Zeit* if *Dasein* had not been able to recognize itself in it so clearly. The *ego* appears to *Dasein* as a deficiency but more particularly as a danger whose fascination is still sufficient to impose norms and which, for this very reason, has to be resisted, at least more arduously than Husserl did. In its ceaseless struggle to mark off *Dasein* from the *cogito*, *Sein und Zeit* therefore had to go over its inadequacies step by step, undo its decision and reverse its orientations. However belligerent it might be, such a confrontation cannot avoid a certain mimetic rivalry where the conqueror sometimes appears to have been conquered by his victim, in some way or other. In short, precisely because *Sein und Zeit* never ceases to call it in question, the *ego cogito* appears more enigmatic in itself and closer to *Dasein*. Because the analytic of the one only proceeds by way of a destruction of the other, it confirms the continued validity of the former.

> If the '*cogito sum*' is to serve as the point of departure for the existential analytic of *Dasein*, then it needs to be turned around, and furthermore its content needs new ontological–phenomenal confirmation. The '*sum*' is then asserted first, and indeed in the sense that 'I am in a world'. As such an entity, 'I am' in the possibility of Being towards various ways of comporting myself – namely, *cogitationes* – as ways of Being alongside entities within-the-world. Descartes, on the contrary, says that *cogitationes* are present-at-hand, and that in these an *ego* is present-at-hand too as a worldless *res cogitans*.
>
> (§43/211, 13–20)

It is simply stupefying that, at the end of the preparatory analytic of *Dasein* and after carrying through his 'destruction' of Descartes, Heidegger should still be sketching out the possibility of a retranscription of the analytic of *Dasein* in terms – certainly displaced and reinterpreted – of the Cartesian *ego*. Undoubtedly, this historical figure must have exerted a powerful fascination if he still found it necessary to refer to him after his critique of historical avatars and of the phenomenological tradition. *Dasein* is itself disentangled from the figure of Husserl's constituting consciousness by a repetition of the *ego sum* against Descartes' *ego cogito*. Far from disappearing in one or another *Kehre*, this attempt at a repetition covers Heidegger's entire thinking as is confirmed by a seminar held in 1968.

> The paragraphs devoted to Descartes in *Sein und Zeit* constitute the first attempt to escape from the prison of consciousness, or rather not to get into it. It is certainly not a question of restoring realism against idealism; for, by limiting itself to establishing the reality of a world for the subject, realism remains dependent upon Cartesianism. It is much more a question of thinking the Greek meaning of the ἐγώ.
>
> (*Questions IV*, p. 222)

Heidegger had certainly undertaken something in the order of a topical overcoming of the *ego* in the direction of the ἐγώ when he commented on the *Protagoras* (*Nietzsche II*, p. 135, etc.); but he surely carried this through more radically with his analytic of *Dasein* – a non-Cartesian *ego* with which perhaps he went even further than the Greeks ('*über das Griechische hinaus*', *Zur Sache des Denkens*, p. 79). In short, *Dasein* represents a fulfilment just as much as a destruction of the *ego* since such a destruction comes down to determining the *sum* – which Descartes left undetermined. That this ontological determination is carried through by way of a multiform ontic indeterminateness reinforces the appearance of a new 'affinity' – between Descartes and Heidegger and against Husserl.

This Cartesian haunting of *Sein und Zeit* can be illustrated by two other arguments. More exactly, it provides two other questions with an argument.

(1) The penultimate paragraph of *Sein und Zeit* introduces a strange formulation of what is normally called the *cogito*. 'This absolute negativity [sc. Hegel] offers a logically formalizable interpretation of Descartes' *cogito me cogitare rem* in which he sees the essence of consciousness' (§82/433, 12–16). The lecture course of Summer 1927, *Grundprobleme der Phänomenologie*, will persist with this claim: 'The *cogitare* is always, according to Descartes, a *cogito me cogitare*' (*GA* 24,

p. 177). Heidegger knew perfectly well that Descartes had never presented the *cogito* in this way.[19] Why then did he advance and uphold this new claim? Because, if he did not reproduce the letter of the Cartesian texts, he did at least produce the metaphysical essence of what, with the primacy of the *ego cogito* over the *cogitata*, came to be in the history of being – namely, the essence of representation. In fact at this point, and just before it got lost in inconclusiveness, *Sein und Zeit* still makes possible that long and continuous mediation of representation which finds expression first in the principle of reason and then in technology.[20] The continuity between the interrupted effort of 1927 and the essays on the history of metaphysics which culminate in *Nietzsche* and *Holzwege* is sustained, despite the *Kehre*. But it is sustained through the intermediary of Descartes. Not only does the Cartesian theme traverse the whole of *Sein und Zeit* (to whose homogeneity it contributes considerably), it also prepares the analytic of *Dasein* and the 'destruction of the history of ontology' for the lengthy meditation to come on the theme of *Seinsgeschichte*. The *ego* of *cogito me cogitare* (*rem*), as the intimate adversary of *Dasein*, projects *Sein und Zeit* towards what nevertheless recedes from it.

(2) But, precisely, the ghostly presence of the Cartesian theme also prevents *Sein und Zeit* from advancing further along the way which leads beyond metaphysics. Even if one admits that it can be invoked in the singular, the *Kehre* makes itself known through two carefully researched, if not unequivocally established, disappearances: that of the language of metaphysics, that of the 'subject', including thereunder, in the end, *Dasein* itself. To be sure, *Dasein* will only be eliminated slowly, but it seems indisputable that the ontological difference will only find its classic formulation by eliminating the mediation between being and beings. Certainly, the language of metaphysics will persist, both as a point of departure and as a residue; but it seems to be more or less established that the phenomenological vocabulary of *Sein und Zeit*, whether transcendental or ontological, is, in every possible instance, demolished after 1935. *Sein und Zeit*, on the contrary, makes use of the vocabulary of metaphysics (which it pretends to question) through and through and so remains affiliated with subjectivity (even if only to destroy it). Amongst the motives for these impediments the least significant is certainly not the powerful shadow of the *ego cogito*, which ceaselessly obscures the phenomenological dis-coveries which *Dasein* is only capable of achieving against it. The adversary (singled out and only too well known) – the *ego* – conquers by the very mimicry which it imposes upon its conqueror, *Dasein*. In fact, Heidegger was only able to get away from his point of departure in *Sein und Zeit* by breaking with *Sein und Zeit* itself. But just as this break was never complete, it was not consummated with

Heidegger's dismissal of Descartes, who continues to speak loud and clear in the last *Seminars*.

In the context of ambiguities such as these two conclusions are clearly called for. First, even the most historical or systematic of Descartes' interpretations cannot dispense with a discussion of the Cartesian hermeneutic offered by *Sein und Zeit*. Second, the understanding of *Sein und Zeit* in the light both of its phenomenological point of departure and its 'destruction of the history of ontology', as also in its analytic of *Dasein* and right through to its inconclusive conclusion, must remain closed just as long as the Cartesian theme of the *ego* is not, in all its multiple dimensions, placed at the centre of the interpretation. In *Sein und Zeit*, Heidegger and Descartes are both interpreters each of the other.

Translated by Christopher Macann

Notes

1 *GA* 61 (Frankfurt, 1985), Anhang I, p. 173. In the earlier texts, references to Descartes are, to our knowledge, very incidental (for example *GA* 1, p. 43).

2 *Questions IV* (Paris, 1976): the original is given here in French. See ibid., pp. 122, 220, 245, 289 and 320. On the relation of Descartes to Fichte and Hegel one should consult the recent research of A. Philonenko 'Sur Descartes et Fichte' and B. Bourgois 'Hegel et Descartes' (in both cases more reserved than Heidegger) in *Les Etudes philosophiques*, 2 (1985), pp. 205ff. and 221ff.

3 When does Husserl begin to discuss Descartes? We find a reference to the latter as early as *Logical Investigations I*, *LU*, t. 2, 64, and he is discussed at length in an Appendix, added as a complement to the 6th Logical Investigation, *LU*, t. 3, 223, 235, 240, 241. But he is only considered here as an opponent. On this see F.-W. von Herrmann, *Husserl und die Meditationen des Descartes* (Frankfurt, 1971).

4 On the importance of the difference between finite and infinite substance which Heidegger, like Husserl, overlooks, see von Herrmann, *Husserl*, pp. 17–20 and, from the point of view of this study, my work *Sur le prisme métaphysique de Descartes* (Paris, 1986), chap. III, §13, pp. 161ff.

5 Regarding the bearing of this accusation, see our essay 'Being and the phenomenon,' in *Phénoménologe et métaphysique* (Paris, 1984).

6 'Here we can already recognize an affinity [*Verwandschaft*] with Descartes. What is worked out, certainly at a more elevated level by phenomenological analysis, as pure consciousness is the field that Descartes confusedly anticipated under the title of *res cogitans*, the global field of the *cogitationes*, while the transcendent world, the paradigmatic index of which is furnished for Husserl by the fundamental layer of the world of material things, is characterized as *res extensa* by Descartes. This affinity is not limited to a contingent fact. Husserl explicitly assumes a relation to Descartes when he declares that this mediation has reached its peak.' ('Prolegomena zur Geschichte des Zeitbegriffs', SS. 1925, *GA* 20, p. 139). A note by Heidegger in his personal copy of *Sein und Zeit* confirms the permanence of his conclusion about this 'affinity'. While criticizing the Cartesian reduction of the phenomenon of the world to material nature, he

adds 'Critique of Husserl's construction of "ontologies"!' *Sein und Zeit* §21/98, n. a).

7 This analysis should be completed and confirmed by the parallel represented by 'Prolegomena zur Geschichte des Zeitbegriffs', §22. 'Das traditionnelle überspringen der Frage nach der Weltlichkeit der Welt am Beispiel Descartes' (*GA* 20, pp. 231ff.).

8 See *Sein und Zeit*, §123/58, pp. 33–8 and the note from the personal copy 'Rückdeutung, regressive interpretation'. Conversely, the *Abkehr/hinkehren* game in the context of anxiety §40/186, pp. 3–8.

9 On its posterity in the later work see H. L. Dreyfus, 'De la techne à la technique: le statut ambigu de l'ustensilité dans *L'Etre et le Temps*', in *Heidegger* (Paris: L'Herne, 1983), pp. 202ff.

10 See *Sein und Zeit*, §21/100, pp. 7–14. The apriori character of the Cartesian doctrine of substance cannot be overestimated, see *Sur le prisme métaphysique de Descartes*, chap. III, §§13–14.

11 On this point, see our sketch: 'Lunique ego et l'alteration de l'autre', in 'Intersoggettività, socialité, religione', *Archivio di Filosofia* liv, 1–3 (1986).

12 Similarly in 'Prolegomena zur Geschichte des Zeitbegriffs', §22/*GA* 20, p. 239.

13 The familiar formula 'being can never be explained by way of beings' (208, 3–4 = 207, 30 and 34, §2/6, 18, §41/196, 17f.), received decisive confirmation in a note to Heidegger's personal copy: 'Ontologische Differenz' (ibid., 208). Thus we find explicit confirmation that the indeterminateness of the meaning of being leads to (or results from) a misunderstanding of the ontological difference by Descartes.

14 This formula – decisive – only appears in the *Meditationes*; however, Heidegger does not seem to make of it a special case.

15 Similarly in *Sein und Zeit* §6/24, 30f.: §20/92, 6f.: §21/95, 5–25; §44/229, 36–40.

16 That Cartesian 'egoity' anticipates Heideggerian 'mineness' is confirmed by the similarity of the objection brought against them by Pascal (Pensées 397 and 597) and E. Lévinas (*Totalité et infini*, p. 61, etc.) respectively – the objection of 'injustice'. For other more positive conceptions of the 'Ich bin' see *Sein und Zeit*, §58/281, 25–7; §60/297, 15–17; §63/313, 28–30; §64/317, 27–8f.

17 For a confirmation of this interpretation of Cartesian liberty as the possibility of the impossible, one might refer to my: *Sur le prisme métaphysique de Descartes*, chap. III, §15, pp. 203–16.

18 Similarly *Sein und Zeit*, §62/308, pp. 16–40.

19 Heidegger adds: 'obzwar nicht eigens und ausdrücklich gemeint' (*GA* 24, p. 177). In fact several of Descartes' statements could be employed more or less to validate his claim though he does not cite them. For instance, AT VII, 33, 12–14; 44, 24; 352, 1–18; 559, 6–7: AT V, 149 (see *Sur la théologie blanche de Descartes* (Paris, 1981), 391f.).

20 The principal mediations on the *cogito me cogitare* (with, it is true, the frequent omission of the final *rem*) are to be found successively in 1938, 'Die Zeit des Weltbildes', in *Holzwege*, *GA* 5, pp. 108–9 (n. 9), 'Der europäische Nihilismus', in *Nietzsche II*, p. 48 etc., and in 1936–46, 'Berwindung der Metaphysik', in *Vorträge und Aufsätze*, I, p. 65, etc. One should also add all the developments devoted either to the *subjectum* or to the *re-presentatio*. Some further references and indications are to be found in my sketch: 'Heidegger et la situation métaphysique de Descartes', *Bulletin Cartésien IV*, in *Archives de Philosophie*, 38(2) (1975).

4

Heidegger's Kant interpretation

Christopher Macann

Heidegger's *Kant and the Problem of Metaphysics* is a unique contribution to philosophical literature. At the time of writing, it was the only example of an attempt by a philosopher to interpret the thinking of a major historical figure in such a way that the basic structures of the interpreter's own philosophy emerged in the course of the interpretative transformation of the work under examination. No doubt this is why it attracted so much attention in its day[1] and why it has continued to prompt voluminous critical attention right up to the present time.

In this paper, I would like to do three things; first, to show the connection between the hermeneutical principles laid out in *Being and Time* and the putting into practice of these theoretical principles with regard to Heidegger's interpretation of the *Critique of Pure Reason*; second, to assess the validity of Heidegger's Kant interpretation; and third, to recommend to the attention of the reader an alternative procedure embodied in my own Kant interpretation.[2]

At the end of the Introduction to *Being and Time*, Heidegger outlines a programme which he never completed as anticipated. Part One is the systematic part of the programme. It falls into three parts: (1) the preparatory fundamental analysis of Dasein; (2) Dasein and temporality; (3) Time and being. The first two sections of Part One make up the two parts of *Being and Time*. The third section was never completed as originally envisaged. First delivered as a lecture much later in 1962, it opens up an entirely new way of thinking about Being – as Maria Villela-Petit has stressed in her paper on Space (chap. 5, vol. I in the present work). Part Two falls under the head of a so-called 'phenomenological destruction of the history of ontology'. Again, it falls into three parts: (1) a study of Kant's doctrine of the schematism. (2) An investigation into the ontological foundations of Descartes' *cogito*. (3) A study of Aristotle's essay on time.

At the time of writing *Being and Time*, Heidegger already had a great deal of material accumulated towards an interpretation of Aristotle, material which served as the basis for his promotion to the rank of *professor extraordinarius*, and which was later published in such volumes of his *Gesamtausgabe* as the *Logik* (*GA* 21) or the *Aristoteles* volume (*GA* 33). *Being and Time* itself contains extensive analyses of the ontological foundations (or lack of them) of Descartes' dualistic philosophy and the discussion with Descartes continues right to the end – as Marion's paper shows. But it was the Kant material which underwent the most radical transformation, basically from a study of the schematism into three entirely distinct bodies of material each of which occupies an entire volume of the *Gesamtausgabe*.

Though Heidegger's debate with Kant permeates other texts which do not take Kant as their specific theme,[3] it is the three volumes specifically devoted to Kant which merit special attention. First, there are the so-called Marburg lectures of 1927/8, now published as volume 25 of the *Gesamtausgabe*. Second, there is the famous *Kant and the Problem of Metaphysics*, published in 1930, shortly after the publication of *Being and Time*, and now issued as volume 3 of the *Gesamtausgabe*. Finally, there are the so-called Freiburg lectures, delivered in 1935/6, and now published as volume 41 of the *Gesamtausgabe*. Though this paper will bear almost exclusively upon the published Kant book of 1930, a word on the other texts is called for.

The Marburg lectures differ from the Kant book in a number of ways. First, Heidegger uses the Introduction not only to offer his own ontological interpretation of Kant's Introduction to the *Critique* but also to present his own conception of ontological phenomenology or, as he already terms it, of 'fundamental ontology'. Second, the main body of the text works out in much greater detail the specific points of Heidegger's Kant interpretation. Third, although the lectures conclude with a section on the schematism, volume 25 of the *Gesamtausgabe* really takes the expositiion of Kant's text no further than the transcendental deduction. This latter limitation is made up in the Kant book which deals extensively with the schematism. Indeed, Heidegger goes so far as to claim that 'these eleven pages of the *Critique of Pure Reason* form the heart of the whole work'.[4] However the Kant book, in its turn, does not carry the analysis into the Analytic of Principles, let alone the Dialectic. Again, in part this limitation is made up in the Freiburg lectures, now entitled *What is a Thing?*[5] which focuses its Kant interpretation upon the second main section of the Transcendental Analytic, or, in other words, on the Analytic of Principles. Like the Marburg lectures (and unlike the Kant book), the Freiburg lectures begin rather than end with the explicit articulation of the ontological understanding that makes the work of interpretation possible.

In one sense therefore, these three major contributions to Heidegger's understanding of the Critical Philosophy could be seen as successive attempts to cover the entire corpus of the *Critique*, at least as far as the Dialectic. In fact however, these three works differ not just in scope or in detail but in their basic intention, not to mention the way in which they work out their respective intentions. Both the Marburg and the Freiburg lectures share a certain stylistic simplicity, the simplicity befitting the context of communication, that of a university lecture. And so both volumes of lectures open (rather than close) with an account of the philosophical orientation which establishes the context for the interpretation. But whereas Heidegger's Marburg lectures take their start in a presentation of the fundamental principles of phenomenological ontology in general, the Freiburg lectures take their start in a more specific question concerning the thing.

The relative difficulty of the Kant book is however due not to any incidental obscurantism but to certain *methodological* necessities, necessities imposed by the hermeneutical procedure itself, which is much more strictly adhered to in the Kant book than in the lectures. Whereas the lectures first offer an ontological interpretation of transcendental philosophy, or of the thing, and then go on to show how the relevant sections of the *Critique* confirm this interpretation, the Kant book stages the interpretative transformation in such a way that, starting fairly close to a recognizable rendering of Kant's intentions, Heidegger is able to move the Critical philosophy ever further away from any conventional rendering and in the direction of his own, ontological interpretation. This is why the Kant book is organized around four sections, each of which is entitled a 'Laying of the foundation' (the use of the concept of 'laying' carries with it an essential connection with the concept of 'laying out' which in German means interpretation – *Auslegung*). Instead of beginning with a section in which he sets out his interpretative hypotheses, he begins with a presentation of the traditional concept of metaphysics, the concept which, in a certain sense, Kant overcomes. To be sure, the possibility of a priori synthetic judgments is already laid out as the possibility of 'ontological knowledge', but this latter is still somewhat ambiguously expressed as the 'precursory comprehension of the being of the essent'.[6] More significantly, it is in the fourth and last section (not the first section) that Heidegger develops, in what he calls a 'repetition', the ontological philosophy which was actually presupposed from the very beginning. In other words, the Kant book is organized in a manner calculated to highlight the procedure of interpretation itself.

But in order to see in what sense this is so, we first need to take a preliminary look at Heidegger's conception of the method of interpretation, as it is set out in *Being and Time*.

A The hermeneutical method

The sections in which Heidegger lays out his theory of understanding and interpretation are the three sections 31, 32 and 33. These sections are however not just thematically but also structurally integrated into the work as a whole. The basic division of *Being and Time* is into two parts, the first devoted to being, the second to time. The first part is itself organized around the basic structure being-in-the-world. The unitary configuration 'being-in-the-world' is split up, for analytical purposes, into its three constitutive components; the *world* (which is examined under the head of 'The worldhood of the world'), the one *who* is in the world (which is examined under the head of 'Being-with and being one's self'), and *being-in as such*. It is in the context of the third of these components, being-in as such, that we find the three sections in question here.

The question of interpretation is located in chapter V, for the simple reason that interpretation is here connected with understanding, one of four *existentialia* of which the other three are state-of-mind, falling and discourse. But although the correct procedure would seem to be to begin with an examination of the three *existentialia* which operate at the level of experience and to proceed on from there to an examination of their expression in and through language, this is not how Heidegger does actually proceed. Rather, state-of-mind and understanding are examined first as ontologically equi-primordial structures in which the Being of the 'there' maintains itself. Interpretation is then examined as a phenomenon grounded in understanding. The analysis of assertion arises as a derivative mode of interpretation, one moreover wherein the primordiality of interpretation is covered over. The investigation of assertion then leads on naturally to an inquiry into language, more specifically, the grounding of language in discourse. Only after this discussion of language has been concluded is the everyday being of the 'there' presented in terms of the existential structure of falling which, appropriately enough, begins with an account of language as fallen, i.e., idle talk (*Gerede*).

The two sections (32 and 33) devoted explicitly to interpretation belong within the exposition of understanding. However, since interpretation is grounded in understanding and since the analysis of assertion is devoted to the levelling down of the primordial possibilities inherent in interpretation, it is the section on being-there as understanding (§31) and understanding and interpretation (§32) which are most relevant for our purposes.

Heidegger opens §31 with an explicit affirmation of the equi-primordiality of state-of-mind and understanding. State-of-mind always has its understanding, and understanding always has its mood. In as much as Dasein is its 'there', the world is always there for it too. On the side of Dasein, being-in is disclosed to it as the 'for-the-sake-of-which' (*Worumwillen*). On the side of the world, being is disclosed as significance (*Bedeutsamkeit*). 'Significance is that on the basis of which the world is disclosed as such.'[7] Having recuperated, for his analysis of understanding, structures taken account of previously, Heidegger moves on to make the connection between the existential comprehension of understanding and possibility. Possibility, understood as potentiality for being, is explicitly contrasted with logical possibility or the contingent possibility of what is not actual but might be. 'Understanding is the existential Being of Dasein's own potentiality-for-being; and it is so in such a way that this Being discloses in itself what its Being is capable of.'[8] In turn, potentiality-for-being is analysed out in terms of the structure of 'projection'. 'As projecting, understanding is the kind of Being of Dasein in which it *is* its possibilities as possibilities.'[9] Further, projection of possibilities can be either authentic or inauthentic in so far as Dasein either does or does not understand itself out of the world in which it finds itself, or rather out of its own self as existing being-in-the-world.

Heidegger opens §32 with a reaffirmation of the connection between understanding, projection and possibility. 'As understanding, Dasein projects its Being upon possibilities.'[10] But the theme of being-towards-possibilities is no sooner announced than it is qualified in a way which leads directly over into interpretation. This qualification is expressed in terms of the notion of a counterthrust (*Rückschlag*). That is to say, understanding, as projection of possibilities, encounters a resistance which forces it to develop itself in relation to. . . . The realization of possibilities of being does not consist in the mere projection of such possibilities but in the effective working out of such possibilities. The key concept in terms of which Heidegger analyses the essence of interpretation, as the development of understanding, is that of what he calls the 'as-structure'. That which is there for interpretative understanding is always taken 'as'. This hermeneutical 'as' is not to be understood as a signification which is thrown over the object. Rather, any involvement with entities encountered within the world is guided in advance by a prior understanding which can be articulated in terms of three fore-structures – fore-having, fore-sight and fore-conception. In so far as meaning gets its structure from a fore-having, a fore-sight and a fore-conception, and in so far as meaning is that in terms of which the intelligibility of something maintains itself, it follows that whatever is understood 'as' is not *discovered* to possess such a meaning but is always already understood in terms of just such a meaning structure. Hence, interpretation necessarily moves in a circle. That which one *seeks* to understand has always already been understood in advance, though this understanding in advance may not have, and usually has not, been rendered thematic. So far from such a circle proving vicious (*circulus vitiosus*) and as such to be avoided, it is only in so far as interpretation gets into the hermeneutical circle in the right way that the understanding which is thereby developed can assume the form of a genuinely primordial kind of knowing.

In these sections on understanding and interpretation the primary objective is to lay out that sense of interpretation which is relevant to an understanding of entities encountered within the world, or indeed of the world itself. However, there are passages in which Heidegger moves from the plane of being to that of textual interpretation. That such a move is called for is of course founded in the fact that the ontological articulation of understanding itself results in a text which must be interpreted in order to be understood. Unfortunately however, the principal passage in which Heidegger talks about textual interpretation is one wherein he restricts himself to a negative critique of a supposedly presuppositionless understanding.

> If, when one is engaged in a particular concrete kind of interpretation, in the sense of exact textual Interpretation, one likes to appeal to what 'stands there', then one finds that what 'stands there' in the first instance is nothing other than the obvious undiscussed assumption of the person who does the interpreting.[11]

However, this brief and indecisive passage will suffice to furnish us with a clue as to the way in which interpretation takes place at the level of the text.

An inauthentic understanding of a text is one in which the interpreter simply assumes that there is something there to be understood and that such an understanding not only can be, but ought to be undertaken in abstraction from the 'being-there' of the one who interprets. By contrast, authentic understanding of a text occurs when the interpreter recognizes the inevitability of pre-conceptions, which pre-conceptions can however be made explicit in the course of the interpretation and in such a way that, in working out an understanding of the text, the interpreter also comes to an understanding of himself or herself as the one undertaking the interpretation. Textual interpretation is, for Dasein in general, just one among many other possibilities of being and indeed one of the least significant. For the philosopher however, that is, for the one for whom an understanding of the essence of interpretation is of critical significance, textual interpretation assumes a privileged position. For it is precisely through an understanding of the texts of other philosophers that a philosopher develops his or her own self-understanding and in so doing finds him or herself in a position to lay out this self-understanding explicitly in the form of a philosophy. In turn, this 'philosophy', as the explicit working out of primordial possibilities inherent in the being-there of the philosopher, will serve as the predetermined framework for any further textual interpretation.

With this remove to the level of textual interpretation, we find ourselves upon the plane required to come to terms with Heidegger's Kant interpretation. The interpreter always and invariably comes to a text with certain theoretical presuppositions. The task of interpretation will require that he *neither* simply let these presuppositions direct the work of interpretation in an unselfconscious fashion (that is, without any recognition of the presuppositions as such), *nor yet* that he attempt to suppress these presuppositions in the interests of a neutral, detached and so impartial, assessment. For Heidegger, the latter attitude is an interpretative attitude like any other and already involves a projective decision which is all the more insidious for being unrecognizable as such.

A much more complicated interaction between interpreter and text comes to take the place of these two *naive* approaches. First, the interpreter must hold himself open to the text, receive the meaning conveyed in the reading of the text and make sense of it in *its own* (not yet *his own*) terms. In a second moment, he must respond to the text in a manner which is implicitly guided by his own 'pre-ontological understanding'. In a third and final moment, he must seek to build into the unity of a distinctive viewpoint the insights engendered through his interaction with the text, insights peculiar to his own way of reading the text. What comes at the end is therefore only the explicit articulation of what was already there implicitly from the beginning. This, I suggest, was the kind of procedure involved in Heidegger's own interpretation of Kant's text.

B The Kant book

But why then did Heidegger never say that, in his Kant book, it was his intention to subject the Critical philosophy to an interpretative procedure which would make it possible for him to bring to light structures which match and reflect the fundamental structures of *Being and Time*? This is no idle question. For although Heidegger must have known what it was he was trying to accomplish, he never really acknowledges that *this* is what he is doing but rather indicates, repeatedly, that his own *highly idiosyncratic* interpretation represents *the* revelation of Kant's most basic intentions. 'The fundamental purpose of the present interpretation of the *Critique of Pure Reason* is to reveal the basic import of this work by bringing out what Kant "intended to say".'[12] Implied in statements of this kind is a claim to the effect that Kant's basic intention had *never before* been recognized as such, since never before had a critic attempted anything like an ontological interpretation of the *Critique*. Later on we shall try to evaluate this claim. For the moment, it will suffice to consider how he goes about the work of interpretation.

There are three movements going on simultaneously throughout the entire Kant book. The first is a movement *forward* in the expository treatment of the *Critique of Pure Reason*. Heidegger does not stick rigidly to this agenda. But, on the whole, his interpretation proceeds through the *Critique* in the order in which it was written. Second, there is a movement *back* in the direction of an ever more primordial, or original, interpretation of the *Critique*. Hence, the 'violence' which Heidegger does to the text tends to increase with each succeeding section as his interpretation comes ever closer to that conception of metaphysics which is his own rather than Kant's. And finally, we find what might be called a movement *around*, a circular movement which reproduces the directives of the hermeneutical circle itself. That comprehension of the project of metaphysics which is simply assumed in a preliminary way at the very beginning gets eventually set out in the last section as the result of what Heidegger calls a 'repetition'.

The Kant book is set out in four sections with the rather resounding titles: (1) 'The point of departure of the laying of the foundation of metaphysics'; (2) 'The carrying out of the laying of the foundation of metaphysics'; (3) 'The laying of the foundations of metaphysics in its basic originality'; and (4) 'The laying of the foundation of metaphysics in a repetition'. The recuperation of the Kantian architectonic in an architectural metaphor ('Laying of the foundation') is not only deliberate but serves to emphasize the importance of Heidegger's specifically ontological interpretation. The *teleological* mode of Kant's transcendental investigation (where the 'step back' is in the direction of a higher, transcendental realm) is transposed in an *archeological* direction, thereby becoming an inquiry into the *arche*, the origin or ground of knowledge.

Heidegger opens his analysis with a distinction drawn from school metaphysics. The point of recurring to the distinction between *metaphysica generalis* and *metaphysica specialis* is however only to show how the latter leads on to the former through the typically Kantian 'Copernican revolution', as a result of which one of the branches of *metaphysica specialis*, namely, the study of man (the other two being God and Nature) becomes the foundation upon which the entire inquiry into being in general is based. In what sense this is so is made plain in the next section in which Heidegger interprets the possibility of a priori synthetic judgments (as presented in Kant's own Introduction) as the possibility of the precursory comprehension of the being of the essent. Thus, from the very outset, Kant's *transcendental* investigation is interpreted as a body of *ontological* knowledge, indeed as a *Daseins analytik*.

This is particularly evident in those passages in which Heidegger interprets the transcendental character of the *Critique* in terms of the phenomenological problematic of transcendence and, moreover, interprets the latter in an ontological rather than a transcendental manner. Taking B 25 as his text ('I entitled *transcendental* knowledge all knowledge which is occupied not so much with objects as with the mode of our knowledge of objects in so far as this mode of knowledge is to be possible *a priori*') Heidegger interprets as follows:

> Thus transcendental knowledge does not investigate the essent itself but the possibility of the precursory comprehension of the being of the essent. It concerns reason's passing beyond [transcendence] to the essent so that experience can be rendered adequate to the latter as its possible object.[13]

Section 2 forms the core of the work and indeed covers the greater part of the *Critique* from the Transcendental Aesthetic and the Logic through the Transcendental Analytic and so on to the Highest Principle of All Synthetic Judgments. It is divided into two parts (A and B), the first of which is concerned with establishing a thesis with regard to the finitude of human knowledge. Not only does §2 *begin* with a preliminary specification of the two sources of knowledge (intuition and understanding), but Heidegger also uses this preliminary specification to announce the primacy of the former over the latter. 'Thinking is simply in the service of intuition.'[14] Intuition stands in an essential dependence upon the object and can only reveal what is already there to be intuited. That this dependence upon the object is not intrinsic to intuition as such but is a mark of the finitude of our human intuition is brought out by way of a contrast with divine intuition, i.e., *intuitus originarius*. Human, as opposed to divine, intuition is non-creative. Non-creative intuition furnishes understanding with a material from which first concepts and then judgments can be composed. But no matter how remote from its source finite knowledge may proceed it always stands in an essential dependence upon intuition and therefore upon objects which must first be received in sense before they can be understood.

An interesting interpretation of Kant's concept of the thing in itself serves to reinforce yet again the ontological character of Heidegger's interpretation. Drawing upon a citation from the *opus postumum* where Kant suggests that the thing in itself is not something different from the appearance but merely the same thing viewed under a different aspect, Heidegger argues that what lies 'behind' the appearance (*qua* thing-in-itself) should be interpreted not as what lies 'beyond' the appearance (in a transcendent sense) but rather as what lies concealed in the revealing characteristic of the appearance.

The preliminary affirmation of the finitude of human knowledge calls in question the legitimacy of the very possibility of metaphysics in so far as it has already been defined in terms of the precursory, experience-free knowledge of the ontological structure of the essent. Thus the original question as to the possibility of the a priori synthesis narrows down to this: 'How can a finite being which as such is delivered up to the essence and dependent on its reception have knowledge of, i.e., intuit, the essent before it is given without being its creator?'[15] Understanding forms its concepts from itself and therefore functions as an autonomous faculty, save in so far as its material is drawn from intuition. Unless therefore intuition can furnish a material from itself, that is, without receiving it from objects, the project of ontological knowledge will fall to the ground. In accordance with this requirement, space and time are then disclosed as two pure intuitions which are capable of generating a manifold of pure intuition spontaneously. Although his presentation of the two pure forms of intuition is at this point entirely provisional (as is Kant's own presentation in the Aesthetic) Heidegger advises us in advance that, in the course of the laying of the foundation of metaphysics, time will come to dominate more and more.

For the time being however, it is not so much time as the imagination which is brought to the fore. The isolation of intuition and understanding and, more significantly, of pure intuition and pure understanding raises the question of how these two faculties join together to make knowledge (both ontic and ontological) possible. Pure intuition, as pure, and pure understanding, as pure, are, as it were, already appropriate to a synthesis in which they should co-operate. But since intuition is a sensible faculty and understanding an intellectual faculty, the synthesis of the two cannot be understood in terms of the intrinsic nature of these two faculties in and of themselves. Something else is needed. Although the first introduction of the faculty of imagination is entirely provisional, still, from the first, Kant does introduce imagination as a faculty of synthesis.

> Synthesis in general, as we shall hereafter see, is the mere result of the power of the imagination, a blind but indispensable function of the soul, without which we should have no knowledge whatsoever but of the existence of which we are scarcely ever conscious.[16]

Heidegger makes a double use of this citation, to bring out the synthetic character of the imagination and to bring out its essential primordiality. The primordiality of the imagination, which is only indicated here by the *obscurity* of the workings of the imagination, is further reinforced with reference to the metaphor of a root which puts out two branches.

It would take us too far out of our way to consider in detail how Heidegger establishes his case. It is worth noting however that, quite characteristically, he proceeds in a series of stages each of which represents a further step back in the direction of the ground. He begins by acknowledging pure intuition and pure thought as the *two essential elements* of pure knowledge. He then enquires into that *unity* of pure knowledge which is made possible by the imagination. He then enquires into the *intrinsic possibility* of this very unity. His analysis, which focuses largely upon the A Edition of the Deduction, accomplishes amongst other things a necessary devaluation of the faculty of apperception (the other obviously unifying faculty) in favour of the imagination. He then goes on to examine the schematism which he terms the 'heart of the whole work'[17] and which he interprets as establishing the *ground* of the intrinsic possibility of the unity of pure ontological knowledge. Finally, and as a sort of summation of all that has gone on before, he uses the Highest Principle of All Synthetic Judgments to effect a *complete determination* of the essence of ontological knowledge.

The third section is the place where, according to Cassirer, Heidegger no longer speaks as a commentator but as a 'usurper'. This third section is divided into three parts but, effectively, the division is into two, a first part focusing upon the faculty of the imagination as the ground of unity and a second part devoted to time – *Being* and *Time*. In part A, Heidegger investigates the formative and unifying capacity of the imagination – the imagination as forming the horizon of objectivity in general, as unifying intuition and thought and as furnishing the root of that structure of transcendence through which the elements are not only unified originally but spring forth in their derivative separation. In part B he effects a truly extraordinary derivation of all the other faculties from the imagination. Pure intuition is shown to be, essentially, imagination (§28). Pure theoretical reason is shown to be, in essence, imagination (§29). Pure practical reason is shown to be, fundamentally, imagination (§30).

In part C, Heidegger begins by taking the previous analysis one step further. The transcendental imagination is shown to be primordial time. There follows a fascinating interpretation of the temporal character of the triple synthesis whereby each of the three dimensions of the triple synthesis is aligned with a different dimension of time – the synthesis of apprehension with the present, the synthesis of reproduction with the past and the synthesis of recognition with the future, an alignment which immediately reminds us of the corresponding strategy in *Being and Time*, where each of three *existentialia* (understanding/mood/falling) is aligned with a different dimension of time. Finally, Heidegger connects time with the self in such a way that the self is shown to be temporal in its being.

In the fourth and last section, Heidegger draws all the conclusions which follow from the analysis conducted up to that point. More specifically, he draws from his previous analyses conclusions which align the *Critique*, fairly straightforwardly, with the metaphysical project attempted in *Being and Time*. He begins by introducing the concept of a repetition. 'By a repetition of a fundamental problem', he tells us, 'we understand the disclosure of the primordial possibilities concealed in it.'[18] The key word here is 'possibilities'. For the previous analyses have revealed the transcendental imagination as the ground of the intrinsic possibility of the ontological synthesis, i.e., transcendence. But no sooner does he state this result than he insists that the result is not what has actually transpired in the course of the interpretation. Instead, he broadens the discussion to the point that the laying of the foundation can be seen as the establishment of metaphysics as anthropology, to be sure, a philosophical anthropology which, as such, can have nothing to do with any empirical study of Man.

And right away the discussion is now set on a tack which will permit Heidegger to introduce all the central themes of his Dasein's analysis, which now becomes that philosophical anthropology towards which all the interpretative analyses have been tending. Thus the repetition of the primordial possibilities inherent in the Critical philosophy turns out to be a reproduction of the central theses of *Being and Time*. It would be pointless to go through this reproductive procedure in detail. Suffice it to say that, in this fourth and final section, we find, yet again, the finitude of human being, as also the definition of the being of Dasein in terms of existence and being-in-the-world, the temporality of Dasein, the structure of projection, the concepts of forgetfulness and re-membering, of care and anxiety. We seem to be worlds away from Kant, and yet it is this move away from Kant which permits Heidegger to rejoin the themes first announced at the very beginning of the study where he talked of the traditional concept of metaphysics and its division into *metaphysica generalis* and *metaphysica specialis*. This closing of the circle is a typically Heidegerrian move and sets his signature upon the entire study.

In order to hammer home even more forcefully the parallel between *Being and Time* and the Kant book, it would be worth reproducing briefly the successive stages of this repetition. The Introduction to *Being and Time* is devoted to an exposition of Heidegger's new conception of phenomenology and, as such, lies outside the scope of the parallel. The first section of Part One (devoted to Being) introduces the notion of a philosophical anthropology as the analytic of Dasein and so corresponds to the analysis of the relation of *metaphysica generalis* to *metaphysica specialis*. The second section introduces the unitary configuration being-in-the-world as the leading theme. This corresponds, in the Kant book, to the ontological interpretation of Kant's question: how are a priori synthetic judgments possible? in terms of the problematic of transcendence. In the third, fourth and fifth sections the unitary configuration being-in-the-world is broken up into its constituent components, the *world* in which (the Worldhood of the world) the *self* which is in (the Who) and *being-in* as such. In the Kant book, this corresponds to the resolution of the question concerning the possibility of ontological knowledge, or transcendence, into the component elements which make up the faculty theory of knowledge, more specifically, intuition and understanding. In the first instance the co-operation (i.e., the ontological unity) of these two faculties is explained in terms of the imagination as a 'between'. But in the second instance this 'between' of the two essential components is re-presented as a 'beneath' of the between. Imagination is shown to be capable of connecting intuition and understanding only because it functions as the primordial root from which the two derivative branches stem. This second step corresponds to what is accomplished in *Being and Time* when being-in as such is grounded in the structure of care. And it brings the analysis developed under the auspices of being to a close. Part Two of *Being and Time* is devoted to a temporalization of the structures disclosed in the course of the previous analysis of Dasein. This corresponds, in the Kant book, to the analyses devoted to the temporalization of the fundamentally unifying function of the imagination and to the gradual emergence of time as the primary theme of the *Critique*.

C Transformational hermeneutics

In this third part of my paper, I want to bring out the limitations of Heidegger's Kant interpretation and to draw alternative conclusions from these same limitations. In so doing, I hope to turn against Heidegger the very sentiment which he expressed when he justified his own interpretation in the light of the Kantian phrase 'understanding a thinker better than he understood himself'.

What is to me most surprising about the way in which Heidegger goes about his business in the Kant book is that, despite the hermeneutical revolution for which he was himself in large part responsible, he *still* tends to depict his interpretation as the real, the underlying, the conclusive truth of the *Critique*. For example, in the second section, he writes: 'To lay the foundation of metaphysics in totality is to reveal the internal possibility of ontology. Such is the true sense of that which, under the heading of Kant's "Copernican revolution", has been constantly misinterpreted.'[19] Such passages are to be found all over the book, for example, where he writes: 'All transformation of the pure imagination into a function of pure thought is the result of a misunderstanding of the true nature of the pure imagination',[20] or again: 'The fundamental purpose of the present interpretation of the *Critique of Pure Reason* is to reveal the basic import of this work by bringing out what Kant "intended to say".'[21] Why could he not have presented his interpretation as an interpretation, that is, as a *possible* way of envisaging the *Critique*, a way confirmed and justified by the ontological phenomenology set out in *Being and Time*? Could it be that he was afraid of not being taken seriously if he did not present his interpretation in the same *definitive* manner as most other commentators? But then, by the time he came to write his Kant book, he was already a philosopher of international stature, one who moreover, from the very beginning, never ceased to claim for the thinker, as opposed to the scholar or the critic, special prerogatives. Notoriously, some of the worst comments made upon historical philosophers are made by the most creative thinkers (one thinks of Kant's own remarks on Leibniz or Locke or Berkeley), worst because, effectively, the thinker presents his predecessors as attempting, unsuccessfully, to do what he himself has succeeded in doing effectively – in Kant's case as proto-Critical philosophers. It is not the violence done to the texts of historical philosophers which is worrisome but the fact that the interpreters seem to have been blissfully oblivious of the violence they had themselves inflicted. Here Heidegger could have worked a salutary corrective had he not proceeded *in the same way*, affirming his own interpretation as the *correct* understanding and dismissing other, often much more orthodox interpretations, as *misinterpretations*.

There are two particularly unorthodox biases expressed in the Kant book. The first is his dismissal of any epistemological interpretation of the Critique. 'The purpose of the *Critique of Pure Reason*', he tells us, 'is completely misunderstood, therefore, if this work is interpreted as a "theory of experience" or perhaps as a theory of the positive sciences. The *Critique of Pure Reason* has nothing to do with a "theory of knowledge".'[22] In view of the fact that most of the analytical interpretations of the *Critique* (which means almost all of the studies written in English) do assume that the *Critique* is, above all else, a theory of knowledge, Heidegger's heresy comes as a refreshing corrective. But it implies a quasi-total rejection of almost everything that has ever been written on the *Critique of Pure Reason*, by far the greater part of which does at least assume that this work has *something* if not *everything*, to do with epistemology. By simply replacing one bias with another, he called in question the most valuable legacy of the hermeneutical revolution, the explicit recognition of the unavoidability of multiple interpretations.

The second, extra-ordinary bias expressed in the Kant study consists in his *identification* of transcendental philosophy with ontology. Again, this standpoint is to be found throughout the study but it is found expressed in a particularly sharp and clear-cut fashion in a passage where he writes: 'the laying of the foundation of ontological knowledge strives to elucidate this transcendence in such a way that it can be developed into a systematic whole (transcendental philosophy = ontology).'[23] Or again: 'For Kant, what matters above all, is the revelation of transcendence in order thus to elucidate the essence of transcendental (ontological) knowledge.'[24]

Moreover, this hermeneutical identification of transcendental with ontological phenomenology is only a repetition (or application) of the position already assumed in *Being and Time*, as is evident from the following passage from the Introduction. 'With regard to its subject-matter, phenomenology is the science of the being of entities – ontology.'[25] Heidegger might have chosen to present his phenomenology as an alternative to, or indeed as the complement of, Husserl's transcendental phenomenology. Instead, he re-defines phenomenology in such a way that it becomes (at least for him) equivalent to ontology. Could it have been respect for his master which led Heidegger to reduce his critical comments upon Husserlian phenomenology to the minimum?[26] Effectively however, the absence of any explicit attack upon Husserlian positions need not leave us in any doubt as to his intentions. For the battle with transcendental philosophy, a battle which might have been waged upon the Husserlian field, was in fact fought out against Kant. So Heidegger's transformation of Kant's transcendental philosophy into ontology must be seen alongside his attempt to win his freedom from Husserlian phenomenology by first carving out, from within the Husserlian domain, an ontological preserve of his own and then *extending* the bounds of this preserve until it came to coincide with the discipline of phenomenology in general – thereby excluding the Husserlian conception altogether.

In my Kant book, I took as the starting point for my own ontological interpretation of the *Critique* these evident inadequacies of Heidegger's interpretative position. I asked myself whether it might not be possible to effect a series of presentations of the *Critique*, each of which would represent a different way of interpreting the *Critique*. And further, I asked myself whether it might not be possible to set out these different interpretations not just in what might be called a 'lateral' frame of reference, as so many alternatives to be juxtaposed one alongside the other, but rather in an integrated succession. In other words, I asked myself whether it might not be possible to lay out the successive presentations in such a way that any given presentation might be seen as the necessary pre-condition for its successor, and so that the interpretation which ensued would display a *logic of the transformation* of one presentation into another.

Merely by refusing the Heideggerian exclusion of any epistemological and any distinctively transcendental interpretation of the *Critique* whilst, at the same time, accepting the Heideggerian ontological interpretation, I was able to generate three distinct ways of interpreting the *Critique*, an epistemological, a transcendental and an ontological. However, like Heidegger, I had an end-point in mind, a goal towards which the entire interpretative transformation would be directed and which would both make explicit, and so also confirm, the standpoint from which the entire work of interpretation was undertaken. This presupposed end-point, or goal, consisted in what I call a 'genetic ontology'. The idea of a genetic ontology was based upon a developmental conception of phenomenological philosophy which, as such, would move through the several stages represented by the three methodologies of epistemology, transcendental philosophy and ontology, and so would be capable of integrating these three methodologies in one unitary frame of reference.

The goal to be attained in turn recommended an alternation between a static and a genetic procedure, and this not merely at the end but along the way to the end. Since the interpretative method employed by Heidegger turns largely upon Kant's faculty theory, it proved necessary to define the distinction between a static and a genetic procedure in terms of just such a faculty theory. A static procedure was defined as one based upon the *simultaneous co-operation* of the fundamental faculties, a genetic procedure, by contrast, was defined as one based upon the *successive instantiation* of the fundamental faculties.[27]

The interpretative schema made possible by the recognition of the three methodologies, together with the alternation between a static and a genetic procedure is one which, in principle, generates six alternative ways of viewing the *Critique*: ontico-static (analytical epistemology) ontico-genetic (genetic epistemology), phenomenologico-genetic (Hegelian phenomenology), phenomenologico-static (Husserlian phenomenology), ontologico-static (Heideggerian ontology) and finally ontologico-genetic.

By the very nature of things, an *ontic* presentation is one which does not venture beyond the objective plane or which, when it does so, only does so by way of a regressive question into the *conditions of the possibility* of what is already actual. In the light of such a venture, the faculty of understanding has to be taken (more or less as we find it in the Transcendental Logic) as the faculty representative of the higher faculties in general,[28] and the scope of Kant's transcendental argumentation is consequently strictly limited to a regressive question concerning the *sine qua non* of what is empirically actual, namely, an already constructed experience of objects. With regard to the possibility of an *ontico-genetic* investigation, we find, interestingly enough, in Piaget's child psychology, a genetic epistemology which exhibits a three-step genesis (sensori-motor, concrete and formal operations) and which also assumes that formal thought figures at the apex of the entire epistemological hierarchy (The Highest Principle of all Analytic Judgments). Indeed, a Piagetian genetic epistemology might have been used to investigate the process by which an objective reality is constructed in the first place.[29] However, precisely because this kind of genetic epistemology utilizes a *psychological* rather than a *philosophical* method, I made no attempt to interpret the Critical philosophy in this manner. Instead, I used the Hegelian progression (basic to the organization of parts A and B of the *Phenomenology of*

Spirit) from sense, through understanding, to self-consciousness (apperception?[30]) to carry the interpretation out of the objective sphere (broadly defined) and into the sphere of a properly reflective consciousness (*phenomenologico-genetic* presentation). Thereafter, and along lines which are already prefigured in Heidegger's interpretation, understanding disappears as one of the fundamental faculties.[31] Its place, as the highest faculty, is now taken by apperception (in relation to pure imagination and to pure intuition).

From this point on, the Critical project is resumed upon a strictly transcendental plane through an examination of the inter-relation of the three transcendental faculties of apperception, imagination and intuition[32] and with a view to instituting a transcendental phenomenological interpretation of the faculty theory. This kind of comparison (between Kant and Husserl) is one which is familiar to the literature from Iso Kern's study of *Kant and Husserl*. However, whereas, by and large, Kern's procedure consists in bringing out the *differences* between the two great transcendental philosophers from a standpoint outside the two main bodies of thought, my method consists in finding affinities through a work of interpretation which seeks to view Kant from a Husserlian standpoint.

In order to bring out the Husserlian character of the kind of transcendental analyses conducted by Kant (especially in the A edition of the Deduction), the distinction between appearance and representation has to be interpreted in such a way as to bring to light something in the order of a phenomenological reduction.[33] An appearance is always the appearance of something (substance) which does not itself appear in the appearing, and in this sense presupposes the existence of just such a something. But a representation is so constituted that nothing may correspond to what is represented, *vorgestellt*, or held *before* consciousness. Thus the concept of representation is indicative of the disclosure of a sphere of immanence within which, and within which alone, a principle of transcendence can, and has to be, found. Second, in place of the analytic or regressive procedure (from the conditioned to the condition of its possibility), appropriate to the epistemological interpretation, the emphasis is switched to the synthetic or progressive procedure (from the condition to the conditioned) in order to exhibit the constitutive capacity of the analyses conducted in the Deduction. This synthetic or progressive procedure can be justified with regard to the so-called 'subjective deduction'[34] and yields an understanding of Kant's enquiry into the objectivity of experience which already anticipates Husserlian phenomenology.

Perhaps the most obvious indication of such an affinity is to be found in the concept of the 'transcendental object', a concept which is only to be found in the A edition of the Deduction. This concept of the transcendental object mediates between two alternatives, one of which, one might say, creates too great a distance between appearance and reality while the other brings the two too close to each other. The transcendental object is not a *thing in itself* lying over and beyond the limits of sensible experience but precisely something which manifests itself in and through appearances. On the other hand, the transcendental object is not to be reduced to the epistemological notion of *substance, qua appearance*. Thus, by neither overstepping the bounds of the phenomenal nor yet reducing the phenomenal to the substantial, as *substrate of appearance*, Kant opens up a way of envisaging the essential unity of a manifold of appearances which leads straight into Husserlian phenomenology. There can be no doubt that Husserl had the Kantian model in mind when, in *Ideas I*, the text in which he made his major breakthrough into transcendental phenomenology, he (Husserl) took over, at a critical point, the Kantian terminology of a transcendental object.[35]

However, the point of carrying through a phenomenologico-static presentation is not just to re-construct the *Critique* along strictly transcendental lines but to lay the basis for what I call an 'ontological transposition'. It is a central contention of my Kant interpretation that an ontological interpretation of the *Critique* can only be arrived at by 'transposing' or carrying over the transcendental dimension of the fundamental faculties into an inverted ontological mode. This is effectively what Heidegger did when, for example, he interpreted the a priori synthesis as a precursory comprehension of the horizon of objectivity in general – but without acknowledging the source from which this ontological derivation actually stems. Thus instead of simply interpreting transcendental truth as ontological fore-knowledge, from the very outset, I prefer to make a distinction between the a priori and the genuinely *prior*. By an a priori investigation is meant the *ultimately conclusive* disclosure of those structures of consciousness which make the objectivity of an already constructed experience possible. By an investigation into the *prior* construction of experience is meant a *genuinely original* enquiry into the process by which such an experience gets built up in the first place. Thus, the opposition a priori–*prior* goes along with such equivalent oppositions as found–ground, constitute–construct, all of which not only permit a distinction between an ontological and a transcendental interpretation of the *Critique* but also allow for the establishment of an essential connection between these two, sharply contrasted, interpretations.

For instance, Kant's theory of space and time effects a reversal of the conventional conception of space and time as frames of reference for that in which we find ourselves. Instead of thinking of ourselves as situated in space and time, Kant invites us to think of space and time as situated 'in us'. But this 'being in us' of space and time is susceptible to a double interpretation, the one characteristically transcendental, the other characteristically ontological. Space and time may be 'in us', as *forms of the mind*. Alternatively, we may conceive of ourselves as spatial and temporal *in our very being*. The pure forms of space and time which are initially interpreted along more conventionally Kantian lines as pure forms 'in the mind' are finally interpreted along ontological lines to mean embodiment (the body as the space that is in me) and action (the temporalization of my being as a body).

Strictly speaking, this means, in the end, that the ontological domain will figure twice. In the first instance, the pure forms will function as so many practical structures ('schemas of action' to use a Piagetian terminology) through whose operations an objective reality is constructed in the first place, of course, in a wholly immediate and unreflected fashion. Once an objective reality has been constructed, it can then be subjected to analysis. The philosophical methodology appropriate to the investigation of such an already constructed reality is epistemology. Transcendental philosophy emerges, in the first instance, as radical epistemology, an epistemology that opens up the distinction between the empirical and the transcendental in order precisely to trace the objectivity of the object back to constitutive structures of consciousness. This reduction *to* consciousness brings about the 'destruction' *of* an already constructed reality, a destruction which prepares the way for something in the order of a 're-construction'. In this sense, what is ordinarily thought of as 'phenomenological constitution' comes to take on the meaning of a 're-construction'. Only in the light of just such a transcendental philosophical project does a properly ontological philosophy become possible. And the task of such a philosophy consists then in the attempt to bring to full self-conscious awareness those very processes and procedures which were originally responsible for the construction of that very reality which forms the starting point of any transcendental investigation.

Simply to articulate such a programme is however already implicitly to be committed to an ontologico-genetic interpretation, not merely of the *Critique*, but also of the several methodologies brought to light in the course of the attempt to articulate all the various ways in which the Critical philosophy can be interpreted. Interestingly, this new ontologico-genetic presentation can be represented as a extension of the phenomenologico-genetic presentation. Since the latter carries the analysis from an objective to a reflective plane, and since the more specifically Husserlian phenomenological interpretation leads on to an (Heideggerian) ontological conception, this latter (the last in the order of analysis) can, in turn, be regarded as the first (in the order of being) stage in a three-stage genesis which moves *from* the ontological, *through* the epistemological and so on *to* the transcendental stage.

Such a programme of *interpretative transformation* is, by the very nature of things, *much more complex* than that carried out by Heidegger. And so a question arises as to whether the effort involved (not to mention the violence done to the text) can be justified in the light of the conclusions that can be drawn therefrom. And here I would simply like to offer a few concluding remarks.

First, the richness of Kant's thinking becomes a positive force to be reckoned with, not a negative factor to be explained away. Kant has often been criticized for the apparent contradictions which abound in the *Critique*. In my view, many of Kant's central concepts should be treated as symbols rather than concepts, symbols in the sense that they unify in one term a multiplicity of meaning and so offer a context for textual interpretation – 'le symbole donne à penser', to use Ricoeur's apposite phrase. This multiplicity of meaning must remain confusing unless and until it can be disentangled. A disentangling of the multivocity of certain central concepts is already effected in as much as the concepts in question are assigned to different theoretical contexts, contexts in which their distinct meanings are separately voiced. Thus each presentation can be regarded as an internally consistent configuration, many of whose key terms will, in the context of other configurations, acquire meanings which may not be consistent with the meaning they assume in the given context.

Second, the exclusively ontological orientation of Heidegger's interpretation forces him to devalue, indeed virtually to disqualify, the faculty of apperception in favour of imagination. And yet, on the face of it, apperception is not only presented by Kant as the highest faculty but as the unifying faculty *par excellence*. Kant calls this key faculty the transcendental unity of apperception and, as such, it possesses two distinctive traits. It represents the highest unity of consciousness on the one hand and the reflective self-identity of consciousness on the other. Moreover, as that self-identity (I = I) which identifies itself with the unity of consciousness, it is also the faculty primarily responsible for integrating the other fundamental faculties within itself. Whereas Heidegger's interpretation concentrates upon the imagination to the *exclusion* of apperception, an interpretation which accords a pivotal role to apperception will also be one which is required to take account of the *inclusion* of intuition and imagination under apperception in the general structure of an a priori synthesis. Moreover, and thanks to the structure of an ontological transposition, apperception is required to figure *both* as a transcendental *and also* as an ontological faculty. The highest founding faculty becomes the lowest grounding faculty. Unification from above is converted into unification from below. Thus, the substance of Heidegger's own ontological interpretation is retained but in a way that does justice to the dominant role of the faculty of apperception.[36]

The dismissal of apperception belongs along with Heidegger's more general depreciation of transcendental philosophy. And this brings with it implications which far transcend the scope of his Kant interpretation.

For instance, it helps to explain Heidegger's tendency to interpret the history of Western philosophy as leading up to and so becoming consummated in technology. Technological thinking is thinking in view of a manipulative practice, and we are becoming ever more aware of the dangers which attend an uncritical extension of calculative–manipulative thinking. But by substituting his own ontological, for Husserl's transcendental, phenomenology, Heidegger failed to take account of the sense in which Husserl's phenomenology is already an overcoming of calculative–manipulative thinking and perhaps a more effective overcoming than that represented by the recollective (*andenkende*) thinking of late Heidegger. To be sure, Husserl's phenomenology radicalizes, and indeed *absolutizes*, the sphere of subjectivity. But the transcendental subjectivity which emerges therefrom is anything but calculative or manipulative in intent. Indeed, in his late work *Crisis*, Husserl traced many of the aberrations of the times through which he was then living to a naive regression to wilful partiality and held out, as a redeeming hope, the classical ideal of a purely disinterested, theoretical reason. Not only is this ideal dismissed by Heidegger and his disciples as a product of subjectivism, the other great subjectivist ideal, the ontologico-theological ideal of an absolute knowledge or, at least, an absolute spirituality is also disqualified (see Souche-Dagues, chap. 25, vol. II in the present work).

Coupled with this dismissal of the spirit and intent of transcendental philosophy there goes a depreciation of its ethical implications. Cassirer, in his debate with Heidegger, was quick to fasten upon this feature of Heidegger's Kant interpretation – as Pierre Aubenque has shown in his paper on the subject (chap. 23, vol. II in the present work). Though, on the surface, it might not seem that Husserl had much to say on the subject of ethics, those who are familiar with what, to my way of thinking, represents one of the very greatest contributions to ethical theory of this century, Scheler's *Materiele Wertethik*, will know how deeply indebted Scheler was to transcendental philosophy in general (the first part of Scheler's work is devoted to a critique of Kant's formalistic ethics) and to phenomenological philosophy in particular.[37]

The kind of interpretation which I undertook in my Kant book seems to me to come closer to the spirit, and the theoretical ambitions, of the hermeneutical revolution than does Heidegger's own version. First, the working out of a multiplicity of alternative presentations forces upon the reader an awareness of that very 'as-structure' in terms of which Heidegger laid out his own theory of interpretation. Whoever says interpretation says *more than one* possible way of understanding. It is precisely this multiplicity which is missing from the Heideggerian account. But the question is whether the recognition of multiple possibilities of understanding means that the work of interpretation is committed to the necessity of *indefinitely many* alternative ways of understanding – in which case we would seem to have avoided the naive conclusiveness of *one* for the chaotic inconclusiveness of *many*. By generating a *finite* number of alternative presentations in accordance with a *well-defined* principle, and by staging the succession of presentations in such a way that something like a *logic of the genesis* of one presentation from another emerges in the course of the interpretative transformation, it becomes possible to envisage the presentations in question as forming a *systematic totality* which effectively exhausts all the methodological possibilities available to the work of interpretation.

Finally, this methodological logic is one which not only describes a circle and but which also finishes up by closing the circle, and this in a double sense. At the specific level of textual interpretation, the fore-knowledge which was presupposed in advance is eventually laid out as the goal towards which the several steps of the interpretative transform-tion tends throughout. In this sense, my own interpretative transform-ation moves in the same direction as Heidegger's ontological interpre-tation. At a much more general level however, a thesis is developed with regard to the respective relations of epistemology, transcendental philosophy and ontology, which are now themselves shown to move in a circle, and precisely because, in a certain sense, ontology figures twice, as the *first* in the order of being and as the *last* in the order of analysis. Heidegger's distinction between a pre-ontological way of being of Dasein and the discipline of ontology helps to bring out this twofold location of ontology. We are (pre-)ontological in our being, and from the very beginning. However, it is only in so far as we move away from the (pre-)ontological origin that we are capable of developing the conceptual resources needed to make sense of this origin and to do so in terms of that discipline which is called ontology.

Moreover, it is also clear that, in some sense, this methodological circle has actually already manifested itself at least twice in the course of the history of modern philosophy; first, in the movement from rational-ist and empiricist epistemology (based upon Aristotelian logic) through Kantian transcendental philosophy and so on to Hegelian ontology and then again in the move from positivist epistemology (based on a much more powerful symbolic logic) through Husserlian transcendental philo-sophy and so on to Heideggerian ontology.[38] That a certain reading of the history of modern philosophy confirms the logic of a transformation of epistemology into transcendental philosophy and transcendental philo-sophy onto ontology seems not only to offer support for this conception of the relation between the various methodologies in question, it also makes it possible to envisage the all-embracing methodology of 'interpret-ative transformation' as a *science*, in that time-honoured sense in which, for Hegel, the essence of scientific philosophy lies in its *systematic* character.[39]

Notes

1 See the paper by Aubenque for an account of the Cassirer–Heidegger debate over Heidegger's Kant interpretation.

2 Christopher Macann, *Kant and the Foundations of Metaphysics* (Heidelberg: Winterverlag, 1981).

3 See especially the extensive presentation of Kant's doctrines in the *Logik* (*Gesamtausgabe* (*GA*) 21) and the volume on human freedom (*GA* 31).

4 Martin Heidegger, *Kant und das Problem der Metaphysik*, *GA* 3, tr. James Churchill as *Kant and the Problem of Metaphysics* (Bloomington: Indiana University Press, 1962). This work will be cited hereafter as The Kant book.

5 Martin Heidegger, *Die Frage nach dem Ding. Zu Kants Lehre von den transzendentalen Grundsätzen*, *GA* 41, tr. W. B. Barton and Vera Deutsch as *What is a Thing?* (Chicago: Henry Regnery, 1967).

6 The Kant book, p. 20.

7 Martin Heidegger, *Sein und Zeit*, tr. John Macquarrie and Edward Robinson as *Being and Time* (New York: Harper & Row, 1962), p. 182 (H. 143).

8 Heidegger, *Being and Time*, p. 184 (H. 144).

9 Heidegger, *Being and Time*, p. 185 (H. 145).

10 Heidegger, *Being and Time*, p. 188 (H. 148).

11 Heidegger, *Being and Time*, p. 192 (H. 150).

12 The Kant book, p. 206.

13 The Kant book, p. 20.

14 The Kant book, p. 28.

15 The Kant book, p. 43.

16 Kant, *Kritik der reinen Vernuft*, tr. Norman Kemp-Smith as *The Critique of Pure Reason* (London: Macmillan, 1929), A 78 = B 103, cited by Heidegger, The Kant book, p. 66.

17 The Kant book, p. 94.

18 The Kant book, p. 211.

19 The Kant book, p. 17.

20 The Kant book, p. 202.

21 The Kant book, p. 206.

22 The Kant book, p. 21.

23 The Kant book, p. 93.

24 The Kant book, p. 171.

25 Heidegger, *Being and Time*, p. 61 (H. 37).

26 Despite frequent references to a 'worldless subject', to a self-enclosed sphere of immanence and the impossibility of conceiving of transcendence as a transcending of such a sphere and so on, statements which clearly imply a reference to Husserl, Husserl's name is only mentioned, in a purely informative way, at two points (H. 38 and H. 47), the other references being hidden away in the notes.

27 Macann, *Kant and the Foundations of Metaphysics*, p. 16.

28 In the first instance the epistemological hierarchy is surmounted by formal thought in accordance with the 'highest principle of analytical judgment', see Macann, *Kant and the Foundations of Metaphysics*, p. 43.

29 Note the title of one of Piaget's earlier works: *La construction de la réalité chez l'enfant*.

30 As is well known, in his *Phenomenology*, Hegel takes as his clue to the stages set out in section A (consciousness) and B (self-consciousness), the Kantian faculty theory. From a starting point in the realm of sense, the exposition moves

through the secondary sphere of understanding before finishing up in the domain of self-consciousness. To be sure, the tautology I = I, in terms of which Kant formulates the reflectivity of apperception is, for Hegel, the mark of the inadequacy of this preliminary concept of self-consciousness. For all that, it is the highest faculty of apperception which Hegel has in mind with his concept of self-consciousness.

31 The first section of Part Three of The Kant book considers the 'three-fold division of the fundamental faculties' and finds grounds, in Kant, for the replacement of the provisional triptich (sense–imagination–understanding) by a more fundamental triptich (sense–imagination–apperception).

32 Although, strictly speaking, this third part should be divided into two, a part devoted to the phenomenologico-static and a part devoted to the ontologico-static presentation of the essential connection of the fundamental faculties, I have, for reasons of economy and in the light of a structure I call the 'ontological transposition', regrouped the two parts under the one head of an *ontologico-static* presentation.

33 The notion of a reduction is worked out in the section entitled 'Immanence'. As a result of the substitution of the concept of representation for that of appearance, the relation (of correspondence) to the object has to be determined by way of a structure of coherence.

34 Kant, *Critique of Pure Reason*, A xvii, p. 12.

35 The language Husserl uses in §131 is that of the 'determinable X'. In the synthesis of recognition in a concept Kant uses similar language to talk of a something in general = x (A 104) or the 'representation of the object = x' (A 105). He will also talk of this transcendental object as a 'correlate of apperception' (A 250), which is presumably why it is also legitimate to talk of apperception as the 'transcendental subject of our thoughts = X' (A 346 = B 404).

36 Implicitly, though only implicitly, Fichte's *Wissenschaftslehre* (Hamburg: Felix Meiner, 1956) effects just such a re-interpretation of the faculty of apperception. Not only is the starting point of Fichte's philosophy the I = I, the efficacy of the I is defined as a practical activity (*stellen*) rather than a theoretical representation (*vorstellen*).

37 In the preface to the first edition of *Der Formalismus in der Ethik und die materiale Wertethik*, Scheler has this to say: 'I owe to the significant works of Edmund Husserl the methodological consciousness of the unity and sense of the phenomenological attitude.' *Formalism in Ethics and Non-Formal Ethics of Values*, tr. Manfred Frings and Roger Funk (Evanston: Northwestern University Press, 1973), p. xiv.

38 Part II of my overall ontological programme envisages an 'epochal interpretation' of the history of modern philosophy from Descartes on. The principle underlying such an 'epochal interpretation' is very simple, to find epochs corresponding to the several stages of the ontological genesis.

39 For example, in a passage from the preface to the *Phänomenologie des Geistes* Hegel writes: 'daß das Wissen nur als Wissenschaft oder als *System* wirklich ist und dargestellt werden kann'; G. W. F. Hegel, *Phänomenologie des Geistes* (Hamburg: Felix Meiner, 1952), S. 23.

5

Critical remarks on the Heideggerian reading of Nietzsche

Michel Haar

In a short and surprising marginal note to the 1936–7 lecture on 'The will to power as art', Heidegger writes: 'The bitterness of the strife [*Auseinandersetzung*] is possible here only because it is supported by the most intimate kinship, by the Yes to the essential.'[1] What kinship? What is this 'essential' he admits he shares with Nietzsche? There is no further explanation here, nor in the later works, about the nature of this secret agreement, which is indeed very rarely acknowledged, and nevertheless must underlie the manifest, long and harsh *Auseinandersetzung*. Is the affinity with Nietzsche perhaps much older than the strife, in the early admiration for the radicality of Nietzsche's philosophical solitude and atheistic way of philosophizing? In *Being and Time*, whereas the Hegelian concept of time is harshly deconstructed, the Nietzschean concept of historicity is highly praised, and we find for the first time an explicit allusion to something 'essential': 'In his *Second Untimely Consideration* (1874), Nietzsche recognized *the essential* and expressed it in a penetrating and unequivocal way.'[2] In the analysis of the three dimensions of historical culture, the Antiquarian, the Critical and the Monumental, Nietzsche had understood that the unity of the three ekstases of historical time comes essentially from the future.

But isn't there an even more original affinity? Heidegger often quotes and comments on Nietzsche's famous sentences: 'Man is the not yet determined animal', or 'Man is something that must be overcome'. Both question radically and from the outset traditional *anthropocentrism* and *humanism*. As early as *Being and Time*, Heidegger seeks to overcome the metaphysical definitions of man as *subjectum*, *ego*, reasonable animal, and thinks that Nietzsche's critique of the 'fictions' of substance and subject, and in particular his attacks on the overestimation of consciousness, conscience and interiority have led the way towards a *decentring of man*.

Another important and fundamental kinship is the rediscovery of the Greeks and the primacy given to the pre-Socratics, which goes hand in hand with an anti-Platonism often violent on Nietzsche's side and which Heidegger shares, up to a certain point. This kinship is deeper than all the reservations expressed about Nietzsche's readings of the Greeks. His penetrating insight into the first Greeks 'is transcended only by Hölderlin'.[3] Contrary to Hegel who looks back, Nietzsche, like Hölderlin, 'sees ahead and opens the way'.[4] This praise is without doubt the highest that Heidegger can bestow. 'All the great problems have been raised before Socrates.'[5] Nietzsche had said this, but he had been the victim of more than one illusion or error: the Romantic illusion of a 'physical' return to the Greeks in the sense of a resurrection of Greece ('One day, let us hope, we will become *physically* Greeks'[6]); and the error principally of transcribing the thinking of the first Greeks in the categories of Plato and Aristotle, taken as evident and normative, even when they are inverted.

> It is certain that Nietzsche has been a victim of the opposition currently and wrongly established between Parmenides and Heraclitus. Here lies one of the essential reasons why his metaphysics absolutely never reached the decisive questioning, though in another sense Nietzsche did understand the great beginning of the whole Greek *Dasein* in a way which is transcended only by Hölderlin.[7]

Nietzsche stayed entangled inside the Platonic opposition between being and becoming that plays a fundamental role in the very definition of the Eternal Return, as well as inside the opposition between truth and appearance, entangled in such a way that he could never reach 'the true medium [*Mitte*] of philosophy' and think the Greek *Anfang* at its true depth. Neither Hegel nor Nietzsche was able to think the Beginning in an original and initial way; they see it only 'in the light of platonic philosophy'.[8] In other words, Nietzsche stays prisoner of tradition: he confirms and maintains the essence of truth as *homoïôsis, adequatio*. He reveals this when he finally affirms that we should imitate not the Greeks, but the Romans.

As astonishing as the initial affinities is the way in which Heidegger, in spite of his main project to contain Nietzsche within the mould of traditional metaphysics, discovers an unexpected *justification* of certain Nietzschean positions. Indeed in his lectures, he is often inclined to transpose several Nietzschean concepts into the categories and the problematics of *Being and Time*. Thus art as the will to transfigure life is interpreted, in phenomenological terms, as 'radiant appearing'; the Nietzschean *Scheinen* as perspectivist illusion is transposed into appearing as a manifestation of being conceived as life showing itself in a higher degree in the artistic phenomenon. The intensification of strength through intoxication in artistic creation is understood in terms of *Stimmung*, i.e. of transcendence. Thus also Eternal Return is fundamentally interpreted through the concept of *instant* (*Augenblick*), a sudden and complete unification of present, past and future with an ekstatic character which cannot be deduced of any 'now' (*Jetzt*). The authentic resoluteness which keeps *Dasein* in the 'repetition' (*Wiederholung*), not of facts, or concrete events with all their small details, but of basic possibilities, seems to be an echo, not of Kierkegaard, but rather of Nietzsche's most abysmal thought.

Such a justification is possible only from the 'yes to the essential'. But what finally constitutes this *essential* which would be held in common? Beyond the spontaneous or chosen affinities, beyond the *Wahlverwandschaften*, beyond the struggle with nihilism and metaphysics, beyond the rejection of anthropocentrism, beyond even the criticism of the primacy of theory and logic, the essential agreement for Heidegger seems to situate himself with Nietzsche in a *passage* (*Ubergang*). This word defines for Nietzsche the very essence of man: a 'transition', a 'bridge' (between animality and the Overman, but also between the reactive forces, the resentment and the new future affirmation). For Heidegger *passage* is a name for the present epoch, as a transition between the endless end of metaphysics and a 'new beginning' of thinking and of history. When Heidegger describes the historical situation of Nietzsche, he describes his own, taking up the Nietzschean expression: 'a precarious passage that points forwards and backwards and that for this reason is ambiguous for everyone even as far as its very nature and meaning as passage'.[9] But why did Heidegger, instead of proposing as he does in this passage a 'dialogue of thinking' with Nietzsche, try, at least at a certain period, to reduce him to the traditional essence of metaphysics, and keep him only within the past and its dead-ends? Is it perhaps – a hypothesis which would need to be verified – in order to set outside of himself the nihilism of absolute subjectivity, the voluntarism, almost the pure will to will that he has been very near to sharing (e.g. in the *Rectorats Rede*), in order to concentrate upon this adversary the failure of this absolute subjectivity and the potentially catastrophic end of the History of Being that it is supposed to prepare?

The central part of the Heideggerian reading of Nietzsche is an attempt to demonstrate that Nietzsche's philosophy remains caught and enclosed within the traditional essence of metaphysics. In chapter VI of the *Nietzsche II*, Nietzsche's philosophy is reduced to five fundamental metaphysical terms.

Will to Power gives the name for the Being of beings as such, the *essentia* of beings. *Nihilism* is the name for the History of the truth of beings thus determined. The *Eternal Return of the Same* means the mode [*Weise*] in which Being in totality is, the *existentia* of beings. The *Overman* characterizes the type of mankind [*humanitas*] which is demanded by such a totality. *Justice* is the essence of the truth of beings as Will to Power.[10]

Leaving aside the more complex question of Nihilism and of the essence of truth which would require a longer analysis, I propose to discuss to what extent and at the price of what distortions Will to Power, Eternal Return and the Overman are violently reduced to the traditional concepts of *essentia*, *existentia* and *humanitas*. I do not intend to show that the Heideggerian reading is wrong or arbitrary, or that Nietzsche totally escapes metaphysics, but rather to make more explicit some of the presuppositions upon which that reading is built.

Will to Power as essence

There can be no doubt that Will to Power is the name for the Being of beings since Nietzsche calls it 'the most interior essence of Being' (*das innerste Wesen des Seins*). But is it, as Heidegger claims, the same absolute Will as that asserted by Hegel or Schelling, or 'the Absolute that wills itself'? Is it a *Grund*, a *substantia* and *subjectum*, a metaphysical basis in which all representations are rooted? And can the values instituted by the Will to Power, according to its 'various points of view', be understood as its representations and, so to speak, as the *cogitata* of the Will? What does the perspectivistic character of the Will to Power imply? In short, what does the Nietzschean Will to Power mean for Heidegger?

In fact, we find in the Nietzsche lectures as well as in the *Holzwege*, three rather different and successive definitions:

(1) In the 1936–7 lecture on 'The will to power as art', Heidegger underlines the *transcendence* of the Will to Power. It is both self-affection, emotion or passion of the will commanding itself (*Affekt des Kommandos*), and movement aiming beyond itself. But as much as it is neither the mere passivity of self-affection, nor the activity of the objectifying will, it is ekstasis, as it is first of all to be lifted up beyond oneself towards Being. This analysis of the Will serves Heidegger to show next that the creative artistic state of intoxication (*Rausch*) as *Stimmung*, is transcendence, movement towards figures, forms, hyperlucidity, ekstatic opening and not self-complacence of the subject. 'Intoxication', writes Heidegger, 'explodes the subjectivity of the subject.'[11]

(2) In chapter VI of *Nietzsche II*, 'Nietzsche's metaphysics' (1940), the Will to Power is defined as the *existence* of every being, but mainly as

the *will to will*; power is nothing exterior to will, it is not something the will strives for, as if it did not possess it, but its very essence. Power means the inner necessity of the ever widening self-affirmation of the will. The expression 'Will to Power' makes manifest 'the unconditional essence of the will, that as pure will, wills itself'.[12] It is pure self-positing, detached from every grounding and with no goal other than its own conservation and augmentation. It must will to will, in emptiness – and finally will nothingness rather than not will. Moreover, Will to Power is the principle of the *'calculation of values'*: the word calculation is repeated seven times in four pages. Will to Power is the subjectivity that counts only on itself, and that posits the values that can support it, while it reckons the quantity of forces necessary to maintain and increase itself. (3) In the *Holzwege* essay, 'Nietzsche's word "God is Dead" ', Heidegger exposes again the ontological meaning of the Will to Power as the Being of beings and the definition of power as the essence of the will that knows and wants itself. But he underlines and develops mainly the theme of the establishment of values, which constitute a *stock of presence* that prefigures the technological stock. As it pretends to grasp Being, to lay hands on it, Heidegger calls the very thinking in terms of values a blasphemy and even a 'murder of Being'![13]

The boldest and the most convincing of these three definitions is certainly the second, which shows the circular structure of the Will to Power as will that wills itself. This circularity allows the establishment of the parallel with the Hegelian Absolute Knowledge as 'circle of circles': it shows the supposedly total nihilism of the will that constantly comes back to itself and whose power lies in the constant overpowering of its own power over itself. It explains the essential link between Will to Power and Eternal Return; the latter is understood as the ultimate consequence or exigency of this eternally repeated return of the will to itself. This circularity finally anticipates the techno-economical circles of consumerism and the techno-political ones of directivism.

Some aspects of these definitions are highly problematic. *First*, when Heidegger interprets the Will to Power in a phenomenological fashion as transcendence, he seems to want to hide its truly metaphysical dimension. His reading underestimates the physical and metaphysical realism of forces, forgetting his own idea that all metaphysics is basically physics. Heidegger interprets the Nietzschean phrase about *'plus von Macht'* as the simple widening of the horizon open to intentionality; whereas Nietzsche, in his 'Physiology of art' insists that the Will to Power as art depends upon a 'real increase' of strength, the intensification of the powers of the body, a feeling of nervous and muscular quickness, a swiftness and lightness of movements, and so on.[14] *Second*, the reduction of the Will to Power to essence neglects and keeps silent about the

Nietzschean critique of the traditional concepts of essence, substance, subject and identity. For Nietzsche, there is no essence in the Platonic sense of *eidos*, that is in the sense of a constant unity which would precede every multiplicity. There is no substantial essence either within or deriving from the Will to Power. 'The question, "what is it?" amounts to imposing a meaning from a certain point of view. Essence is something perspectivistic that already presupposes a multiplicity.'[15] Will to Power should, in fact, always be said in the plural: the Wills to Power; a plurality which cannot be totalized or substantially unified, of forces engaged in complex and variable relations of struggle, commandment and obedience.

Every centre, every focus of meaning is fictitious, or the momentary expression of a balance of forces which is constantly changing. If this is the case, the metaphysical notions of *Grund* and *subjectum* are shattered and relativized. There is neither a grounding nor an absolute subject in Nietzsche, no *Grund*, but *Abgrund*, chaos. And finally the principle of the *calculation of values*, the key or core of the Heideggerian demonstration (especially as the stock of values prefigures the *Bestand*) raises the difficult question of the meaning of perspectivistic evaluation in Nietzsche. For Heidegger, evaluation only continues the work of reason since Descartes: to measure, to calculate beings, to give account to the subject which is both the stage where everything appears so to speak in court, or stands before the supreme judge. The thought in terms of values would not question the traditional stage of reason and representation: Heidegger calls values 'representing productions' (*Vorstellende Hervorbringungen*). Values are calculated to be adequate to the will ('you will only have the values that suit your degree of strength', says Nietzsche). The rationalism of the calculating Will to Power in art and science would be the prefiguration of the perfect oblivion of Being in the will to will. The perfection of calculation would hide the sombre emptiness and the absence of the goal of power exerted for the sake of power. But, can the Nietzschean idea of value as interpretation be reduced to the concept of rational representation? Nietzsche is clearly struggling with the tradition of reason as accountable to a normative and law-making authority. But when he writes, 'We cannot refuse the world the possibility of yielding to an infinity of interpretations', he states that the Will to Power is an indefinite process of interpretation which never arrives at a final and adequate representation, at a 'seventh day's rest' or 'sabbath of all sabbaths'. He breaks with the principle of reason. For every reason, whether Leibnizian, Hegelian or technological, does not pretend to achieve an infinity of *possible* calculations, but the only calculations which are the truest, that is the most correct, adequate . . . the best. Reason has to exclude the false, whereas interpretation imposes neither the application of the principle of contradiction, nor even that of the principle of reality. A fictitious interpretation can have immense strength – such is the case with Eternal Return. The phrase 'calculation of Values' is metaphysical, and it is made up by Heidegger, as it cannot be found expressed *verbatim* in Nietzsche. Will to Power can never place values in front of itself and compare them objectively. All values are necessary. But because they are answers to constraints, or rather to situations of constraint in which the interpretative forces are themselves caught. An interpretation is not a theory. It is not calculated in the sense that it would constitute a detached representation, a scene. It has the spontaneous, ambiguous, unstable character of the attempt, the essay. Values are transitory. They cannot be seized or secured as can be the objects of science and technology. The models which Nietzsche uses to characterize interpretation (deciphering medical symptoms, or philological readings) simply cannot be applied to the non-ambiguous rationality of Technology.

Eternal Return and the theology of existence

The simplifying identification of the Eternal Return with the traditional category of existence is surprising, especially if we consider the multiple versions that Nietzsche gives of his doctrine. Indeed, Eternal Return apparently does not refer to the given-ness of being in totality, or to the mere fact that it is, but rather in its first formulation in the *Joyful Science* (§341), 'The heaviest weight', to the *hypothesis* of an infinite reaffirmation by the singular will of a singular moment, according to a question: 'Would you want *this* once more and an innumerable number of times?' This question also supposes a thought suggested by a demon: 'This life as you live it now, you will have to live it again.' The *demonic* and terrifying thought is the idea that whatever the attitude of the will in the face of this revelation may be, acceptance or refusal, the factual necessity of the eternal repetition will prevail. But this factual necessity is itself inscribed in the equally hypothetical 'pre-' question that opens the text: 'What would you say if one day a demon . . . ?' Therefore, the twofold hypothetical or twofold fictitious character of the Eternal Return seems to set it far apart from the traditional category of existence and make it participate simultaneously in the three categories of modality distinguished by Kant: *possibility, existence* and *necessity*. Among these categories, the category of possibility in a broader sense than the logical possibility considered by Kant (something whose contrary is contradictory) seems to prevail. Heidegger is ready to admit that Eternal Return is the thought of a possibility; 'the possibility which is asked is, as a possibility, more powerful than any factual reality would be'.[16] One should add that if Eternal Return is presented as an interpretation, it is also strongly characterized as a *belief*, or as Heidegger says, an *anti-*

belief,[17] a sort of secret religion which is meant to make a selection among men and which constitutes, therefore, the ultimate trial in the process of overcoming nihilism. But the Return is also indissolubly linked to the experience of the ecstatic *instant*, the supremely affirmative instant of *joy*. It is equally attached to the experience of the *amor fati*, the experience of the supreme affirmation of the universal bond, of the ring encircling and uniting all things in a circle which is imperfect, 'vicious', because it includes evil, and is nevertheless divine: the *circulus vitiosus deus*.[18] Finally, but it is not the last possible meaning, there is a cosmological sense of the Return, as an attempt to give a scientific explanation of the relation between the finitude of the totality of the forces constituting the universe and the infinity of time. Heidegger knows this plurality of aspects, which he mentions in his lecture, but he reduces all of them to the modality of *existence*. Why?

Because of a structural necessity inherent to the essence of metaphysics, so it seems. The Will to Power as *essence* of the world, as a *what*, must also have its *existentia*, its *how*. The circular or the cyclical movement is its most perfect replica or its closest image: the circle is, according to Heidegger, 'the most constant stabilization of the unstable',[19] of the becoming, or of the chaos of forces and perspectives. It is the greatest fixity for mobility, or as Nietzsche says, 'the most extreme closeness of a world of becoming to the world of Being'.[20] At this point, which is called the 'summit of contemplation', the Eternal Return is indeed conceived as the 'widest actualization of the Will to Power'. Conversely, according to Heidegger, it is only from this doctrine of the Eternal Return that the Will to Power can be understood. The Return is the epitome of Nietzsche's philosophy. Nevertheless, Heidegger mentions that whereas the Will to Power is constitutive of the Being of beings, Eternal Return is only a modality. Will to Power 'exists' as Eternal Return. But how can that be the case? How can a thought, and moreover the thought of a possibility, be the modality of the existence, be the 'facticity' and the effectivity of the world. Must men not, as in Pascal's *Wager*, decide in favour of the Return? The Heideggerian reading underestimates the dimension of virtuality, of attempt, of fiction, but also of *choice* which is at work in the idea of the Eternal Return.

Moreover, it raises the difficult question of the passage from the ontological character of the *existentia* to its theological character. By a kind of levelling of differences, the 'katholou' or the *koïnotaton* (that is according to Aristotle the most common character of being) and its highest, noblest, most divine character (*theïon*) melt into one another, so to speak. Ontology is theologized, in as much as the Return as modality of the essence of the world receives the attributes of divinity. Nietzsche's God would be both 'a state of maximum', the maximum of strength of the Will to Power, its highest concentration, and the habitual, current state of the world. In any case, God or the divine can no longer be submitted to the traditional determinations of the metaphysical God: Nietzsche's God is neither the first being (is he even a being?), nor the *causa sui*, nor the prime mover, nor the *demiourgos*, nor the creator. Heidegger notes that to speak of 'pantheism' ('God' in this case would be understood as the dionysian world itself considered as the supreme being), is not very illuminating, since the 'pan' and the 'theos' are both unknown, or undefinable, or impossible to reduce to concepts. We could add the fact that Nietzsche criticizes the very idea of totality when he writes for instance: 'We must make the Universe crumble into pieces, lose the awe before the All. . . . There is no All. Profound aversion to reposing, once and for all in any one total view of the world.'[21]

Heidegger characterizes Nietzsche's theology in two ways:

(1) The divine as such is not dead. Only the 'moral God', that is, God reduced to a supreme judge who rewards and punishes, the God of the weak and the suffering, is dead. God survives beyond good and evil.
(2) The Nietzschean thought of the Return constitutes 'a negative theology from which the Christian God is absent'.[22] The phrase, 'negative theology' sounds strange but it can be defended in many ways. The most abysmal thinking is, if not unsayable at all, at least the object of a silence, a reservation. *Zarathustra* hesitates to communicate it and Nietzsche himself expresses it only in three passages of his published works. On the other hand, the Return implies the concept of world as chaos, i.e. with the negation of all its positive, anthropomorphic determinations, especially order, beauty and finality. This negative theology, in dehumanizing totality, saves the possible coming of a new god that Heidegger calls a 'more divine god'.

But is not this reading too one-sided? For if the 'too human' concepts of order, finality and beauty are negated, other attributes, absolutely positive attributes, are conferred upon totality – namely permanence and necessity. 'The overall character of the world is . . . chaos *not* because of the absence of necessity, but *because of the absence of order*'.[23] There is, therefore, a necessity of totality, and so a *positive theology* in Nietzsche, who calls many things divine. Heidegger seems to avoid discussing Nietzsche's positive thinking about divinity.

The Janus-head of the Overman

The analyses concerning the Overman show a striking contrast between the manifest content of Nietzsche's texts and their unthought. Heidegger's changing of his interpretation of the Overman is particularly radical. In 1940, he defines him both as the penultimate figure of the *animal rationale* and as the *Master of the Earth* who would anticipate a calculating domination under the veil of the artistic will in the 'grand style'. The type of the Master of the Earth is interpreted as the future planetary ruler, later called the 'civil servant of technology'. On the contrary, in *What is called Thinking?* in 1951/2, the Overman no longer possesses any nihilistic qualities. He is nearly the prefiguration of the Shepherd of Being: 'The Overman is poorer, simpler, more tender, harder, calmer, more generous, slower in his decisions and more sparing in his speech.'[24] He stays away from the masses and from the techno-economical and political power. He represents 'a higher man',[25] who is 'qualitatively different from traditional man',[26] far from being his mere 'enlargement'.[27] How can we understand this Turn?

The first definition tries to show that the Overman belongs totally to the general essence of metaphysics. His meaning is *deduced* from the inner necessity that governs this essence and its realization in technology. The repetition of the word *must (müss)* underlines this essential necessity (*Wesens-notwendigkeit*).[28] The Hegelian subjectivity of the Spirit, Heidegger remarks, *must* still be inverted in the subjectivity of the body conceived as 'great reason';[29] the absolute subjectivity *must* be embodied in the highest type of man, the Overman. Heidegger insists on the continuity between mankind and the Overman (understood as the perfection of mankind), whereas Nietzsche speaks of a rupture and outright juxta-position of the two. 'Not mankind, but the Overman is the goal', says *Zarathustra*. The Last Man and the Overman, Nietzsche states, 'will live side by side (in the distant future) separated as much as possible, the latter similar to the Epicurean gods who have no preoccupation with men'.[30] The Last Man, as stated in *Zarathustra*, is needed in order to let the Overman appear as his strongest opposite. Eternal Return does not *eliminate* the Last Man, even if it always selects the more 'super-human' types who can bear such a thought.

There is another contradiction with the manifest meaning of Nietz-sche's text: for him, the Overman cannot exist in the singular, but only as the plurality of exceptional individualities.[31] For Heidegger, on the contrary, the Overman is interpreted as 'the supreme and unique sub-ject'[32] that embodies the most affirmative Will to Power.

'The Overman', he writes, 'does not know the barren isolation of the simple exception',[33] but constitutes for him the collective will of a man-kind that knows how to *calculate* the mastery of the earth.

Finally, there is a contradiction between the Overman as the prefigur-ation of the technocratic ruler and the Nietzschean idea of a secret, non-violent, non-dominating reign of the future 'Masters of the Earth', who would reign in their own creative sphere apart from the masses. Indeed the whole technological unthought of the Overman is linked to the unthought of the notion of 'grand style'. Why does the 'grand style', which Nietzsche does not associate with the Overman, but with 'classical art' (that is, every art with an economy of means, with clarity, with laws, with mathematical sobriety, with the strongest concentration), why does grand style reveal the future essence of technological power? Precisely because of the artistic *reign* attributed to the Overmen. But for Nietzsche, they will reign, however secretly, invisibly, over men, without governing, as 'artistic tyrants'. They will be artists in the largest sense, by their power of seduction. Nietzsche does not say that they will necessarily practise the 'grand style'. But the real hermeneutic violence in Heidegger's reading is the link he establishes between the grand style and the essence of technology. 'The grand style which includes, in advance, universal domination, includes the gigantic.'[34] Here there is another break with the literal sense: the grand style, according to Nietzsche, is turned towards what is 'pretty, short, light, delicate',[35] whereas the giganticism of technology supposes exaggeration of effects, accumulation of power, constant overpowering.

Is there any analogy between the autonomy of aristocratic artists and the planetary domination of technology? In Nietzsche's texts, the allusions to industrial production are very rare, and he hardly speaks of industrialization as a means of levelment. But the presupposition of the Heideggerian analysis is that the unthought of the Will to Power is calculation. It is true that Nietzsche speaks of a surplus of force, of the 'quantity of power', of 'scales', of 'measures of force', but the Overmen are presented as personalities with a spiritual or affective radiance: 'it would be a Caesar with the soul of Christ', or the ' unity of the thinker, the creator, and the lover', or the 'gathering of the poet, the lawmaker, the scientist, and the hero, capable of deciphering enigmas'.[36] In any case, the Overman according to Nietzsche is radically detached both from political action and economic production. He does not calculate. Calculation can only be general, that is to say, applicable to the masses. How can a totally solitary type, whom Nietzsche compares to the gods of Epicure, be the prefiguration of managers and planners? The Overman is clearly an anti-universalistic figure. Why would the Overman have to select men? Men, for Nietzsche, select themselves according to their attitude towards the Eternal Return.

This is why the image and the definition given by the 1952 lecture seem nearer to the Nietzschean texts. According to the second version, the Overman is totally disinterested towards government and planification. He wisely steps aside from the political world. One must not look for him 'in the marketplaces of a manufactured public opinion'.[37] He has given up intervening in the affairs of the world, acting *in* or *on* the technological world. 'The Overman never shows up in the clamorous escorts of the so-called powerful men, nor in the prearranged meetings of the heads of State.'[38] Heidegger does not describe the non-technological activity of the Overman, but evidently, since he is 'sparing in his speech', this activity could be related to poetry and thought.

In spite of this change, Heidegger hesitates to acknowledge – even in the second version – the radical novelty of the Overman versus man. Though he constitutes a 'rejection of traditional mankind', he leads traditional mankind to its perfection and full accomplishment.[39] It seems that the ultimate figure of the Overman remains ambiguous. Nevertheless, the change is not arbitrary and is not due to the political changes. National socialism is gone, but technology stays. On the level of the unthought, the double face of the Overman corresponds to the Janus face of technology, to the link between *Gestell* and *Ereignis*. Is it pure chance that the *Blitz* (flash of lightning) is both the symbol in the Nietzschean text of the apparition of the Overman and in the Heideggerian text of the coming, invisible to most men, of the *Ereignis*? But can the same men be the servants of unbridled rationality and the preservers of the enigma of Being? The actual use of power and the powerlessness of thought seems incompatible. The Heideggerian opposition between the 'civil servant of technology', and the 'Shepherd of Being' seems to repeat the Nietzschean cleavage between the Overman and the Last Man.

Again Heidegger seems to hesitate between two interpretations. On the one hand, in a Nietzschean, 'pessimistic' way, he presents the theme of a *co-existence* between two ontological types of humanity which are destined to incommunicability. On the other hand, looking for a reconciliation in the name of the unity of Being, he refuses any analogy with the extreme dualism of the herd type and the affirmative type. Nevertheless, the complete cleavage reappears when Heidegger foresees an 'extreme danger'[40] which would be tantamount to the 'death of human essence': that those who are imprisoned by calculative thinking and those who are still open to the secret and to the withdrawal of things, would no longer meet, no longer communicate, would move away from each other at an ever faster rate. The two dimensions would be then, according to Heidegger, like two completely foreign constellations.

But in a less dramatic interpretation, the co-existence of the two Nietzschean types would only mean that two possibilities are simultaneously offered to man in his relation to technology. It is the same man who should be calculative and meditative, capable of planning and of letting be, able to say yes *and* no to technical objects. In spite of the Nietzschean temptation of a cleavage, Heidegger maintains the unity of the essence of man because of the unity of the essence of Being.

In building up deliberately Nietzsche's philosophy into a metaphysical system, Heidegger does violence to his text; in trying to reject it totally in the past, in transforming the main themes into rigid theses, he covers up the novelty of Nietzsche's method of interpretation.

Nevertheless, the very resistance of Nietzsche's text to this unilateral reading makes it all the more powerful and enigmatic. Its irreducible character puts in question the very notion of a transhistorical 'essence of metaphysics' and its all too simple continuity.

Notes

1 *Gesamtausgabe (GA)* 43, p. 277.
2 *Sein und Zeit*, p. 396.
3 *Einführung in die Metaphysik (EM)*, p. 97.
4 ibid.
5 *Groß Oktav Ausgabe*, Leipzig *(GOA)*, XIII, p. 4.
6 *GOA*, XV, p. 445.
7 *EM*, pp. 96–7.
8 *Nietzsche I (N I)*, p. 469.
9 *Was heißt Denken? (WD)*, p. 21.
10 *Nietzsche II (N II)*, p. 260.
11 *N I*, p. 145.
12 *N II*, p. 266.
13 *Holzwege*, p. 246.
14 See e.g., *Wille zur Macht (WM)*, §800.
15 *WM*, §556.
16 *N I*, p. 393.
17 *N I*, p. 434.
18 *Beyond Good and Evil*, §56.
19 *N II*, p. 287.
20 *WM*, §617.
21 *WM*, §470.
22 *N I*, p. 353.
23 *Joyful Wisdom*, §109.
24 *WD*, p. 67.
25 ibid., p. 33.
26 ibid., p. 67.
27 ibid.
28 *N II*, p. 302.
29 ibid., pp. 306–7.
30 *GOA*, XVI, §901.
31 'One Overman would not be a god, but a devil.'
32 *N II*, p. 302.
33 *N II*, p. 312.
34 ibid., p. 310.
35 ibid. Heidegger quotes here *WM*, §849.
36 *GOA*, XIV, §16.
37 *WD*, p. 69.
38 ibid.
39 ibid., p. 26; p. 67.
40 *Vorträge und Aufsätze*, p. 34.

6

Heidegger's conception of space

Maria Villela-Petit

Space and the incomplete character of *Being and Time*

How is one to interpret the incomplete character of *Being and Time*, the absence of this third section which should have been called 'Zeit und Sein', given the further development of the Heideggerian work? Should we not ask ourselves what this incompleteness was implicitly bound up with? Was it simply, as appears at first sight, bound up with the question of being and of time, which *Sein und Zeit* seeks to connect in one single question? And what if this incompleteness also had to do with the third term that the dyad *being* and *time* had, in a certain manner, obscured, namely space and, in particular, the respective relations of space and time in the economy of *Sein und Zeit*?

An interrogation of this kind does not proceed solely from my interest in the question of space; it is also suggested by some remarks which Heidegger himself makes in the text of the lecture 'Zeit und Sein' (1968),[1] a lecture which adopted, let us not forget, the very title intended for the third section of *Sein und Zeit*, that which, precisely, had never been brought to completion.

The reading of this lecture calls for two acknowledgements. The first is that Heidegger names space and time together by employing the nomenclature *Zeit-Raum*. This titular procedure (whereby time and space are brought together through a common characteristic) is not to be understood as a tribute paid to relativist science. Rather, it signals, on the one hand, the inappropriateness of the propositional structure of language and, on the other, the incapacity of any physical theory to express what has to be thought here, namely, the deployment, the truth of being apprehended on the basis of the experience of what Heidegger calls *Ereignis*. But we are getting ahead of ourselves. For the moment, let us simply note that, by way of such a nomenclature, Heidegger undoubtedly wanted to warn us against any attempt (including his own earlier attempt) to effect a transcendental appropriation of space by time or, in opposition to the former, and in the Hegelian manner, to attempt a sort of dialectical identity between space and time.

The second acknowledgement which a reading of the lecture 'Zeit und Sein' brings to light has to do with this remark: 'The attempt in *Being and Time*, §70, to trace the spatiality of Dasein back [zurückführen] to temporality cannot be sustained'.[2] What is at issue in this §70, to which Heidegger refers here? And is what he says here, in the form of a retraction, intended to cover this paragraph alone or does it not rather suggest, at the same time, the unsatisfactory character of the ontologico-phenomenological analysis of the spatiality of *Dasein* and of space proposed in the first section of *Sein und Zeit*?

Let us consider the first of these questions to begin with. In what does this withdrawal from what is no longer tenable (*Unhaltbar*) consist, in Heidegger's own words? To focus upon the title of this §70 alone: 'Die Zeitlichkeit des daseinsmässigen Räumlichkeit', one is obliged to recognize that there is nothing untenable to be found here. A phenomenologico-existential analysis of spatiality could very well be led to take account of temporalizing aspects, of the dominant implication of this or that temporal dimension, in the diverse modalities of the spatialization of Dasein.[3] So the difficulty will have to be located somewhere other than in what, taken in isolation, is announced in the title of this paragraph alone. Once one gets into the reading of the paragraph, one quickly appreciates that Heidegger was trying to eliminate the possibility of adding to this title an 'and reciprocally' which would make it possible to write another paragraph entitled: 'Die Räumlichkeit der daseinsmässigen Zeitlichkeit.' It was precisely the possibility of just such a reciprocity which it was important for Heidegger to exclude. For it would, in addition, compromise his project of deriving historicality (*Geschichtlichkeit*) and inner-time (*Innerzeitlichkeit*) from originary temporality (*Zeitlichkeit*) alone, to the exclusion of an element of spatiality. As Didier Franck remarks, 'if "spatiality" has to intervene in the derivation of inner-time from originary temporality, the whole project called *Being and Time* would thereby be called in question'.[4]

That Heidegger himself had seen the problem presented by spatiality for his attempt to found the being of Dasein upon its ekstatic temporality, is evidenced by the claim he makes at the beginning of §70: 'Thus with Dasein's spatiality, existential–temporal analysis seems to come to a limit, so that this entity which we call "Dasein", must be considered as "temporal", "as also" as spatial coordinately.'[5] However, for him it was precisely a matter of circumventing the menace presented by 'spatiality' by reducing this menace to a kind of semblance against which one should be protected. Couldn't such a 'semblance' lurk in this 'und auch', leading to an alignment (*Nebenordnung*), to an identification of the spatiality and the temporality of Dasein? But such an identification would have led to nothing less than the emergence of temporality as determining, in the final analysis, the meaning of the being of Care (*Sorge*) in as much as it structures Dasein existentially. Against the risk of such an identification, of just such a linkage (*Verkoppelung*), §70 is going to try and confirm the structure of temporality as the ground (*Grund*) of the ontological constitution of Dasein and of its modalities of being, amongst which spatiality figures.[6]

It is the temporal *distentia* which is going to found the spatializing *dispersion* (*Zerstreuung*) and therefore the spacing of the dis-tancing and of the orientation characteristic of the spatiality of Dasein. At the end of §70, this foundational primacy of time, where the out-of-itself of existing as 'temporality' founds the *Da* of Dasein, is underlined in these terms: 'Only on the basis of ekstatico-horizonal temporality is the irruption of Dasein in space possible.'[7]

But surely this understanding, moving as it does from the *Da* of Dasein, stands in the way of a fuller and more complete assumption of corporality (*Leiblichkeit*), a corporality implied by all the various modes of spatialization of being-in-the-world? A difficulty of this kind was suspected early on by Erwin Straus, this phenomenological outsider, for whom: 'The *Da* in which, in Heidegger's own words [*Anspruch*], our being is thrown, is our corporality with the structure of the world which corresponds to it.'[8] In other words, with a view to getting rid of the dualism of mind and body (which is certainly one of the principal objectives of the fundamental ontology of *Sein und Zeit*), was it really necessary for Heidegger to subordinate the spatiality inherent in corporality to ekstatic temporality?

According to *Sein und Zeit*, nevertheless, the foundation of spatiality upon temporality not only serves to secure the independence of space with reference to time but also makes it possible to understand the dependence of Dasein with regard to space and, in this way, 'the well known fact concerning the abundance of "spatial images" in language'.[9] This 'fact', let us recall, had been thematized by H. Bergson in *Time and Free Will* where space and language are found to be intricately interconnected. As for Heidegger, he claims to be able to explain it with reference to temporality itself. Does he not see in it, after all, the sign of a dominance of the *present* as the temporal dimension of concern (*Besorgen*),[10] which is the mode of being of Dasein delivered over to its concernful everydayness, by way of which, for him, its spatiality is also made manifest?

Since we are not in a position to discuss this interpretation at length, an interpretation which touches upon both language, space and time, we will limit ourselves to pointing out that Heidegger himself will not hesitate later to circumvent it, even to pronounce it wrong. In fact however, referring the spatialized images of language solely to the spatiality of everyday praxis might well have been an indication of the deficiency of the thinking on language in *Sein und Zeit* and, more especially, of the mystification of what, due to our belonging to the earth, to our habitation between heaven and earth, 'takes place', leaves its trace in language.

But let us get back to the development of §70 as a whole. What does the insistence upon designating temporality as a foundation (*Grund*) mean if not the persistence of the gesture, even the qualified gesture, of transcendental foundation?[11] The allusion to Kant in §70 – and even though Heidegger expresses a concern to take up a distance with regard to the posing of the problem by the latter – is indicative of the surreptitious continuation of this gesture. For what is it in fact that Heidegger objects to in Kant? Certainly not the intellectual gesture which seems to assure a certain primacy of time over space. But rather that deficiency in the Kantian ontology which, blinded by the metaphysics of representation, fails to gain access to a true ontologico-existential comprehension of human finitude. It goes without saying that in §70 one is very close to the reading Heidegger will give of the *Critique of Pure Reason* in his *Kant and the Problem of Metaphysics*. Written at the same time as *Sein und Zeit*, this work praises Kant for having seen that the question of man belongs to the question of being. The interpretative accent is placed upon the transcendental imagination as the root of the transcendental transcendence of the imagination which, according to Heidegger, is, in the final analysis, to be identified with originary time as pure self-affection. As he sets it out at §35: 'Time is the condition of the possibility of every act which is formative of representation, that is to say, it makes pure space manifest.' And further on, he adds: 'To admit the transcendental function of pure space does not in any way imply a refusal of the primacy of time.'[12]

It is impossible to overlook the fact that such an interpretation (debatable because unilateral) precisely tended to accentuate the primacy accorded to time over space in Kant. For this primacy was one which, in a certain sense, had already been accorded to time in the *Transcendental Aesthetic*, that is, if one considers the criterion in accordance with which time, as the condition of the possibility of all representations, has a greater extension than space, since it is a prerequisite of the representations of external as well as of internal sense. To the former should be added his underestimation of the fundamentally spatial, as well as temporal, power of schematization. A primacy which, however, the *Refutation of Idealism* will serve to undermine. In any case, what concerns us here is to see how the Heideggerian interpretation of Kant, at the time of *Kant and the Problem of Metaphysics*, went along with (was congruent with) the way in which *Sein und Zeit* had envisaged the relationship between spatiality and temporality.

From the foregoing it follows that if, as we find in §22 of *Sein und Zeit*, 'space, in a sense which has still to be determined, constitutes the world',[13] this world, which is revealed to Dasein as belonging to its own proper structure of being (cf. Dasein as 'being-in-the-world'), would remain dependent upon Dasein (and not even, or at least only laterally, upon *Mitsein*). One sees here a subtle continuation of the privilege of interiority over exteriority, that very privilege which the understanding of Dasein, as being-in-the-world, tried to place in question. . . .

These difficulties, these apories and their consequences for the question of being were certainly foreseen, even if only in part, by Heidegger. From the beginning of the 1930s he sets out in a direction which will be thought through later as the 'turn' (*Kehre*), a turn which can be situated around 1935. But this change of direction within the frame of the same quest, that of being, is both preceded and prepared by a massive hermeneutical investment in Greek philosophy. And so begins that interpretation of Plato and of Aristotle as a function of what Heidegger understands by 'the beginning of metaphysics'. In connection therewith, he turns his attention to the question of the 'truth of being', which question now takes the place of that of the 'meaning of being', the question proper to *Sein und Zeit*. This is also the context in which we have to situate his meditation on *physis*, where he tries to rejoin pre-Socratic Greek thinking. In accordance with this 'initial' comprehension, it is being which offers itself as (*als*) *physis*, as he points out repeatedly in *Introduction to Metaphysics*.[14] However, the deepening of the question of being will of itself bring with it a change of attitude with regard to the question of space. As we are now in a position to confirm on the basis of a reading of the *Beiträge zur Philosophie*, a work published in 1989 but which Heidegger composed around 1936–7. It is at this point in time, and not simply at the time of the lecture 'Zeit und Sein', that the wording *Zeit-Raum* impressed itself upon him.

Having made these points, we are left with two directions in which to proceed. The first consists in going back to the analytic of spatiality in *Sein und Zeit*, with a view to trying to bring out its limits; the second, in considering the effects of the turn (*Kehre*) on the thinking about space.

Space in the first section of *Sein und Zeit*

Let us turn to chapter III, entitled 'The worldhood of the world' (§14 to §24). Here Heidegger refuses to envisage the world as simply subsisting in space, therefore making a break with the classical attitude for which the world did subsist, reduced to being nothing but the totality of bodies in the objective space of Euclidean geometry. In this way a critique of the attitude of modern philosophy is implied in as much as it forgets that geometrical space is itself constituted by an objectifying operation which can only be carried through on the basis of a world to which we are attached existentially and whose intrinsic spatiality we have to understand.

On the other hand, the approach to spatiality is not accomplished, as one might have expected, by way of a phenomenology of perception. The ontological strategy of *Sein und Zeit* makes this impossible. For, to isolate and privilege perception would be to abandon the concrecity of the being-in-the-world of Dasein in favour of a subject split up into a diversity of faculties or capacities. Heidegger, on the other hand, claims to have disclosed the world phenomenologically in the thickness of its concrete significations which, according to him, are first of all those which proceed from the daily practice of Dasein as being-in-the-world. From which it follows, as Franco Volpi has shown very clearly under the auspices of a 'reappropriation', that is, a creative translation of notions proceeding from the practical philosophy of Aristotle, that a certain priority has to be accorded to action and to doing in as much as, in everyday praxis, the latter both encompass and go much further than perception.

To understand such a step with regard to the problem of space, it is worth remembering that it has to be situated explicitly in the context of an attack upon Cartesian ontology which, under various forms, has not ceased to make itself felt throughout the course of modern philosophy. The confrontation with Descartes is so decisive here that it takes up the entire middle section of chapter III; from the very outset, it is stated that the exposition of the Cartesian ontology 'will furnish, by way of its antithesis [*negativen Anhalt*], a theme for the positive explication of the spatiality of the surrounding world [*Umwelt*] and of *Dasein* itself'.[15] Thus, from the very beginning ontological dualism is called in question. The distinction between *res cogitans* and *res corporea* is rejected to the extent that this distinction would, if operative, obscure the spatiality proper to human Dasein while reducing the beingness of every natural being to *extensia*. With regard to a physical thing, all that is taken to be true is what manifests itself as subsisting (*Vorhandene*) for a theoretical consciousness, what can be rendered intelligible in physico-mathematical terms; the phenomenality of the world is thus relegated to the status of a subjectivo-relativistic appearance.

But whereas in Husserl's *Krisis* the critique of the forgetfulness of the *Lebenswelt* goes together with an attempt to understand the process of idealization which underpins the 'mathematization of nature' in modern physics where the interest focuses on Galileo (cf. §9), in *Sein und Zeit*

Heidegger tries above all to think the ontological legacy of such a procedure in Descartes and he interprets these ontological consequences in terms of a 'de-mundanization' of the world. This term designates the eclipse of any understanding of the effective modalities of our being in the vicinity of things with reference to the horizon and on the basis of the world. Correlatively, he talks of the de-mundanization of Dasein in modern times since thenceforward the latter takes its stand *vis-à-vis* an a-cosmic world, as a subject 'out of the world' and therefore capable of ignoring its originary spatiality.

With a view to re-discovering the spatiality of Dasein, Heidegger sets out from a description of the spatiality of the surrounding world (*Umwelt*). He takes as the guiding thread for this phenomenologico-ontological description, the being of those entities which present themselves with a primordiality which precludes their reduction to *res extensa* or the in-itself of objectivist ontology. This kind of entity is one with which Dasein is concerned in virtue of the use (*Umgang*) which he makes of it in his daily life, with regard to which he is present in the mode of concernful involvement (*Besorgen*). It is those things which are close at hand (*Zur Hand*) which are ontologically determined by their availability (*Zuhandenheit*) for utilization. Thus they present themselves as tools or instruments (*Zeuge*) in their character of being-in-order-to (*Um . . . zu*): for instance, the hammer for the fabrication of the table or the construction of the house. In virtue of this structure of being which carries with it the determination of a reference to . . . (*Verweisung*), each instrument is revealed as always already inserted into a whole, an instrumental totality (*Zeugganzheit*).[16] By way of an example of a totality of things structured with a view to their utilization, Heidegger evokes what happens in an office. The things which are to be found there are not disposed in such a way that each can be taken in isolation from the others. Together, and on the basis of their relations with others, they determine the 'physionomy' of the room. What we encounter in the first place is the room in that susceptibility for signification which belongs to it: an office and not just a volume geometrically defined by the four walls which its simple things fill up. We discover the room, Heidegger also tells us, as a residential instrument (*Wohnzeug*). Is it really necessary to point out that this expression betrays a thinking about dwelling, about housing, which does not go much further than a certain functionalism – which latter reminds us of what Le Corbusier was to recommend a little later, with this qualification that, in the context of an industrial civilization, Le Corbusier preferred to talk of a 'residential machine'.[17]

In sum the uncovering of the environment in *Sein und Zeit* shows it to be a totalization of meanings and objectives, the same as those constitutive of the connection linking instruments one with another (*Zeugzusammenhang, Zeugganzes*). The analysis never ceases to implicate both the spatiality proper to the being of an instrument and that inherent in the whole into which it is inserted. Those entities which are available for utilization are entities whose 'proximity' cannot be determined primordially by any system of measurement, but with reference to an oriented proximity which arises out of that concern which characterizes Dasein in its everydayness. The being of the instrument only acquires its meaning with reference to a practice and its proximity is therefore that of its instrumental accessibility. This does not mean that, as it were, it has to be dragged around, for it does have its place, a place where it can be found, and this implies that it is not to be regarded as a simple thing subsisting somewhere in a space which is unqualified and which has not been differentiated into subsidiary places. And just as an instrument is never encountered in an isolated fashion so a place is only what it is with reference to other places together with which it constitutes a network or a 'totality' of places (*Platzganzheit*).

In turn, since it has itself to be situated, the condition of the possibility of a totality of places lies in a wherein (*Wohin*) in general, a wherein which concernful involvement has in mind from the first. Thus every place has to be referred to a 'region', to a 'side', all of which is already implied every time one specifies the place of a thing from 'this side' rather than from 'that side'. The word we are translating by 'region' or by 'side' is *Gegend*. At the time of *Sein und Zeit*, Heidegger is still far from having thought about *Gegend* or *Gegnet*, as he will do, on several occasions, after the *Kehre*. Here these *Gegende* are still thought as a function of the spatiality inherent in everydayness. However, for the determination of these regions which, for their part, confer a more general orientation upon the space of the surrounding world, one being, the sun, plays a privileged role. For its places, though changing, are places which are constantly and regularly available for the diverse and variable uses to which we put the light and the heat which they yield. They serve to differentiate the celestial regions which furnish pre-established points of reference for the terrestrial regions which these places occupy and articulate.[18]

That such a purely pragmatic consideration of the sun and its 'orients' by no means exhausts the existential meaning that its course has for us is clearly recognized by Heidegger when he adds: 'Churches and tombs are disposed according to East and West, the life and death parameters which determine Dasein in its inalienable possibilities of being.'[19] But should he not then have gone on to question this availability, the *Zuhandenheit* of entities as the privileged *leit motif* of the uncovering of the spatiality of the world? Before trying to do justice to this question it is worth pointing out that the spatiality of the surrounding world is only existentially relevant because it is founded on the spatiality of Dasein. In other words, the spatiality of the surrounding world presupposes the being of Dasein, to whose spatiality it belongs essentially to adopt an orientation and to make distances disappear. Its encounter with intra-mundane entities implies a making space (*Raum geben*), an arrangement (*Einräumen*) which makes possible a range of places upheld by gestures such as 'displace', 'remove', gestures which do not require the intervention of a theoretical attitude or the constitution of a geometrical space.

The analyses of §22 to §24 proceed as we have seen, in a regressive fashion, on the basis of an uncovering of the spatiality of the world in the direction of its ontological presupposition, namely, the spatializing being of Dasein. This now permits us to formulate more exactly the questions which the approach to spatiality in *Sein und Zeit* raises.

Without recurring to the importance of highlighting the existential primacy of the practical over the theoretical, there are grounds, nevertheless, for asking ourselves whether our way of encountering the spatiality of the world and of intra-mundane entities really should be restricted to that mode of involvement which Heidegger takes account of here which, obviously, takes as its paradigm the labour of the craftsman and the world which corresponds to it. To take only one of the essential features of the *Umwelt* disclosed by Heidegger's analysis of spatiality, 'totalization': *Zeugganzes, Platzganzheit*. It is a matter of integrating each instrument, and the place which belongs to it, in a sort of system of reciprocal reference on the basis of which each can be uncovered in its usefulness for . . . , in its pragmatic significance. This was already implied in the *Um* of *Umwelt*, which has to be understood in its double meaning of *um* – 'surrounding' and of *um* – 'in order . . .'. But what then becomes of our exposition of the open space of a countryside which suspends, 'disorients', even if only for a moment, the prevision which characterizes 'everyday praxis'? Is it not the case that concernful preoccupation (promoting the 'hold' and the hand as the organ of prehension), even if it does make possible a revealing of the spatiality of the world of everyday praxis, nevertheless puts into effect something like a 'reduction', to wit, a 'neutralization of its phenomenal appearance'? What are we to make of the presentation or of the donation of nature in its 'grandiose spectacles' (sky, sea, mountain, waterfalls, etc.), those very aspects which Kant takes account of in his analytic of the sublime in the third Critique, where it is already a question of poetic vision?[20]

But it is not even necessary to leave the space of the home[21] with its affective and identificatory investments to recognize the limitations of an analytic which only considers the spatiality of the world from the standpoint of its significance and of its practicality as a function of that specific existential which is involvement.

Besides, what is one to say of those worlds in which instrumentality cannot be isolated in as much as the available entity (the tool) incorporates from the start other determinations and references than those of its utility alone? And how, on the basis of its *configurational* aspects, can one fail to attribute to the spatiality of the world a metaphorical and symbolic tenor which, to some extent, already encompasses and surpasses the pragmatic significance which is uncovered across our daily praxis?

Last but not least, the analytic of spatiality in *Sein und Zeit* suffers from the absence of any investigation bearing on the constitutive spacing of *Mitsein*, which latter impacts not only upon our understanding of the space of the world (spaces and distances of a social order), but also upon any consideration of the spatiality of Dasein itself as well as upon the question of *Jemeinigkeit*, that is to say, the question of selfhood or identity.[22] How is one to understand Dasein's character of being 'mine' if one does not take into consideration the 'here' and the 'there' constitutive of intersubjectivity which, from the start, manifests itself as an intercorporeal phenomenon – as Husserl made amply clear in his *Vth Cartesian Meditation*? Once again we rejoin the question of embodiment which the very project of *Sein und Zeit* failed to articulate more exactly in its connection with the question of spatiality and of the *Mitsein*. The articulation of this question is however anticipated, but in a largely negative way, as emerges from §10 of the Summer 1928 lectures on *Leiblichkeit*, entitled 'The problem of transcendence and the problem of *Sein und Zeit*', where *Leiblichkeit*, *Mitsein* and the phenomenon of *Raumbedeutung* as the primary determination of every language (*Sprache*), are presented as having to be understood on the basis of spatial dispersion (*Zerstreuung*).[23]

However, if, at the heart of the Heideggerian meditation, this tangle of crucial questions remains undeveloped, this is not true of other issues which we shall now go on to mention. Two digressions which, in *Sein und Zeit*, follow upon the course of the analyses of the spatiality of the world will serve to confirm the above. The first of these digressions arises in the context of entities which are not produced, natural beings the recognition of which is presupposed by any product whatsoever. This recognition of non-produced goods arises, Heidegger points out, as a function, or in view, of (*Wozu*) the work to be produced. 'But when this happens, the Nature which "stirs and strives", which assails us and enthrals us as landscape, remains hidden.'[24] It is therefore not always possible to reduce nature to the *Zuhandenheit*, as is explicitly underlined in §44.[25] These remarks in their turn relativize the choice of the *Umwelt* or of the instrument (*Zeug*) as the only available clues to any elucidation of the spatiality of the world and of Dasein.

The other digression goes in the same direction. It takes into account the hypothesis of a 'primitive world'. In this regard Heidegger remarks that 'what is ready-to-hand within the world just does not yet have the mode of Being that belongs to equipment'. And he adds: 'Perhaps even readiness-to-hand and equipment have nothing to contribute as ontological clues in interpreting the primitive world. . . .'[26] But if these remarks place his interpretation of everydayness in a new perspective they do not, for all that, suffice to dissuade Heidegger from treating entities encountered within such a world under the negative sign of a 'not yet'. 'It does not yet have the mode of being that belongs to equipment.' And he does not even bother to ask what 'reduction' (of symbolic attributes, etc.) might correspond to just such an 'accession'. However, in the Second Section of *Sein und Zeit* (where the analytic of the First Part is reconsidered from the standpoint of the foundational element of temporality), intra-mundane entities, together with nature itself (as landscape, field for agricultural exploitation, etc.), are uncovered in their historical (*geschichtlich*) character, which latter goes along with, and is indeed inseparable from, the historicity (*Geschichtlichkeit*) of Dasein as being-in-the-world.[27]

Nevertheless, the assumption of the historical character of the world of everyday life in this Second Section, entitled 'Dasein and temporality', an assumption which could not remain without its consequences for the question of the spatiality of the world, does not bring Heidegger to return to the disclosure of the latter; and that, as we already pointed out, because it pertained to the very project of *Sein und Zeit* that historicality should be derived from temporality alone. Be that as it may, it is no less true that the two digressions of chapter III from the First Section, that on nature and that on the primitive world, appear 'supplementary' with regard to the elucidation of spatiality as already explicitly carried through.

It is however worth noting that in *Vom Wesen des Grundes*, Heidegger tried to explain, even to give, in his own words, 'precise reasons' for the exclusion of nature from the analytic of spatiality. This is because, he tells us, the question of nature could only be introduced on the basis of the analysis of *Befindlichkeit*,[28] which latter is only pursued later on, namely, in the context of the analysis of that fundamental existential structure which is Care (*Sorge*). But these 'precise reasons' leave the real question entirely on one side: what of the spatiality inherent in *Befindlichkeit*, that is to say, in each of the affective moods (*Stimmungen*) by way of which Dasein experiences itself and finds itself in its being in the midst of beings? The absence of any interrogation on the spatiality of moods such as anxiety, joy, fear, boredom[29] can only be explained as a function of the very project of *Sein und Zeit* to found spatiality upon temporality. . . . But then, in what concerns the thinking about space, the incompleteness of this project, as well as leading to a deepening of the question of being, is going to mean, at one and the same time, an opening and the opening move of a new attempt.

Space after *Being and Time*

Even though it is always possible to find several 'turns' along Heidegger's path of thought, the critical shift is that executed in the famous turn, the *Kehre*, around 1935. With regard to what concerns space, it makes itself known in the lecture: 'The origin of the work of art' and in the course of lectures: *What is a thing?* (*Die Frage nach dem Ding*), and especially as it is only now possible to appreciate, in the text which has remained unpublished for so long, *Beiträge zur Philosophie*. Let us consider the course of lectures first of all. In the first part, Heidegger reviews the different ways in which philosophy has attempted to determine the being of the thing. He questions the relationship between the identity, the particularity of the thing and the categories of space and of time. To summarize: what is the relation of the *this* to the *here* and the *now*? Is space a simple framework, a system of co-ordinates making possible the determination of the spatial position of one thing relative to others? What are we to make of the limit, in things, between a without and a within? In the second part of the course Heidegger tries to characterize the field, the historical ground upon which the determination of the being of the thing rests in the *Critique of Pure Reason*; which determination now appears to Heidegger as the metaphysical centre of Kant's work. The point to stress concerns the gap between the Greek conception of movement and of locus and that of 'modern times', the position established by Galileo and Newton and on which Kant himself relies. For the Greeks, Heidegger recalls, thinking especially of Aristotle, 'the type of movement and the locus of the body are determined by the nature of the latter'. 'For any characterization and any estimate of movement, the earth is the centre . . . the stars and the heavens in general move *peri to meson*, around the centre, their movement being circular.'[30] On the other hand, with Newton, 'any body left to itself moves in a straight line and in a uniform fashion'.[31] It is important to appreciate the consequences of such a transformation. For it not only affects the understanding of movement and of nature but also the position of Dasein at the heart of being. Among the consequences mentioned, let us consider, in particular, the change which the concept of *locus* undergoes. 'The locus', writes Heidegger, 'is no longer the place to which a body belongs in virtue of its intimate nature but simply a position which it assumes from a purely relative standpoint, that is to say, in relation to other positions.' Henceforward, 'the difference between terrestrial and celestial bodies becomes otiose'.[32] What could this mean if not that the gap between the sky and the earth is abolished and that loci are now only neutral positions? The result is a flattening of physical space which, in accordance with a purely geometrical representation, is, from now on, nothing but a homogeneous medium whose attributes can only be derived from mathematical representation. Conceived in this way, space does not have much to do with the spatiality of the world in which we find ourselves. What is more, it conceals this spatiality. This concealment, which touches both the spatiality of the world and that of Dasein, was thought by Heidegger in *Sein und Zeit*, on the basis of the Cartesian ontology and its dualism. In the course of lectures *Die Frage nach dem Ding*, on the other hand, where the interpretation of the history of philosophy is tied together around Kant, he envisages it on the basis of classical physics while at the same time recognizing, as Catherine Chevalley's paper (chap. 63, vol. IV of the present work) shows, that this physics is itself, at least in part, called in question by the new physics. Such then is the hermeneutical background against which Heidegger takes command, little by little, of a thinking about dwelling which proceeds along the same lines and conjointly with his thinking about being.

In addition, the lectures already announce two themes which are absent from the analysis of the spatiality of the surrounding world in *Sein und Zeit*, namely, that of the Earth and that of place (*Ort*). While in *Sein und Zeit* it was above all a question of 'place' (*Platz*), and of a 'network of places' (*Ganzheit von Plätzen*) seen as a function of the readiness-to-hand (*Zuhandenheit*) of an equipmental whole, it will from now on be a question of place (*Ort*) and of the relation between space and place. He goes back to the lecture, 'Der Ursprung der Kunstwerk', contemporary with the course of lectures, to deepen these themes. In this lecture, Heidegger further pursues his investigation into the thinghood of the thing and into the equipmental being of equipment but with this difference, that he now does this with a view to bringing to light the truth of the thing, or of equipment, on the basis of its manifestation in the work of art.

The inadequacy of the traditional determinations of the being of thing stands out most evidently when one questions the work of art. Thus the different philosophical conceptions of the thing stemming from the tradition, whether as 'informed matter' (*geformter Stoff*), or as 'support of qualities' (*Träger von Merkmale*, substantia + accidens), or as the 'unity of a multiplicity of sensations' (*Einheit einer Mannigfaltigkeit des in den Sinnen Gegebenen*) give themselves away as so many obstacles to any approach to the true being of the thing, and a fortiori to the truth of the being of the work of art. This obstacle has to be set aside as the condition without which it is impossible to open the way to an alternative approach to the question of truth. Normally tackled as arising out of the domain of science, as an epistemological affair, the question of truth is here paradoxically posed in terms of the work of art. Art is going to be set up by Heidegger as the phenomenological site where the truth of the being of entities makes its appearance. But if, as he says, art is the realization of truth, this can only be because the truth is not first and foremost the object of a theoretical attitude, that it does not consist initially in an *adequatio rei et intellectus*. Rather than being conveyed by an objectifying judgment, the truth takes place as an event in the work of art. Thus Heidegger offers an alternative to the dramatic Nietzschean opposition between art and truth, an opposition summed up in *The Will to Power* with the adage: 'We possess art lest we perish of the truth',[33] namely, an alternative which might be expressed as follows: art as the realization of the truth.

This occurrence, this taking place of the truth is in turn set in relation to what Heidegger identifies as structuring the work of art. This 'structure' is not something internal to the order of 'representation' and which would be connected with the formal aspects of the work. It is identified by way of a contrast with what in *Sein und Zeit* was said on the subject of production: equipment (*Zeug*) or work (*Werk*). Here, what is produced refers back to what is not produced as to a simple material; for such is the understanding of natural beings brought to light from the standpoint of everyday praxis. The forest is considered as wood, the river as yielding hydraulic energy. The 'material' is absorbed into the product, the work itself being grasped in its being-for . . . depending on the use to which it is put. But in breaking the chain of utilitarian references in which the 'product' is caught up, the work of art opens up a more essential access to the truth of the product, a truth which is also the truth of the world to which the product belongs; in other words, that of the site to which it bears witness. As a guide to his meditation Heidegger chooses a canvas of Van Gogh in which shoes are depicted, shoes which he takes, in a way which is both debatable and has been largely debated,[34] for the shoes of a peasant. This meditation, which neglects the aesthetic aspects of the work in order to come to terms with its theme, to the point of making it impossible to identify the work in its singularity, can be summed up in two affirmations: 'Across these shoes', Heidegger writes, 'there passes the silent appeal of the *earth.*' And further on: 'This product belongs to the earth. It harbours the *world* of the peasant.'[35]

By relating to the thing in this way, the shoes are made to appear in the work and in relation to what is co-signified in the work, that is, an Earth and a world. Thus Heidegger's meditation on Van Gogh's canvas makes Earth and world appear as the polarity which both holds open and furnishes our dwelling space with its dimensions. It does therefore point towards the rootedness of dwelling in a soil, a theme which, at the time, was not exempt from ideologically ambiguous connotations but which, at least in Heidegger's writings, was not associated explicitly with the theme of blood or with racism.[36]

The second example of a work of art invoked by Heidegger will permit him to give a further and more adequate account of his thinking about dwelling while at the same time furnishing him with an opportunity to consider the nature of the relation of *place* and *space*. Now the work in question is a Greek temple. This is what he has to say.

> It is precisely the temple as a work which disposes and collects around itself the unity of the ways and relations through which birth and death, misery and prosperity, victory and defeat, endurance and ruination confer upon human being the shape of his destiny.[37]

It is clear that the 'Greek temple', taken with this kind of generality, is not being considered from an architectonic standpoint but as a *place* that unites around itself an entire network of ways and significations which articulate its space and give a meaning to dwelling. This meditation invites the reader to move beyond the point of view of what would be an aesthetic objectification and so to see the temple at work in its efficacity as a work. The temple installs a mortal world, that of the Greeks, in as much as it articulates its topology and its signifying configuration at the same time as it makes the Earth manifest and, without annihilating its obscure face, makes manifest its power of withdrawal, its reserve, the gateway opening upon being. The temple therefore constitutes the link, the unifying trait between an Earth and a world. It is thanks to this landmark that an earth can manifest itself and appear as native soil (*der Heimatliche Grund*), and that a space of dwelling is thereby outlined. To sum up, a space *qua* dwelling, has to be thought on the basis of the places which it articulates.

Starting from the lecture: 'Der Ursprung des Kunstwerkes', dwelling impresses itself as one of the most constant of Heidegger's meditative themes. This is attested in a much later text which merits our attention not only because it condenses a number of previously conducted analyses but also because it rings the changes on the terms employed in the lecture of 1935. We are talking of the lecture 'Building dwelling thinking', given in 1951 at the 'Second Darmstadt Symposium', a symposium devoted to 'Man and space'.

Before we begin, let us note that in the period between the lecture of 1935 ('Die Ursprung der Kunstwerk') and that of 1951 ('Bauen Wohnen Denken'), Heidegger's thinking on space is nourished by considerations stemming from the notion of *chora*. This is a very typically Heideggerian move. Greek thought, and especially pre-Socratic thought, provides him with the occasion for a remarkable meditative prolongation but one which, in reality, takes him further away rather than bringing him closer to the Greek text. Moreover, to all appearances the meditation sets out from a pre-Socratic expression while leading to something else, without this something else ever being consciously assumed. To take Heraclitus' fragment 109: in his course of lectures *Heraklits Lehre vom Logos*

(Summer term 1944), while criticizing the usual translations of *kechoris-menon*, Heidegger remarks that in *chorizein*, *chora* is to be found. This furnishes him with a pretext to 'translate' the Greek in a creative fashion, that is to say, not only to find in it a linguistic equivalent, namely, *Gegend* or *Gegnet* in the sense of surrounding world (*Umgebung, die umgebende Umgegend*), but, on the basis of this 'finding' to develop a meditation taking as its guide the distinction between *topos* (*Ort*) and *chora* (*Gegend, Gegnet*).[38]

The meditation on *die Gegend* and its old form *Gegnet* is developed and deepened in 'Conversations along a country path' ('Feldwegge-spräch'), written a little after the course on Heraclitus to serve as a 'commentary' on *Gelassenheit*.[39] In this work, the accent is placed hence-forward on the opening of *Gegend*. It names the opening which surrounds us (*das umgebende Offene*) and on the basis of which everything that is, is able to make its appearance. It is the *Gegnet* as 'free extent' (*die freie Weite*), with which we can enter into a relation of resonance, provided only that the things (*die Dinge*) which appear therein 'should have lost their objective character'.[40] The thinking about the *Gegend* is therefore the passage required in order to leave the terrain of representative thinking to which, according to Heidegger, Husserl's thinking about the transcendental horizon still belonged. In this sense, to take up again Heidegger's own words, it has to be seen as signifying 'the end of philosophy' and inaugurating (as the title 'conversation on thinking' sug-gests), 'the beginning of thinking', one might even say, of poetic thinking.

What distinguishes the region, the *Gegend*, is its gathering character. It holds together (*versammelt*) and unifies a plurality of places. Heidegger's thinking experience around the notion of *Gegend*, an experience which marks a break with an objectifying representation of space in favour of a meditative (rather than contemplative) approach arising out of concrete (non-abstract) language, must not be lost sight of when one tries to understand the lecture 'Bauen Wohnen Denken'. As its title indicates, this lecture is directed towards the question of dwelling. But the activity of building will have to be taken account of in a manner quite different from that implied by the means–ends schema which, he now tells us, 'closes off any access to essential relations'.[41] We are certainly far from *Sein und Zeit. . . .*

What then does 'building' mean? To this question the answer would seem to be obvious: to construct according to a plan. But the answer undertakes a detour which brings to light the several layers of meaning encompassed by the word 'build'. For the root of the word *bauen*, *buan* means 'to dwell'. If this is so, the normal order of understanding (one builds to dwell) has to be inverted, and not because dwelling, or *bauen*, would come first chronologically but because, in *bauen*, building, *wohnen*, or dwelling is already in question. By that is meant that we build according to the manner in which we dwell which is, in turn, the manner in which we *are* on the earth. By means of *bauen*, in the sense of dwelling, an unusual link is instituted between dwelling and being. Just such a link had already been outlined in the context of §12 on *In-Sein.* . . . But the implications of this link in what concerns space had not been drawn. Here, it is thanks to the etymological resources of language that the link can be made.

> 'I am' [*ich bin*], 'you are' [*du bist*] mean: I dwell, you dwell. The manner in which you are and in which I am, in which we other humans are on earth is dwelling. To be human means to be on earth as mortal, that is to dwell.[42]

It is clear that 'being-in-the-world' is henceforward to be understood in terms of dwelling and that, in consequence, our dwelling and the spatiality which belongs to it can no longer be uncovered on the basis of everyday *praxis* alone. It encompasses all the dimensions of our human sojourn here on earth. It is therefore the configuration essential to that very sojourn which it is a question of clarifying. 'Bauen Wohnen Denken' refers back to the lecture 'Das Ding' which precedes it by about one year. In the two lectures, the configuration of dwelling is thought as a fourfold game. To dwell is to sojourn here 'on earth' and 'under heaven' which is its overhang. But to be on earth and under heaven means, in addition, 'to dwell in the presence of Gods [*Göttlichen*]' and to belong 'to the community of men'. Such are the names given to the terms in accordance with which the game of the world takes place and which have to be thought not separately but in line with the unity which they constitute. This is what is expressed by the prefix *ge* of the singular form *Geviert*. Dwelling now appears in the light of the game which gives it its dimensions, which is its measure. The polarity earth–world from 'The origin of the work of art' gives way to the world no longer understood as one of the terms of this opposition but as the unity of that game which joins earth and heaven, mortals and divinities.

From a schematic point of view one sees here a kind of 'square', which, by the way, is one of the most ancient figures of space, referring back as it does to the four cardinal regions (*Gegende*). All the same, for Heidegger, the *Geviert* is not a spatial representation. It signifies the gathering, the non-separation of terms which are distinct but between which a dwelling is played out. Unquestionably, though he makes no such allusion, Heidegger's meditation on the world reminds one of that passage from the Gorgias where Plato has Socrates say:

> Wise men, Callicles, say that the heavens and the earth, gods and men, are bound together by fellowship and friendship and order and

temperance and justice, and for this reason they call the sum of things the 'cosmos', the ordered universe, my friend, not the world of disorder or riot.[43]

But what with Plato was motivated by considerations pertaining to equality, the harmony necessary to instil wisdom in the individual and justice in the city takes on with Heidegger the meaning of an implicit critique of uni-dimensional dwelling, that kind of dwelling which no longer accords a place to the sacred in as much as it reduces the truth within the limits of scientific objectification. The figure of the *Geviert* allows him to break down what he himself had called the 'spherical character' of modern metaphysics, meaning that sphere of subjectivity which absorbs the world into the sphere of representation, thereby preventing Being from being considered on the basis of the Openness of Being.[44]

Let us get back to building and to dwelling. Once dwelling has been thought in the light of a world-play, of *Geviert*, which latter stands opposed to *Gestell*, that is to say, to any imposition of technico-scientific rationality upon the world as a whole, it becomes possible to address the question of the constructed thing without running the risk of missing the belonging of building to dwelling. The constructed thing is in this case the bridge, any bridge. The meditation does not take it into account as might the engineer or the architect but in such a way as to let the totality of relations which attach it to the earth stand out. For the bridge gathers together the banks (while still permitting the river to flow) and the heavens (from which it receives its waters). Furthermore, it gathers together men (to whom it affords a passage) and the Gods (whose patron saint dwells there in effigy).[45] Only in this way, that is to say, provided one takes account of the plenitude of its signifying relations is the bridge truly thought on the basis of dwelling. The constructed thing has as its essence the management of places or, as he writes: 'The place does not exist before the bridge.' In other words, a place *qua* dwelling place cannot be defined by simple geometrical co-ordinates and on the basis of a homogeneous representation of space. It is not in space. On the contrary, it is on the basis of such places as a bridge that 'places and the various ways in which space is managed can be determined'.[46]

This way of thinking about space on the basis of place was already present in 'The origin of the work of art' in the considerations relative to the subject of the Greek temple. However, the text 'Building dwelling thinking' places the main accent upon the specificity of the constructed thing which, *qua* place (*Ort*), is capable of generating space. As one of his recapitulative proposals puts it: 'The spaces we negotiate daily are "managed" by places whose being is founded on things like buildings.'[47] The simplicity of the meditation should not be allowed to obscure the displacement which it aims to put into effect. It is a matter of tearing our thinking about space away from the horizon of a mathematization which reduces it without, for all that, going back to a 'physics' in the Aristotelian sense of the term. What he has in mind is another way of thinking place, whereby it is both given and expressed at one and the same time as dwelling place. For what was said of the thing is also valid of place, namely, that, from all antiquity, our thinking has been habituated to assess its being too poorly.

In 1969, in one of his last texts, *Die Kunst und der Raum*, Heidegger returns to the necessity of thinking the space installed by art in terms other than a subjectively conditioned transformation of the objective space of a physico-technical project. The key here are the plastic arts, a term which, in accordance with the German aesthetic tradition, applies equally well to architecture as to sculpture. Once again he appeals to that comprehension of art which emerged from 'The origin of the work of art', namely, art as the work of truth, in as much as truth means here the non-retreat, the uncovering of being (*die Unverborgenheit des Seins*). But if space managed or installed by a work of art can be called true in the sense that it is the place where an uncovering of being takes place, the question arises whether it is possible to discover what really constitutes the reality (*Eigentümlichkeit*) of this space. For Heidegger, this comes down to asking what lies concealed in the word *Raum*. He finds in the latter the dynamic trait of spacing, of *das Räumen*, in the English sense of 'making room'. This spacing is a liberating, a detaching with a view to the establishment of a dwelling. It is therefore a liberation with a view to the emergence of a dwelling place, of an apportionment of places. This meditation on spacing does not invert the relation place–space as it was thought in the previously quoted texts but brings out yet more forcibly the necessity for an inhabited space, founded on constructed things, to take place on the basis of the open space of a region (*Gegend*). Thus *Die Kunst und der Raum* interweaves the two threads of Heidegger's meditation on space: that which, starting out from an investigation of the being (*Wesen*) of the work of art, renews the thinking of the relation place–space and that which considers the region (*Gegend*), the free Extent (*die freie Weite*), on the basis of *Ereignis*. We shall return to this.

But what does the 'plastic' bring to the thinking about place and space, subject, of course, to the qualification that, as we stressed above, Heidegger's analyses are never directed toward a phenomenal appearing of individual works but attempt to read across art and its works a common structure of truth? While admitting the inadequate character of his remarks Heidegger attempts to think the plastic arts (architecture and sculpture) as 'places which become embodied and which, by opening a region and taking it into their safe-keeping gather together around themselves a free space which accords to each thing a sojourn and to man a dwelling amidst things'.[48] In this way, the abstract character of an approach which makes of a work a simple volume with an enveloping surface which brings out the contrast between an interior and an exterior space is called in question. This point of view is abstract in the sense that it separates the edifice or the sculpture from the dwelling and ignores its capacity to gather man together at the very heart of a region. In addition, the work makes the place appear in its relation to the void. A void which is not a lack or a defect but whose productive efficacity has to be shown in the coming into being of a place.

Leaving architecture behind (the Greek temple) and turning towards sculpture, could we perhaps find a body of work which corresponds to Heidegger's meditation? Even though his text does not include any reference to a specific work, we shall at this point risk the name of Henry Moore. Surely the works of Moore are able to play with the void in such a way that, by defying the principle of organic continuity, they often introduce a discontinuity into the body, even a void? In addition, surely they resist the enclosure of a museum and seek to give birth to a place which gathers around itself the space of a region? This at any rate is what Roland Penrose suggests when he writes:

> No site seems to defy sculpture more radically than the sky and the open horizon of a countryside and yet it's here that Moore finds the greatest affinity between nature and his own works. The wild slopes of the Scottish moors where several of his bronzes have been erected reinforce the grandeur and the dignity of this presence.[49]

At the end of *Die Kunst und der Raum*, the reference to the plastic arts is revoked. The realization of the truth which reveals space in the work of art can do without any support, any plastic incarnation, and simply float in the air or vibrate in song, in the voice or in the sound of church bells. This is the meaning of the quotation from Goethe with which this meditation comes to an end:

> Es ist nicht immer nötig, dass das Wahre sich verkörpere; schon genug, wenn es geistig umherschwebt und ubereinstimmung bewirkt, wenn es wie Glockenton ernst-freundlich durch die Lüfte wogt.[50]

Other passages by Heidegger from about this same period are in agreement with this saying by Goethe. So, for example, we find him writing in 'The end of philosophy and the commencement of thinking': 'However, the clearing, the open, is not only free for brightness and darkness, but also for resonance and echo, for sounding and resounding. The clearing is open for everything that is present and absent.'[51]

Texts such as these insist upon an experience of space as the Openness which is revealed just as well by the place instituted by the work of art (whose surface vibrates to the play of light and shade) as by the resounding of sound (the church bell, for example) or of the voice. The possibility of thinking about art without resorting to the banal opposition of the temporal and the spatial arts is hereby subtly announced, since sound or voices call for that very openness of space which they at the same time bring to light.

The formula *Zeit-Raum* refers to just this experience, this temporal as well as spatial proof of the Open, as the medium in which the donation of being occurs. Already employed in *Beiträge zur Philosophie*, that is to say, in the earliest outlines of a thinking about *Ereignis*, it is in 'Zeit und Sein' that this formula takes on its full meaning. In fact, it is in this text that there arises the equivalence: *Es gibt Zeit, Es gibt Raum*: an equivalence which itself refers back to the experience of the donation of being: *Es gibt Sein*. Since for Heidegger it is the primary task of thinking to be the guardian of being, this task requires that the relation of space to *Ereignis* be taken care of.

As regards the nomenclature *Zeit-Raum*, a question remains as to whether it has anything to do with *you-zhou*, the term by means of which Chinese thinking calls 'space–time' the universe. Is the posing of such a question an underlining of the necessity of what Heidegger himself terms the ineluctable dialogue with the East? But such an unavoidable alignment also seems to mean that the thinking of the donation of being with Heidegger definitely turns its back on any thinking about a transcendence beyond space and time. This is all the more evident in view of the fact that Heidegger, in his project of the 'destruction' of metaphysics, abolishes any philosophical distinction between cosmology, psychology and theology, thereby wishing to suppress any 'creaturely' dependence between *cosmos* and *theos*, between the *cosmos* and the creative *logos*.

Let us leave these questions in abeyance, no matter how critical they might be and conclude more modestly with the question of inhabited space. There can be no question that the Heideggerian meditation frees the question of space from the disciplinary boundaries within which it used to be incarcerated (geometry, physics, geography, cosmology) or the limits which continued to be assigned to it by transcendental philosophy and by the philosophies of interiority. In this sense it still remains to be shown how Heidegger distanced himself little by little from the kind of Augustinian thinking which was so near and dear to him right up to *Sein und Zeit*, especially in what concerned time. As we have tried to show, thinking about space in its inseparable connection with time became with him a thinking about dwelling, which latter is in itself a thinking about Being. To get to this point called for a conversion of the utilitarian and controlling viewpoint into a viewpoint consonant with the Opening of Being, a Being which is announced in every being but to which only poetic speech and meditative thinking is capable of responding, of appropriating in the manner required by *Ereignis*.

It nevertheless remains true that in his path of thought, his *Denkweg*, Heidegger left to one side all the social and political aspects of the space of dwelling. He missed their hidden dimensions. Moreover, the transformation in our ways of dwelling, of communicating, brought about by the scientifico-technical complex, were only envisaged by him from the negative standpoint of the forgetfulness of Being, the inverse of the positive standpoint of the domination of beings. It was Heidegger's personal idiosyncrasy that he refused the experience of the city, no doubt seeing in cosmopolitanism and cultural pluralism nothing but a rootlessness which might be captured in the expression 'the desert extends'. One certainly has no right to object to his preference for country paths and little towns like those German university towns in which he taught. And yet, without minimizing the defects of the cities and their degradation of our civilization, can one not also see therein the crucible of a unique experience, that of a plural society in which a new consciousness of self and of humanity might eventually emerge? This too deserves to be thought. Without wishing to underestimate the significance of his thinking about dwelling and the experience appropriate to it, should we not nevertheless recognize that, in the cities too, not to mention the planetary village, the Gods, as well as poets, may very well be present?

Translated by Christopher Macann

Notes

1 'Zeit und Sein', in *Zur Sache des Denkens* (Tübingen: Niemeyer, 1969).

2 ibid., p. 24.

3 As in the wake of *Sein und Zeit* (Tübingen: Niemeyer, 1976), English tr. J. Macquarrie and E. Robinson (New York: Harper & Row, 1962), the Dasein's analysis of a Binswanger links the style of certain modes of behaviour to the hypertrophy of one temporal dimension (generally the past) in the way of being-in-the-world of the patient.

4 D. Franck, *Heidegger et le problème de l'espace* (Paris: Editions de Minuit, 1986), p. 115. See also P. Ricoeur, *Temps et Récit III* (Paris: Seuil, 1985), chap. 3 ('Temporalité, Historialité, intra-temporalité') on the aporie of the Heideggerian hermeneutics of temporality. Finally, we should note that without ever thinking of Heidegger, Merleau-Ponty, in connection with the visual subject, refers to a 'unique space which separates and reunites, which upholds every cohesion (even that of the past and future) since this cohesion would not exist if it were not rooted in the same space', thereby rendering invalid any approach to the past and future which tried to dispense with space or which failed to recognize the interconnection of time and space.

5 Heidegger, *Sein und Zeit*, S. 367.

6 Cf. *Sein und Zeit*, S. 367: 'Dann muss aber die spefizische Räumlichkeit des Daseins in der Zeitlichkeit gründen.'

7 *Sein und Zeit*, S. 369.

8 E. Straus, *Vom Sinn der Sinne, Ein Beitrag zur Grundlegung der Psychologie*, 2nd edn (Berlin: Springer, 1956), S. 292.

9 *GA* 26, S. 174.

10 §69, (a) 'Die Zeitlichkeit des unsichtigen Besorgens' which privileges the 'present', as the temporal dimension of concernful preoccupation.

11 *Einführung in die Metaphysik* (Summer term 1935) contains the following remark which appears as a response to an objection to the subject of the strategy of transcendental foundation in *Sein und Zeit*, a response by means of which Heidegger aims in particular at distinguishing himself from Husserl: 'Aber das dort gemeinte "Transcendentale' ist nicht dasjenigedes subjektiven Bewusstseins, sondern es bestimmt sich aus der existenzialen-ekstatischen Zeitlichkeit des Daseins.' (Cf. *GA* 40, S. 20.) But in this way the ultimately foundational character of the temporality of Dasein is simply confirmed.

12 Cf. *Kant und das Problem der Metaphysik*, *GA* 3, S. 254.

13 *Sein und Zeit*, S. 102.

14 Cf. *Einführung in der Metaphysik*, *GA* 40, S. 134, S. 148, etc.

15 *Sein und Zeit*, S. 89.

16 ibid., S. 68–9.

17 It is worth noting that in *Einführung in der Metaphysik* Heidegger does not use the expression *Wohnzeug* when he evokes the 'school' as a 'dwelling place'.

18 *Sein und Zeit*, S. 103.

19 ibid., S. 104.

20 See Kant, *Kritik der Urteilskraft*, §29; tr. James Meredith as *Critique of Judgment* (Oxford: Oxford University Press, 1952).

21 A sketch of this problematic is to be found in my essay: 'Le chez-soi: espace et identité' in *Architecture et Comportement*, vol. 5 (Lausanne, 1989), pp. 127–34.

22 In a passage from *Vom Wesen des Grundes* (*GA* 9), Heidegger tries to explain the approach to the Me and the You on the basis of being-self by noting that in *Sein und Zeit* it was only a question of being-self, of neutral selfhood, even when the sexual difference was in question. What interests us here is to note that at no time does he articulate the question of selfhood in connection with intersubjective spacing, which latter is however implied in the distinction of 'mine–thine'.

23 See *GA* 26, S. 173–4. The work by D. Frank, *Heidegger et le problème de l'espace* turns around these questions.

24 *Sein und Zeit*, S. 70.

25 Cf. ibid., S. 211.

26 ibid., S. 82.

27 See ibid., §75, in part, also S. 389.

28 *Vom Wesen des Grundes*, French tr., p. 130.

29 See on this question the excellent work by Pierre Kaufmann, *L'Experience emotionnelle de l'espace* (Paris: Vrin, 1967).

30 *Die Frage nach dem Ding*, French tr., pp. 95–6; tr. W. B. Barton and Vera Deutsch as *What is a Thing?* (Chicago: Henry Regnery, 1967), pp. 84–6.

31 ibid., p. 97.

32 ibid., p. 98. See here also the article by Catherine Chevalley (chap. 63, vol. IV of the present work.)

33 Cf. *The Will to Power*. See on this question Erich Heller's essay: 'Nietzsche's last words about art versus truth', which constitutes chap. 9 of *The Importance of Nietzsche – Ten Essays* (Chicago: Chicago University Press, 1988).

34 See Meyer Schapiro, and the discussion of this text by J. Derrida in 'La verité en pointure' in *La verité en peinture*.

35 Cf. 'Der Ursprung des Kunstwerkes' in *Holzwege* (Frankfurt: Klostermann, 1972), S. 233. English tr. Albert Hofstadter in *Poetry, Language, Thought* (Harper & Row, 1971).

36 On rootedness.

37 'Der Ursprung des Kunstwerkes', S. 31, in *Holzwege*.

38 Cf. 'Heraklits Lehre vom Logos' in *Heraklit*, GA 55 (Frankfurt: Klostermann, 1979), S. 335.

39 Cf. 'Zur Erörterung der Gelassenheit – Aus einem Feldweggespräch über das Denken' in *Aus der Erfahrung des Denkens*, GA 13, S. 45ff.

40 ibid., S. 47.

41 'Bauen Wohnen Denken' in *Vorträge und Aufsätze*, 4th edn (Tübingen: Neske, 1978), S. 140. English tr. Albert Hofstadter in *Poetry, Language, Thought*.

42 ibid., S. 141.

43 Cf. Plato, *Gorgias*, 508a.

44 Heidegger, 'Wozu Dichter?' in *Holzwege*, S. 283.

45 Heidegger, 'Bauen Wohnen Denken', S. 143ff.

46 ibid., S. 148.

47 ibid., S. 151.

48 Heidegger, 'Die Kunst und der Raum' (St Gallen: Eiker. Vlg, 1969), S. 11/GA 13, S. 208.

49 R. Penrose, 'Au coeur de la terre natale' in *Hommage à Moore* (Paris: éd. XXième siècle, 1972), p. 12.

50 Goethe, cited by Heidegger, 'Die Kunst und der Raum', GA 13, S. 210.

51 Heidegger, 'Das Ende der Philosophie und die Aufgabe des Denkens' in *Zur Sache des Denkens* (Tübingen: Niemeyer, 1976), S. 72. English tr. Joan Stambaugh in *On Time and Being* (New York: Harper & Row, 1972), p. 65.

7

The ekstatico-horizonal constitution of temporality

Françoise Dastur

The title of this paper is borrowed from *The Fundamental Problems of Phenomenology*.[1] In the name of this title, I would like to raise some questions concerning the meaning and role of the concept of horizon in the Heideggerian thinking between 1926 and 1928, i.e. during the years immediately preceding and following the publication of *Being and Time* in February 1927.[2] For it is precisely on this subject that the lecture course from the Summer semester 1927 gives us explanations that were not forthcoming in *Being and Time*. In spite of the fact that the complete title of the first part of *Being and Time* – the second part was never published – runs: 'The interpretation of Dasein in terms of temporality and the explication of time as the transcendental horizon for the question of Being', the last sentence of the second section – i.e. the last sentence of the text published in 1927 – still assumes the form of a question: 'Is there a way which leads from primordial *time* to the meaning of *Being*? Does *time* itself manifest itself as the horizon of *Being*?'[3] The explication of time as the transcendental horizon for the question of Being should have constituted, in fact, the theme of the third section, under the title 'Time and being', as it is indicated in the plan of the book presented in section 8.[4] A marginal note in Heidegger's own copy (the famous *Hüttenexemplar*), a marginal note which is reproduced in the text published in 1977 in the *Gesamtausgabe*, refers the reader to the Marburg lecture course of the Summer semester 1927 entitled *The Fundamental Problems of Phenomenology* for an explication of time as the transcendental horizon for the question of Being.[5] At the beginning of this lecture course there is a note indicating that these lectures constitute 'a new elaboration of the third (section) of the first part of *Being and Time*'.[6] We know, on the report of the editor of the *Gesamtausgabe*, Friedrich von Herrmann, that Heidegger burnt the first elaboration of this third section soon after it had been written.[7] It has been necessary to recall these detailed references in order to emphasize the fact that the 1927 lecture course throws a new light on what Heidegger calls, in *Being and Time*, the *Temporalität des Seins*, which should be strictly distinguished from the *Zeitlichkeit des Daseins*.[8] The theme of the horizon as the correlate of a temporal extasis, on one hand, and the theme of the *Temporalität* of Being, on the other hand, are tightly knit together, as we can see from this sentence from the 1927 lecture course that reads: '*Temporalität* is *Zeitlichkeit* with respect to the unity of the horizonal schemas which are its own.'[9] We can of course find some indications about this in *Being and Time*. The expression *Temporalität des Seins* appears in §5 when, after having exposed the preliminary character of the existential analysis, i.e. of the theory of the Being of Dasein as care, Heidegger emphasizes that the temporal interpretation of care, which constitutes the second section (*Dasein und Zeitlichkeit*) does not yet furnish the answer to the leading question, that is, the question of the meaning of Being in its entirety (*Sein überhaupt*), but only provides an initial basis for arriving at such an answer.[10] But in fact §5 (together with §8 which sets out the plan of the whole treatise), is the only passage in *Being and Time* where we can find a reference to the leading problematics of the book. The latter does not consist – it is necessary to recall – in furnishing the basis for a philosophical anthropology, but in the explication of time as the horizon for any comprehension of Being, starting from temporality as the Being of Dasein, i.e. of the being characterized by a comprehension of Being.[11] Only this explanation of *Temporalität* can give a concrete answer to the question asked in *Being and Time*, the question concerning the meaning of Being.[12] But to inquire about the meaning of Being does not consist in looking for what lies behind Being, but in questioning Being itself in so far it is included in the comprehensibility of Dasein.[13] For 'meaning' is an existential of Dasein and not a property of a being; it is that within which the comprehensibility of something maintains itself, the horizon (the *Woraufhin*, literally, the 'whither') of the project from which something as such is comprehended.[14] It is therefore comprehension itself and the conditions of its possibility which have to be questioned in order to bring to light the horizon for the donation of Being. And the condition of the possibility of such a comprehension is, precisely, temporality. But *Being and Time* does not show how all comprehension implies a comprehension of Being as such, which is itself possible only on the basis of the temporality of Dasein.[15] This point is developed in §20 of *The Fundamental Problems of Phenomenology* under the head 'Zeitlichkeit und Temporalität'.

Being and Time also offers some indications about the ekstatico-horizonal structure of temporality. It is in §65, where temporality is characterized as the ontological meaning of care,[16] that temporality is defined as sheer *ekstatikon* (*ekstatikon schlechthin*).[17] But it is only in §69, which deals with the temporality of being-in-the-world that, in less than three pages (§69 C), the temporal problem of the transcendence of the world is explicitly treated, i.e. what, in temporality, makes the event of the world possible – the horizonal 'schema' that constitutes the 'whither' (*Wohin*), the 'rapture' (*Entrückung*) in terms of which the *ekstasis* takes place.[18] This analysis of the ekstatico-horizonal character of temporality is taken up again and developed in *The Fundamental Problems of Phenomenology* and it is completed in the lecture course from the Summer semester 1928 entitled *The Metaphysical Foundations of Logic*.[19] The first part of this lecture course consists of an analysis of transcendence and intentionality and is a prefiguration of the problematics of the text written in the same year (which Heidegger dedicated in 1929 to Husserl for his seventieth birthday) under the title *Vom Wesen des Grundes*. In a passage from this 1928 lecture course (where we find the very first auto-interpretation of *Being and Time*[20]), Heidegger seeks to show, in a retrospective manner, that the entire second section of *Being and Time* is dedicated to the elaboration of a transcendence which is in fact only explicitly mentioned in §69 C. He recalls therefore that, in a note from page 263 in *Being and Time* (which deals with the Husserlian primacy of intuition), it is explicitly said that the intentionality of consciousness is based upon the temporality of Dasein.[21] This note indicates moreover that the showing of the relation between intentionality and ekstatico-horizonal temporality will be dealt with in the next section, i.e. in the famous third section. It is the only indication in *Being and Time* concerning the connection between the phenomenon of intentionality and ekstatico-horizonal temporality, a connection which is also mentioned, but not explicitly developed, in *The Fundamental Problems of Phenomenology*.[22] What is characteristic of the Marburg lectures (held in the period when Heidegger wrote *Being and Time*[23]), is the continuity of the discussion with Husserl and the emphasis on the problem of intentionality, a problem which the lecture course from 1925 already recognizes as a phenomenon which will furnish contemporary philosophy with its own proper dynamic.[24] The lecture course from 1927, like the one from 1928, gives an essential place to the notion of intentionality. In the discussion of Kant's thesis stating that 'Being is not a real predicate', which can be reformulated in a more positive way as 'Being is position or perception', Heidegger declares that the constitutive elements of the intentionality of perception are not only the *intentio* and the *intentum* but also the comprehension of the mode of Being of what is aimed at in *intentum*,[25] showing therefore that the ontological condition of the possibility of all intentionality as such is the comprehension of Being. He further emphasizes that the possibility of bringing to light the ontological difference also calls for an investigation of intentionality, i.e. of the mode of access to Being.[26] The investigation of intentionality is necessary because, as Heidegger says (in his foreword to the *Lectures for a Phenomenology of Inner Time Consciousness*, edited by him, at Husserl's request, in April 1928), intentionality is not a key word, but the title of a central problem.[27] To dwell inside this problem does not mean that intentionality should be regarded as a master-key capable of opening all doors,[28] but grasped in its principal and philosophically central signification.[29] On the one hand, it is necessary to see that the idea of intentionality refers (beyond Brentano's conception of intentionality as the central notion of his Psychology from an empirical point of view) to the question posed by Plato and Aristotle, i.e. to the ontological question,[30] and precisely because the notion of intentionality annihilates the apparent problem of the subject–object relation[31] considered by the theory of knowledge of the nineteenth century as the basis of its problematics and therefore breaks with the classical conception of subjectivity, i.e. with the opposition of consciousness and world understood as the juxtaposition of two equally present-at-hand beings. But on the other hand, it is necessary to become aware of its limits, i.e. of the fact that intentionality is understood by Husserl as *noesis*, as a rational determination which should not be referred to the entire personality – as Max Scheler thought was the case.[32] As a dimension of existence itself, intentionality is therefore only an 'ontic transcendence', a transcendence in the vulgar meaning of the word, which, as a relation to beings, has itself to be founded upon an 'archi-transcendence', the transcendence of Being-in-the-world.[33] For the intentional relation is only the factual mode of an actually required appropriation of what is already surpassed, i.e. revealed on the basis of transcendence.[34]

By way of the theme of intentionality, and so subject to the condition of seeing in intentionality a problem and not a solution,[35] the question of transcendence, as a dimension of existence, still therefore has to be raised. For to exist means nothing else than to bring about the distinction between Being and beings.[36] To the Husserlian phenomenology that sees in intentionality the archi-phenomenon, ontology therefore stands opposed as this other transcendental science[37] which, on the contrary, sees in transcendence, *qua* archi-transcendence, the condition of the possibility of all 'ontic transcendence', i.e. of all intentional behaviour. But this essential determination of Dasein, i.e. of the fact that it transcends itself by itself, depends upon the ekstatico-horizonal character of temporality. It is therefore now necessary to unfold the relation of transcendence to temporality. The term 'transcendence' is certainly not taken by Heidegger in its philosophical (medieval or modern) sense but only in the original sense of the word for which *transcendere* means to go beyond, to get across, to pass over.[38] What Heidegger calls the onto-logically 'authentic' meaning of transcendence,[39] understands the *transcendens* as what goes over as such and not as that in the direction of which a 'passing over' is undertaken. It is therefore not possible to consider Dasein as immanent nor the objects as transcendent, as is the case with the vulgar, i.e. Husserlian, meaning of transcendence, because such a transcendence is not the ontic transcendence of the subject–object relation, but the comprehension of oneself from that world which constitutes the true correlate of the surpassing movement. Dasein is a being that is in the modus of self-surpassing, in the modus of *epekeina*.[40] That is the reason why Dasein's selfhood does not imply a substantial centre from which the transcending movement is supposed to start, but is, on the contrary, founded upon transcendence itself – as the condition of its very possibility. But what makes the transcendence of Dasein possible is the ekstatic character of time.[41] In order to understand what that means, it is necessary, first of all, to pay attention to the transformation inflicted upon the classical opposition between objective and subjective time by the Heideggerian thinking, once the subject–object relation has become invalidated as a plausible problem. In his 1928 lecture course, Heidegger emphasizes that he deliberately names original time 'temporality' in order to give expression to the fact that time is not a predonated being (a *Vorhandene*), but, on the contrary, something whose essence is temporal.[42] This means that, strictly speaking, time is not, but temporalizes itself and so can never be imprisoned in an ontological concept.[43] To think time as temporalization means giving up the attempt to elaborate a physics, or even a psychology, of time. Featuring neither as a frame for worldly events, nor for the internal processes of the psyche, it has to be accepted that time does not exist in any way at all. The 1925 lecture course closed with this conclusive statement: 'Nicht: Zeit ist, sondern: Dasein zeitigt, qua Zeit, sein Sein' (Not: time is, but Dasein temporalizes its Being, as time).[44]

This implies that the unfolding of time coincides with the unfolding of Dasein and that the movements of nature are, as such, completely free with regard to time: they acquire an intra-temporality only when they are encountered 'in' the time that we ourselves are.[45] The 1928 lecture course is even more explicit and declares that temporality is the *Urfaktum*, the originary fact, and that entering into the world of beings is the *Urgeschichte*, the originary history.[46] Such an identification of Dasein and time allows us to understand why Heidegger is much less interested in the analysis Husserl gives of the phenomenon of time itself (in his lectures on *The Phenomenology of Internal Time Consciousness*) than in the elucidation of intentionality through the analysis of phenomena like perception, remembrance, expectation, etc. Many years later, when Heidegger gave a short speech at a conference organized for the thirtieth anniversary of Husserl's death, he peremptorily declared that his own question concerning time was wholly determined by the Being question and had been developed in a direction that always remained foreign to the Husserlian investigation of time consciousness.[47] We find the same judgment in the 1928 lecture course, at a time when Husserl's lectures had just been published by Heidegger. Heidegger acknowledges, as he had already done in a note to *Being and Time*,[48] that Husserl's investigations on time constitute a measure of progress relative to contemporary psychology and the theory of knowledge, but he sees Husserl's essential achievement in the analysis of the intentional structures of time consciousness. For as far as the problem of time itself is concerned, nothing has changed relative to the tradition because time is still taken as something immanent, something internal to the subject. For Heidegger, what Husserl names 'temporal consciousness' is precisely time itself in its originary sense.[49] To understand that originary time is in fact nothing other than the totality of the modalities of temporalization belonging to existence means precisely to understand the ekstatic character of time. The phenomenon of 'expectation' as well as that of 'remembrance' are not only a way of perceiving the future and the past, but a way of interrogating the very sources of these modalities of time, not only a mode of time consciousness but, in an originary sense, time itself.[50] In the 1927 lecture course, Heidegger distinguishes clearly between the primary concept of future, past, present, i.e. the existential sense of temporality as unfolded by Dasein itself, and the expression of time that has always to do with intra-temporality. To characterize pure transcendence without the subject, that is, as Dasein, Heidegger makes use of the term *ekstasis* which, in its non-philosophical sense, simply means to stand out, which makes it a term appropriate to the literal sense of the word ex-istence. The 1928 lecture course is even more explicit in presenting originary temporality as a triple transport (*Entrückung*) without a centre, that is, without any substantial nucleus from which a temporal ekstasis could spring out, as a *raptus* through which the temporal dimensions are opened, or as a spring or swing (*Schwung*) that makes of temporalization the free swinging (*die freie Schwingung*) of originary temporality in its entirety, which alone can explain the Being-in-the-throw of Dasein, i.e. of the connection in Dasein of thrownness and projection (*Geworfenheit und Entwurf*).[51]

But this ekstatic character of originary temporality cannot be separated from the horizonal character that belongs to all ekstasis as such. It is important to emphasize that the relation of the ekstasis to its horizon cannot be of the same kind as the relation of *intentio* and *intentum* (or *noesis* and *noema*) in ontic transcendence, that is, in intentionality. In this case, the correlate cannot be something determined because transcendence is precisely defined as the movement by which all limitations are exceeded. But the ekstasis is however not a transport towards nothingness, or a completely undetermined rapture. Rather, it projects an horizon which presents itself as a specific openness or as a schematic pre-tracing (*schematische Vorzeichnung*) of what transcendence is aiming at.[52] The term 'schematic' is an allusion to the Kantian transcendental schematism, about which Heidegger speaks in his lecture course from the Winter semester 1925–6 and again, in 1929, in *Kant and the Problem of Metaphysics*.[53] The Kantian schema is the representation of a general procedure of the imagination with a view to procuring an image for its concept;[54] in the same way, the horizonal schema of the temporal ekstasis is the condition of the possibility of the comprehension of Being.[55] But what is the exact meaning of horizon in this context? The 1928 lecture course gives the answer. Despite its usual meaning of a circular visual limit, the term horizon is not originally connected to seeing and intuition. It means, in accordance with the Greek verb *horizein*, what limits, surrounds, encloses.[56] The ekstasis, as pure rapture, surrounds and limits itself under the form of an horizon that makes it possible. Such an horizon, in spite of the fact that it belongs to ekstasis, is neither located 'in' the subject nor 'in' time or space, because it is not something that is, but something that temporalizes itself as pure possibility. Heidegger speaks of the horizon as constituting the *ekstema* of the ekstasis in analogy with the correlation of *noesis* and *noema* in the structure of intentionality, but in a completely different sense from that characteristic of the immanent structure of the noetic–noematic unity that remains internal to consciousness. The structure of transcendence, one that brings together the unity of all ekstases in the ekstematic unity of their horizons reveals the 'internal productivity specific to temporality', a productivity whose product is nothing else than the world itself. It is this productivity that Kant encountered for the first time in his theory of the productive transcendental imagination. And in spite of the fact that this genial intuition got forgotten later, it still testified to the fact that the Being of Dasein possesses the internal possibility of self-enrichment, not in an ontic, but in an ontological sense. This capacity for self-enrichment that characterizes Dasein is, in fact, nothing other than transcendence itself and it produces nothing ontic, but only this nothingness that is the world, a world which can never be understood as the sum of beings. Even though this nothingness is not a *nihil negativum*, it is, as Heidegger stresses, the *nihil originarium* that arises with and through temporalization.[57] Temporality finds its end in the horizonal schemata whose unity constitutes the nothingness of world. Since the very finitude of time precludes the possibility of its being projected upon something else, it is able to provide the ultimate light for the knowledge of beings and for the comprehension of Being. But we find no justification of the finitude of time in the 1927 lecture course since this would require a return to the question of Being-towards-death, a question developed in the second section of *Being and Time* and which alone permits us to understand what is said in §65, namely, that original time is finite precisely because it temporalizes itself from the authentic future as anticipatory resoluteness (*vorlaufende Entschlossenheit*), i.e. as authentic Being-towards-death.[58] But death is not an end in the sense of what puts a stop to Dasein but is, on the contrary, the foundation of its finite existence. In the same manner, the finitude of time (the corollary to the finitude of Being mentioned only in the Freiburg inaugural lecture of 1929: 'What is metaphysics?'[59]) is not an extrinsic limitation of Dasein but, on the contrary, the origin and starting point of its very own Being, i.e. of all possible projection – a limitation which, because it is internal, makes possible its own surpassing, i.e. makes possible both ekstasis and transcendence.

The *Temporalität des Seins* therefore constitutes the unity of that horizon from which each being can present itself in the world. It is true that in §21, in *The Fundamental Problems of Phenomenology*, Heidegger accords an apparently excessive importance to the horizon of *praesens* which latter constitutes the condition of possibility of the comprehension of the Being-ready-to-hand of the instrument, and it is equally true that the thesis developed in *Being and Time* to the effect that the future furnishes the direction for temporalization and is the primary phenomenon for originary temporality[60] is not reaffirmed in the 1927 lecture course, precisely because there is no mention of the finitude of time. But this does not mean that this thesis is given up or called in question, since it is taken up again in the 1928 lecture course.[61] Moreover the primacy of the future is relative: it only characterizes the sense of originary temporalization, and that is the reason why such a primacy can be transferred to another ekstasis, depending upon the mode of existence of Dasein. Heidegger speaks in this respect of the unsteadiness of existence, an unsteadiness which comes from the fact that temporality is capable of modification and that the sense of temporalization can be changed by giving the primacy to an ekstasis other than the futural.[62] The relation to the *Zuhandenen*, to the ready-to-hand, can occur only in the horizon of *praesens* which is the corollary of the primacy granted to the present (*Gegenwart*) and to presentation (*Gegenwärtigen*). In the *determined* perspective of a temporal interpretation of Being as Being-ready-to-hand,[63] the horizon of *praesens* is the leading horizon because it is the one which commands all relation to inner-worldly beings of any kind whatsoever – and in this sense it also commands the relation to the *Vorhandenen*, to the merely present being.[64] But it has to be stressed that only the unity of the horizons (not only of the *praesens* but also of what should logically be called the *praeteritum* and the *futurum*[65]) can accommodate what the 1928 lecture course already names as the event of the entrance into the world of beings (*das Ereignis des Welteinganges des Seienden*). Because this event is the primordial event (*Ureignis*), originary temporalization can only be the temporalization of the world itself as the ekstematic horizon for temporality in its entirety.[66]

In the context of such an analytic of the *Temporalität des Seins*,[67] Heidegger still seems to be developing his project of an ontology as a temporal and transcendental science.[68] But the 1928 lecture course also declares that this temporal analytic is at the same time *die Kehre*, the turning which brings ontology expressly back to the ontic metaphysics in which it has implicitly always stood.[69] Is this reversal to meta-ontology (mentioned in the 1928 lecture course) already, and of itself, the announcement of a *Kehre* which will allow us to think the epocality of Being and the foundation of this epocality under the name of *Ereignis*? It is difficult to answer this question as long as we do not have access to all the texts from the beginning of the thirties, and especially to the first version of 'The essence of truth' from 1930. It seems in any case that the transcendental perspective that allows the constitution of the 'metaphysics of Dasein' (developed in the writings published in 1929) as a continuation of the meta-ontological turning of 1928 must, on the contrary, be abandoned – so that the *Kehre* can be achieved. But 'abandoned' is perhaps not the correct word here: 'surmounted' says a marginal note from the *Hüttenexemplar* regarding the title of the third section in the plan presented at the end of §8 of *Being and Time*. This marginal note seems to suggest that only the surmounting of the horizon could allow a return to the origin.[70] Is this not an indication that the concept of horizon has finally proved to be inadequate to think the domain of openness, the *Spielraum* within which all beings can be encountered?[71] In a text from the years 1944–5 that bears the title *Gelassenheit*, such a 'space' is given the strange name of *Gegnet*.[72] Here representative and 'transcendental-horizonal' thinking is called in question as the dominating mode of thinking and a transformation of representative thinking into a waiting for the *Gegnet*, i.e., into an open extent[73] oriented toward the 'region'.[74] Such a transformation does not in fact require that the former point of view be abandoned, but rather that it should be seen in another light, after an effective change of position with regard to it. The horizon as such is also only the side, turned towards us, of an openness[75] which surrounds us and this openness should, as such, be named *Gegnet*, 'region' in the sense of a gathering locus for all extended and enduring things.[76] Surely the *Kehre* consists in considering the *Kehrseite*, the reverse side of that horizon which remains concealed from us and to any representative thinking that only draws the meaning of the terms 'horizon' and 'transcendence' from objects opposed to it?[77] To experience what 'lets' be – *sein lässt* – horizon leads us beyond such a representational, transcendental-horizon thinking to a waiting that can never be understood as an anticipationg because it has no object,[78] a waiting for the opening of the *Gegnet* to which we all belong. In the same manner, in 1949, the neccessity of thinking the ekstasis more adequately will lead to the experience of endurance (*Ausstehen*), of the openness of Being. In this new light, the ekstatic essence of existance can no longer be understood as a Being-out-of-itself[79] because this could still imply a reference to the substantial centre of the self. Rather it now has to be understood as the Being *in* the truth of Being, as *Innestehen*, standing inside, *Inständigkeit*, instance.[80].

That is why the ekstatico-horizonal constitution of temporality has to be reconsidered in the light of what Heidegger, after the *Kehre*, no longer calls the 'meaning of Being', but the 'truth of Being', the truth of a Being that is no longer understood as an *existential* of Dasein and as the goal of Dasein's transcendence, but as the origin of Dasein. For, as *The Letter on Humanism* puts it, if Being is brought to light for human being in the ekstatic project, this project does not however create Being. And so what throws into the project is not human being itself. Rather, it is Being itself that destines human being to be its own ek-sistence, to be the 'there' of Da-sein as its very own essence.[81]

Notes

1 See Heidegger, *Die Grundprobleme der Phänomenologie* (Frankfurt am Main: Klostermann, 1975), *Gesamt ausgabe* Band 24 (abbreviated *GA* 24), p. 279: 'die ekstatisch-horizontal Verfassung der Zeitlichkeit'. The term *Verfassung* which is here translated in a conventional manner by 'constitution' refers more precisely to the idea of 'composition' and has the meaning of an articulated totality.

2 On the circumstances of the publication of *Being and Time* see 'Mein Weg in die Phänomenologie' in Heidegger, *Zur Sache des Denkens* (Tübingen: Niemeyer, 1969), p. 88.

3 Heidegger, *Sein und Zeit*, p. 437 (abbreviated *SZ*).

4 *SZ*, p. 39.

5 See *GA* 2, p. 41.

6 *GA* 24, p. 1.

7 See *GA* 2, p. 582 (Nachwort des Herausgebers).

8 The distinction between *Temporalität* and *Zeitlichkeit* is essentially a terminological distinction: see *GA* 24, p. 324. But this distinction was not drawn from the very beginning. In the lecture course from the Winter semester 1925–6, Heidegger still uses the term *Temporalität* to characterize the Being of Dasein. He explains that *zeitlich* means to happen in time, whereas temporal means to be characterized by time (*GA* 21, p. 199). At that time Heidegger still understands *Zeitlichkeit* in the 'vulgar' sense of intra-temporality and that is the reason why he then prefers the term *Temporalität* to characterize the mode of Being of Dasein. He speaks there of the *Temporalität* of care, whereas in *Being and Time Temporalität* refers to Being and *Zeitlichkeit* to Dasein.

9 *GA* 24, p. 369.

10 *SZ*, p. 17. It is not possible to translate 'Sein überhaupt' by 'Being in general' because Heidegger, following Aristotle, insists on the fact that there is no generic unity of Being. That is why I propose to translate it by 'Being in its entirety', and this in line with the primal meaning of 'überhaupt' a word that

originally belonged to the vocabulary of the cattle keepers and so retains the meaning of 'the whole' in opposition to 'in detail'.

11 See *SZ*, p. 17.

12 See *SZ*, p. 19.

13 *SZ*, p. 152.

14 *SZ*, p. 151.

15 There is in fact an analysis of the temporality of comprehension to be found in *Being and Time* at §68a but it tends only to elucidate the temporal meaning of comprehension in general and not to elucidate the fact that temporality is the condition of the possibility of the comprehension that Dasein has from itself.

16 *SZ*, p. 323.

17 *SZ*, p. 329.

18 *SZ*, p. 365.

19 Heidegger, *Metaphysische Anfangsgründe der Logik, GA* 26.

20 As Jean Greisch emphasizes in his presentation of the complete edition of Heidegger's works in *Martin Heidegger* (Paris: Cahier de L'Herne, 1983), p. 467.

21 *GA* 26, p. 215: 'Und daß die Intentionalität in der Transzendenz grundet, ist gerade hier [§363, Anm.] gesagt und als ontologisches Grundproblem fixiert.' The note itself says only: 'Daß und wie die Intentionalität des "Bewußtseins" in der ekstatischen Zeitlichkeit des Dasein grundet wird der folgende Abschnitt zeigen.' The term 'transcendence' does not appear in the note itself in spite of the fact that it can be found on the same page, 363.

22 *GA* 24, p. 448.

23 Heidegger recalls in *Unterwegs zur Sprache* (Pfullingen: Neske, 1959), p. 95, that he began to write *Being and Time* in 1923 and we know that the book was finished in 1926.

24 *Prolegomena zur Geschichte des Zeitbegriffs, GA* 20, p. 34.

25 *GA* 24, pp. 100ff.

26 *GA* 24, p. 102.

27 See E. Husserl, *Vorlesung zur Phänomenologie des inneren Zeitbewußtseins* (Tübingen: Niemeyer, 1928), p. 1: 'Auch heute noch ist dieser Ausdruck kein Losungswort, sondern der Titel eines zentralen Problems.' It is necessary to recall that it was Husserl himself who asked Heidegger to edit his lectures and not the reverse. Regarding the history of the manuscript of these lectures see R. Böhm's Introduction to volume X of the *Husserliana* (The Hague: Nijhoff, 1966) and W. Mieskiewicz's article in *Revue de Métaphysique et de Morale* (1984).

28 See *GA* 26, p. 166.

29 See *GA* 26, pp. 167–8.

30 See *GA* 20, p. 184.

31 See *GA* 26, p. 168.

32 *GA* 26, pp. 167 and 169. In this lecture from the Summer semester 1928 during the course of which Max Scheler died (19 May 1928), Heidegger emphasizes Scheler's mediating role between Husserl and himself. Scheler refuses to see in intentionality a character of knowledge but does not go so far as to consider it a dimension of existence itself. He insists on understanding intentionality as a character of the still not thoroughly elucidated notion of personality.

33 *GA* 26, pp. 194 and 169.

34 *GA* 26, p. 253.

35 According to Heidegger, Husserl in *Ideen I* sees in intentionality a solution because he understands intentional being as the fundamental region of being, the region of pure consciousness and its correlates. Intentionality is then no

longer a question of presence but provides the 'final' solution for modern philosophy, i.e. the accomplished system of transcendental subjectivity. See the *Letter to Richardson* (1962) in W. Richardson, *Through Phenomenology to Thought* (The Hague: Nijhoff, 1963), p. xiv: 'Meanwhile "phenomenology" in Husserl's sense was elaborated into a distinctive philosophical position according to a pattern set up by Descartes, Kant and Fichte.' On this point see Brisart's excellent paper: 'L'intentionalité comme "titre d'un problème central" selon Heidegger', *Cahiers du centre d'études phénoménologiques* (*CEP* 2) (Louvain la Neuve: Cabay, 1982), pp. 32–84.

36 *GA* 24, p. 254.

37 *GA* 24, p. 374. See also *SZ*, p. 38 where phenomenological truth is said to be *veritas transcendentalis*.

38 ibid., p. 423.

39 ibid., p. 425.

40 ibid.

41 ibid., p. 428.

42 *GA* 26, p. 264.

43 ibid.

44 *GA* 20, p. 442.

45 ibid.

46 *GA* 26, p. 270.

47 See M. Heidegger, 'Uber das Zeitverständnis in der Phänomenologie und im Denken der Seinsfrage' in *Phänomenologie – lebendig oder tot?* (Karlsruhe: Badenia Verlag, 1969), p. 47.

48 See *SZ*, p. 433.

49 *GA* 26, p. 264.

50 *GA* 26, p. 263.

51 *GA* 26, p. 268.

52 *GA* 24, p. 435.

53 To show how the 'horizonal' thematic is dependent on a still transcendental questioning would require a thorough examination of all the texts Heidegger dedicated to Kant between 1925 and 1930. For the moment we can only stress the importance of transcendence in the Kantian sense and point out that this was as decisive for the elaboration of the Being question as Husserlian intentionality.

54 *Kritik der reinen Vernunft*, B. 180.

55 *GA* 24, p. 437.

56 *GA* 26, p. 269.

57 *GA* 26, p. 272.

58 *SZ*, §62.

59 *Was ist Metaphysik?* (Frankfurt am Main: Klostermann, 1960), pp. 39–40. Being is finite because it 'needs' the transcendence of Dasein in order to be revealed, because (as *Sein und Zeit* puts it on p. 212) 'there is' (*es gibt*) Being only as long as Dasein is.

60 *SZ*, p. 331.

61 *GA* 26, p. 273.

62 *GA* 24, p. 408.

63 See the title in *GA* 24 of §21 a.

64 See *SZ*, p. 363, where it is stressed that the objectivation, which is the operation through which the mere presence (*Vorhandenheit*) of beings is given, has the sense of a distinctive presentation (*ausgezeichneten Gegenwärtigung*).

65 It should be stressed here that, on the one hand, and in a certain sense, every horizon, as a project of Dasein, has the sense of a future from which it

is possible to come back to the beings given within such an horizon but also, on the other, that the (implicit) primacy of the horizon of the *praesens* is the foundation for all traditional ontology. That is why Heidegger accords such importance to the temporal interpretation of Being as *Vorhandenheit*.

66 *GA* 26, pp. 273–4.
67 ibid., p. 201.
68 *GA* 24, p. 201.
69 *GA* 26, p. 201.
70 *GA* 1, p. 39. The whole marginal note runs as follows:
    'Die transzendenzhafte Differenz
    Die Überwindung des Horizonts als solchen
    Die Umkehr in die Herkunft
    Das Anwesen aus dieser Herkunft.'
71 See *Kant und das Problem der Metaphysik* (Frankfurt am Main: Kloster-mann, 1973), §16, p. 67.
72 *Gelassenheit* (Pfullingen: Neske, 1979), p. 31.
73 ibid., p. 41. The old form *Gegnet* for *Gegend* means literally what stands opposite and comes from *gegen*, meaning against or opposite to, and had to be formed on the model of the Latin *contrata*, region. Compare the French *contrée* and the English 'country'.
74 ibid., p. 52.
75 ibid., p. 39.
76 ibid., p. 42.
77 ibid., p. 39.
78 ibid., p. 44.
79 See *SZ*, p. 329 where the pure *ekstatikon* of temporality is understood as 'das ursprungliche "Aussersich"' an und für sich'.
80 See *Der Rückgang in den Grund der Metaphysik* (1949) Einleitung zu *Was ist Metaphysik?* (Frankfurt am Main: Klostermann, 1960), p. 15:

Die Stasis des Ekstatischen beruht, so seltsam es klingen mag, im Innestehen im 'Aus' und 'Da' der Unverborgenheit, als welche das Sein selbst west. Das, was im Namen 'Existenz' zu denken ist, wenn das Wort innerhalb des Denkens gebraucht wird, das auf die Wahrheit des Seins zu und her denkt, könnte das Wort 'Instandigkeit' am, schönsten nennen.

See also *Gelassenheit*, p. 62 and *Humanismusbrief* in *Wegmarken* (Frankfurt am Main: Klostermann, 1967), p. 161.
81 *Wegmarken*, p. 168.

8

Way and method: hermeneutic phenomenology in thinking the history of being

Friedrich-Wilhelm von Herrmann

To Hans-Georg Gadamer
on his 90th birthday

In his first elaboration of the question of being in terms of fundamental ontology Heidegger characterizes the method of this ontology (in Section 7 of *Being and Time*) as both 'phenomenology' and 'hermeneutic phenomenology'.[1] However, not only do the terms *phenomenology* and *hermeneutics* disappear from *Beiträge zur Philosophie (Vom Ereignis)*[2] – where he takes the second way, i.e., elaborates the question of being according to the history of being – but there is also no mention of a 'method' that thinking in terms of the history of being might have. And yet, those who pay attention, not only to the external use of such terms, but also to what is most fitting in phenomenological seeing and the self-showing of the *Sache (Sichzeigenlassen der Sache)* know that thinking in terms of the history of being is *also* phenomenological through and through – that is, is guided by the self-showing of the *Sache* for thinking.

But the question still remains: why does Heidegger retain the principle of phenomenology while he abandons the terms *phenomenology* and *hermeneutics*? In the 'Dialogue on language'[3] he responds to this question: 'This happened, not – as is often thought – in order to deny the importance of phenomenology, but rather to let my own pathway of thinking remain in the realm of the nameless' (*GA* 12, p. 114). At the end of Heidegger's 'My way into phenomenology' there is a still more articulate confirmation that thinking in terms of the history of being remains bound to what is most fittingly phenomenological:

Phenomenology . . . is the possibility of thinking, at times changing and only thus persisting, to correspond to the claim of what is to be thought. If phenomenology is thus experienced and kept hold of, it can disappear as title, in favour of the *Sache* of thinking, whose disclosure remains a mystery.[4]

This says everything that is decisive regarding the point that we are making. Elucidations of the preliminary conception of phenomenology in *Being and Time* already conclude with this remark: 'The only way to understand phenomenology is to grasp it as possibility' (*GA* 2, p. 52). For Heidegger the phenomenological *way of dealing with* 'things themselves' lies in its *enabling character of possibility*. As possibility, phenomenology is higher than its actuality in any given case, because as possibility phenomenology can always be grasped anew and more originally.

Because phenomenology, as the method of self-showing of the *Sache* of thinking, is essentially at the service of this *Sache*, therefore phenomenology as the possibility of thinking transforms itself *along with the transformation of the Sache which shows itself*. If Husserl sees the *Sache* itself as intentional consciousness and transcendental subjectivity, Heidegger sees the *Sache* in a transformed way, as being what gets disclosed in Dasein's understanding of being. But with this transformation in the *Sache* there is also a transformation in the very meaning of phenomenology: as possibility, now understood in a new way. And when the *Sache* is again transformed within Heidegger's thinking of being – such that being as such is no longer thought within the transcendental-horizonal perspective, but as the unity of the relation of the truth of being to Dasein and of Dasein's essential relation to the truth of being – then this transformation yields a new and transformed understanding of phenomenology. And yet, throughout this manifold transformation, phenomenology *remains thinking's possibility*.

At this point phenomenology is characterized as that possibility which 'corresponds' (*entspricht*) to the 'claim' (*Anspruch*) of what is to be thought. By characterizing phenomenology as that possibility of thinking which makes possible this 'corresponding with the claim of what is to be thought', Heidegger clarifies phenomenology precisely as the enactment of thinking in terms of the history of being. For both of these words, *claim* and *correspondence*, are the root-words by which the unity of the *relation* (*Bezug*) of being to Dasein as well as Dasein's *comporting relationship* (*Verhältnis*) to being is grasped conceptually and in language within thinking in terms of the history of being. The unity of this relation and this comporting relationship is what thinking in terms of the history of being thinks as *the unfolding of being itself* (*Wesung des Seins selbst*), as *Ereignis*. In its way of enactment, thinking which thinks being's root unfolding as *Ereignis is* phenomenology. Thinking being in terms of the history of being thus becomes such a pure enactment of phenomenological self-showing of the *Sache* itself that the title 'phenomenology' can fall away.

As we stressed at the beginning, Heidegger calls phenomenology as the possibility of thinking being: *hermeneutics*. In the afore-mentioned 'Dialogue on language' Heidegger declares emphatically that, in the transformation from the transcendental-horizonal perspective to the perspective of thinking in terms of the history of being, phenomenology retains its basic hermeneutical character. There he speaks of the 'hermeneutical relation' and elucidates it as the bringing of a manifestation *in* the hearing of the message as the unconcealing of the twofold of emergent emergence (*Anwesen und Anwesendes*). This wording of the basic hermeneutical feature of phenomenology in terms of the history of being comes out of that context wherein claim and correspondence belong together, i.e., comes out of *Ereignis*. Thus there is no doubt that, in its enactment, thinking in terms of the history of being is determined phenomenologically and hermeneutically. Our *task*, then, is to work out the hermeneutical-phenomenological structure in the thinking in terms of the history of being.

It is true that, as it understands itself, thinking in terms of the history of being no longer talks about *method*. Instead it replaces methodological considerations with reflections on the *way* or *pathway* of thinking. In thinking in terms of the history of being, the words *way* or *path of thinking* are not used as metaphors. If we recall that *way* or ὁδός is the root-word in the word *method* – a coming together of the Greek words μετά and ὁδός – then we are called to understand, in this reflection of 'way', the transformed shape of hermeneutic phenomenology. In thinking in terms of the history of being, the word *way* is the root-word for the 'problem of method' as it fits the thinking of being. But because what is said with the word *way* in the thinking of being cannot be compared with modern thinking on method – either in philosophy or science – and because 'way' here is the direct opposite of 'method' in the modern sense, Heidegger no longer uses the word *method* in his reflections on the way. Rather he employs this term only in the sense of its modern usage. Hence his reflections on the question of the 'way' immediately mark this 'way' off as distinct from the modern understanding of method. Thus the title 'Way and method' indicates the pathway of thinking of being in its difference from the method of modern thinking and representation. With this differentiation the word *way* constitutes the basic hermeneutical-phenomenological feature of thinking in terms of the history of being.

Our task, again, is to work out the hermeneutical-phenomenological structure of thinking in terms of the history of being. But before we can do this, we must bring to mind explicitly how hermeneutic phenomenology functions as the method of dealing with the question of being in terms of fundamental ontology.

1 Hermeneutic phenomenology within fundamental ontology

(a) The three senses of hermeneutics

By interpreting the two root-words of Greek thinking that make up the term *phenomenology*, Heidegger defines phenomenology as 'letting what shows itself be seen from itself, just as it shows itself from itself' (*GA* 2, p. 46). Phenomenology is the manner of dealing with, the mode of access to and the manner of determining the theme of fundamental ontology. The theme of fundamental ontology, however, is Dasein in its *Existenz*, i.e., understanding being. In the enactment of its *Existenz* Dasein understands, along with its own being, the manifold being of beings that are not Dasein as well as the meaning of being in general. Understanding being through existing, discloses being as a whole, existentially-horizonally, or transcendentally. Therefore the task of phenomenology as a method is step by step to let Dasein – in its *Existenz*, i.e., understanding being – be seen as what shows itself of itself from itself, such that Dasein's understanding of being shows itself as the transcendental-horizonal disclosure of being as a whole.

The *logos* of phenomenology, we are told, has the methodological character of ἑρμηνεύειν (*GA* 2, p. 50). Phenomenological description in the sense of showing and demonstrating what is to be seen from itself has the 'methodological sense' of interpretation (*Auslegung*). With this characterization of the methodological sense of phenomenology as interpretation or ἑρμηνεύειν, Heidegger distinguishes *his* notion of phenomenology from that of Husserl, who defines phenomenological description as *reflection* – a reflection which takes place in reflective acts as intentional acts of consciousness of a higher level.[5] Thus interpretation is distinct from reflection.

But this distinguishing characterization is not sufficient, because phenomenological analysis which proceeds reflectively can understand itself as interpretive, too – interpretation of the intentional act of consciousness as the intentional object of the reflective act. The distinction between interpretation and reflection will be adequately made only when interpretation is no longer determined as an intentional act of consciousness, but rather from out of the mode of being of Dasein, i.e., from *Existenz*.

As theoretically explicit enactment, phenomenological interpretation is rooted in the *existential mode of being of interpretation*, as discussed in Section 32 of *Being and Time*. And interpretation understood existentially is essentially the unfolding and laying out of what is projected in advance in a *projecting understanding*. It is because Heidegger considers philosophical questioning itself to be 'a possibility of the being of each existing Dasein' (*GA* 2, p. 18) that Dasein exists as thrown projection – in the *Existenz*-possibility of a questioning which is phenomenological and fundamental-ontological (Dasein as thrown into its *Existenz*, i.e., understanding being) – and as interpreting what is thus projected. Section 63 of *Being and Time* characterizes the root character of ontological interpretation as projection and the unfolding of what is projected. The being which, in the pre-phenomenological enactment of *Existenz* according to the *Existenz*-possibilities of being-in-the-world, is implicitly projected as *Existenz* – and as the being of beings other than Dasein – this being is explicitly and thematically projected in the *phenomenological enactment of Existenz* and gets interpreted in terms of its structural content. In this sense the question of being is 'the radicalizing of an essential tendency of being that belongs to Dasein, i.e., of the pre-ontological understanding of being' (*GA* 2, p. 20).

Hermeneutical-phenomenological thinking is not reflection, but rather a *projecting-interpreting understanding*. Because hermeneutic phenomenology as the method of fundamental ontology thematizes Dasein (in terms of its being, i.e., understanding being) by projecting and interpreting, phenomenology is the hermeneutical phenomenology of Dasein. Through ἑρμηνεύειν as a projecting-interpreting seeing of what shows itself of itself, 'the proper meaning of being and the basic structures of Dasein's own being are *made manifest* to the understanding of being that belongs to Dasein' (*GA* 2, p. 50). Thus Heidegger elucidates interpreting by going back to the Greek sense of the word ἑρμηνεύειν which as interpreting also means proclaiming and making manifest. *Phenomenological interpreting as making manifest* is what Dasein itself accomplishes. In the phenomenology of Dasein and out of an understanding of being which is always already unthematically in enactment in and through the ἑρμηνεύειν which Dasein explicitly enacts, Dasein makes manifest to itself the basic structures of its own being (which are concealed in its unthematic understanding of being), the mode of being of beings other than Dasein, and the meaning of being in general. Dasein's making manifest to itself takes place as interpreting unfolding of the projecting understanding of being which has been explicitly thematized. Because the phenomenology of Dasein has the character of ἑρμηνεύειν in the sense elucidated, this phenomenology is characterized as *hermeneutics*. This is the first sense of the word *hermeneutics*.

The second sense of hermeneutics follows from the first. In the existential root-structures of Dasein, which simultaneously constitute the understanding as *understanding of being*, the being of beings other than Dasein, the manifold modes of beings, and the manifold of what beings are are all horizonally disclosed. But along with temporalization of the temporality of Dasein, the temporalized horizonal time, i.e., *Temporalität*, is disclosed as the unity of the meaning of being of all beings other than Dasein. By phenomenologically uncovering the root-structures of Dasein and of the meaning of being that is understood by means of these structures, the horizon of investigation for an ontology of beings other than Dasein opens up. Considering ontologies of beings other than Dasein, hermeneutics of Dasein as understanding being (hermeneutics in the first sense) becomes hermeneutics in the second sense, i.e., in the sense 'that it works out the conditions for the possibility of every onto-logical investigation' (*GA* 2, p. 50). It is in view of this task that the words hermeneutics of Dasein appear without quotation marks. But when they appear with quotation marks – 'hermeneutics of Dasein' – this indicates that hermeneutics which serves regional ontology.

The third sense of hermeneutics is also included in the first. The meaning of being as such can be phenomenologically interpreted and laid open only after Dasein is interpreted with regard to its *Existenz*, wherein Dasein implicitly understands the meaning of being. Considering the priority of this task within fundamental ontology, hermeneutics gets its third sense as 'the analytic of the existentiality of *Existenz*' (*GA* 2, p. 50).

As far as the sequence of steps is concerned, this third sense of hermeneutics is the 'primary' one, because only by taking this step can hermeneutical-phenomenological fundamental ontology come to an answer to the basic question concerning the meaning of being.

(b) Conditions for the enactment of hermeneutics

Phenomenological hermeneutics *is* interpretation in a certain sense. How-ever, it is called *hermeneutics* because it is not interpretation in its pre-theoretical mode of being nor the theoretical way of comportment known as interpretation of texts, nor 'the methodology of historical humanistic disciplines' (*GA* 2, p. 51). This phenomenological hermeneutics inter-prets Dasein in its being as a projective and interpretive understanding. It is this phenomenology which shows first and foremost that, in its being, Dasein is constituted by projection and interpretation. The phenomenological-hermeneutical insight into the ontological constitution of Dasein also includes an insight into the mode of enactment of any phenomenological interpretation of one's own Dasein, namely that what enables this phenomenology is precisely what it brings forth, i.e., projec-tion and interpretation, as they belong to the ontological constitution of Dasein.

The *mode of being* of the hermeneutic phenomenology of Dasein and its understanding of being is *explicit projection* and *explicit interpretation* of what is projected. There is no interpretation without projection and no projection without interpretation. Thus at the beginning of Section 32 of *Being and Time* we read: 'The projection of understanding carries within itself the possibility of self-unfolding. We shall call the unfolding of understanding: *interpretation*' (*GA* 2, p. 197). Moreover we read: 'Existentially, interpretation is based in understanding, not the other way around' (ibid.). Interpretation does not shape the understanding; rather, as appropriation, interpretation emerges from that primary understanding which takes shape in projection. For this reason hermeneutics of Dasein is a projective-interpretive understanding of Dasein and its understanding of being.

However, projection is what it is as projection only in conjunction with the existential mode of being of *thrownness*. Projection can only disclose projectively what it is thrown into. For the hermeneutics of Dasein this means that explicit projection projects Dasein unto its *Existenz*, i.e., understanding being – an *Existenz* given in advance to projection by thrownness, as what is explicitly projectable.

Moreover, co-original with thrownness and projection is *Rede*,[6] the root unfolding of language. Both of these basic existentials 'are co-originally determined by *Rede*' (*GA* 2, p. 177). For the hermeneutics of Dasein this means that when thrown projection is explicitly enacted – when Dasein is projected unto its *Existenz*, i.e., understanding being – this projection holds what is projected in an articulated understandability that stems from *Rede*.

If interpretation is existentially based in the projective understanding and if this understanding is what it is in conjunction with thrownness and articulated *Rede*, then the *totality* of explicit projection, thrownness and articulated *Rede* is where the phenomenological interpretation of hermeneutics is based.

Only when we see these subtle interconnections clearly do we grasp the extent to which interpretation is subject to the three conditions of enactment, namely fore-having, fore-sight and fore-grasping. We might say: what is projected in the explicit projection – or: what is projected in the *hermeneutic enactment of the thrown and articulated projection* – is what is primarily understood as *fore-having*. As appropriation of understanding, phenomenological interpretation moves within a being that understands Dasein, which is projected unto its *Existenz*, i.e., understanding being. It is this Dasein that has become fore-having for interpretation. Interpretive disclosing carries out the appropriation of what is primarily understood (thought still in a hidden way) under the guidance of a regard for that unto which what is projected is to be interpreted. This 'regard' which guides interpretation in advance is the *fore-sight*. In accord with its ontological relationship to its fore-having, interpretation already reaches ahead into a graspability which it (interpretation) draws from fore-having and into which it (interpretation) brings what gets interpreted. The third condition of enactment of phenomenological interpretation is *fore-grasping*. Because phenomenological interpretation is based within the totality of thrownness, projection and *Rede*, the conditions for the enactment of this phenomenology are fore-having, fore-sight and fore-grasping. Thrownness is carried out in fore-having; projection, in fore-sight; and *Rede*, in fore-grasping (cf. *GA 2*, p. 200).

(c) The circle of hermeneutics

Fore-having, fore-sight and fore-grasping are the conditions for enacting *any* interpretation and thus also for enacting the phenomenological interpretation of hermeneutics. All interpretation – including hermeneutic interpretation – moves within this threefold structure. This structure implies that, when something is phenomenologically interpreted by hermeneutics, hermeneutics must have understood this something in advance – in an understanding which takes shape in a primary projection. With fore-having, fore-sight and fore-grasping as conditions for enactment, interpretation dwells in a *fore-understanding* of what interpretation is to interpret and make its own. For this reason no interpretation – and thus also no phenomenological hermeneutic – is 'a pre-suppositionless grasping of something given in advance' (ibid.). Interpretation of hermeneutics, too, operates essentially within a fore-understanding which takes shape and unfolds in the *hermeneutic projection* of Dasein, which projects Dasein unto its *Existenz*, i.e., understanding being. In so far as interpretive understanding nourishes itself from the projectible fore-understanding, in a certain sense it moves in a circle, though not an empty one. Rather, this circle deepens and differentiates understanding. This circle of understanding, the *circle of hermeneutics*, 'is the expression of the existential fore-structure' (*GA 2*, p. 203).

Because the circle of hermeneutics is the essential structure for interpretive understanding, this understanding requires that we 'enter' this circle 'in the proper way' (ibid.). Interpretation of hermeneutics must have understood

> that its first, constant, and final task is not to let fore-having, foresight and fore-grasping be given by flashes of inspiration and popular conceptions, but to solidify the scientific thematic by working out these fore-structures in terms of the things themselves.
>
> (ibid.)

This is a characterization of the enactment of interpretation in view of its basic *phenomenological* feature and its three conditions for enactment. Interpretation must see to it that what is understood in fore-having, foresight and fore-grasping is obtained from the things themselves, i.e., from what shows itself by itself. Only when projection projects Dasein in its existing understanding of beings – as Dasein shows itself by and from itself – can the interpretation of what is thus phenomenologically projected be in turn enacted phenomenologically.

As stated already, philosophizing Dasein *makes manifest* to itself the basic structures of its own being, the mode of being of beings other than Dasein, and the meaning of being as such through ἑρμηνεύειν of the phenomenology of Dasein and out of its non-thematic understanding of being. For the sake of this hermeneutic proclamation (*hermeneutische Kundgabe*) philosophizing Dasein explicitly projects the existing understanding of being, which is otherwise enacted only implicitly. Hence we can call this project the 'hermeneutic project', which belongs essentially to the interpretation of hermeneutics.

2 The basic hermeneutical-phenomenological feature of thinking in terms of the history of being

(a) The hermeneutic relation

Heidegger's oft afore-mentioned 'Dialogue on language' is of extraordinary significance for our inquiry, because in that text with a few sharp strokes he marks out *the transformed structure of hermeneutic phenomenology in thinking in terms of the history of being*. In this dialogue we read that 'ἑρμηνεύειν is that revealing which brings tidings because it is capable of hearing for a message' (*GA* 12, p. 115). A little later we read: 'All of this makes it clear that hermeneutics does not mean just interpretation, but goes even deeper than that and means bringing of a message and tidings' (ibid.). What Heidegger then calls 'hermeneutic relation' is, as relation, the bringing of a message by way of listening to it. Bringing tidings is ἑρμηνεύειν, which takes place in hearing for a message. The message which is passed along to listeners is 'being itself', i.e., 'the emergence of the emergent, the twofold of the two out of their onefold' (*GA* 12, p. 116). We are told that it is this twofold that lays claim on 'humans in their root unfolding' (ibid.). And the root unfolding of humans consists 'in corresponding to the claim [*Zuspruch*] of the twofold' (ibid.). Humans correspond to this claim by listening to the message of the twofold, by proclaiming the message that they hear, and by bringing tidings of it.

This characterization of the hermeneutic relation articulates thinking in terms of the history of being – a thinking that thinks the relation (*Bezug*) of being to Dasein and the comporting relationship (*Verhältnis*) of Dasein to being, thinking this whole relation as *Ereignis*.

But which *experience* of thinking is it that transforms the initial posing of the question of being in terms of fundamental ontology into the approach to this question in terms of the history of being? What is called 'claim' (*Anspruch*) and 'appeal' (*Zuspruch, Zusage*) in thinking in terms of the history of being has the same structure of relation as the 'throw of being' (*Wurf des Seins*) in the *Letter on Humanism*.[7] It is the 'throw of being' that gives rise to the 'thrownness of Dasein'.[8] Thus it is the phenomenological experience of the *origin of thrownness in being's throw* (*'throwing forth'*) *of the truth of being* that opens up the way for thinking the question of being in terms of the history of being.

However, we cannot enter the pathway that works out the question in terms of the history of being without having gone the way of elaborating that question in terms of fundamental ontology. The way-opening experience of existential thrownness as coming from the throw of the truth of being is, finally, the decisive insight into being's root unfolding as *Ereignis*.

In this context there is a key passage from that work of Heidegger's which, by way of a sixfold, conjoined lay-out, opens out the elaboration of the question of being in terms of the history of being, namely *Beiträge zur Philosophie (Vom Ereignis)*. This key passage states that:

> the thrower of projection experiences itself as thrown, as appropriated by being. The opening which is achieved through projection is an opening only when it occurs as the experience of thrownness and thus as a belonging to being. This is the essential difference *vis-à-vis* all *transcendental* ways of knowing with regard to the conditions of possibility.
>
> (*GA* 65, p. 239)

One cannot fail to hear here that thrownness of projection is the same as its *being-appropriated* through being for the sake of the root unfolding of the truth of being. *Appropriating* means that humans are determined as 'proper to being' (*GA* 65, p. 263) in terms of being's relation to them. The thrown projection which occurs in terms of appropriating takes place in such a way that it picks up the 'counter-movement of appropriating' (*GA* 65, p. 239). But depending on how projection picks up this 'counter-movement', the *free* character of projection comes into play.

Already in *Beiträge* Heidegger sees the relation of appropriating (being-thrown) as *needing* (*Brauchen*) and the projective relationship to the appropriating truth of being as the *belonging* (*Zugehören*) of humans to being's root unfolding: 'In order to unfold, being needs humans. And humans belong to being so that they accomplish their uttermost calling as Da-sein' (*GA* 65, p. 251). The onefold of appropriative needing and projective belonging makes up the 'innermost occurrence' in *Ereignis*. It is this innermost occurrence, the *unfolding of being as Ereignis*, that Heidegger calls 'the turning in *Ereignis*' (*GA* 65, p. 407). In one of the most precise formulations Heidegger says: 'The turning unfolds between the call (to the one who belongs) and hearing the call (by the one who is being called). The turning is a re-turning' (ibid.). Thus *Beiträge* thinks the *basic structure of thinking in terms of the history of being*, which from now on undergirds, guides and governs all of Heidegger's writings, including what is properly called his 'later philosophy'.

When thinking thinks being as such in its unfolding as *Ereignis* and as the returning *in Ereignis*, then this thinking gets accomplished as a listening which hears for the appropriating call of being, i.e., hears for the message, and as a manifesting of what is heard. In hearing-for, thinking receives the truth of being as what throws itself forth. Thinking experiences its *thrownness* in this receiving. By bringing tidings of what it receives, thinking comports itself *projectively* towards and preserves the truth of being which throws itself forth (cf. *GA* 12, p. 119). In the language of thinking and in the word of the work of thinking, thinking preserves/shelters being's root unfolding as *Ereignis* and the turning in *Ereignis* – whose root unfolding is thrown forth and projected. In hearing for the call, thinking comports itself phenomenologically-hermeneutically: *phenomenologically*, in so far as thinking lets the self-showing of things themselves or being as such be seen; *hermeneutically*, in so far as in projection thinking brings tidings of the self-showing and, in preserving/ sheltering, interprets what throws itself forth and is projected, bringing it into the articulated word of the work of thinking.

The transformation of hermeneutic phenomenology in the thinking in terms of the history of being follows from thinking the root unfolding of being as *Ereignis*. In hearing-for a message, hermeneutic bringing of tidings shows in itself the structure of *Ereignis* as an occurrence. When Heidegger says that humans stand within the twofold through the *hermeneutic relation*, the term *Bezug* (relation) does not mean *Beziehung* (connection). Rather it means *Brauch* (need) in the sense that we discussed above: human being in the root unfolding as *Ek-sistenz* is needed by the truth of being and for this truth, so that humans belong to 'a need which claims them' (*GA* 12, p. 118).

The hermeneutic relation in which humans stand takes place when the appropriating-needing relation to the truth of being and the appropriated relation belonging to the truth of being come together. This becomes clear when Heidegger says that the relation in which humans stand, in accordance with their root unfolding, is called 'hermeneutical, because it brings tidings of that message' (*GA* 12, p. 128). This message 'claims humans in order that they correspond to it' (ibid.). In the word *message* we must think solely the truth of being which in its throw to humans discloses them as Dasein and throws them into Dasein, such that they exist as thrown. Similarly we must think the bringing of tidings by the message solely as claimed, i.e., as a thrown projection which corresponds to the appropriating throw of the truth of being. Correspondence is the mode of enactment of projection. Thus the word *message* is the fundamental word in hermeneutics for the *throw*, i.e., for the 'bringing of the tidings'. This word is also the fundamental word in hermeneutics for the *projection* as projected from within the throw of the truth of being. In so far as in their projective thinking humans bring tidings of the message that they have heard, they are 'messengers of the message' (ibid.). Bringing tidings of the message is also 'a course/pathway taken by the message' (ibid., p. 148).

Within the fundamental-ontological perspective, phenomenological hermeneutic is characterized as an ἑρμηνεύειν which, as the explicit, projective interpreting that lets-be-seen-from-itself, makes the fundamental structures of Dasein's ownmost being and the meaning of being as such manifest to the understanding of being that belongs to Dasein. What is disclosed through hermeneutical (philosophical) projection is given in advance (by thrownness) as projectible and interpretable. What is given in advance to this projection is Dasein as it exists implicitly in its understanding of being – Dasein which as such is projected hermeneutically onto its existential structures and onto the meaning of being as such, disclosed existentially and horizonally.

If we now turn to the experience marked by the history of being, according to which Dasein's *thrownness* into the disclosure of being as a whole stems from the *throw* of the disclosure of the truth of being, then what is projectible by hermeneutic projection is no longer solely given in advance in thrownness, but comes from out of the throw of the truth of being. But then ἑρμηνεύειν no longer means *making* manifest, but rather *bringing* tidings of what throws itself forth.

But why did the thrownness which was phenomenologically-hermeneutically laid out in the transcendental-horizonal perspective prove inadequate for the thinking that determines being as such? Because the transcendental-horizonal perspective could not let the *historicality of being itself and its truth* be thought. To be sure, the fundamental ontology of *Being and Time* thinks through the historicality of Dasein, its existing in the possibilities of being-in-the-world, comprehended either as appropriate or inappropriate. But what is left unthought in this ontology is the historicality of the disclosure of being as a whole. And it becomes necessary for Heidegger to think the historicality of being itself when he undergoes the phenomenological experience that *the WAY that beings emerge gets historically transformed.* We can think the mode of emergence of beings as standing reserve (*Bestand*) in the root unfolding of technique only when we phenomenologically-hermeneutically think the historicality of the truth of being as the *historically transformed unfolding of being.* We gain an insight into the historical unfolding of being itself when we experience and think thrownness into the disclosure of being from out of the appropriating throw of being.

(b) The way of regioning

Phenomenological-hermeneutic thinking, bringing tidings of the message heard in listening, takes place as a 'way' of thinking. The question now concerns this 'way' as a pathway and how this pathway relates to thinking and to what is to be thought. The elucidation of these questions takes place in a reflection on 'way'.

A decisive reflection on 'way' is found in the series of lectures entitled *Das Wesen der Sprache*: *The Root Unfolding of Language*[9] (*GA* 12, p. 167). The question concerning the root unfolding of language occupies an eminent place in the elaboration of the question of being by thinking in terms of the history of being. In the 'Dialogue on language' we read in this regard: 'Language, accordingly, is the predominating and sustaining element in the relation of human beings to the twofold. It (language) determines the hermeneutic relation' (*GA* 12, p. 116). We mentioned at the beginning that reflection on the 'way' as a pathway of thinking being differs from method as it is understood in the modern sense. The fact of this differentiation already makes clear that, in dealing with the 'way', we are dealing with the incomparable 'question of method' as it pertains to the thinking of being. Because the word *method* gets its determination in terms of the modern understanding of method, the thinking of being renounces the word *method* when it reflects on 'way'. This is true, even though, when considered in its literal sense, the word *method* means 'along the way' and would be an appropriate word for the kind of going that occurs as thinking of being on a 'way'.[10]

How does Heidegger characterize the root unfolding of method in modern science? As a way of knowing, scientific method is not just an 'instrument at the service of science' (*GA* 12, p. 167). The modern conception of method does not have the character of serving, but of dominating. This character shows itself in the manner in which for its part method 'takes sciences into its service'. The relationship between *subject-matter* and *method* in the sciences indicates a priority of method over subject-matter. The domineering character of the scientific method reflects the domineering position of the subject in the modern sense, which in its representational and domineering relation to beings represents and produces them solely as objects, eventually reducing beings to an orderable standing reserve. Method controls subject-matter, i.e., the beings to be examined scientifically, in such a way that not only does method determine the subject-matter, but also 'places the subject-matter into the method', thus making subject-matter 'subordinate' to method (ibid.). Gathering up, Heidegger characterizes the relationship of method to subject-matter in modern science by saying: 'All power of knowing lies in the method. The subject-matter is taken up and absorbed by the method' (ibid.). The method prescribes *what* is to be considered a valid object of knowing and *how* this object is to be known. Beings themselves do not provide the pattern for access to them. Rather, method forces beings to show themselves according to method's instructions. This domineering way in which modern method unfolds is an essential way for the modern subject to establish its reign over beings.

Considering how thinking being differs from scientific representation, we might expect to see in the thinking of being a simple reversal of the relationship of method to subject-matter. But this is not the case. Heidegger says: 'Here there is neither a method nor a subject-matter' (ibid.). This is to say that in the thinking of being there is neither a method nor a subject-matter as these terms are posited in scientific representation. That thinking of being has no subject-matter does not mean that this thinking is without a matter for thinking. That thinking of being has no method does not mean that this thinking is without a pathway. It simply means that the relation between matter for thinking and pathway of thinking in the thinking of being is a totally different relationship from that of subject-matter to method in the thinking of the sciences.

Instead of method and subject-matter, thinking of beings thinks 'way' and 'region'. Whereas in characterizing scientific thinking Heidegger puts method ahead of subject-matter, in characterizing the thinking of being he first mentions 'region' and then 'way'. Region is called a region 'because region regions and makes free what is to be thought by thinking' (*GA* 12, p. 168). As in all basic words from Heidegger's later thinking, the word *Gegend*/region, too, at first seems strange. But as in all basic words from Heidegger's later thinking, the word *Gegend*/region, too, is drawn from letting the matter show itself. When Heidegger says *Gegend gegnet* (region regions), he is reaching back to the Middle High German word *gegenen* – a word which is lost in the modern High German – which means *entgegenkommen* (coming over against) or *begegnen* (meeting). When *Gegend* takes place in the regioning of the region, what is to be thought comes over against thinking; it meets thinking. Regioning of the region frees up for thinking what is to be thought.

But 'regioning of the region' as 'coming over against' shows the same structure as the message that belongs to the *hermeneutic relation*, i.e., from the disclosing of the twofold of emergence and emergent that thinking takes up. The basic disclosing character of the regioning of the region is what Heidegger thinks as freeing or freeing up – from out of concealment into the open of unconcealment.

In the same way 'regioning of the region' shows the same structure as the call (*Zuruf*), appeal (*Zuspruch*) or claim (*Anspruch*). But this is nothing other than the 'throw' of being from which the thrownness of Dasein emerges into the truth of being. In that it regions, region frees up 'what is to be thought by thinking', i.e., the matter to be thought. In a broad and formal sense region and what it always frees up is the 'subject-matter' of thinking. But this subject-matter is not just posited by the 'method' which controls it; rather, it is freed up by a preliminary appeal for thinking as what is to be thought. What is freed up as the matter for thinking is what shows itself by itself; and this self-showing lets thinking hear the call, the message. Because what is to be thought is freed up by the regioning of the region, therefore thinking comports itself to it as the self-showing of the matter itself, as a *phenomenological* thinking.

This way of thinking, which receives what is its to think from the freeing up that occurs in the region, 'dwells in the region by going the ways of the region' (ibid.). To the extent that thinking grasps what is in each case freed up, it *becomes* a way for thinking. The genitive 'ways *of* the region' is a *genitivus possessivus*. These are ways which belong to the region in as much as this region frees them up. When thinking hears, understands and unfolds what is freed up as what meets thinking, then thinking sets upon a way that gets shown from the region. In the thinking of being, 'the way belongs in the region' (ibid.).

It is important to note this determination of the relationship between way and region, in order to distinguish *this* relationship from the relation of method and subject-matter in modern thinking and representation. Whereas in modern thinking subject-matter belongs to method, in the thinking of being way always belongs to the region. In scientific representation subject-matter submits to the method which controls it. By contrast, in the thinking of being the way is joined to the region, because it is the region which, in its freeing up the being which it must think, lays out the way to be gone. For such a thinking the 'method', now thought as 'way', gets its determination from within the matter to be thought, in so far as this matter opens access to itself in a preliminary way.

What in 1959, in the lecture trilogy *Das Wesen der Sprache*, Heidegger thought in the phrase 'ways of the region' he had first worked out in *Beiträge zur Philosophie*, his second major work, after *Being and Time*. In *Beiträge* he worked out the phenomenological-hermeneutic thinking of *Ereignis* in terms of the history of being. *Beiträge* refers to thinking in terms of the history of being as '*Gedanken-gang*': 'a pathway of thought which runs through and lights up the hitherto concealed realm of being's unfolding and obtains this realm in its ownmost character as *Ereignis*' (*GA* 65, p. 3). The 'work of thinking' which occurs as thinking in terms of the history of being can and must be 'a *pathway*, with all the ambiguities of that word: a going and at the same time a way – thus a way which goes itself' (*GA* 65, p. 83). And this way is the way of access to being as *Ereignis*. Of course, being the way it is, this way is freed up by the appropriating throw of the truth of being; and only as always freed up in appropriated projection can it be grasped and gone.

For this reason the way of thinking's projection 'does not have the firm contours of a map' (*GA* 65, p. 86). Instead the land/region *emerges* only *through the way*, granted that this way 'is determined by being itself', i.e., is freed up in the appropriating throw as a projectible and goable way (*GA* 65, p. 80).

In making this sharp distinction between way and method, Heidegger is not engaging in self-criticism regarding his initial account of the 'phenomenological method'. From the outset Heidegger's understanding of method in the 'letting what shows itself by itself be seen from itself' is contrary to the modern understanding of method. The phenomenological method that is worked out in Section 7 of *Being and Time*, as a method of letting what shows itself be seen from itself, is precisely *not* the same as a method which controls the subject-matter of scientific knowing. Rather it is a method which is joined to the philosophical subject-matter, namely the meaning of being as such and the ontological make-up of Dasein, i.e., understanding being. As far as the phenomenological method of *Being and Time* is concerned, the matter for thinking has the first and last word. As self-showing of the matter itself, phenomenological method is completely and diametrically opposed to the modern understanding of method. The modern understanding of method is as far removed as is possible from the basic phenomenological attitude. This understanding of phenomenological method, which Heidegger also calls the *formal* concept of phenomenology, was instituted by Husserl and summed up in the maxim 'to the things themselves'. Heidegger's thinking from beginning to end lives off this understanding of phenomenology – an understanding which the later Heidegger formulated simply as 'letting the matter show itself'. For this reason the only proper way of access to Heidegger's thinking is the way of *phenomenological* interpretation.

(c) The turning in Ereignis *and the circle of hermeneutics*

As it is outlined for the first time in *Being and Time*, phenomenological hermeneutic includes in essence a fore-understanding, given in fore-having, fore-sight and fore-grasping, and – along with this fore-understanding – the circle-structure of hermeneutics. How do both fore-understanding and the hermeneutic circle-structure fit in the *hermeneutic relation* of thinking in terms of the history of being?

We find instructive responses to these questions again in the 'Dialogue on language'. As Heidegger specifically points out, what is discussed in this dialogue – particularly with regard to the question of language's root unfolding – is significant for *all* the issues of thinking in terms of the history of being. In that dialogue Heidegger characterizes the question concerning the root unfolding of language, as well as the question concerning being as such, as putting a question to (*Anfrage-bei*) and asking after (*Nachfrage-nach*). In the question of being we put a question to being and ask after being itself, i.e., being's root unfolding. In order to initiate this questioning and inquiry, we must open ourselves to a 'regard' or 'sight' which, as Heidegger emphasizes, is not limited to the questions just touched upon (*GA* 12, p. 164). That to which we put the question and ask after 'must already have been addressed to us' (ibid.). The structure of having already been addressed by what is to be taken into the question is the structure of the necessary fore-understanding within which every question originates.

This regard which must open up questioning as putting-the-question-to and asking-after, in order to see through its own conditions of enactment – this regard we can call the *hermeneutic regard*. Heidegger formulates this in a general way when he says:

> Putting the question to something [*Anfrage*] and asking after something [*Nachfrage*] need here and everywhere first to be addressed by that which touches them in questioning and which they pursue in questioning. The starting point of any question always already dwells within the appeal of that to which the question is put.
>
> (ibid.)

In the realm of thinking in terms of the history of being every question receives its essential and necessary fore-understanding from the appeal or that which first of all enables questioning as such. As a putting the question to something or asking after something, questioning would run into a vacuum, were it not guided in advance by what questioning asks about and searches for (cf. *Being and Time*, Section 2). The question of being as such has its fore-having in the appeal of that to which the question is put and which is asked after. As a questioning, this question looks to this *fore-having*, within a *fore-sight* and a *fore-grasping*. This questioning that always already dwells within the appeal is the structure of the *hermeneutic circle*.

If questioning in the realm of thinking in terms of the history of being is so decisively made possible from out of the appeal, then questioning is not 'the genuine gesture of thinking . . . but rather hearing the appeal of what must come into question' (ibid.). Such an *essential hermeneutic insight* into the basic posture of thinking in terms of the history of being does not abolish questioning as questioning, in favour of a mere listening. This by no means denies the questioning character of thinking in terms of the history of being. It is simply and solely a matter of detecting the condition for initiating and enacting the question. If it turns out that the starting point for the question has the appeal of fore-having as its condition, then *mere questioning* can no longer be the basic posture of thinking, but rather an understanding that hears what is offered for questioning and asked after. Only if thinking above all is an understand-

ing hearing of that which lights up as what is to be thought and questioned – only then can thinking begin its questioning in the right manner
(as putting a question to something and asking after it) and enact it
step by step. In the enactment of questioning, thinking is primarily an
understanding hearing of that which thinking inquires into.

The thinking which thus makes its basic posture transparent to itself
is not at all a thinking without questioning, but attempts to gain clarity
about that which *makes possible this thinking's ability to question.*

Thinking of being which receives its fore-having for its enactment from
a hearing understanding of what is offered to it has the character of a
self-joining. This thinking does not exercise control *over* the matter that
this thinking has to think. Rather, this thinking is joined to the matter
for thinking which is thrown toward thinking as something to be thought.
The basic *phenomenological* attitude of this thinking speaks from out of
that joining, in which the matter to be thought shows itself for this
thinking's enactment of questioning. But the basic phenomenological
attitude of this thinking is at the same time its basic *hermeneutic* character. Hearing understanding of the appeal of that 'to which all questioning
is put by asking after the root unfolding' (ibid.) is the same hearing that
we are familiar with in the 'hermeneutic relation' as that hearing of the
message which brings tidings of it.

Thinking in terms of the history of being accounts for the essential
hermeneutic insight into the hearing understanding of the appeal of that
which is put into question when, as is the case in questioning the root
unfolding of language, this thinking formulates the following directive for
the continuation of its questioning thinking: root unfolding of language:
language of root unfolding. The expression which follows the latter colon
is the formal indicator of the *fore-understanding* of what is asked after.
Thus thinking in terms of the history of being is also held within that
peculiar movement which *Being and Time* calls the *circle of understanding.*

There is an instructive passage in *Beiträge zur Philosophie* in which –
as is to be expected from everything that we have said so far – the *circle
of hermeneutics is transformed and re-rooted into the 'turning in Ereignis'.*
This passage reads:

> The innermost occurrence in *Ereignis* and its widest reach lies in the
> turning. The turning that unfolds in *Ereignis* is the hidden ground for
> all other turnings and circles – each one subordinated, unclear in its
> origin, remaining unquestioned, and wanting to be taken as the 'very
> last' turn or circle. (Cf. the turn in the contexture of the guiding
> question and the circle of understanding.)

(GA 65, p. 407)

As presented earlier, *the turning in Ereignis* is the appropriating relation of being to Dasein and the appropriated-projecting belonging of Dasein to the unfolding of the truth of being. The appropriating relation, or as Heidegger puts it in *Beiträge*, 'being's breakthrough [*Anfall*] as appropriating the *Da*' (ibid.) is that appeal which has always to be heard and understood before thinking can put a question to being or ask after it. Questioning as putting-a-question-to and as asking-after gets enacted according to the hearing understanding of the appeal as a thinking projection. Only what is projected in the hermeneutic project out of hearing the appeal can be interpreted in the narrower sense as a thrown-projection. The *circle of understanding* is rooted in the turning which unfolds in *Ereignis* as the counter-movement of the appropriating-throw and appropriated-projection.

Thinking in terms of the history of being which thinks the root unfolding of being (being as such) as *Ereignis* and as the turning in *Ereignis* – and which is understood in its character of enactment as appropriated from out of *Ereignis* – is a phenomenological and then a hermeneutic thinking. Not only does phenomenological hermeneutic or hermeneutic phenomenology think the root unfolding of being as *Ereignis*, but it also has its enabling ground in *Ereignis* and in the turning that belongs to *Ereignis*.

The interpretive glimpse into the basic phenomenological-hermeneutic feature of thinking in terms of the history of being leads to this insight: in its manifold ways Heidegger's thinking can be appropriately and adequately interpreted only if each stage of interpretation heeds the *basic hermeneutic-phenomenological* character of this thinking. We owe hermeneutic phenomenology as *phenomenology* to Edmund Husserl's original establishment of this basic philosophical posture. Only one who has thoroughly mastered Husserl's phenomenology in the sense of its actual maxim 'to the things themselves' and who has worked through this phenomenology by enacting it – only such a one is called upon and capable of entering into a philosophical dialogue with Heidegger's thinking, as caretaker of this phenomenological-hermeneutic thinking and of the two ways of elaborating the question of being.

Notes

1 *Sein und Zeit, Gesamtausgabe (GA)* 2.
2 *Beiträge zur Philosophie (Vom Ereignis)*, *GA* 65.
3 'Aus einem Gespräch von der Sprache', in *Unterwegs zur Sprache*, *GA* 12, pp. 79ff.
4 Martin Heidegger, 'Mein Weg in die Phänomenologie', in *Zur Sache des Denkes* (Tübingen: Niemeyer, 1969), p. 90.

5 Edmund Husserl, *Logische Untersuchungen*, vol. II, Part 1, Husserliana Bd. XIX/1, ed. U. Panzer (The Hague: Martinus Nijhoff, 1984), para. 3.

6 Given the central role that *Rede* has in Section 34 of *Sein und Zeit*, this word moves deeper than any meaning or connotation it has in its ordinary usage. For reasons as to why in Heidegger's German *Rede* cannot be taken simply at face value and identified with 'discourse', 'speech' or 'talk' see F.-W. von Herrmann, *Subjekt und Dasein* (1985), p. 103.

7 Martin Heidegger, *Brief über den Humanismus* (Frankfurt am Main: Vittorio Klostermann Verlag, 1981), p. 18.

8 ibid., p. 33.

9 'Das Wesen der Sprache', in *Unterwegs zur Sprache*, *GA* 12, pp. 147ff.

10 For a discussion of the difference between *way* and *method* see also Martin Heidegger, 'Der Fehl heiliger Namen', in *Aus der Erfahrung des Denkens*, *GA* 13, pp. 231ff.

The end of philosophy as the commencement of thinking

Samuel IJsseling

In the middle of the sixties, Heidegger wrote a few texts which take the end of philosophy as their express theme.[1] They can be read as the development of earlier texts which deal with the overcoming of metaphysics and in a broader context they can be understood as a development and radicalization of what in *Being and Time* and in the 'Marburg Lectures' was still characterized as the destruction of traditional ontology. What is at issue in this discussion of the end of philosophy, Heidegger tells us, is 'the attempt, repeatedly undertaken since 1930, to reformulate the questions of *Being and Time* in a more original way'.[2] The carrying through of the destruction of the ontological tradition in which, according to *Being and Time*, 'the question of being first achieves its true concreteness', belongs essentially to this posing of the question.[3]

The frame of reference into which Heidegger fits the problem of the end of philosophy, generates, on the one hand, a thinking exchange or dialogue with Hegel and, up to a certain point, also with Husserl and Nietzsche; on the other hand, it gives rise to reflection on, or an entry into, the essence of technology and modern science and, before all else, of computer science. The opposition Heidegger establishes between philosophy and thinking also belongs within this frame of reference. And finally, there belongs within this framework the attempt to achieve 'a determination of the matter of thinking'. And – as we hope to show – *one* aspect at least of this matter of thinking is, for Heidegger, what remains concealed in the end of philosophy, that is, what really happens when philosophy comes to an end. It belongs to the matter of thinking to ponder what is peculiar to the end. We want to try and throw some light on these three points.

In the frame of reference in which Heidegger poses the problem of the end of philosophy, there belongs, in the first place, the thinking exchange, or the dialogue with Hegel. What is astonishing is not, as Heidegger notes in *The Fundamental Problems of Phenomenology*, that philosophy is, 'in a certain sense, thought to an end by Hegel';[4] and that the theme of the end of philosophy is expressly raised. In the Preface to the *Phenomenology of Spirit*, Hegel sets himself the task of 'bringing philosophy nearer to the form of science – that goal whereby it can lay aside the name of love of knowledge and be actual knowledge'.[5] In actual or absolute knowledge philosophy arrives at its completion. According to Heidegger, this completion is the radicalization and realization of the whole original project of philosophy since the Greeks, and in particular of the Cartesian philosophy. Theme and method have become one and the same, and in absolute knowledge the being of beings as presencing has, in the form of substantiality and subjectivity, reached the fully developed certainty of self-knowing knowledge. According to Heidegger, there is a tendency to suppose that philosophy has achieved its highest perfection here at its end. Heidegger is of the opinion however, that it is not possible to talk of perfection. He writes:

> Not only do we lack any criterion which would permit us to evaluate the perfection of one epoch of metaphysics as compared with any other epoch. The right to this kind of evaluation does not exist. Plato's thinking is no more perfect than Parmenides'. Hegel's philosophy is no more perfect than Kant's. Each epoch has its own necessity. We simply have to acknowledge the fact that a philosophy is the way it is.[6]

For Heidegger, completion of philosophy does not mean perfection but rather 'being gathered in its most extreme possibility'.[7] It may be noted here that in *Being and Time* the 'most extreme possibility' of Dasein is death and that it gives expression to the finitude of Dasein. If Heidegger talks about the completion of philosophy as 'being gathering in its most extreme possibility' the finitude of philosophy is also announced therewith.

A thinking conversation with Hegel oriented around what is peculiar to the end of philosophy is not a matter of criticizing Hegel, or even of contradicting him. In the essay 'Who is Nietzsche's Zarathustra?' Heidegger says: 'The business of mounting refutations never succeeds in getting on the path of thinking. It belongs to that smallness of spirit whose expression is required for the maintenance of publicity.'[8] And a few pages earlier he says: 'The unique thing that thinking is capable of saying can be neither logically nor empirically proved or disproved.'[9] It is a matter not of mounting refutations but of a 'dialogue', as Heidegger calls it in the appendix to the Nietzsche volume in the *Gesamtausgabe*.[10] There he tells us that this dialogue is not a fault-finding or an underlining of failures. It is the establishment of limits, not with a view to denying the latter as limiting or to doing better or trying to show that one has done better. The limits belong to its greatness. The limits of anything great are the margins of what is other and created. These limits are constitutive for philosophy and belong to the finitude of philosophical thinking. This finitude – again itself an aspect of the end of philosophy – is not based solely, or in the first instance, upon the limitedness of human faculties but upon the finitude of the matter of thinking or upon the finitude of being itself.[11]

In this connection Heidegger speaks of the unthought, of the unthought *in* thinking. Here too the 'reference to the unthought in philosophy is not a criticism of philosophy'.[12] The unthought is not a lack but belongs essentially to philosophy. In *What is Called Thinking?* Heidegger writes: 'The more original a thinking is, the richer will its unthought be. The unthought is the most precious gift that a thinking has to convey'.[13] And in *The Principle of Reason* he writes:

The greater the work of a thinker, the richer is what is unthought in this work, that is to say, what initially and exclusively through this work emerges as having not yet been thought. Of course, this unthought has nothing to do with what a thinker might have overlooked or not mastered and which his more knowledgeable successors have to make good on.[14]

The unthought increases, so to speak, to the extent that more is thought. For this very reason, according to Heidegger, the unthought is greatest with Hegel, who thought everything that could only be thought. In my opinion, a reading of Heidegger is not possible in which this unthought does not in any way possess a positive content. It is true that with Heidegger the unthought is sometimes ambiguous and there are texts which convey the impression that it is something positive. In any case, it is never what in the metaphysical tradition is called the *ineffable* or what surpasses our thinking. It is rather what reveals itself in anxiety, in the depths of boredom, or at and in the end of philosophy. This becomes still clearer with Heidegger's deliberations about the essence of technology and modern science.

The end of philosophy manifests itself most evidently in modern technology or, as Heidegger expresses it,

as the triumph of the controllable institution of a technologically scientific world and the social order which corresponds to this world. The end of philosophy means: the beginning of that world civilization which is founded in Western European thinking.[15]

The end of philosophy is therewith now understood as the *resolution* of philosophy into technical science. In a certain sense, a first step towards this resolution is the *release* of the sciences from philosophy and the institution of their independence.[16] A technologically scientific interpretation of thinking is bound up with this. Thinking becomes philosophical and the latter is conceived and developed in a technologically scientific fashion. This already comes to light in the Greek era as a decisive trait, as a direction. Many other steps are important in this development, as, for example, the translation of Greek thought into Roman, which is imperialistic and has the character of power-oriented knowledge – truth is what holds out and possesses power – and further on, the translation of Roman into the Roman-Christian, in which the being of beings is understood as brought into being in the sense of creation. A decisive step is the formulation of 'The principle of sufficient reason' with Leibniz, which latter required a long 'incubation period', as Heidegger tells us, but which was already announced in certain features of the entire metaphysical tradition. From now on, everything is in principle susceptible to calculation and control, planning and mastery. *At the End* now means this, that being is no longer understood as subject or object, as was the case with Descartes, Hegel and Husserl, but as disposable reserve. The so-called subject–object schema as the basis for an explanation of all appearances loses its significance. Industrial society is, as Heidegger tells us, neither subject nor object,[17] and what is known as the enframing (*Gestell*) no longer belongs within the horizon of representation, and so remains foreign to traditional thinking. Today's world is guided by technological science in which truth is equated with efficiency and in which, through such cybernetic key-words as information, regulation and feed-back, primary concepts such as ground and consequence, cause and effect, subject and object, theory and practice, concepts which played a leading role in science hitherto are transformed in an almost uncanny manner. A new basic attitude comes into being, a new relationship, and the key word for this basic attitude is *Information*, whereby Heidegger remarks somewhat cynically that we have to hear the word in its American-English accent.[18] This information, as for example the data stored up in DNA which determines the manner in which the organism develops, can be understood neither as subject nor consciousness nor as object nor matter. It is neither the same, as was the Platonic ειδοζ nor the Aristotelian μορφη nor *forma*. All of our philosophical categories have lost their meaning. It is a monstrous, uncanny possibility, a 'most extreme possibility', that all philosophical concepts have become meaningless. This possibility belongs to the essence of the end of philosophy.

To reject or to criticize Hegel is as unimportant for Heidegger as it is to pass judgment upon technology or the entire development which has led to it, although Heidegger is sometimes the victim of his own rhetoric. He writes in *Identity and Difference*: 'To be sure, we cannot repudiate the technological world of today as the work of the devil nor should we destroy it, assuming that it does not do this to itself.'[19] There is no evil genius of technology but only the secret of its essence. This essence is being itself[20] which, to a very large extent, remains ambiguous. It is, so to speak, that which makes possible and permits the appearance of what we today call reality, but it also conceals within itself the most extreme danger. *We* cannot destroy technology or overcome it, let alone reverse it, but it can destroy itself, either through a nuclear war or through the total destruction of the environment, as Heidegger wrote in 1950. It can also bring with it the needlessness of that complete thoughtlessness which Heidegger takes to be much more dangerous. Technology and science would then lose their meaning. Here we run up against that most extreme limit which can no longer be thought.

Technologized science is that into which philosophy is resolved, and according to Heidegger, that is a *legitimate advance*.[21] At the end of philosophy, that direction which philosophical thought has been pursuing in the course of its history from the very beginning makes itself known.[22] This history is the history of being itself and, in a certain sense, it is the technicians who are most true to this history and who follow its direction most faithfully, although Heidegger never formulated it quite so explicitly. In this history or in the coming-to-its-end of philosophy something still remains hidden: a task of thought. This task consists, in the first place, in *pondering* what really comes to pass at this end. To ponder this belongs to the matter of thinking.

In connection with this entire problematic, the opposition Heidegger draws between philosophy and thinking plays a large role. And here it should be noted that Heidegger often uses the word thinking for philosophy and the word philosophy for what he understands by thinking. Moreover, it is not a matter of an absolute opposition. On the one hand, there remains in philosophy something which is still *always* kept from thinking and, on the other, thinking can probably never occur entirely without philosophy.

Philosophy is for Heidegger metaphysics, or, in the end, ontology. And this then possesses an onto-theological constitution. Metaphysical thinking is an explanatory and a grounding thinking. It inquires into causes and grounds, into motives, conditions of the possibility and it never rests content with the thing itself because it is always looking for something else behind the thing, a more original thing. It is – especially since Descartes – a representational thinking which, because it always understands its subject matter as that of a representing subject or as represented object, is even less capable of sticking with it. It may also assume the form of a reasoning process, a logical progression that also keeps on going right past the subject. Metaphysical thinking can, in addition, take on the form of a conceptualization which seeks to see everything in one large connection or in a unity and which is characterized by a making-own (*sich-eigen-machen*) or appropriation (*Aneignung*) or by interiorization. This conceptualization – a word that Heidegger otherwise seldom employs – is directed to the freeing of everything from its alienness, its strangeness and to taking it up into itself as being-with-itself. It is domestication. Philosophy is, above all since Descartes, a seeking after security, after certainty, a safe-keeping. Truth then becomes the complete certainty of self-knowing knowledge. This understanding of truth is characteristic of modern times and so it is also not accidental that modern philosophy begins with doubt and no longer with wonder and moreover with a view to transforming this doubt into certainty as soon as possible. One form of metaphysics at the end is calculative thinking, which has been especially successful since Leibniz and which claims sovereignty over everything, computes everything and takes account of everything. This thinking can, according to Heidegger, proceed better and much more quickly through thinking machines, computers which in one second flawlessly calculate thousands of relationships. In connection with such a thinking, human being is an inconvenience. At the end, or with the completion of philosophy, this thinking will simply become data storage and data processing. At that point, traditional metaphysical concepts have lost their meaning.

This metaphysical thinking with its – according to Heidegger – secretive history and development makes it possible for modern man to master and control everything. At the same time, this very man is mastered and bewitched by this thinking and it is precisely this that slips out of his command and control in an almost uncanny fashion. That means that in this thinking something still lies concealed which remains alien to it, something to which the thinking in question has no access and which escapes it. In other words, metaphysical thinking is enveloped by a limit, by a margin which makes this thinking possible, which limits it and determines it and, at the same time, also continually threatens it.

To metaphysical thinking, Heidegger counterposes another kind of thinking which he calls recollective (*andenkende*) thinking. Under Hölderlin's influence, it is also associated with celebrating, greeting, remembering, thanking. It is an abiding-with, a wonder-ful tarrying, a holding out, an ability to wait – indeed for a lifetime – a stepping back, an abode. It reminds us perhaps of Far Eastern wisdom which was not alien to Heidegger or of a probing of reality of the kind to be found in Paul Klee, a man who astonished Heidegger and whose theoretical and pedagogical writings the latter perused thoroughly. In my opinion, it can also be understood as the realization and the radicalization of the original idea of phenomenology. Thinking as the enduring of being, as an abiding with beings in their being, an abiding with thinking and precisely in view of the fact that we really do think in this way and finally, as an abiding with what determines our thinking, what calls us to think, what commands our thinking and so points the way.

One question which keeps on arising is: is such a thinking (still) possible? Does it not once again and necessarily amount to a metaphysico-technical thinking? If we are dominated by metaphysico-technical thinking and, in the end, are solely directed by the key concepts of computer science, is another kind of thinking then still possible? One should not underestimate this difficulty and Heidegger is himself fully aware of the seriousness of this problem. He will contend that this other thinking can *only* be prepared, that it is essentially, and indeed remains, untimely and can *always* only be a task. It requires quite specific strategies to guard it and to protect it against the danger which threatens it to an ever-increasing degree from the side of the sciences and their cybernetic organization within a self-regulating world civilization. Heidegger knows that this other thinking can never be a purely university or academic affair because these organizations, with their indigenous research operations, their conferences and their literary directives are carried along by the metaphysico-technical thinking and themselves belong to world civilization. Still less can it subsist outside of a particular historical, technico-economic, politico-scientific, institutional and linguistic frame of reference. For this reason, the greatest possible care has to be taken to prevent it from being the victim of the attempt to interpret it and to integrate it within the existing frame of reference. Much of Heidegger's rhetoric must be viewed in this light.

Heidegger's strategy – if one may use this word for his path of thought – is a matter of transgressing the limit, a transgression which, in general, is immediately reproved or neutralized by the dominant thinking. A transgression with respect to which a limit, an end, must first be established and with respect to which, finally, a question has to be asked with regard to the determination of this limit, this end. For Heidegger, a limit is never the place where something comes to an end but, on the contrary, where it begins. A limit is constitutive for what is. The establishment of a limit, its transgression and the question concerning the determination of the limit, belong to the problematic of the end of philosophy. The question concerning the essence of the limit of thinking or concerning the finitude of all thinking is the question concerning the determination of the matter of thinking which – according to Heidegger – is itself finite and whose finitude is much more difficult to experience than the previous positing of an absolute.[23]

Heidegger employs many and various names to describe the matter of thinking, as for example, being itself, the event of appropriation (*Ereignis*), αληβεια, distinction, clearing, difference as difference, decision and many, many others. All these names and their multiplicity have in turn a strategic significance, that is, they refer not to a positive content but simply point in a specific direction. They incline the glance. They are *pointers* (*Winke*) or *paths* (*Wege*).

Here, it might be thought that one runs up against a transposition into another language, and into another frame of reference of what, in the Marburg lectures, Heidegger still called the 'phenomenological reduction'. There he distinguishes it markedly from that of Husserl. Whereas for Husserl the phenomenological reduction is a method for leading the phenomenological viewpoint from the natural attitude of human being living in the world of things and persons back to transcendental consciousness and its noetico-noematic experiences (experiences in which the object is constituted as a correlate of consciousness), for Heidegger, the phenomenological reduction leads the phenomenological viewpoint back from the always *determined* conception of beings to the understanding of the being of these beings.[24] Whereas for Husserl the wonder of wonders is transcendental subjectivity, a subjectivity 'beyond which it is pointless to question back', and which proves to be 'the one and only absolute being',[25] for Heidegger, the *wonder of all wonders*, as one can read in the Postface to *What is Metaphysics?* is 'that entities exist'.

The reduction or the leading back becomes, in the later Heidegger, *way*, or better ways. In the multiplicity and the character of these ways lies the 'step back'. Way and 'step back' cannot be understood here as a method, because the concept of method belongs within the realm of metaphysico-technical thinking. The becoming-a-method of the way – a process which, in the epoch of the completion of thinking, is, in a certain sense, brought to a close in the conclusion of Hegel's *Science of Logic* – is constitutive for metaphysics and for the end of philosophy.[26] Way and 'step back' mean here not an isolated movement of thought but the way in which the movement of thought takes place, and a long way which demands a duration and endurance whose scale we cannot know.[27]

The 'step back' moves out of metaphysics into the essence of metaphysics and is, from the standpoint of the present and the insight one has into it, the step out of technology into that *essence* of modern technology which can now be thought for the first time.[28] Metaphysics and, at its end, technology constitute a determinate conception of beings or a determinate way of dealing with things and with human beings. The *essence* of metaphysics or technology – Heidegger calls it what is 'to be thought' – is being itself and points in the direction of ἀλήθεια, of clearing, of difference, etc. Ἀρχή or ἄρχειν, that is, the mastery of metaphysics or technology is what makes possible, determines and limits metaphysics and technology. It is, as it is called in *What is Metaphysics?* the *ground* of metaphysics and technology. At that time, step back still meant 'regression into the ground of metaphysics' – in the words of the title of the Introduction, subsequently added. Later, the word *ground* becomes problematic, because it still belongs to metaphysical thinking, just as does the word being.

The *essence* of metaphysics is probably also the *end* of metaphysics as what is to be thought, and end is here to be understood in a spatio-temporal sense. In *Identity and Difference*, where the problematic of the 'step back' is extensively handled, Heidegger says that with the step back it is a matter of a step out of the already thought into an unthought from which the thought receives its *essential space (Wesensraum)*.[29] Heidegger frequently thinks the essence and the end of metaphysics in terms of the categories space, spatiality, place, limit. Clearing too, the free openness, is supposedly that in which pure space and everything in it which is present and absent receives its all-gathering and preserving place.[30] Space, place and end belong together.

Heidegger writes: 'With the step back philosophy is neither abandoned nor does it disappear into a memorial for thinking human being.'[31] The step back out of metaphysics into its essence does not mean that the discipline gets thrown out of the cultural circuit of philosophical 'formation'. It is much more a matter of the attempt to make of philosophy an 'over against' with respect to itself, a factum, a work, a work of language – I would like to say here: as text, and text must here be regarded as an abode, as a place or a *there* where being occurs as discovering and covering up, as revealing and concealing (both necessarily *and* accidentally). The step back out of metaphysics can for this reason only be carried through as an analysis of metaphysics, as an analysis of technology. And this analysis can only be endless because it is directed towards and upon an unthought which essentially remains unthought and which becomes more extensive to the extent that more is thought and thought in a more original manner. Most of Heidegger's texts after *Being and Time* consist in endless analyses of great texts out of the history of philosophy, analyses whose goal is not to say better what was said there, to criticize, and still less to refute them but rather to get on the track of what *happens* in these texts.

When one tries with Heidegger to approach philosophy as a work, as a work of language, one must avoid at least three things; first, this work should not, and cannot be regarded as the pure product of humankind. That would be a form of subjectivism, whereas the philosopher tries to say what is given to him to say and tries to show what shows itself from itself. Second, the work of philosophy should not, and can not be regarded as a more or less adequate reproduction or presentation of a reality given from outside philosophy. To conceive of truth as adequation may well be correct but belongs to the finite sphere of metaphysics and never succeeds in seeing what is accomplished along the way in philosophy as a work. Third, the words and sentences out of which the work is constructed cannot be viewed as signs or a complex of signs, which is supposed to indicate a reality given outside the work. 'The essence of speech is not determined out of the sign-character of words', Heidegger writes in *What is Called Thinking?*[32] '*Saying is showing.*' Indeed, Heidegger claims that the moment in which the word's *showing* became a signifying was one of the most important moments in the history of truth, of the understanding of truth as adequation and of the understanding of being as present at hand or 'continual presence'. In 'The origin of the work of art' we read:

> Where no language prevails . . . there is also no openness of beings and also, accordingly, no openness to what is not and to emptiness. In as much as language first names beings, such naming first articulates beings and makes beings appear. This naming first nominates the entity in its being and out of its being.[33]

And another passage. 'Through the word, in language, things first are and become what they are.'[34] 'Language first grants the very possibility of standing in the midst of the openness of beings.'[35] And 'if our essence did not take up its stand in the power of language, the totality of beings would remain closed to us, the entities which we are ourselves no less than the entities which we ourselves are not'.[36] What is said here about language is especially valid for the language of the thinker and for that linguistic work which is philosophy.

Philosophy as a work can be understood neither as a human product nor as a more or less adequate reproduction of a reality present at hand nor as a constellation of signs. More positively expressed, it can be said that every great philosophy is a building, a construction. As a construction, it is not an image or a representation of the world. Rather, it institutes or grounds a world. The building of philosophy stands there as the temple at Paestum stands there and, in this standing there, it opens up a world, confers a visage upon humans and Gods and makes things visible. Philosophy is a finite and limited place where reality is revealed and, at the same time, concealed. On the basis of this revealing and concealing, there arises something like what we call a world. The building that philosophy is cannot subsist without human beings but, for all that, it does not find its origin in human beings. The construction of a philosophy is, before all else, a matter of receiving and remaining open, hearing and listening. In a certain sense, philosophy constitutes itself. It is not however a *creatio ex nihilo* but is necessarily put together out of pre-given material. This material is not, as in architecture or painting, made up of stones or of colours but, as in poetry, of *words*. The fragments and sections which are taken over from, and have to be taken over from, already existing philosophical texts also belong to that material out of which a philosophy is built. Not one work, not one text stems completely from itself. Rather, it continually refers to other texts to which it is related. A text is always taken up in a context of meaning or a referential totality. The network of references to other works is a condition of the possibility for the emergence and the understanding of a work. At the same time, it also creates the greatest obstacle for this emergence and this understanding, and it establishes its confines. As Heidegger writes: 'Modern thinking is in its basic traits much less accessible than Greek thinking, for the writing and works of the modern thinker are built differently, more intricate, intermingled with tradition and everywhere inserted into Christianity.'[37] On the basis of this 'developed state of affairs', philosophy runs the danger of deteriorating into 'groundless chatter' and becoming totally incomprehensible, and that means that instead of *uncovering*, it *covers up*. This danger, or so says Heidegger, is inherent in the language by which philosophy is guided. Language is – according to a famous text from Hölderlin which Heidegger is happy to cite – 'the most dangerous of the goods given to human being'. In Heidegger's opinion, it is the danger of dangers and indeed for several reasons. First, because 'the greatest good fortune of the first, instituting speech is at the same time the deepest pain of loss'.[38] Second, because any, even the purest, the most original and the deepest forms of expression can be taken up into a readily accessible way of talking. Words get used, used up in being used, and indeed necessarily so. And third: in the course of reproducing, of repeating, it is never established whether the original words still put into effect what they were formerly able to effect. This belongs to that which Heidegger calls the 'dis-essence [*Un-wesen*] of language' and, as he expressly remarks, it can never be avoided.[39]

Because philosophy is a construction it can also be subject to a *destruction*, or perhaps better, a de-construction. This leads us to the question concerning the relationship between the end of philosophy and what, in the Marburg period, was called the destruction of traditional ontology. Heidegger has frequently repeated that this destruction will not bury the past in oblivion and that it is not a negation or condemnation of the past to oblivion. It is a critical taking apart of concepts which were handed down and, in the first instance, necessarily applied and, at the same time, it is a regression to the sources from which they were drawn.[40] In *Being and Time* Heidegger speaks about an investigative exposition of the 'birth certificates' of ontological concepts and he says:

> But this destruction is just as far from having the *negative* sense of shaking off the ontological tradition. We must, on the contrary, stake out the positive possibilities of that tradition, and this must always mean keeping it within its limits.[41]

It is clear that this destruction can only be carried through as an analysis of the factically present ontology. It runs parallel with the analytic of Dasein which belongs, together with the destruction, to the dual task of *Being and Time*. Dasein's analysis and destruction are two sides of fundamental ontology or the question of being.

The most important, though often overlooked, feature of the destruction is that it is guided by the question: what does really happen in the history of philosophy? What happens when a philosophy constitutes itself as a specific philosophy? The answer to this question runs: being itself happens, αληβεια as uncovering and covering up, clearing, etc. but that brings with it in the first place ever new questions. More concretely: at the end of his Kant book Heidegger writes with reference to his interpretation of Kant: 'Don't ask what Kant says but what *happens* in his laying of the foundation of metaphysics. The interpretation of the *Critique of Pure Reason* carried out above is aimed solely at the laying bare of this *happening*.'[42] He says much the same thing with regard to his interpretation of Schelling and Hegel, of Leibniz and Descartes. More generally expressed: Heidegger poses questions like *What is Metaphysics?* and *What is Philosophy?* Here, the *is* must be understood transitively, as he himself remarks.[43] That means: what allows the, or a, philosophy to be what it is and to be as it is? Or *What is meant by Thinking?* whereby 'means' is meant something like require, evoke, call into existence, orient, etc. Or again: 'Regression to the ground of metaphysics' and return to the source. These questions question into the *matter of thinking*. And precisely the same problematic, though now thought out in a more original fashion, comes back again in the question concerning the end of philosophy. What happens when philosophy comes to an end, is gathered up in its most extreme possibility? The answer to this question runs again: being itself, here thought as withdrawal, expropriation. In this sense, the problematic of the end of philosophy is the same as that of the destruction of ontology. But there are differences. There is a tendency to see the difference in the fact that, for philosophers, destruction was still a task and that philosophy in the end destroys itself. It is true that the role and responsibility of the thinker in *Being and Time* are greater than with the later Heidegger. But if one formulates the problem in this fashion, one only too readily assumes that the destruction and the end of philosophy are an annihilation. More important is perhaps the fact that the destruction is directed towards reaching an *original level*, a ground in which philosophical concepts are rooted and grounded or a source from which they were drawn, whereas that cannot be the case with the end of philosophy. Still, one has to proceed carefully with words like origin, ground or source in connection with *Being and Time* – in any case, this is my view, though such an interpretation is perhaps disputable. Indeed, the original has always already been lost and refers in the last instance to a past which never was present. In other words, the origin, the ground or the source is, according to *Being and Time*, Dasein itself, which is essentially finite, never in possession of its self and never really with its self. Besides, *the* question of *Being and Time* is how something like Dasein is possible. Dasein is the being that is *there*. On the other hand, the question concerning the end of philosophy is also directed towards something more original, towards what makes this end possible. Even here *the* question runs: what *is* the end of philosophy?

To conclude, I would like to come back once again to the Heidegger–Hegel relationship in connection with the problematic of the end of philosophy. In the end, one can pose the question whether Heidegger's thinking is an inverted Hegelianism. This is a severe reproach, and all the more so since Heidegger somewhat cynically remarks that 'since Hegel's death everything has simply become a movement in reverse'.[44] And he specifically wants to get away from this movement. Heidegger: an inverted Hegelianism? Even Derrida hinted at this years ago when he posed the question of whether Heidegger's thinking might not constitute the deepest and most powerful defence of what he sought to bring to discussion under the title 'philosophy of presence'.[45] Derrida would no longer express himself in this way but the problem remains. Heidegger's thinking – a Hegelianism because he followed Hegel in still trying to think what Hegel's thinking actually makes possible, namely, what it means to say that philosophy reaches its completion in technology and what lies hidden in this end. An inverted Hegelianism, because Heidegger always starts out from history, with the supposition – in opposition to Hegel – that the commencement is what is most strange and powerful, and that what comes thereafter is not a development but a levelling down in the form of simple diffusion, a not being able to remain within the commencement in which philosophy does not proceed toward absolute knowledge but much rather towards technology, a technology which neither understands itself nor masters itself nor calls itself into question nor is even able to call itself into question. It is not difficult to cite texts from Heidegger which say this kind of thing. Everything depends on the question of what Heidegger means by *end* and by *commencement*.

Commencement (*Anfang*) is clearly distinguished by Heidegger from beginning (*Beginn*). One can say that philosophy begins with the Greeks and that calculative thinking begins with Leibniz. This beginning lies behind us. The commencement however lies before us precisely as the to-be-thought and the unthought. It is not a matter however of an unthought which can be thought. It is far more of a *limit* and in this sense also an *end*; a limit which makes thinking possible in limiting. This limit cannot be thought in the sense of an appropriation. But if one pays attention to precisely what happens when thinking takes place, if one abides by what happens in philosophy when thinking dwells, one runs up against the limit, against the 'other' of thinking. Even the expression 'the other of thinking' which Heidegger intentionally avoids can easily be misunderstood if one views the other in the light of the dialectic, or if one links it up with the limitations of the human faculties. It is much more the finitude of being itself. Just as a distinction obtains between beginning and commencement so also does it between end (Ende) and end (*Ende*). The end of philosophy can mean that philosophy ceases, either in the nineteenth century, with the absolute knowledge of Hegel, or in the twentieth century, with technology. This is however not the end of philosophy with which Heidegger is concerned. The end which concerns Heidegger is already there with the Greeks, at that moment in which philosophy establishes itself. In our time, it has reached a culmination or has been gathered into its most extreme possibilities, but it accompanies all thinking.

What remains *most questionable* with Heidegger is perhaps that he always thinks the outset and the outcome in the light of history and historicality. The concept of 'history' (*Geschichte*) is, in my view, the most questionable in Heidegger's thinking and a concept which can only be phenomenologically justified with great difficulty. Perhaps Heidegger already appreciated that and, for this reason, speaks of 'destiny' (*Geschick*). According to Heidegger, destiny is not to be thought out of a happening which can be characterized by means of a course of events and through a process. Sending (*Schicken*) means preparing, arranging, bringing each thing to that place where it belongs, making room for, assigning. Destiny is what furnishes the temporal play-space (*Zeit-Spiel-Raum*) in which beings can make their appearance and in which philosophy in general first becomes possible. This furnishing is a self-proffering and self-withdrawal and therefore also essentially bound up with commencement and end. The phrase 'destiny of being' is however not an answer but a question, amongst other things, the question concerning the *essence* of history, the *essence* of commencement and end.[46] To think this belongs to the task of thinking at the end of philosophy.

Translated by Christopher Macann

Notes

1 The most important are: 'Das Ende der Philosophie und die Aufgabe des Denkens', in *Zur Sache des Denkens* (Tübingen: Niemeyer, 1969), pp. 61–90, and *Zur Frage nach der Bestimmung der Sache des Denkens* (St Gallen: Erker Verlag, 1984).
2 'Das Ende der Philosophie', p. 61.

3 *Sein und Zeit, Gesamtausgabe (GA)* 2, p. 26.
4 *Grundprobleme der Phänomenologie, GA* 24, p. 400.
5 Hegel, *Phänomenologie des Geistes* (Hamburg: Meiner, 1952), p. 12.
6 'Das Ende der Philosophie', p. 62.
7 ibid., p. 63.
8 *Vorträge und Aufsätze, GA* 7, p. 121.
9 ibid., p. 119.
10 *Der Wille zur Macht als Kunst, GA* 43, p. 277.
11 *Zur Frage nach der Bestimmung*, p. 20.
12 'Das Ende der Philosophie', p. 76.
13 *Was Heißt Denken?, GA* 8, p. 72.
14 *Der Satz vom Grund, GA* 10, pp. 123–4.
15 'Das Ende der Philosophie', p. 65.
16 ibid., p. 63.
17 *Zur Frage nach der Bestimmung*, p. 12.
18 *Der Satz vom Grund, GA* 10, p. 202.
19 *Identität und Differenz, GA* 11, p. 33.
20 *Die Technik und die Kehre*, p. 38.
21 *Die Frage nach der Bestimmung*, p. 13.
22 ibid., p. 7.
23 ibid., p. 20.
24 *Grundprobleme der Phänomenologie, GA* 24, p. 29.
25 Husserl, *Formale und transzendentale Logik*, Husserliana XVII, p. 278.
26 *Aus der Erfahrung des Denkens, GA* 13, p. 233.
27 *Identität und Differenz, GA* 11, pp. 46–7.
28 ibid., p. 48.
29 ibid., p. 49.
30 'Das Ende der Philosophie', p. 73.
31 *Die Frage nach der Bestimmung*, p. 20.
32 *Was heißt Denken?, GA* 8, p. 123.
33 *Holzwege, GA* 5, pp. 60–1.
34 *Einführung in die Metaphysik, GA* 40, p. 63.
35 *Erläuterungen zu Hölderlins Dichtung, GA* 4, p. 35.
36 *Einführung in die Metaphysik, GA* 40, p. 63.
37 *Der Satz vom Grund, GA* 10, p. 123.
38 Hölderlins Hymnen 'Germanien' und 'Der Rhein', *GA* 39, p. 60.
39 ibid., pp. 63–4.
40 Cf. Samuel IJsseling, 'Heidegger and the destruction of ontology', in *Man and World*, 15 (1982), pp. 3–16. Included in J. J. Kockelmans (ed.), *A Companion to Martin Heidegger's 'Being and Time'* (Washington, DC, 1986), pp. 127–44.
41 *Sein und Zeit, GA* 2, p. 22.
42 *Kant und das Problem der Metaphysik, GA* 3, p. 193.
43 *Was ist das – die Philosophie?*, p. 22.
44 *Vorträge und Aufsätze, GA* 7, p. 76.
45 J. Derrida, *Positions* (Paris: Minuit, 1972), p. 75.
46 *Der Satz vom Grund, GA*, 10, pp. 108–9.

10

Does the saving power also grow? Heidegger's last paths

Otto Pöggeler

The one hundredth anniversary of Martin Heidegger's birth is also a conspicuous reminder that Heidegger's life slips ever more deeply into the past. In order for Heidegger's thought to have an influence, the tasks towards which he sought an approach must first be more clearly understood. Through his publications Heidegger exerted an influence upon people who never had personal contact with him. The force of the appeal lay in the concentrated earnest with which he forced himself and fellow philosophers into the decisive questions of human life. The systematic elaborations remained fragments; the confrontation with the history of thinking was the contrary of historical erudition, but also often an overlooking of concrete historical reality. Yet Heidegger's effect was due to the impetus he stimulated and he thereby elicited significant accomplishments from others: work as various as the new theological approach of the Bultmann school and Oskar Becker's philosophy of mathematics or the work on the metaphysical tradition and the relation to a painter like Cézanne. In the conversations which extended beyond the preliminaries of the first hours, Heidegger tried to steer his interlocutor towards his own path. For that reason the best encounters with Heidegger perhaps have been such conversations.

Each person takes from these conversations that which corresponds to his or her own horizon of expectations. Conversations across several days in Freiburg in 1959 and 1961 helped me of course above all to prepare the presentation which then appeared in 1963 as *Der Denkweg Martin Heideggers*.[1] Since this presentation was originally supposed to contain also a second part with confrontations on several exemplary topics, I submitted for discussion for example (each time after consulting with Oskar Becker in Bonn) the question of whether Heidegger did not overlook the achievements of mathematics and thereby also portray technology in a skewed light. Heidegger was so interested by these questions that he sought out Becker in Bonn for a personal conversation.[2] In terms of art, Heidegger above all commented on Paul Klee in our conversations, and I in turn alluded to the lyric poetry of Paul Celan. However, my question concerning certain formulations in Hölderlin's hymn 'Der Einzige' made it clear for me that Heidegger did not follow Hölderlin's last steps. During a return visit (which was enriched by the presence of Keji Nishitani) Heidegger read us his 1964 lecture 'Das Ende der Philosophie und die Aufgabe des Denkens';[3] the visit concluded with Heidegger reading the 'Eisgeschichte' from Stifter's story 'Die Mappe meines Urgroßvaters'.[4] The celebration of Heidegger's eightieth birthday in the Heidelberg Akademie took place (after Heidegger suffered a serious illness) at a time which had lost contact with Heidegger's questions, and therefore placed academic discussions in the foreground. The conversational openness was again present in the last personal meeting in the Spring of 1972. Because of American experiences, but also due to German initiatives, I raised the question of whether the scientific-technical world by its own constitution could come to a test of the necessary and the dangerous; Heidegger's resolute exhortation was to position oneself immediately in the confrontation with this world – without the detour into digressive and deferring discussions of the 'history of Being'. The liveliest attention and agreement centred on considerations of the relationship of Paul Celan to Friedrich Hölderlin. Heidegger was contemplating undertaking an edition of his works. Was Heidegger not exterior to the impetus of the times? Shortly before his death, I thought I'd bid him farewell in an appropriate fashion with a greeting from Delphi.

When Heidegger edited his Nietzsche lectures and texts,[5] he finally gave up the attempt to produce the documented path of his thinking in a larger introduction. With that it was clear that it wasn't Heidegger's concern to comprehend retrospectively the path of his thought and to relate it to the themes and questions of the present. Rather he sought to develop further his thought in the immediate confrontation with the specific questions already posed. In 1959–60 the 70-year-old philosopher left no doubt that his task lay before him: to provide that essential main work, for which he had collected all his thoughts, but for which he lacked a language. The lecture 'Der Weg zur Sprache' of 1959[6] says of Wilhelm Humboldt that he worked on his study of the diversity of human language, according to his brother, 'alone, in the vicinity of a *grave*' until his own death. Humboldt was able to find a popular influence through his letters to a friend and through his sonnets; yet the pioneering treatise always lay ahead. Are we lacking Heidegger's last work? Seminar protocols and occasional writings indicate yet another modification of approach; moreover Heidegger left behind him a wealth of drafts and notes. Yet is that an *opus posthumous*? We cannot yet know the answer.

In his first forays, Heidegger had combined the metaphysics of medieval Aristotelianism with Kant and Hegel. However, by the First World War he was already concerned with a hermeneutic of factical experience of life and wanted to develop it by means of a remodelling of phenomenological philosophy. Aristotle could be a teacher in a new way, since, in the sixth book of the *Nichomachean Ethics*, he also ascribed to the situational orientation here under the changing moon an *aletheuein* and therefore a particular *logos*. Could a formal-indicative hermeneutic, an existential conceptuality, provide access to the situation, even to the liminal situation (*Grenzsituation*) and the unavailable *kairos*? With this the question of Being and time was raised anew. Yet in 1929 Heidegger earnestly proposed that the guiding sense (*Sinn*) of Being in Aristotle must not be defined as *ousia* (as Brentano maintained), but rather as *energeia*, which bears in it potential and therefore is a being-at-work (*Am-Werk-sein*). Doesn't this being-at-work assert itself as unbridled technology, as the total mobilization of all energies, as Ernst Jünger suggested? Does man touch the mythical, which gives his life meaning, perhaps only still in art, which has not shed its cultic rootedness? Heraclitus, so imputes Heidegger, posed the question of a Being, which (somewhat as the linguistic root indicates, in that it still bears the 'I am') is also at once a Becoming – namely that *physis* to which the *aletheia* belongs. Nietzsche alluded to this dimension when he conceived of that which is particularly Greek as the antagonism between the Dionysian and the Apollonian, i.e. when he wanted to wrest the forms of Being from Becoming itself. Hölderlin developed this approach more purely, in that he comprehended the eternity of the divine as the 'stride past' (*Vorbeigang*), which always has its own respective place and hour, and therefore cannot be opposed to time. When the struggle of the great totalitarianisms for world domination openly took the stage in the Second World War, Heidegger in the Nietzsche lectures of 1940 no longer analysed 'Idealism' as the failure of truth, but rather 'Nihilism'. The 'seinsgeschichtliche Bestimmung des Nihilismus'[7] from the sombre years of 1944–6 appears to combine Nothing and Being in an almost mystical fashion. What 'mystical' might mean here Heidegger clarified for himself when he began to translate Lao-Tzu in 1946–7. And thus from the Bremen lectures of 1949[8] onward he could interpret the world in its contemporary constellations from the antagonism of 'enframing' (*Gestell*) and 'the fourfold' (*Geviert*). Is that which is here called *Gestell* still conceptualized from that disposal (*Verfügung*) of being (*das Seiende*) in the representing (*Vorstellen*) and delivering (*Zustellen*) of Being, which Husserl treated as the original foundation of philosophy through Plato and Descartes? How can the co-presence of the divine and the mortal in the fourfold today indicate the saving power (*das Rettende*)? Obviously Heidegger felt himself called upon by the age to rethink yet again his philosophical approach, namely to juxtapose art to world civilization and its technology or 'artificial intelligence' in a new way.

Though it remains today still premature to say anything completely reliable about the paths taken by Heidegger in the last twelve years of his life, this paper will briefly consider two texts from this period: the *Spiegel* interview of 1966 and the Athens speech of 1967. With all the provisionality rightly reserved for the genre of the discussion, these texts will be used to put a question to Heidegger's thought: does the care (*Sorge*) for the proper (*das Eigene*) and the authentic (*das Eigentliche*) not lead to the premature rejection of the contemporary world as a closed structure (*Verschlossenheitszusammenhang*), and thereby as well to an inappropriate definition of the co-operation (*Miteinander*) of art and technology? When Heidegger used the fame which *Being and Time* brought him to break out of academic philosophy, this question of art and technology as a decisive one had fallen to him. The following reflections should make clear that Heidegger even on his final path yet again thought through this question anew.

I Two late texts

On 23 September 1966, three days before his seventy-seventh birthday, Heidegger was interviewed by the news-magazine *Der Spiegel*. According to the agreement the text was to be published only after the philosopher's death; at that time it had a worldwide echo as scarcely any other text.[9] A passage from the discussion's minutes, which was replaced by a less personal formulation at Heidegger's request, portrayed the aged philosopher at work, endeavouring to introduce his fellow-thinkers into the essential questions, and thus to bring them onto his path of thought: 'I believe I am on the path, though I don't know whether I will complete it.' Heidegger elucidated what provoked him to his work when in May 1976, a few days before his death, he sent the *Spiegel* editor Georg Wolff his manuscript 'Modern natural science and modern technology' ('Neuzeitliche Naturwissenschaft und moderne Technik') with the dedication: 'A question as of yet unthought' (*Eine noch nicht bedachte Frage*).[10] The confrontation with the 'unbridled beast' (as Heidegger put it in his last Marburg lecture) had at least since the crisis Winter of 1929–30 pushed Heidegger in a direction which also made possible the temporary alliance with the National Socialist Revolution. That Nietzscheanism, which at once both joined and juxtaposed life and spirit (*Geist*) to each other, seemed to conceptualize the constellation of the time: a new transfigured figure (*Gestalt*) for the pain of becoming (*das Werden*) was to be wrested out of the antagonism of the Dionysian and the Apollonian. However, with the young Nietzsche's thoughts on art,

Heidegger sought not only an historical greatness in a world reconfigured by myths; he also accepted how the later Nietzsche juxtaposed Dionysus against the world-negating Christian eschatology, yet nevertheless proclaimed the death of traditional God. Ernst Jünger at that time gave this Nietzscheanism the final edge: in the total mobilization of all energies was to be won that contact with the 'mythical' which also through death in the *matériel* battle was to enable the experiencing of the identification with a meaning-giving and surviving figure (*Gestalt*): the soldier and the worker.[11] When Heidegger broke off his direct political engagement, he saw the constellation of the times more validly addressed in Hölderlin's discourse of the truth, which eventuates (*sich ereignet*) despite the 'long' time. The Germans, this restless and threatened people (*Volk*) in the endangered midst of Europe, appeared called upon to find a new future from its relationship to the Greeks. Yet even before National Socialism openly trod the path of struggle for world domination, Heidegger, in the lecture course *Einführung in die Metaphysik* from Summer 1935,[12] posited the retrograde tie (*Rückbindung*) of the still only mechanical mobilization and organization to the question of race alongside the retrograde tie of Bolshevism to the notion of 'class', although also in tandem with the collusion of groups in Western liberalism. Heidegger labelled all of these externalized formations of a common life as being completely oblivious to the actual task at hand. The *Spiegel* interview of 1966 repeats this view of things: National Socialism, as it were, had 'gone in the direction', of searching for a relationship to the essence of technology; 'these people, however, were far too unreflective in thinking to attain a truly explicit relationship to that which today happens and which is underway for the last three centuries'.

In a famous annotation to the lecture course from Summer 1935 Heidegger contrasted the actual National Socialism with its 'inner truth and greatness', namely the attempted confrontation with modern technology; the *Spiegel* interview still claimed an 'inner truth' for the confrontation of poetry and thought (*Dichten und Denken*) with the destiny (*Geschick*) which determines our time. The universal scientific-technical grasp (*Zugriff*) of what is (including the human being), should be shown its limits; in the Being of beings the withdrawal (*Entzug*) should be found, which withdraws the assigned (*das Zugewiesene*) from disposal (*das Verfügung*) and thereby allows to flash up that which grants meaning and binds, which is named the holy and the divine. Metaphysics, which found its culmination in a philosophical theology,[13] is dismissed as an illusion. Thus Heidegger maintains that philosophy and in general 'all the merely human musings and endeavours' on their own cannot bring about a direct transformation of the present state of the world.

Only a god can yet save us. The single possibility remaining for us is in thinking and in poetry to prepare a readiness for the appearance of god or for the absence of god in the downfall; that we go down in the face of the absent god.

Heidegger says only 'a' god, but that means: a 'god' such as showed itself high over the city of Athens in the meaning-bestowing form of Athena of the Parthenon and who orientated the entire life of the *polis*. Thus art as a counterforce to the technological disposal (*Verfügung*) comes into play, an art which still or once again possesses a cultic significance for life. The question remains of whether we are vouchsafed such an art, which allows the saving power to appear or which wakens a preparedness for it. Does Heidegger in the cited sentence mean that the 'appearance of god' (*Erscheinung des Gottes*) could save, but the 'absence of god' (*Abwesenheit des Gottes*) is ensnared in a downfall, which after the self-destruction of Europe as the former centre of the world also distorts the essence of man itself there? A few sections later Heidegger speaks of the 'preparation for the readiness of one's self-exposure for the arrival or the absence of god' (*Vorbereitung der Bereitschaft des Sich-Offen-Haltens für die Ankunft oder das Ausbleiben des Gottes*): 'Also the experience of this absence is not nothing, rather a liberation of man from that which in *Being and Time* I called the deterioration to being [*das Seiende*]'. In any case this indicates that one cannot reckon history according to happy or unhappy peoples or periods. He who flounders can also learn what he should have lived by, and towards which task his life was actually oriented. In its very downfall Europe can teach the world something! The Greeks knew that the downfall of a tragic figure is no mere loss: in her downfall Antigone showed a new experience of the divine, through which another time could be born (at least in Hölderlin's translation and reinterpretation of this tragedy, which was definitive for Heidegger).[14]

Half a year after the *Spiegel* interview, on 4 April 1967, Heidegger took his leave from public activity before the Academy of Sciences and Arts. His speech 'The provenance of art and the determination of thinking' ('Die Herkunft der Kunst und die Bestimmung des Denkens')[15] reminds the age of the sciences and technology that the Greeks founded as the beginning for the Western European sciences and arts. The inception (*Anfang*) of a destiny (*Geschick*) however is the greatest power, which prevails before all belated followers and also awaits us as the future. Athena, 'the erstwhile protectoress of the city and the country', is to accompany the lecture. The first step of the speech asks: what does the goddess say of the provenance of art? Athena is she who advises in manifold ways (in Homer, in the metope of the temple to Zeus in Olympia). For that reason she could assist those who weren't yet technicians but also not mere craftsmen (*Handwerker*), that is, the artists.

Besides the *techne* the *technites* needed a knowledge (*Wissen*) which looks ahead toward the standard-rendering invisible power (*das maßgebende Unsichtbare*). Athena can bestow counsel because she has the shining bright eye that also penetrates the night and renders the invisible visible. She who gives counsel and illuminates at once is also the meditating one (*die Sinnende*). She gazes at the border stone (as in the holy relief in the Acropolis museum). Only from the border does that, which is, find its essence: the mountain and the island, the glistening olive tree as the goddess's gift to her country. The *techne* belongs to the rising (*das Aufgehen*) and the abiding (*das Verweilen*), that is, to the *physis*. In order for *physis* and *techne* to come together, an element is needed, which even archaic Greece only cautiously touched on: the lightning of Zeus, which directs everything. According to Aeschylus, Athena guarded the key to the house in which this lightning lies locked and sealed.[16] Thus could art earn its provenance from the rule of this goddess.

In a second step of the speech Heidegger needs to prove that the gods have fled: 'Delphi slumbers' (*Delphi schummert*). Art is no longer work (*Werk*) in the sense of Heidegger's artwork essay.[17] Art no longer provides through its works the orientation to 'a world of the folkish and the national' (*eine Welt des Volkhaften und Nationalen*); rather art now belongs with the sciences and technologies in a 'world civilization'. In the world of this civilization science itself, to speak with Nietzsche, has been conquered by method, namely by the secured disposal (*Verfügung*) of all that is. Method unfolds as cybernetics. As futurology, cybernetics also draws into the programmable the single possibility of interference, the apparently free human action. The presupposition of these cybernetic-futurological graspings is the society which, relying exclusively on itself and its power of disposal (*Verfügungsmacht*), posits itself as an industrial society above its institutions as the constructed spheres of the lived world. In a third step Heidegger asks from where in this world a thinking might come which can reflect upon the provenance of art. Cybernetics encloses the human being and his relations to the world in the most extensive feedback control system of inter-relation between human and world; the futurology brings that captivity into the programmable, and the industrial society exists only 'on the basis of its incarceration within its own construct' (*auf dem Grunde der Eingeschlossenheit in ihr eigenes Gemächte*). Does modern art as well fall prey to the self-regulating artistic process? In that case, the claim, from which it lives, comes from the scientific-technological world; art too becomes an autonomous (perhaps compensatory) feedback of information in the feedback control system of industrial society. Heidegger searches for another path. Indeed he must ask whether the hope, as it is posited by Ernst Bloch as a principle,[18] is 'not the unconditional selfishness of human subjectivity'. But even Heidegger does not want to renounce world civilization, rather he wishes to take a step back from it; and from the distance gained he wants to perceive it as a destiny (*Geschick*), without being pulled back into its tendency towards its self-enclosedness (*Sichverschließen*). For that reason he recalls the inceptive (*das Anfängliche*), that from which art could become art, yet also that from which thinking (*das Denken*) is claimed, if it accepts that which was foretold, yet which remained unthought. The Greek light, which sets everything within its borders, indicates a concealment (*Verborgenheit*), which conceals, in that it reveals (*entbirgt*) at the borders. The temporal period of this unconcealment is a clearing (*Lichtung*); yet this clearing is not only light (*Licht*) (as the metaphysics of light and reason intended), but also at the same time darkness; one can also stride through darkness. The word *aletheia* points in this direction, yet this indication in the age of nuclear physics, genetic technology and astronautics must remain something slight and inconspicuous. Heidegger however can end his discourse with a verse of Pindar: the word determines life further in time than the deeds, if language brings it up out of the depths of the meditating heart.[19]

II Technology and politics

Heidegger's thought struck a chord, because it was not learned discussion, specialized analysis or hasty actualization, but because with concentrated seriousness it led to first and last questions, and thus from the point of view of the one and only question of Being problematicized the possibility of philosophy itself. Under a certain necessity Heidegger was led to return to the beginnings of philosophy in the tragic age of the Greeks; he saw this beginning of thinking in close proximity to poetry (*Dichtung*), especially tragedy. One notices in Heidegger's Athens speech that it addresses the Greeks as the founders of our science and arts, but then does not speak of the philosophy and sciences of the Greeks, rather it elucidates the definition of thinking from the provenance (*Herkunft*) of art. Heidegger proceeded in this way, because he increasingly tended to the conviction that the beginning of thought was unable to incorporate its inceptiveness (*Anfänglichkeit*) into itself and therefore was unable to comprehend itself from out of the event (*Ereignis*) of truth. Thus philosophy was able to become the metaphysical grasp of being (*das Seiende*); it was of itself and with the sciences defined as 'technical' (*technisch*). Plato's doctrine of ideas is seen in this way in the light of Nietzsche's reflections on the history of nihilism, even though Nietzsche himself thereby becomes more and more hopelessly entangled in the metaphysical viewpoint. Thereby thinking (*das Denken*) itself cannot wish to remain 'Greek', but rather must lead its inception, which forgot its inceptiveness, to another inception. One of the last achievements of bourgeois culture, tourism by ship, made it possible for Heidegger at an advanced age to visit the sites of the erstwhile Greek life, for example, on the first trip in April 1962, to walk through the lion's alley (*Löwenalle*) in Delos. Yet his very visits to Greece led Heidegger to revise his endeavours to think the beginning of thought: in the last of his four *Seminare* (1973 in Zähringen)[20] Heidegger made it known that he had again changed his interpretation of Parmenides. In Parmenides too there was no trace of the concealing (*Verbergung*) in the unconcealment (*Unverborgenheit*) and thus no trace of the essence of *aletheia*! That was a revocation of the approach with which Heidegger in his 1932 lecture course on the beginning of Western philosophy had articulated a new passage in this path of thought; without any support from the earliest obliterated traces Heidegger had to develop his theme, the clearing for the self-concealing (*Lichtung für das Sichverbergen*). Was not thereby the uni-linear drama of the history of Being also given up, which saw this history of thought yet again 'substantially', that is, solely from the vantage point of the single posited and failed task (of thinking)? For Heidegger's thesis, that the modern natural sciences are already technical in their very approach, one can also adduce parallel reflections in Max Scheler and the neo-Marxists. The development of the nuclear sciences and technologies especially is a convincing example that the scientists are, to a large extent, powerless and helpless, caught in the net of political and economical forces. One can find an early intimation of the victory of method over science in the conclusion of Hegel's *Logic*, where method is absolutized into the development of one logical relationship.[21] The young Marx related the self-sufficient industrial society to a utopian goal, when in his Paris manuscripts for the public ownership of production and a humanized nature he proclaimed even the ontological proof of God.[22] None the less the question arises of whether the first thesis of the victory of method over science is too undifferentiated and thereby finally false. When Heidegger locates the technical approach in modern natural sciences in its mathematicalization, then it must be noted that the Greeks had already made the move to pure mathematics and that Hellenistic astronomy created a mathematical natural science that is not a technical grasp. In point of fact the modern scientific approach is characterized by the analytical experiment which, for instance in the case of motion, abstracts the effective forces of resistance (such as friction) and thus through a methodological abstraction arrives at 'pure' phenomena and their laws. The methodology relativizes scientific labour towards the conceptualization of delimited and abstracted characteristics of reality; for this reason as well Heisenberg's later endeavours will be misunderstood, if they are characterized in a vulgar fashion as a struggle for a totalized 'universal formula'. In his lecture 'The question concerning technology',[23] Heidegger imputes to Heisenberg the thesis that in a physics which takes account of the physicist and his experimental structure, man only encounters himself. Heisenberg however had to contradict this radicalization: physics, in its methodological abstraction and in the critical knowledge of its own boundaries, only interprets certain aspects of our being-in-the-world; the Platonic doctrine of ideas and the correctly understood mathematicalization have abiding validity for this comprehension of reality and exist on good terms with the interpretation of reality by artistic productions.

Being and Time in its confrontation with the Greeks sought to elaborate philosophically a 'science of Being', and thus to make possible a logical and existential differentiation between sciences such as physics, history and theology. Later Heidegger conceived of scientific labour as a single unified process which, as a grasping of the world in itself, is technical and thus inextricably linked with technology. Yet when the essay 'Die Frage nach der Technik' attempts to discuss and situate technology in its 'essence', then technology is interpreted not anthropologically or instrumentally, but ontologically. Technology (*die Technik*) is a disclosure (*Erschließung*) of being (*das Seiende*) according to its Being and therefore indicates the constellation of the truth of Being itself. The modern science of atomic energy would be impossible without nuclear technology; it is bound up with the dangers of military and industrial uses of this technology, yet it also discloses unfamiliar underlying dimensions of reality itself. However, such an articulated knowledge remains here limited to certain aspects of our being-in-the-world, and only this methodological abstraction lends to the disclosure of reality its scientific character. The uncanniness of the newly disclosed dimension of reality reminds man drastically of his powerlessness and finitude; the struggle against the dangers made possible by this new technology indicates that this human finitude has its practical dimension.

When Heidegger speaks of cybernetics, then he is indirectly recalling that the mathematical physics cannot sustain unchallenged the role of a paradigmatic science, as it was earlier believed. If biology has received a new significance, then genetic technology indeed demonstrates the advance of mechanistic ways of thinking; yet along with these tendencies in microbiology can be found the holistic characteristics of macrobiology, which on the other hand speaks of the uniqueness and the unavailability (*Unverfügbarkeit*) of life and its 'niches'. Astronautics as well reminds man of the limits of his expansion into space and of the openness and inexplicability of his situation (if there were a conversation, indeed an encounter with other intelligent beings in the universe, then the situation of humanity would drastically change). In the *Spiegel* interview Heidegger finds terrifying the televised view of the earth from the moon, and sees it as an indication of the deracination of man; but doesn't this image also show how improbable and how full of beauty, though also full of dangers is this niche of life on this small blue planet? Nowhere is the concrete technology the unfolding of a single will to power which, eternally recurring, wills itself and thereby demands from humanity its self-sufficient 'industrial society'. This totalizing discourse of society perhaps conceptualizes a tendency in contemporary humanity; but a critical analysis of society must proceed with greater differentiation and can then relinquish such discourse to the vulgar beliefs, which have nothing more to do with science.

Nietzsche saw in the philosophers of the tragic age of the Greeks the testimony that philosophy could also exist among a 'healthy' people. Philosophy in this sense however presupposes the unitary style of a culture. Such a unitary style Heidegger finds only in the negative characteristics of a world civilization. Politics becomes meaningful only when it makes possible through its guaranteeing of delimited life-spheres a disruption of this disastrous universal network. Before the question therefore, of how the present world is apportioned into various dominions, is the question, for instance, of how the opposition of technology and art is vouchsafed a necessary scope of action. The *Spiegel* interview does not want to decide whether one day in China and Russia 'ancient traditions' (*uralte Überlieferungen*) will not contribute to 'making it possible for man to have a free relationship to the technical world'; it is significant that the hopes for the USA are more subdued. Heidegger, who in 1937 in the last public gesture of communication in a newspaper article had called for 'paths towards discussion' (*Wege zur Aussprache*)[24] with France, worked further toward a German–French encounter after the self-destruction of Europe; admittedly Heidegger, who in *Being and Time* still constructed the central concepts of the 'temporal interpretation' with words derived from Latin, wanted to oblige Romance language philosophy to a thinking in the original Greek and its echoed articulation in German. The resistance to the 'unbridled beast' of technology can be formulated with words of Heidegger's friend, the French poet René Char, the 'poet and resistance fighter', who let Hölderlin echo in the pathos of his poems and who united his native Provence with the Mediterranean realm and with Greece:

> In Provence rocket bases are now being built, and the country is being devastated in an inconceivable fashion. The poet, who certainly is not to be suspected of sentimentality or a glorification of the idyllic, told me, the deracination of man, which there is taking place, is the end, if poetry and thought do not once again come to non-violent power.

The question remains, whether this 'contra' (*Gegen*) can be translated into a reasonable political *praxis*. In the *Spiegel* interview Heidegger maintains: 'It is a decisive question for me today how a – and which –

political system can be related to the technological age. I have no answer to this question.' The next clause is indeed fearful: 'I am not convinced that it is democracy.' Heidegger, who at least supported his students in their endeavours to create a new relationship between philosophy and politics, had for himself as well not completely ruled out political activity. Thus, despite the abstinence he imposed upon himself in the political realm after his aberration (*Verirrung*) in 1933, Heidegger joined a people's referendum in late 1975, which demanded a moratorium on nuclear reactor construction.

The decisive question remains of whether the totalitarianism of National Socialism should be seen as a prelude to a perhaps more terrifying future and whether it should be ascribed to a trivialization (that is, determined by the supremacy of instrumental reason, as the Frankfurt School exegesis, similarly to Heidegger, would have it). Is the 'inner truth', through which poetry and thought seek to answer a destiny (in a rupture or in the subversive endeavour to locate inconspicuous beginnings), really only the antithesis to totalitarianisms or rather often a tendency of them? The French Revolution and, more than a hundred years later, the October Revolution wanted to help humanity to achieve a better life; the conviction that history must lead to something absolutely new soon led to the view that in such an exceptional situation every form of terror is permitted, even necessary. This tendency may also have had its role to play in the National Socialist Revolution; a philosophizing, which knew itself committed to the hour and the historical upheaval, could join with the very first uncertain departure. In the *Spiegel* interview Heidegger claims that his lecture course of 1951–2 *Was heißt Denken?* strives for the inner truth of poetry and thought (*Dichten und Denken*), and yet for that reason is so little appreciated. Yet in this lecture course does not the inner truth turn suddenly and without mediation into a perverted triviality, when with Nietzsche and with a glance at the example of old Russia those institutions are recommended which could still be 'anti-liberal' 'to the point of malice'? Hölderlin's short ode is quoted, in which Socrates favours Alcibiades, that is, which portrays the union of wisdom with youthful and fervent beauty.[25] Hölderlin's point of departure is the *Symposium*, but he then conceives of beauty as a tragic process. But Thucydides can instruct us how the youth of Athens brought their city to ruin through their military adventure in Sicily, and how Alcibiades himself could offer his political art first to the Athenian, then to the Spartan and Persian, then finally to the Athenian faction again. Even Hölderlin's political dreams came to an end in that he would have been brought to trial and charged with high treason by Sinclair, had the poet's mental collapse not protected him. The appeal to Hölderlin's verse would be mere palliation, if one overlooks this crass reality and doesn't take it as an admonition for the path through the twentieth century.

III Art and the saving power

The Greek light (*Licht*), as Heidegger says in his Athens speech, places
the simple within its borders: the island, the mountain, the olive tree.
Can this light also lead us to the clearing (*die Lichtung*), as Heidegger
conceives of it from its meaning as a demarcated woodland clearing?
Heidegger relates the Greek light to the lightning of Zeus which directs
everything. In the Heraclitus seminar which Heidegger held with Eugen
Fink[26] he remembers one afternoon of his sojourn on the island of
Aegina: 'Suddenly I heard [sic] a single stroke of lightning. My thought
was: Zeus.' The key to the lightning, which directs the emergence of the
Greek world, is in the safe keeping of Athena; yet if anything, art
and not thinking remained close to this mystery (*Geheimnis*). Thus the
beginning, which the Greeks made for history, is to be related to the
actually posited task only through another beginning of thinking. The
question arises where at all in Greek history one is to establish this
beginning. A goddess such as Pallas Athena who comes to us from
temple reliefs and archaic poetry exhibits murky beginnings, no doubt
pre-Socratic: the tutelary spirit of cities, the aid in battle only gradually
took on its later form, after the Indo-Europeans came to the Aegean
Sea four thousand years ago. That Athena sprang fully armed from the
head of Zeus, or that she safeguards the secret of his lightning, these
are beliefs that were attributed to the goddess only much later. She first
received her name from the Boetian and later Attic Athens and thus
demonstrates how the gods of myths and epics were only retroactively
associated with definite locales and regions. Is there at all anything simple
and inceptive (*ein Einfaches und Anfängliches*) in this history, which one
can hold onto and that can still give us an orientation?

On the one hand the Mediterranean peninsulas and islands must have
seemed to the various groups of migrating Greeks like the land of
Phaeacians, who hosted and fêted Odysseus; on the other hand they
must have been overpowering with blazing sun and storm, and ever-
surging sea and earthquakes, and the elemental forces of nature. The
emigrant newcomers brought with them their supreme sky-god, who also
safeguards the lightning; this god had to join with the earth and mother
divinities already present there. In these conjunctions the simple and the
inconspicuous could have played its role. For instance one of the oldest
shrines, the Temple of Hera at Samos, lay not only in the fertile plain;
the divinity for it was also found in the lygeum (or esparto) bush, which
even today protects fertility (without such hormonal assistance many
children would not be born). Perhaps Zeus came to this goddess as a
cuckoo, which might well mean: with the call of spring. In any case the
Samian Hera is not simply the Hera of Argos; the Artemis of Ephesos
is not (as Heidegger assumes in his Heraclitus lectures[27]) the Artemis of

Delos and sister of Apollo. These figures of Greek divinity were in constant transformation; they existed only in a diversity, which in turn entailed confrontations: even Athena first had to wrest the Attic land from Poseidon, the sea-god and earth-shaker. The Greeks remained exposed to this diverse and conflictual multitude of divine powers in their small cities, which for their part were likewise in continual struggles with each other and thus equally exposed to downfall and arduous rebuilding. When the Age of Goethe sought a new art and literature for its new life-experiences, it wanted to draw its orientation from Greece; can we today assume this orientation, after Nietzsche has lent it a tragic intensity?

When Nietzsche spoke of the Dionysian and the Apollonian, he assumed that Schopenhauer had interpreted the view of Greece and aesthetics in general through the overturning of the metaphysical tradition: it is music which discloses the *an sich*, the ideal forms are finally only an illusion, which makes bearable the pain of becoming. Yet can epic and sculpture really be ascribed simply to the Apollonian, and can tragedy then be interpreted as the mediation of these elements with Dionysian music? Only heroic battle and death counted for Homer's heroes; what happened *in* death was irrelevant. Yet later the graves of heroes and the remembrance of the founding figures were again cultivated and the gods again united with the country; thus could all those tendencies appear anew, including the Dionysian. Nevertheless the Dionysian tragedy began – in the *Oresteia* of Aeschylus – with the invocation of Zeus. When Heidegger in the Winter of 1929–30 enlisted Nietzsche's antagonism to the interpretation of the argument about 'life and spirit' (*Leben und Geist*), he also took up Nietzsche's late slogan 'Dionysus contra the Crucified'. Nietzsche's friend Overbeck had impressed him with the 'world-denying' element of Christian eschatology; therefore with Hölderlin Heidegger inquired after the gods of the earth and the homeland (*die Heimat*) and after the demi-god, who like the Rhine makes an entire land fertile and habitable.

When the catastrophe which had occurred long ago finally became manifest in the Second World War, the saving power remained only as the slightness of inconspicuous beginnings; finally Hölderlin was heard from the echo which he had found in Trakl. If Trakl has him, who is called into the downfall (*Untergang*), encounter the spiritual blueness of the sacred (*die geistliche Bläue des Heiligens*),[28] then Cézanne 'realizes' in the autonomous medium of art as nature does, in that he allows inconspicuous things to emerge out of the blue shadows. The artist, who confined himself to Provence, found his theme not in the disquiet of Paris nor in the contrast between the poverty in the coal-mining region and the solitude of Bretagne, but rather in the peaceful Montagne St Victoire. When Heidegger spoke of Provence as the bridge to Greece, then one wonders to what extent he saw Greece and the inceptiveness of its hills, islands and olive trees with Cézanne's eyes. One should not search out a place in the many centuries for that which is inceptive (*'das Anfängliche*) in Greek history, in which for example Athena first becomes the figure we encounter in the temple pediments and the literary texts. The inceptiveness lies rather in that modest area, in which *mythos* and *logos*, *Dichten* and *Denken* separate from each other, yet according to Heidegger always remain in the vicinity of a common striving for a native (*heimatlich*) dwelling on this earth. However, perhaps thought in the tragic age of the Greeks was also more various than Heidegger wants to perceive it, yet always marked by a colonial push for world conquest, which must be separated from the traditional embeddedness in *mythos*. Thus Plato's doctrine of ideas in a genuine way might continue 'Greek' motifs, which for us today have a practical relevance. Philosophizing incidentally is related not only to poetry (*Dichtung*) and to a cultic form of art; it has its beginnings also in its diverging from other life-spheres. Therefore there can be no single beginning of philosophy at all. When work for everyone grows scarce and leisure time becomes problematical in an industrial society, then art for its part cannot be so intertwined with the active life, as once may have been the case in the Greek dawn.

Heidegger tried to remove Athens from its contiguity with Jerusalem, Carthage and Rome; thus he had to overlook how Hölderlin in the final phase of his creativity relativized the relation of German to Greek and the hope for an immediate return of the divine. In 1939–40 Heidegger put aside the problematic of the hymn 'Wenn am Feiertag' with Norbert von Hellingrath by deleting the fragmentary conclusion of the poem; in 1959 he simply omitted the thematically more complete early version of the late draft for the hymn 'Griechenland'. Yet that version shows that by then for Hölderlin the *mythos* of the Greeks had become only one of the guises of God and that the poet's concern was rather the transition over the Alps, indeed the Hesperian festivals such as the wedding of the heir to the Württemberg duchy in London. Thus the verses of 'Patmos' that speak of the danger, in which the saving power also grows, are reversed by Heidegger: the verses no long warn against seeking a rupture and breakthrough to the divine at any cost, rather they refer to the nihilism in which every trace of the divine is gone. According to the Patmos hymn, however, the danger lies in the fact that the peaks of time (*Gipfel der Zeit*) are distressingly near. These peaks, which remain separate from each other, are those above which the eagle flies in the hymn 'Germanien': the mountains of Asia, where patriarchs and prophets encountered their god, the sacred mountains of Greece and Italy, the Alps, which led to Northern Europe and its history. Only the faithfulness, which keeps the one and the other and which mediates all that is bestowed, furthers the growth of the saving power. For that reason

Hölderlin flies with the Genius not only to Taurus in Asia, but also returns to the Aegean: above the shadowless straits of the sea, which are familiar to the sailor, he finds among the beloved Greek islands near Samos and Delos also Patmos, the island monastery. There Saint John, in a cave on the precipice of a mountain, underwent and recounted that revelation, which teaches endurance in dark times.

With Hölderlin's elegy 'Brot und Wein' Heidegger charged poets with the task of bringing back to mortals the trace of the absent gods. But he never considered how Hölderlin spoke of the trace in the hymn 'Der Einzige': in the desert as the place of temptation toward hubris Christ preserves 'the trace of a word' (*die Spur eines Wortes*), namely that of law, which is already written but once again is becoming a mere trace. The Hesperian especially, who perforce stands in an open history, should not reject the helpful trace. However, in 1942–3, when Heidegger in his lecture course *Parmenides*[29] tried to dissolve the opposition of *mythos* and *logos* and to regain a tragic experience of god, he was only concerned with Sophocles and the Greeks; the poet who placed Shakespeare next to Sophocles is depicted thus: 'Goethe is a disaster' (*Goethe ist ein Verhängnis*). According to Heidegger humanism mixed together that which is incomparable and made Greek antiquity 'completely' inaccessible. Certainly one needn't think immediately of Shakespeare's persiflage of the Greeks in *Troilus and Cressida*; but Shakespeare and Goethe belong to us. And in fact from the 1950s onward one sees Heidegger again and again presenting the path to that which is simple with a citation from Goethe, yet the gesture of rejection and the retreat to a proper and authentic (*ein Eigenes und Eigentliches*) remained. Thus can Heidegger, who none the less introduced 'deconstruction' (*die 'Destrucktion'*) into phenomenological philosophy, speak of contemporary literature in the *Spiegel* interview only as 'largely destructive'. When Heidegger was in Bremen once he made a rare visit to the theatre and there saw Lorca's *Dona Rosita*, in which the old professor Don Martin is mocked cruelly by his students and only the old housekeeper finds his question, 'What is an idea?' still meaningful. At this point Heidegger whispered to his companion, 'Yes, that's me'. Thereby he seemed to interpret himself – 'with an expression of composed sadness', as Lorca's stage directions put it. Yet only with difficulty could the critic of humanism have adopted the humanity of Molière, who has the extravagant Sganarelle in *L'escole des maris* say that it is 'better to belong to the multitude of fools than to be wise and stand alone against all the rest'. It is inconceivable that Heidegger could have recognized the grotesquerie of those statements from his *Parmenides* lecture course, which in the sombre winter of 1942–3 after the establishment of the 'Final Solution' and in the face of Stalingrad yet portrayed the Germans as 'invincible', if only they would repeat

the Greek inception (*Anfang*) and remain 'the nation of poets and thinkers' (*Volk der Dichter und Denker*).

In his 'Rektoratsrede'[30] of 1933 Heidegger repeated the old legend of
the Greeks, that Prometheus was the first philosopher; with reference to
the *Prometheus* of Aeschylus Heidegger claimed that all knowing
(*Wissen*) remained exposed to the predominance of fate (*Schicksal*). In
the meantime man in another Promethean feat had acquired atomic fire,
but also the atomic constituents of life itself, which is now threatened in
its entirety, world-wide. Because of this humanity is now forced into a
new solidarity and responsibility, and thus Heidegger's discourse on 'the
planetary nature' (*das Planetarische*) of world civilization can be taken
not only negatively as a reference to deracination. Out of the very
dangers now arisen must man not bring his new intellectual and practical
abilities to bear on prospects which Heidegger himself in 1927–8 with
Max Scheler in a fully positive way had called 'metaphysical' or 'meta-
ontological'? In this dimension philosophizing might enter into a new
proximity to art; this proximity signifies however neither an overtaking
of the mythical through *logos* nor the presupposition of an absolute
inceptiveness (*Anfängliche*) in art. Hegel's discourse on 'the end of art'
is qualifiably correct, in so far as art and poetry (*Dichtung*) constitute
only one particular human pursuit alongside others (for instance the
scientific-technical). Sometimes it seems as if in his final years Heidegger
in his reflections on his companion in misfortune, Cézanne, had forgotten
Paul Klee, from the perspective of whose theoretical writings Heidegger
had wanted in 1959 to write a 'pendant' to his artwork essay.[31] With all
the inclination to the lyrical, the phantastic and also the farcical, Klee
developed an art which consciously constructs and composes its figures
out of the simplest elements. Thus in his art Klee incorporates the
technological (*das Technische*), so as finally to induce from it the acceptance of finitude and fatefulness (for example the acceptance of one's
own death in the last picture *Tod und Feuer* (*Death and Fire*), which
Heidegger included with Trakl's poems and Heisenberg's formulae in his
foreword to *Being and Time*[32]). The saving power can grow only when
humanity as a whole assumes responsibility for an always precarious and
always finite and limited life on this concrete planet. The future name
of the divine must derive its meaning from this adoption of a fateful
finitude. The simple and the initial can only be found from within the
overarching situation. For that reason Paul Celan in a poem, which at
first was to be a poem of Hiroshima, also related the simpleness of the
cherry blossom to that 'here', which remains determined by Hiroshima:
'Here – where the cherry blossom wants to be darker than there'.[33]

Translated by Henry Pickford

Notes

1 Translator's Note (hereafter T.N.): *Der Denkweg Martin Heideggers* (Pfullingen: Neske, 1963); *Martin Heidegger's Path of Thinking*, tr. Daniel Magurshak and Sigmund Barber (Atlantic Highlands, NJ: Humanities Press International, 1987).

2 Cf. the Afterword to the second edition of *Der Denkweg Martin Heideggers* (Pfullingen: Neske, 1983), p. 355. The latter account in *Heidegger und die hermeneutische Philosophie* (Freiburg/München: Verlag Karl Alber, 1983) continues the thought of the first book with the attempt to reincorporate Hiedegger's themes into a hermeneutical philosophy.

3 T.N.: in *Zur Sache des Denkens* (Tübingen: Max Niemeyer Verlag, 1969), pp. 61–80; 'The end of philosophy and the task of thinking', in *Basic Writings*, ed. D. F. Krell (New York: Harper & Row, 1977), pp. 373–92.

4 T.N.: cf. Heidegger's text 'Adalbert Stifter's "Eisgeschichte" ' (1964), in *Aus der Erfahrung des Denkens 1910–1976*, GA 13 (Frankfurt: V. Klostermann, 1983), pp. 185–98.

5 T.N.: M. Heidegger, *Nietzsche*, 2 vols (Pfullingen: Neske, 1961); M. Heidegger, *Nietzsche*, 4 vols, ed. D. F. Krell (New York: Harper & Row, 1979–87).

6 'Der Weg zur Sprache', in Martin Heidegger, *Unterwegs zur Sprache* (Pfullingen: Neske, 1959), pp. 157–216; 'The way to language' in *On the Way to Language*, tr. Peter D. Hertz (New York: Harper & Row, 1971), pp. 111–38.

7 T.N.: Title of one of the lectures from *Nietzsche II*. Translated as 'Nihilism as determined by the history of being' in *Nietzsche*, vol. IV, ed. D. F. Krell.

8 T.N.: *Einblick in das was ist*. Bremer Vorträge (1949). 'Das Ding'; 'Das Ge-stell'; 'Die Gefahr'; 'Die Kehre'.

9 'Nur noch ein Gott kann uns retten', in *Der Spiegel*, Hamburg, 31 May 1976, pp. 193–219. English trs, 'Only a god can save us now', tr. D. Schendler, *Graduate Faculty Philosophy Journal*, 6 (1977), pp. 5–27; ' "Only a god can save us": *Der Spiegel*'s interview with Martin Heideggger', tr. M. P. Alter and J. D. Caputo, *Philosophy Today*, 20 (1976), pp. 267–84.

10 *Der Spiegel*, 31 May 1976, pp. 193ff.; 30 August 1976, p. 3. On the question, to what extent a practical or political philosophy might adjoin Heidegger's reflections on the significance of technology, see the controversy between A. Schwan and myself: cf. the Afterword to the second edition of Otto Pöggeler, *Philosophie und Politik bei Heidegger* (Freiburg/München, 1974), pp. 155ff. Cf. also Otto Pöggeler, 'Heideggers politisches Selbstverständnis' in Annemarie Gethmann-Siefert and Otto Pöggeler (eds), *Heidegger und die praktische Philosophie* (Frankurt: Suhrkamp, 1987).

11 T.N.: Pöggeler is referring to two texts by Ernst Jünger; *Der Arbeiter* (1932) and *Totale Mobilmachung* (1934). Cf. Heidegger's response to Jünger in 'Zur Seinsfrage', in *Wegmarken* (Frankfurt: Klostermann, 1967), pp. 379–420; *The Question of Being*, tr. with Introduction by William Kluback and Jean T. Wilde (New York: Twayne, 1958). On Heidegger and Jünger see Michael E. Zimmerman, *Heidegger's Confrontation with Modernity: Technology, Politics and Art* (Bloomington, Ind.: Indiana University Press, 1990).

12 T.N.: *Einführung in die Metaphysik* (Tübingen: Max Niemeyer, 1976); *An Introduction to Metaphysics*, tr. R. Manheim (New Haven: Yale University Press, 1955).

13 T.N.: On this point cf. for example 'Die onto-theo-logische Verfassung der Metaphysik' in *Identität und Differenz* (Pfullingen: Neske, 1957), pp. 31–68; *Identity and Difference*, tr. Joan Stambaugh (New York: Harper & Row, 1969).

14 T.N.: On Heidegger and Antigone cf.: George Steiner, *Antigones* (Oxford: Clarendon Press, 1986), pp. 131–5, 174–7.

15 In *Distanz und Nähe. Reflexionen und Analysen zur Kunst der Gegenwart (Festschrift für W. Biemel)*, ed. Petra Jaeger und Rudolf Lüthe (Würzburg, 1983). T.N.: to my knowledge no English translation of this text exists.

16 T.N.: cf. Aeschylus, *Eumenides* ll. 824–6.

17 T.N.: 'Der Ursprung des Kunstwerks', in *Holzwege* (Frankfurt: Vittorio Klostermann, 1950), pp. 1–72; 'The origin of the work of art', in *Basic Writings*, ed. David Farrell Krell (New York: Harper & Row, 1977), pp. 143–88.

18 T.N.: Ernst Bloch, *Das Prinzip Hoffnung*, now in Bloch's *Werkausgabe* (Frankfurt: Suhrkamp, 1985); *The Principle of Hope*, tr. Neville Plaice, Stephen Plaice and Paul Knight (Cambridge, Mass.: MIT Press, 1986).

19 T.N.: Heidegger at the conclusion of the Athens speech cites Pindar's Fourth Nemean Ode, ll. 6–8:

ῥῆμα ὅ ἐργμάτων χρονιώτερον βιοτεύει,
ὅτι κε σὺν Χαρίτων τύχᾳ
γλῶσσα φρενὸς ἐξέλοι βαθείας.

('Longer than deeds liveth the word, whatsoever it be that the tongue, by the favour of the Graces, draweth forth from the depth of the mind'. Sir John Sandys, *The Odes of Pindar*, Loeb Classics (Cambridge, Mass.: Harvard University Press, 1968), p. 347.)

Heidegger translates the passage as:

Das Wort aber weiter hinaus in die Zeit als die Taten bestimmt es das Leben, wenn nur mit der Charitinnen Gunst
die Sprache es herausholt aus der Tiefe des sinnenden Herzens.

20 T.N.: *Wer Seminare*, *GA* 15, ed. Curd Ochwadt (Frankfurt: V. Klostermann, 1986).

21 T.N.: cf. the final chapter of Hegel's *Wissenschaft der Logik*, 'The absolute idea':

More exactly, the absolute Idea itself has for its content merely this, that the form determination is its own completed totality, the pure Notion. Now the determinateness of the Idea and the entire course followed by this determinateness has constituted the subject matter of the science of logic, from which course the absolute Idea itself has issued into *an existence of its own*; but the nature of this its existence has shown itself to be this, that determinateness does not have the shape of a *content*, but exists wholly as *form*, and that accordingly the Idea is the absolutely *universal Idea*. Therefore what remains to be considered here is not a content as such, but the universal aspect of its form – that is, the *method*.

Hegel's Science of Logic, tr. A. V. Miller (Atlantic Highlands, NJ: Humanities Press International, 1969), p. 825.

22 T.N.: cf. Karl Marx, *Economic and Philosophical Manuscripts* (1844).

23 T.N.: 'Die Frage nach der Technik', in *Vorträge und Aufsätze* (Pfullingen: Neske, 1954), pp. 9–40; 'The question concerning technology', in *The Question Concerning Technology and Other Essays*, tr. with introduction by William Lovitt (New York: Harper & Row, 1977), pp. 3–35.

24 T.N.: 'Wege zur Ausprache', in *Aus der Erfahrung des Denkens 1910–1976*, pp. 15–22.

25 T.N.: *Was heißt Denken?* (Tübingen: Max Niemeyer Verlag, 1954), p. 9; *What is Called Thinking?*, tr. Fred D. Wieck and J. Glenn Gray (New York: Harper & Row, 1968), p. 20. The poem there reads:

> *Socrates and Alcibiades*
> 'Why, holy Socrates, must you always adore
> This young man? Is there nothing greater than he?
> Why do you look on him
> Lovingly, as on a god?'
>
> 'Who has most deeply thought, loves what is most alive,
> Who has looked at the world, understands youth at its height,
> And wise men in the end
> Often incline to beauty.'

26 T.N.: *Heraklit* (Seminar with Eugen Fink) (Frankfurt: V. Klostermann, 1970); *Heraclitus Seminar 1966/67*, tr. C. H. Seibert (Alabama: University of Alabama Press, 1979).

27 T.N.: *Heraklit*, GA 55, ed. Manfred S. Frings (Frankfurt: V. Klostermann, 1987).

28 T.N.: Reference to Heidegger's reading of selected poems of Georg Trakl in 'Die Sprache im Gedicht,' in *Unterwegs zur Sprache* (Pfullingen: Neske, 1959), pp. 35–82; 'Language in the poem: a discussion of George Trakl's poetic work', in *On the Way to Language*, tr. Peter D. Hertz (New York: Harper & Row, 1971), pp. 159–98.

29 T.N.: *Parmenides*, GA 54, ed. Manfred S. Frings (Frankfurt: V. Klostermann, 1982).

30 *Die Selbstbehauptung der deutschen Universität. Rede, gehalten bei der feierlichen Übernahme des Rektorats der Universität Freiburg i. Br. am 27.5.1933. Das Rektorat 1933/34. Tatsachen und Gedanken*, ed. Hermann Heidegger (Frankfurt: V. Klostermann, 1983); 'The self-assertion of the German University: address, delivered on the solemn assumption of the Rectorate of the University Freiburg. The Rectorate 1933/34: facts and thoughts', tr. with an introduction by Karsten Harries, *Review of Metaphysics*, 38 (March 1985), pp. 467–502.

31 T.N.: 'Der Ursprung des Kunstwerks', in *Holzwege* (Frankfurt: V. Klostermann, 1950), pp. 1–72; 'The origin of the work of art', in *Basic Writings*, ed. David Farrell Krell (New York: Harper & Row, 1977), pp. 143–88.

32 On Heidegger's relationship to Klee, cf. H. W. Petzet, *Auf einen Stern zugehen: Begegnungen und Gespräche mit Martin Heidegger, 1929 bis 1976* (Frankfurt: Societäts-Verlag, 1983), pp. 154ff. (pp. 199f. narrate the Bremen–Lorca anecdote). Cf. also Pöggeler, *Die Frage nach der Kunst. Von Hegel zun Heidegger* (Freiburg/München: Verlag Karl Alber, 1984), pp. 26ff. On Heidegger's relationship to painting, cf. Pöggeler's Leiden lecture 'Kunst und Politik im Zeitalter der Technik', in *Heideggers These vom Ende der Philosophie Verhandlungen des Leidener Heidegger – Symposiums April 1984*, ed. R. J. A. van Dijk, M. F. Fresco and P. Vijgeboom (Neuzeit und Gegenwart, Bd. 5) (Bonn: Bouvier/VVA, 1988). On Heidegger's encounter with Celan, cf. the chapter 'Todtnauberg', in Pöggeler, *Spur des Wortes. Zur Lyrik Paul Celans* (Freiburg/München: Verlag Karl Alber, 1986), pp. 259ff.

33 T.N.: Periphrastic citation of the first line of Celan's poem 'Hier' ('Here') from the collection *Von Schwelle zu Schwelle* (*From Threshold to Threshold*).

The first full line reads: 'Hier – das meint hier, wo die Kirschblüte schwärzer sein will als dort' ('Here – that means here, where the cherry blossom wants to be darker than there').

11

Heidegger's idea of truth

Ernst Tugendhat

Heidegger is perhaps the only philosopher of our time who has tried to advance the classical tradition of ontologico-transcendental philosophy in a productive way. That this advance is presented as an overcoming and one in which philosophy is finally brought to a close, has of course made it suspect. The critique of Heidegger's thought is mostly carried out upon a plane which, for its part, is no longer that of the ontologico-transcendental tradition. Assuming that it still makes sense today to hold on to the formal idea of an ontological or transcendental philosophy as a desirable ideal, Heidegger's attempt must be examined specifically with regard to this guiding idea, if we are to arrive at an assessment of our own possibilities.

In this connection, a particular significance can be attributed to the concept of truth. Crudely expressed, one can say that it is a characteristic of the philosophy of the classical tradition that, on the one hand, it is universal (questioning into being in general) while, on the other hand, it starts out from some first, or most original, principle. For ancient metaphysics, this first principle was an absolute being. In modern, transcendental philosophy, the standpoint of knowledge and therewith that of truth comes to the fore, and this from two sides. All beings are questioned with regard to the condition of their possibility in so far as this condition can be known to be true, and the first and most original principle to which this question leads back is not so much an absolute being as rather something which is given with absolute certainty. Thus, Husserl understands his transcendental philosophy as a phenomenological clarification of everything posited as true, with reference to a transcendental subjectivity whose distinctive characteristic lies in its absolute self-givenness, that is, in its character as the sphere of the absolutely evident and therefore of a conclusive truthfulness. Heidegger holds on to the idea of a first and most original principle and, in so far as he does so he remains, formally speaking, in the tradition of transcendental philosophy. However, the self-givenness of subjectivity is for him no longer an absolute principle but rather one that has already been mediated by the ecstatic temporality of Dasein through a precursory openness – its world as history. To this extent the transcendental (thesis) is surpassed. In order to have a word which describes both the continuity and the break, let us call this position 'meta-transcendental'. What is most originally given is no longer characterized by the evidence of an absolute subjectivity but by the disclosure of the finitude of Dasein and – in so far as this disclosure stands out in an open field of play – through the clearing of this very field itself.

I do not want to offer an interpretation of this basic position of Heidegger's but only to ask what it means that Heidegger, for his part, also understands this transformed transcendental 'reference back' in terms of a first and most original truth, even though he abandons the standpoint of certainty and evidence. In *Being and Time* he describes the disclosure of Dasein as the first and most original phenomenon of Truth (*SZ*, 221) and correspondingly, in his later writings, he describes the clearing of the world as the 'Truth of Being'. This is not obviously in line with our normal understanding of truth and actually presupposes Heidegger's own theory of truth, a theory for which truth is determined as 'disclosure' and 'un-concealment'. One therefore has to subject this theory to an interpretation if one wants to understand with what right and with what meaning Heidegger chooses the word 'truth' to characterize his meta-transcendental reference back.

In order to keep the interpretation within a controllable frame, I propose to limit myself to a particular text, section 44 of *Being and Time*. Here Heidegger develops his concept of truth for the first time. To be sure, all the various aspects of his position have not yet been developed and the conception as a whole experiences a characteristic modification later through the so-called *Kehre*. But the essential decisions, those which remain fundamental for everything that follows, are already taken here and can therefore best be grasped here.

The treatment of the concept of truth is carried out in two steps. In a first section (a) Heidegger handles propositional truth and comes to the conclusion that it must be understood as 'uncovering' (or – as Heidegger says later – unconcealing). This finding then allows him in section (b) to extend the concept of truth to all that can be uncovered and to any disclosure. And since it has already been shown, in *Being and Time*, that all uncovering of inner-worldly beings is grounded in the disclosure of world, this latter proves, in the end, to be the 'most original phenomenon of truth'. Section (b) therefore brings us back to our initial question, how, for Heidegger, the concept of truth can be the fundamental philosophical concept. But the decisive step in the argument of §44 is certainly the thesis of section (a) that the truth of an assertion lies in its disclosiveness. Once this has been conceded, everything else follows almost deductively. So first, we have to carefully interpret this analysis of propositional truth.

It is a methodological necessity that Heidegger takes propositional truth as his point of departure here, as also in the only detailed development of the concept of truth to be found later in 'On the essence of truth' (Wegmarken, *GA* 9). To be sure, the philosophical determination of a basic word does not have to be restricted to any natural understanding of this word but it has to start out from such an understanding all the same. From the standpoint of ordinary understanding, propositional truth is certainly not the only meaning of the word 'truth' but it is the most familiar. That a concept of truth agrees with the propositional concept does not perhaps accomplish much. But it does at least furnish the minimal condition that must be met if it is to feature at all as a concept of truth. Heidegger certainly did not recognize this requirement as clearly as this because he was of the opinion that propositional truth was first brought to the fore by Plato and Aristotle (probably the opposite lies nearer to the truth: it is precisely Homer who in general only speaks of truth in connection with an assertion and Heidegger could only arrive at his position because, in his own conception of the Greek pre-philosophical understanding of truth, he let himself be guided less by actual word usage than by a free interpretation of the etymology). Still, this much can be said: Heidegger does in any case take propositional truth to be primary for us, which places us in need of a new concept of truth. And so we do not run contrary to his intentions if we take him at his word in this respect.

He follows another hermeneutical maxim in that he not only starts out from our natural understanding of language but also holds to the traditional philosophical conception, that is to say, to the well-known formula: *veritas est adequatio rei et intellectus.* How, asks Heidegger, is this correspondence really to be understood?

He prepares an answer by way of a critique of various contemporary conceptions, in particular, the so-called theory of ideas: if we ask about the truth of a statement, it is a question not of a correspondence between an immanent representation and a transcendent being; rather, in the statement itself, we are already directed to the state of affairs. And the statement or assertion is now true when it shows the state of affairs 'as it is in itself', when the state of affairs is discovered to be 'in itself just as it is pointed out in the assertion' (*SZ*, 218).

In a remark, Heidegger refers at this point to the phenomenological theory of truth developed by Husserl in his sixth *Logical Investigation*, and quite rightly so. Just as Heidegger's critique of the theory of ideas only reproduces Husserl's line of argument, so does his positive determination of the concept of truth seem at first only to take up again that of Husserl. Through his specifically phenomenological thematic, through his new distinction between the objective content and its intentional mode of givenness, Husserl arrived not only at a rejection of the theory of ideas but also at a comprehensive interpretation of the adequation formula. The distinction of different modes of givenness of the same object led to the knowledge that, according to the adequation formula, that which had to correspond with the facts is neither the subject (as this formula would wrongly have it) nor something else – for instance, the statement as a physical occurrence – but precisely the same thing, only in other modes of givenness. On the one side, we find the state of affairs as it is intended in so-called signifying givenness, on the other precisely this state of affairs, as it is itself. This 'being itself' of the state of affairs is not something transcendent to experience, but is only the correlate of a distinctive mode of givenness. The state of affairs as it is itself is the state of affairs as it manifests itself when it is itself given to us.

So when Heidegger says that the truth of an assertion consists in this, that it points out or discloses the entity 'just as it is in itself', one might at first suppose that he had simply repeated Husserl's thesis. In which case one would only be in a position to appreciate the specificity of his concept of truth if one asked how and why he still distinguishes his own from Husserl's position. Heidegger himself does not explicitly address the subject. Here we run up against an, at first purely incidental, peculiarity of Heidegger's exposition. He develops his own concept of truth in opposition to that of other contemporary theories but only to those Husserl had himself rejected a quarter of a century earlier. What Heidegger arrives at with his own *line of reasoning* is therefore only the position assumed by Husserl. And the decisive step beyond Husserl is not subject to further justification, indeed, is not even presented as his own step.

In what respects Heidegger's conception differs from that of Husserl can only be extrapolated from the different variations which he presents on the side as equivalent formulations to the former. The first specification runs: the assertion is true when it so indicates or discloses the state of affairs as it is in itself. The 'so-as' is here bracketed by Heidegger. Obviously, this 'so-as' is essential to the truth-relation since it describes the correspondence of the state of affairs just as it is disclosed by the assertion with precisely this state of affairs 'as it is in itself'. It is all the more surprising that Heidegger now introduces without justification a formulation in which the 'so-as' is missing. He says: 'The assertion is true, means: it discloses the state of affairs in itself' (*SZ*, 218). Nevertheless, this revised formulation is still entirely legitimate, for it still entirely corresponds to Husserl's conception. For, since the correspondence, when it proves correct, is an identity, one can, when the assertion points out the state of affairs in the same way as it is itself, also simply say: it captures the state of affairs in itself. The 'so-as' is implied in the 'in itself'. In a third formulation however, Heidegger carries the simplification one step further. He cancels, again without justification, even the 'in itself'. The assertion is true now means quite straightforwardly: it uncovers the state of affairs. In this way he arrives at the thesis: 'The truthfulness (truth) of the assertion must be understood as its disclosedness' (*SZ*, 218). Only with this shift does Heidegger explicitly distance himself from Husserl and reach his own concept of truth which, from now on, he upholds in this formulation alone. So it is all the more remarkable that he does not elucidate further precisely this small, but yet decisive, step. How is this to be explained?

Initially, the claim that an assertion is true if and only if the intended entity is 'in itself just as it is pointed out or discovered to be in the assertion' did not seem to place any special weight on the word 'discovered'. For in general Heidegger does understand the assertion in terms of pointing out and discovering (cf. *Being and Time*, §33). And what the truth of the assertion brought out seemed not to be the fact that the entity should be uncovered by it but rather *how* it is uncovered by it, namely, 'just as it is in itself'. In the latter formulation however it becomes clear that precisely this qualification, which appeared to bring out what is essentially at issue, has become dispensable for Heidegger; with the result that the truth consists in the pointing out and the uncovering as such.

In fact, Heidegger's characterization of the assertion as a pointing out and an uncovering makes an essential advance over Husserl's position. The question is only whether this new conception of the assertion also renders redundant any further qualification with regard to the determination of the truth of an assertion. With Husserl, the act of expression is understood statically, as it were, as a mode of intentionality, as the holding before oneself of a specific objectivity, as representation. Just as Heidegger leaps over Husserl's intentionality in general with the concept of 'disclosure', so he also understands assertion dynamically as a mode of disclosure, as an uncovering and specifically as a pointing out (*apophansis*). With the concept of disclosure, Heidegger seeks to thematize the 'clearedness' of human being, a clearedness which is only implicit in Husserl's intentionality and the corresponding concepts of the tradition. Clearedness is not adopted as a ready-made state; rather, the question arises, how it is brought about. Hence, disclosure is to be understood as an occurrence which is actively related to its opposite – closedness or concealment. In the special case of the assertion, it becomes clear that wherever it arises in a concrete connection with life and with science it is not to be understood in a functionless fashion as the rigid positing of an objectivity, but dynamically as a letting be seen in which we point out something as something, in which we lift it out of concealment, both for ourselves and for others so that, as Heidegger says, it is 'un-concealed'.

And now it is also possible to understand the reason why, with regard to the determination of the truth of the assertion, Heidegger omits the supplement 'as it is itself'. As long as one understands the assertion statically, as a representation or meaning, one is, of course, not entitled to say: an assertion is true if and only if it means the entity in question; for the way in which it means the entity can also be false. One is therefore already obliged to say: it is true if and only if it means the entity as it is itself. If, on the other hand, we understand the assertion as a pointing out and an uncovering, it then seems to be sufficient if we say without further qualification: the assertion is true if it uncovers the entity, for, if it is false, it does not uncover the entity at all but 'covers it up' or 'conceals' it. It therefore already lies in the nature of uncovering as such that it must be true if it really is an uncovering.

Heidegger must certainly have reasoned along these lines when he made the attempt to give grounds for thinking why, for him, the sup-plement 'as it is itself' was redundant. As soon however as one lays out in clear steps the reflection which surreptitiously lies at the root of Heidegger's thesis, its weak point already manifests itself. It lies in the ambiguity with which Heidegger employs the word 'uncover'.

In the first instance, it stands for pointing out, the ἀποφαίνεσθαι in general. In this sense every assertion uncovers, the false just as well as the true. At the same time however, Heidegger employs the word in a narrow and pregnant sense, in accordance with which the false assertion is not so much an uncovering as a covering over. Here, it goes without saying that truth lies in uncoveredness. But what does uncovering mean when it no longer signifies a pointing out in general? How is ἀληθεύειν to be differentiated from ἀποφαίνεσθαι?

Heidegger gives us no answer to this question because he, in distinction from Aristotle on whom he relies (*SZ*, 219), does not explicitly distin-guish the broad from the narrow meaning of uncovering. Hence, even after he first arrived at the conclusion that truth consists in uncovered-ness, he can then still speak of an 'uncoveredness in the mode of the appearing' (*SZ*, 222). In this way, the thesis about truth as uncovering only becomes enlightening if one maintains that the false assertion does not uncover. Instead of this Heidegger now says that, in the false assertion, the entity is 'in a certain sense already uncovered and still not represented' (*SZ*, 222). The covering up of the false assertion does not exclude a certain uncovering. But then, in what sense does the false assertion uncover and in what sense does it cover up? Since Heidegger does not qualify more closely either the uncovering of the true assertion or the covering over of the false, the only way out remains a quantitative determination. In the false assertion, the entity is 'not fully hidden' (*SZ*, 222). Should we therefore say: in the false assertion the entity is partly uncovered and partly hidden? In that case, the false assertion would be put together in part out of truth and in part out of ignorance. Of course, Heidegger never meant to say this. But then, if one limits oneself to the two concepts un-concealment and concealment, there remains absolutely no possibility of determining the specific sense of falsehood, and therefore also of truth.

The characterization of falsehood as a covering up is undoubtedly a step forward. But this covering up is neither a simple subspecies of that concealment from which the *apophansis* receives its pointing out nor a mixture of just such a concealment with un-concealment. The false assertion does indeed conceal but what and how? One has to say: it covers up the entity as it is itself and indeed in such a way that it uncovers it in another way, namely not in the way in which it is itself. For this reason there is no possibility of distinguishing the uncovering in the narrower sense which makes up the truth of an assertion from uncovering in the broader sense of *apophansis*, save by saying that it uncovers the entity just as it is itself. It is simply not possible to get around the supplement 'as it is itself' in the course of characterizing the true assertion. And the determination 'uncoveredness', which is supposed to make this point of view superfluous, does, for its part, actually have to make use of it, if it is going to be a determination of truth.

Even in the smaller writings which follow upon *Being and Time* however, Heidegger, in his attempt to trace the truth of an assertion back to un-concealment, continually passes over the very respect which is at issue in the question of truth. In 'On the essence of truth' (*Wegmarken*, *GA* 9), 'On the essence of grounds' (*Wegmarken*, *GA* 9) and 'On the origin of the work of art' (*Holzwege*, S. 40) the thesis is advanced that, in order that the assertion should be in accord with the entity, the entity in question must show itself, must be uncovered. Thus the truth of the assertion as adequation is grounded in the truth of the entity as un-concealment. That one should call that in the entity which the true assertion is directed toward 'the truth' is meaningful and also corresponds to normal word usage. When, for example, we say: 'we are inquiring into the truth', then clearly we are not asking about the correctness of the assertion. Rather, we are asking how the entity is itself. For Husserl too, the primary sense of truth lay in the truth of the entity. But one simply cannot see that towards which the true assertion is directed as merely consisting in the self-showing, in un-concealment as such. For the false assertion is also directed towards something that shows itself. Even semblance (*Schein*) is an unconcealing.

To be sure, one might object, semblance is not a genuine un-concealment.

But then we only run up again against the same ambiguity that made its appearance in *Being and Time* with the concept of 'uncovering', an ambiguity which Heidegger nowhere clarifies. We then have to say that the true assertion is precisely not directed toward the entity as it manifests itself immediately but toward the entity as it is itself. This difference, within the self-showing, between an immediate and, as it were, obtrusive givenness and the thing itself is never taken into consideration by Heidegger. So although, with his concepts of uncovering and un-concealment, he deepens Husserl's intentionality and givenness, the difference between givenness in general and self-givenness escapes him. Heidegger has quite rightly seen that the distinguishing characteristic of Husserl's concept of truth as well as, in another sense, that of Plato and Aristotle lay in this, that truth must here be understood in a circuit of self-manifestation and givenness. He then went straight on to broaden this givenness in and for itself by inquiring into the condition of its possibility, without noticing that truth, for Husserl as well as for Greek philosophy, in no way resided in givenness as such but in the possibility of a distinctive mode of givenness.

Perhaps Heidegger wanted to say that, in Husserl's talk about self-givenness, there still lurks a surreptitious relation to an absolute being in itself transcending experience. That is nevertheless not the case. Self-givenness, 'evidence', is for Husserl nothing but the – in the final analysis only partial – fulfilment of a significative intention and therefore still remains relative to the latter. The given possesses in itself a depth dimension, the so to speak obtrusively given points beyond itself.

On the other hand, if instead of explaining it as experientially immanent, one avoids the reference to self-givenness altogether, then, in the interests of consistency, one also has to drop the concept of truth. Only in so far as the ambiguity in the talk about uncovering is not made explicit can one be misled about this. If the meaning of unconcealing were exhausted in this, that it lifted the entity out of concealment into the light, then we would have no occasion to talk about truth and untruth. Rather, such talk is called for only because our relation to beings is a specifically mediate one, a relation of such a kind that ordinarily it is not given in itself, though we can nevertheless refer to it and *for this reason* also refer to it as being other than in fact it is. If, as Heidegger has shown, assertion is dynamically directed from concealment to un-concealment then it is, at the same time (if its *telos* is not merely *apophansis* but truth), directed from the subject-matter, as it actually manifests itself, to its self-manifestation. And this second direction is in a certain sense the opposite of the first, in that it is here a question not of bringing the subject-matter to givenness but of validating the givenness with reference to the subject-matter. Only through this second direction does the first acquire a validity, so that the revealing, which would otherwise be arbitrary, is directed toward the entity as it is itself. If, on the other hand, one lets the revealing get directed in accordance with the givenness of the entity, as it shows itself, then this arbitrariness is immediately sanctioned. Being itself is the critical instance of revealing. Only when this second direction is recognized as self-sufficient can it be fruitfully explained with the help of the first, so that one can now say that the false assertion covers up the entity, namely in its being itself and that the true assertion alone really does reveal the entity, namely, as being itself.

Heidegger's new conception of the assertion as an uncovering and a revealing seems, on the one hand, and if it is suitably completed, entirely accommodated to a deepening of our understanding of the truth of an assertion. The functional-apophantic conception of the assertion is an advance upon the static intentional. In particular, this dynamic conception makes it possible to understand not merely the conclusive true assertion but the assertion along the way to the truth as an unconcealing of the thing itself and, in this sense, as a truth-relation (not as truth). On the other hand, this conception leaves out what is specific to the phenomenon of truth, at least in the form in which Heidegger actually worked it out. To be sure, it is implied even if only ambiguously, but for this very reason not conceptually articulated. The specific sense of truth is, as it were, submerged in the notion of uncovering as *apophansis*. And even the specific sense of untruth is, if not simply left out of account, then at least only subsequently taken into consideration, not only in *Being and Time* but also in 'On the essence of truth', so that its antithesis can no longer be essential to the meaning of truth but is instead taken up with it into the truth – which is of course only logical when truth is entitled *apophansis*. The specific problem of truth is overlooked but not in such a way that it is simply set aside and so still remains open. Rather, in as much as Heidegger holds on to the word truth but then deforms its meaning and this again in such a way that we still catch a glimpse of its true meaning, it is no longer possible to see what has been overlooked here.

What Heidegger accomplishes with his new determination of the truth of an assertion first becomes clear in section (b) of §44 of *Being and Time*. Here Heidegger arrives at an unusual extension of the concept of truth over and beyond the domain of assertion. This takes place in two steps.

In order to understand the first step, it is necessary to bear in mind that, in *Being and Time*, the word 'uncover' stands terminologically for any disclosure of inner worldly beings and so not merely for that disclosive assertion which points out but also for the circumspective disclosure of concern (cf. §18). It is on this point that Heidegger now rests his case. If the truth of the assertion according to section (a) lies in uncovering, then it follows (or so he reasons), that in fact all letting be encountered of inner worldly beings is 'true' (*SZ*, 220). One sees that the thesis at which Heidegger had arrived in section (a), a thesis with regard to truth as uncovering which is only insightful in so far as one takes the term in the narrow sense, has actually been understood in the broad sense. Had it not been so understood, he would not have been able to reason in this fashion. Only because, for Heidegger, the truth of an assertion does not lie in the way in which it uncovers but only in that it uncovers is he then able to carry truth over to all disclosure in general without further justification. The question is no longer one of determining whether it is possible to find, in the realm of circumspective concern, a difference corresponding to that between the true and the false assertion. Rather, simply because it uncovers, concern is in general characterized as a mode of truth.

That Heidegger should have extended disclosure beyond intentionality, beyond objective representation, is a significant and decisive step. What has thereby been gained for the problem of truth now has to be considered in detail, whether it be that it has proved worthwhile to draw a distinction between truth and falsehood even in modes of disclosure which lie outside the theoretical realm, or whether it be that, in contrast to other modes of disclosure, those which are truth-related acquire a new emphasis. But it is precisely these questions, questions which it has now become possible to raise as a result of the plane upon which he poses the problem, which are cut off by Heidegger in virtue of his simple equation of disclosure and truth. By comparison with the genuine gain in insight which the concepts of uncovering, disclosure and un-conceal-ment bring with them, their equation with the concept of truth only implies a loss. Not only is what has already been discovered in connection with the truth of assertion left in obscurity again, the new possibilities of broadening the truth-relation which were opened up from the point of view of disclosure, are not made use of. Instead of broadening the specific concept of truth, Heidegger simply gave the word truth another meaning. The broadening of the concept of truth, from the truth of assertion to all modes of disclosing, becomes trivial if one sees the truth of assertion as consisting simply in the fact that it is in general disclosive.

Where this all leads only becomes clear with the second step, which now follows. All uncovering of inner worldly beings is grounded, as was shown earlier (§18), in the disclosure of world. Hence, or so Heidegger is now able to conclude, disclosure of Dasein itself as being-in-the-world, the disclosure of its world (*SZ*, 220f.), is the 'most original truth'. We are now provided with an answer to our initial question, how Heidegger is able to describe as the 'most original truth' what is for him the most originally given, even though it is not characterized by evidence. This determination follows from Heidegger's peculiar conception of the truth of assertion. But it also follows therefrom that, just as what Heidegger earlier called truth had nothing to do with the specific phenomenon of truth, so the same applies here too. In fact, this original disclosure or clearing is, for Heidegger, the product of a temporal field which first makes possible any self-manifestation of beings; *any* self-manifestation and not just the specifically true. That Heidegger speaks here of truth is due simply to the fact that he already calls self-manifestation itself truth.

To the above, one might respond with the question: doesn't it all come down to a matter of terminology? Heidegger's question is in any case the more comprehensive. And in as much as it is questionable to what extent one can distinguish between truth and untruth in what pertains to the disclosure of world, to the understanding of our historical horizon of meaning, as well as in the assertion of matters of fact, is it not then legitimate to understand the opening up of a world as the event of truth? No! – and for precisely this reason: because then the question whether and how the disclosure of world can also be related to the issue of truth in its specific sense, would be covered up.

This can no longer be regarded as a special omission but concerns the problem of truth as a whole. If, for instance, any truth-assertion about inner worldly beings is relative to the historical horizon of our under-standing, then the entire truth problem is now concentrated upon this horizon and the decisive question now has to be: in what manner can one inquire into the truth of this horizon, or is it not rather the case that the question of truth can no longer be applied to the horizon itself? This question becomes untenable for Heidegger, in as much as he already calls any disclosive understanding a truth in and for itself. On the one hand, this makes it possible for us to still talk of truth in connection with understanding and its horizons. On the other hand however, it becomes pointless to inquire into the truth of this horizon since that would only mean inquiring into the truth of a truth.

To be sure, we find here the same ambiguity as previously with the assertion. But the distinction between ἀποφαίνεσθαι and ἀληθεύειν is in reality so clear that no one would waive the right to inquire into the truth of an assertion simply because he was already prepared to attribute truth to *apophansis* as such. With regard to the meaning horizons of understanding, on the other hand, it would be necessary to first consider in what respects a question of truth was at issue here. In so far as our horizons are continually given in an opaque fashion, the immediately given refers beyond itself even here to the thing itself but obviously, in a manner other than the assertion. We could say: when we inquire into the matter at issue with a pre-given assertion, we are trying to verify it. When, on the other hand, we inquire into the matter at issue with a pre-given meaning, we are trying to clarify it. An untrue assertion is false, whereas an untrue meaning is confused or one-sided. The truth of an elementary assertion is decidable. It consists in a correctly comprehended 'in itself'. For the clarification of meaning, on the other hand, the in itself of truth, the 'as it is itself' which emerges in the evidence of complete transparency, is only a regulative idea of the process of critical questioning.

These crude indications suffice to show that in the realm in which Heidegger quite rightly grounds all truth, the explanation of what is specific to the truth-relation brought with it new difficulties and the question concerning the truth did in fact prove unsatisfactory in that a plain evidence and certainty, and therefore a positive hold on the truth, becomes unattainable, with the result that the meaning of the truth-relation comes to consist in something negative and critical. Hence the temptation to solve the problem, like the Gordian knot, by simply understanding truth as disclosure itself. Now, in the name of truth, even the challenge of the critique can be resisted, indeed, understood as the result of a subsequent historical restriction which, in its original meaning, was not contained in the truth-relation at all. If truth means un-concealment, in the Heideggerian sense, then it follows that an understanding of world in general is opened up but not that it is put to the test. What must have seemed so liberating about this conception is that, without denying the relativity and the opaqueness of our historical world, it made possible an immediate and positive truth-relation, an explicit truth-relation which no longer made any claim to certainty and so could not be disturbed by uncertainty either.

Therewith however, what is specific to the truth-relation is not only overlooked but is converted into its opposite. In what way this renunciation of the idea of a critical consciousness made itself known and worked itself out in detail can be shown with reference to the later writings, in particular, the paper 'On the essence of truth'. But the interpretation of Heidegger's analysis of the concept of truth in *Being and Time* already made it possible to advance the thesis that Heidegger overlooks the problem of truth precisely because of the way in which he makes the truth into his foundational concept. That he already calls disclosure in and of itself truth leads to the result that it is precisely not related to the truth but is protected from the question of truth.

This result is however not purely negative. It leaves unaffected the essentials of the position through which Heidegger distances himself from Husserl's transcendental position. And the question remains open whether, through his refusal of the critical approach, Heidegger did not give his own view an orientation which was not necessarily contained in it and, to this extent, left other possibilities open. Heidegger's thought is not so homogeneous as it makes itself out to be and we seem today to have gradually achieved that remove from him which permits us, instead of taking sides for or against, to critically differentiate what does not appear to lead further from what should not be abandoned.

Since Heidegger uses the term truth for what is for him the most originally given – the disclosedness of Dasein (i.e., the clearing of being) but then takes truth in a sense other than the specific one, it becomes all the more pressing to try to place what is most originally given in relation to truth. What is most originally given, 'world' in the sense of the clearing of being is, of course, not the world of the moment, in the sense of whatever is contained within the horizon but rather the open field of play – not in the first instance of beings but of this horizon itself. Correspondingly, disclosure is not taken up in any actual world project. If one now takes account of the specific meaning of truth then certainly one could no longer call disclosure itself, i.e., clearing 'truth'. But one could say that disclosure is essentially directed towards the truth (even though it can also prohibit the question of truth) and that clearing is a field of play whose depth dimension refers to truth and that therefore whoever is preoccupied with the latter is called upon to raise questions concerning the truth and concerning the truth not merely of beings but also of the horizon.

In this way, Heidegger's radicalization of Husserl's transcendental position would be retained. The claim to a self-conscious subjectivity which finds itself in possession of an a-historical, absolute evidence would be discarded, without however giving up Husserl's concept of evidence as the idea of a specific givenness of truth. At the level at which Heidegger poses the problem, evidence does not lose its meaning but has simply to be understood (as in part it is already with Husserl) as a regulative idea, and the same naturally also holds of truth. The immediacy of the hold on evidence would be overcome but, instead of making way for a new but now pre-critical immediacy of truth, the critical consciousness would be retained, though held in that suspense which belongs to its essence. Precisely with regard to Heidegger's meta-transcendental position, for which the most originally given is neither substance nor subject but an open field of play, the critical consciousness would have been able to locate its own non-representative suspense. Here, when transcendental philosophy not merely takes in a historical dimension but where it opens itself up to it and gives up the idea of anchoring itself upon a last ground, it became possible to radicalize and to build up anew the idea of a critical consciousness. But, by the same token, it also became possible to give it up in preference for a new immediacy. In fact, the open field of play could not be held in suspense because, without the depth dimension of truth it was only thought as immediate, whether the immediacy in question was that of the project or of the destiny of un-concealment. And the step from the uncanniness of *Being and Time* to the belonging of the *Letter on Humanism* is only a small one because, what is for the truth question the constitutive moment of reflection, is left out from the very outset. For this reason, Heidegger had to develop his position as an overcoming of the modern philosophy of reflection even though it could just as well have become the radicalization of the latter. Heidegger tied the philosophy of subjectivity down to the dogmatism of self-certainty. But it would be more correct to say that, with the idea of certainty, if only it remains a regulative idea, modern philosophy has radicalized the Socratic challenge of a critical justification and that means the challenge of a theoretical responsibility. In this way, there arose the task of developing the concept of truth in its full scope, a scope which had already been indicated with disclosiveness, but without giving up the regulative idea of certainty and the postulate of a critical foundation.

Translated by Christopher Macann

12

Wittgenstein and Heidegger: language games and life forms

Karl-Otto Apel

1 Thirty years on: a retrospective overview

In this paper, I would like to take up once again and develop still further the comparison between Wittgenstein and Heidegger which I undertook at the beginning of the 1960s in a series of papers.[1] In what follows I shall therefore be concerned with such questions as: what new insights have been opened up since the beginning of the 1960s with regard to the evaluation of Wittgenstein and Heidegger? And what follows therefrom for the critical development of the comparison I made at that time between the two thinkers?

(1) First, it seems to me that my positive evaluation of the epochal significance of both thinkers and of their – at that time still surprising – affinity has been confirmed both by the world-wide influence and by the convergence of their thinking. We no longer – as in my student days in the decade after 1945 – have to contend with the hermetically sealed and starkly opposed fields of (Anglo-Saxon and Scandinavian) *analytical* philosophy and (continental European) *phenomenological* philosophy. Rather, a convergence along the lines of a linguistic-pragmatic, or even a hermeneutical, turn has taken place – right up to (post-Kuhnian) philosophy of science – and this situation is due largely to the historical impact of the convergence between Wittgenstein and Heidegger – whereby American pragmatism functions as the sounding-board and amplifier.

(2) On the other hand, it seems to me that my critique of Heidegger and Wittgenstein – or, more exactly, of both thinkers' inadequately conducted reflection upon the logos (i.e., of discursive language games and their unquestionable presuppositions)[2] – which was only intended as provisional at the beginning of the 1960s, has, in the meantime, acquired

an increased relevance. Briefly, the reduction of philosophy to self-therapy, a reduction which Wittgenstein's critique of language and meaning linked with the pseudo-problems of traditional metaphysics, was paradoxical from the very beginning; for it represented a negation of Critical philosophy's own claims to meaning and truth. Precisely this tendency created its own disciples. Moreover, in Heidegger's ever more radical 'Destruction' of Western metaphysics (and more completely in Derrida's 'Deconstructivism' and in Lyotard's 'Post Modernism', which refer back to Heidegger and Wittgenstein) this tendency is strengthened to the point of attesting to something like the self-destruction of philosophical reason.[3] The opportunity opened up by Wittgenstein and Heidegger of effecting a post-metaphysical transformation and reconstruction of philosophy – from the standpoint of discursive language games containing the conditions of the possibility and validity of a critical hermeneutics and a philosophical critique of language and meaning – seems to have gone to ground in a self-destruction of philosophical discourse through an all too uncritical pursuit of the more problematic suggestions of two of the most prominent thinkers of the century.

The theme of my present paper is already indicated in advance with this ambivalent retrospective view of the historical impact of Wittgenstein and Heidegger.

In the first part of my paper, I would like once again to set out the main points of the convergence of the positive achievements of Wittgenstein and Heidegger in the form of a summary and a supplementation of my previous comparison. Admittedly, and due to the lack of space, this cannot be done with reference to the Wittgenstein and Heidegger editions which have appeared in the meantime. Instead, we shall concentrate upon a selection and a description of what is essential in the historical impact of the two thinkers from the remote perspective of the present.

In the second, critical part of my paper which, in this instance, will carry the most weight, I would like to enter more closely into an argument with Heidegger and Wittgenstein. Finally, I would like to show that neither thinker was fully cognizant of, and so failed to measure up to, the primary requirement of philosophical *logos* or language game, namely, a rigorous reflection, in the medium of public language, upon what is undertaken, believed in and presupposed when philosophical questions are raised and theses developed – or even only suggested. These latter, no matter how self-critical they may turn out to be, must after all claim to consist of statements capable of eliciting assent about how things are in general, that is, about the status of philosophy and its relation to the world.

First of all then, let us proceed with our comparison between the positive achievements of Wittgenstein and Heidegger.

II The linguistic and hermeneutical turn in philosophy

As already indicated, what the achievements of Wittgenstein and Heidegger have in common is the rendering possible of a philosophical critique of language and meaning, on the one hand, and a pragmatic hermeneutic, on the other. What is meant by this? Let us first try to point out the paradigmatic function of the critique of language and meaning with reference to a problematic which plays an exemplary role in modern philosophy.

II.i Wittgenstein's and Heidegger's critique of the mentalism of modern philosophy

The way in which the problem is posed in modern philosophizing might be expressed in the following train of thought:

In reality – and this is the basic assumption – only that is certain which is evident to me in inner experience, therefore not the existence of things and persons in the external world but only that I believe I am perceiving something here and now. Thus my sensational experience or at best my representation of the external world is the only genuine object of my consciousness whilst the things and persons which occupy the external world, including thereunder the common world, are at best a result of justified conclusions drawn on the basis of the data of immanental consciousness. Indeed, even the fact that such conclusions are justified in principle must, in principle, remain doubtful for epistemological philosophy. In the end, everything I take to be real could be something which only appears in my consciousness, for example, could only be my dream. Or, the being of things might only consist in their being perceived, and so on.

With this sketch of a problem, which could always be extended and spun out further, I wanted to point to the paradigmatic presuppositions of modern philosophy, which already figured with Augustine and with the Okhamism of the late middle ages, and which have at least served to determine the problem of consciousness in modern philosophy from Descartes to Husserl. Even today philosophers can be found who take the questions mentioned above to be meaningful and pressing. But one may then be sure that they are thinking in accordance with a pre-Wittgensteinian and a pre-Heideggerian paradigm. The 'intellectual revolution' implied in the critique of meaning which has taken place here can be most effectively illustrated with reference to the 'language games' of late Wittgenstein; more precisely, with reference to the famous thesis that a 'private language' is impossible, in other words, that 'a solitary individual' cannot follow a rule.[4]

From this standpoint, precisely what, after Okham, and even more so after Descartes, featured as the only certainty of human knowledge – the evidence of my inner experience – became irrelevant in the framework of an intersubjectively valid world and self-understanding.

With this however the *subjective certainty* of inner experience, for example, the certainty that I have pains or the Cartesian certainty that I think or that I have specific representations, is not called in question. What is denied is only that this purely subjective certainty can be distinguished epistemologically and that an (epistemological) primacy can be accorded to it over any intersubjectively valid knowledge of the external world.

The reason why the epistemological primacy of inner experience cannot be legitimately sustained is that our knowledge-claims are bound up with the assumption of a shared language (not only with regard to their possible truth but also with regard to their intelligible meaningfulness) and, to this extent are, in the course of the language game, bound up with a publicly controllable rule-following procedure. In this linguistically-founded assumption of the intersubjectively valid understanding of something as something lies the new paradigm for philosophy. For it follows therefrom that the never certain but still publicly intelligible (and with regard to criteria controllable and correctable) experience of the external world must assume a primacy over the subjectively private certainty of inner experience.

Should the epistemological primacy of inner experience be upheld, it would have to be possible for the epistemological subject to validate the certainties of inner experience (for example, the certainties of pain sensations or of a reflection about thinking or about representations immanent to consciousness), in a private language, that is, in a language which no one else could understand because it would only be characterized by 'private ideas' in John Locke's sense. Such a language is however unthinkable, because its rules – both syntactical and semantical – cannot be learned and taught with reference to rule-following criteria.

If the certainty of inner experience were to furnish the basis for the introduction and application of semantic rules, there would then, according to Wittgenstein, have to be something like a 'dictionary' which would only exist in my mind; that is, its word meanings would have to be established by means of definitions relating to private sensations or representations. And in order to re-identify these sensations and representations one would have to refer the table of meanings in the dictionary to the representations in question. In other words, with a view to justifying the correctness of my application of the semantic rules I would never be able to appeal to anything independent of my consciousness. Rather,

I would have to rely upon memory. According to Wittgenstein, this would be as if I could only decide about the question of 'whether I had correctly noted the departure time of a train' by remembering an image of the page of the timetable and not by testing this memory image with reference to a publicly accessible timetable.[5] This means however: it is impossible to establish the distinction between right and wrong. For without recourse to an instance independent of my consciousness there could be no distinction between 'following the rule' and 'thinking one is following the rule'.[6]

In fact, the indubitable certainty of inner experience in the post-Cartesian philosophy of modern times exists precisely because the distinction in question between doing and thinking one is doing, i.e., between being and appearing, would be suspended. And this positive paradigm serves to account for the direction of the modern critique of knowledge, namely scepticism. For Descartes' 'problematic Idealism' which was taken so seriously by British empiricism and which Kant accepted as meaningful even if refutable, this doubt fundamental to the modern critique of knowledge rests on the supposition: whatever is not certain in the sense of inner experience, that is, those judgments which are at times true and at times false because they relate to an external world independent of me, these judgments could always be false because there might be no external world, because it might be the case that everything which is taken to be real simply exists as my dream.

At this point, the critique of meaning implicit in the consideration of language games underlying all world and self-understanding will become still clearer than with the destruction of the paradigmatic illusion of the epistemological primacy of 'inner experience'. For it is enough to check the language game with reference to the phrase '*simply* my dream' (i.e., '*simply* in consciousness') in order to recognize the meaninglessness of the statement 'everything . . . could *simply* be my dream' (i.e., could *simply* be in consciousness). For the language game which makes the dramatic meaning of the phrase '*simply* my dream' possible clearly presupposes as a paradigmatic certainty, that not everything is my dream but that a real world exists. For this language game would have to be suspended as a possible language game if everything were simply my dream. But then, in practice, nothing has changed. One has only introduced a new language game of such a kind that in place of what was previously understood by '*simply* my dream' now has to be introduced with the description 'dream²'.

In his last book (unpublished in his lifetime) *On Certainty* (*Uber Gewissheit* (*U.G.*)), Wittgenstein brought out even more pointedly the suspension of the language game in question through the Cartesian dream argument. He says there: 'the argument, perhaps I am dreaming is simply devoid of meaning because in that case I would have had to dream the

expression of it, indeed, that these very words are themselves meaningful'
(*U.G.*, 383). The self-suspension of this language game is, in the final
analysis, traced back here to the performative contradiction inherent in
the argument – a point to which I will return in the second part of my
paper.

The arguments brought forward so far might suffice to elucidate the
point of the revolution brought about by Wittgenstein's critique of language and meaning. It should also be noted however that Kant's transcendental epistemology is no way immune to what is in question in this
critique of meaning. To be sure, Kant tried to refute the primacy
accorded to 'inner experience' and, accordingly, to 'subjective Idealism'.
And Peter Strawson has undertaken a critical reconstruction of this
argument in *The Bounds of Sense*.[7] But at the same time he also pointed
out that the presupposition underlying a 'transcendental Idealism of consciousness', that, namely, of a transcendental realism, of unknowable
things in themselves, itself rests upon a metaphysical claim which is
undermined by a critique of language and meaning.

It is for example simply not possible to distinguish, along Kantian
lines, the concept of 'appearances' or of the 'world of appearances' on
the one hand from that of 'mere semblance' – in the sense of the
'empirical reality' of objects of experience while, on the other hand,
distinguishing the former from the concept of 'unknowable' but still
'thinkable' things in themselves in the sense of pure appearances.[8] A
language game containing these distinctions – or so Wittgenstein would
have said – cannot function because it cannot be learnt. The sense in
which the concept of 'pure appearances' can be learnt presupposes the
concept 'knowable reality' just as much as it does that of 'mere semblance'. Thus, the reality which we can know cannot be distinguished
over again as 'pure appearance' from a 'noumenal' reality. (In fact, Kant
took note of the problem of the consistency of this conceptual usage in
his *Critique of Judgment*, where he found himself obliged to introduce a
'symbolic use of language' with an 'analogical schematism' to accommodate the epistemological talk about 'things in themselves'.[9])

It is now time to consider the correspondences and convergences
between the 'intellectual revolution' implied by this critique of meaning
and the philosophy of Heidegger.

Significantly, a correspondence can be most easily established between
Wittgenstein and Heidegger on the basis of the latter's early major work
Being and Time, even though in this work Heidegger has not yet introduced language as the 'house of being' and as the 'habitation of mankind'
as he will later in *The Letter on Humanism*. But even here the pre-
linguistic, so to speak, visual-eidetic suppositions of Husserlian phenomenology have already been transcended in favour of the hermeneutic of

a being-in-the-world which has always already been linguistically interpreted, as for example in the following paradigmatic statement:

> This everyday way in which things have been interpreted is one into
> which Dasein has grown up in the first instance, with never a possibility
> of extrication. In it, out of it, and against it, all genuine understanding,
> interpreting, and communicating, all re-discovering and appropriating
> anew, are performed. In no case is a Dasein, untouched and unse-
> duced by this way in which things have been interpreted, set before
> the open country of a 'world in itself' so that it just beholds what it
> encounters.[10]

It is evident that this passage cannot be fitted into the context of a
Wittgensteinian critique of language and meaning without further ado.
Rather, it contains the key to a hermeneutic of language and refers to
the so-called 'pre-structure of understanding being-in-the-world' and, as
such, of an 'already' linguistically disclosed and so pre-figured pre-com-
prehension of the life-world. In *Being and Time* a dimension of temporality or historicality is therewith already in question, a dimension which,
with Wittgenstein, is not articulated in this form. For Wittgenstein concedes that language games are historically engendered and are transformed. But he hardly ever investigates the historical dependence of our
thinking upon the tradition of Western philosophy, a tradition which
preoccupied Heidegger throughout his life. Wittgenstein prefers to construct functional models of as many simple language games as possible
– 'objects of possible comparison', as he likes to call them – which are
supposed to facilitate the description of everyday language usage. To
this extent, Wittgenstein remains throughout his life a trained aircraft
engineer who does not have much feeling for the humanities, while
Heidegger continually embodied the *modus vivendi* of a philosophically
and historically oriented scholar.

For all that, this distinction, which is certainly relevant, does not
prevent the two kinds of analysis, the analysis of the 'everydayness' of
understanding being-in-the-world, an analysis drawn from *Being and
Time*, and the analysis of 'everyday' language games, bound up as they
are with activities, concrete expression and world interpretation and
representing as they do 'cross-sections of life-forms', from throwing light
upon each other, substantiating and completing each other, at least in
part.

In relation to the key points of the hermeneutical stance, cited by us,
an even more direct relation between Heidegger and Wittgenstein can be
set up. It is for example clear that Wittgenstein emphatically substantiates
Heidegger's construction in the sense of an entanglement in the linguistic
world interpretation and in the sense of having always already been

seduced by it. He would admittedly have placed less emphasis upon the aspect of a 'concealing-revealing' world disclosure made possible by the foregoing and more upon the aspect of everyday speech patterns and, to this extent, upon the emergence of the *vacuous language games* of philosophy, games which are no longer connected to a meaningful life-*praxis*.

But it is possible to establish direct correspondences with Heidegger even on the plane of just such a critique of meaning. Such a correspondence is for example to be found in *Being and Time* in the hermeneutical indication that we are only able to understand immanental objectivities made up of sense-data or pure presentations on the assumption that our ordinary understanding of the world assumes the form of being-in-the-world and, to this extent, uncovers the real being itself 'as something' in a 'relationship' or 'meaning context' – the 'roaring car', the 'motor bike' and the 'tapping woodpecker', not the corresponding noises in consciousness.[11] If we wanted to try and grasp our being-in-the-world as 'being-alongside' the immanental sounds in consciousness, *qua* sense data, such a 'being-alongside' could only be understood as a 'deficient modus' of being with things themselves – originally disclosed and comprehended as something. (Analytical philosophers would talk here of a parasitic relationship.)

Moreover, Heidegger not only established the Cartesian position with regard to immanental consciousness as a deficient mode of being-in-the-world, but – as an extension of this critique – also that represented by Husserl under the auspices of 'methodological solipsism', that is, the primordial 'solitariness' of the transcendental ego, which now figures as a deficient mode of being-in-the-world under the auspices of being-with-others.[12]

On the basis of this analysis of being-in-the-world and the world-understanding which belongs to it, Heidegger was able to formulate a hermeneutical equivalent to the epistemological critique of Descartes' dream argument in his own critique of Kant's demand for a proof of the 'existence of things outside me'.[13] He shows that Kant set out from the Cartesian assumption of an 'isolated subject present at hand' and from the primacy of the inner experience of this subject and does not get beyond this assumption even in the proof of a necessary coincidence of the changing and the persisting through time. For this very reason, Kant has to concede that 'problematic Idealism' is both 'reasonable and in accordance with a thorough and philosophical mode of thought', and so 'allows for no decisive judgment until sufficient proof has been found'.[14] Against this position, Heidegger contends that both the distinction and the connection of 'inner' and 'outer' in relation to my consciousness can only be rendered intelligible if the primacy of being-in-the-world as being alongside external entities has already been presupposed. (The corresponding analysis of the way in which language games are learnt arrives at precisely the same result.) In this way Heidegger arrives at his conclusion that the 'scandal of philosophy' against which Kant rails consists not in this, that the proof of the existence of an external world has not yet been provided but in this 'that such proofs are expected and attempted again and again'.[15]

It is understandable that Heidegger's analysis of being-in-the-world as being-with should also lead to an equivalent conclusion relative to the traditional problematic of the existence of 'Other Minds'. Heidegger explicitly rejected the theory (represented by middle Dilthey and by Husserl) of the constitution of the other subject on the basis of 'empathy', for example through an analogical inference, because such a conception wrongly presupposes the reflective self-understanding of an isolated 'I' subject.[16] In opposition to such a position Heidegger shows that 'empathy' does not constitute being-with in the first instance but 'is itself first possible on this basis' and 'gets its motivation from the deficiency of the dominant modes of being-with'.[17] Even this phenomenolgical reference can be strengthened and deepened through a language-game analysis which starts out from possible ways of learning the meaning of personal pronouns, and in such a way that statements by Hegel, Humboldt, G. H. Mead and Rosenstock-Huessy on the equi-primordiality and the reciprocity of communication roles thereby become applicable.

II.ii The deconstruction of world understanding and of the idea of truth in Western metaphysics in general

Up to now, the point of departure for my comparison of the positive results of the thinking of Wittgenstein and Heidegger has been the heuristic standpoint of the critique of mentalism and the methodological solipsism which goes along with it. My aim has been to bring out the hermeneutical-phenomenological equivalences in Heidegger. A still broader horizon opens up for the comparison when one sets out from Heidegger's 'destruction' of the ontology of pure 'presence-at-hand' or, in other words, from the standpoint of a hermeneutical-pragmatic analysis of the 'relational' world – more precisely, in Heidegger's sense: from the world as the 'wherein of self-referring understanding', i.e., the 'upon which' of a letting be encountered of entities in the kind of being that belongs to involvements.[18] On one occasion, Heidegger formulates this conception of the pre-theoretical constitution of the life-world in terms of the possible structural pre-stages of any theoretical use of language.

Between the kind of interpretation which is still wholly wrapped up in concernful understanding and the extreme opposite case of a theoretical assertion about something present-at-hand, there are many intermediate gradations: assertions about the happenings in the environment, accounts of the ready-to-hand, reports on the situation, the recording and fixing of the facts of the matter, the description of a state of affairs, the narration of something that has befallen. We cannot trace back these sentences to theoretical statements themselves, they have their 'source' in circumspective interpretation.[19]

It is clear that these passages can be read in the Wittgensteinian sense of a reference to the multiplicity of non-theoretical language games. Even with regard to the Heideggerian point – the founding of 'theoretical statements' about what is present in a pre-theoretical ('circumspective') 'interpretation' of the 'relational-world', it is possible to find a fairly close equivalence in Wittgenstein, namely – as has yet to be shown – in his pragmatically-oriented critique of the traditional absolutizing of that nominative or descriptive function of language in which the latter is referred to objects.[20] The basis of comparison which is in question here goes further than the Cartesian critique of meaning in this sense that, with Heidegger as also with Wittgenstein, it reaches back to the beginnings of Western ontology and philosophy of language in Plato and Aristotle. Let us first consider Heidegger's 'destruction' of the ontological (or objectively theoretical) world understanding.

First of all we need to show that under the assumption of a purely theoretical distancing from beings as simply 'present-at-hand' something like a *de-worlding* has to make its appearance.[21] This means: the connection of the 'significative-references' inherent in the life-world, in the sense of the relatedness or meaningfulness of entities, is dissolved. In so far as there is now only a 'staring' at the present-at-hand, nothing like a 'hermeneutical synthesis' of 'letting something be as something' is conceivable, and this implies that the basis for a predicative synthesis of the apophantical *logos* also falls away. Putting this together one might conclude: the fact that something is confronted as something standing over against presupposes that beings were encountered previously as something in a pragmatically relational-totality. And, according to Heidegger, this in turn presupposes that human Dasein as being-in-the-world is able to disclose the 'significance' of the world out of the horizon of being-ahead-of-oneself in the mode of 'care', and of 'concernful having to do with'. A purely theoretical consciousness of objects of the kind Husserl assumes is given originally is quite incapable of conferring 'significance' upon the world.[22] (This circumstance was not properly thought through by Husserl even with his introduction of the concept of the 'life-world' in *Crisis*, which seeks to respond to Heidegger's *Being and Time*.)

I would however like to note here that this pragmatic conception of the life-world has to be applied even to the constitutional conditions of scientific theorizing and its connection with experimental *praxis*, if one wants to think with Heidegger beyond the Heidegger of *Being and Time*. For the latter cannot be rendered intelligible in terms of Heidegger's purely theoretical limiting case of being-in-the-world, which implies simply staring at the present-at-hand. For example, the meaning-constitution of the categories of proto-geometry and proto-physics can only be re-constructed under the assumption of a human measuring practice, as Hugo Dingler and Paul Lorenzen and Peter Janich have shown.[23] Something similar is to be found with the category of the causal necessity of the succession of two events, for example, the expectation that, when iron is heated, it expands. This understanding of causal necessity, which differs from mere (Humean) regularity (as is seen in the proposition 'when iron is heated, the earth rotates'), can only be constituted – as G. H. Von Wright has shown[24] – on the pragmatic assumption that the experimental praxis of physics (and before that of human labour) is, through our intervention in the course of nature, able to bring about something which, without that intervention, would not have happened.

If one's point of departure is that these pragmatic conditions of the possibility have to be rooted in a world-constitution already presupposed by science, Heidegger's concept of 'de-worlding' can then be supported with a famous example from the history of philosophy, namely, David Hume's conclusion that nothing like a necessary relation between the occurrence of one natural event and a preceding or succeeding event can be discovered. In my view, Hume arrived at this conclusion simply because he conducted his analysis from the standpoint of a purely theoretical remoteness from the world, because he had abstracted altogether from the worldly involvement of experimental *praxis*. His discovery therefore depended upon a *de-worlding*. (I am, like Paul Lorenzen, convinced that even the most abstract relations (those, for instance, of logic and mathematics) would fall to the ground if, through a total abstraction from the life-*praxis*, we effected a de-worlding in Heidegger's sense.)

However, if the above-mentioned conclusions concerning life-worldly constitutional foundations apply equally to science, an important reservation must be voiced against the Heideggerian thesis about the ontological primacy of the relational world of concernful dealings (i.e., everyday being-in-the-world) over any world conception in the sense of *objectivity*, an objectivity founded by Descartes and Kant but already laid down in that understanding of being implicit in Greek ontology (e.g., nature as the being-there of things in so far as they belong together in a law-governed connection). A state of affairs makes itself known which is never taken into consideration in *Being and Time*. *Between* the existential relational-world, a relational-world which is itself related to a being-in-the-world founded in mineness or ourness and which is, to this extent, subjectively perspectival and historically pre-structured, and the limiting case of de-worlding which arises as the correlate of a simple staring at things (therefore of a complete disengagement from any life-*praxis*), between these two poles which were thematically articulated by

Heidegger, a world-understanding which takes on a destinal significance for the West emerges, that of an objective (and this means at least in principle intersubjectively valid) science. This world-understanding does indeed abstract, and in principle, from any 'purely subjective' (and so also from any collectively subjective) presuppositions but it does not abstract – as does the purely theoretical world-understanding outlined in *Being and Time* – from any practical involvement that, as an epistemological interest, might open up the worldly significance of a referential totality of signs. Rather, it does itself rest upon the quite unique 'discovery' of an objectivity which constitutes itself for every 'consciousness as such' and as that which can be measured and causally explained. That 'existential fore-structure' of the historically-determined world-understanding which first made possible the concrete theoretical constructions of science has not prevented scientific theories and experiments from being intersubjectively reproducible, and to this extent, universally valid.

What I have just pointed out was recognized by later Heidegger to the extent that in his concept of the *Gestell*, scientific world-understanding (an understanding whose roots can be traced back to classical ontology) is explicitly related to a *praxis* which furnishes the a priori conditions for the latter – that of technology.[25] But he fails to connect this discovery with any appreciation of the phenomenon of strictly *intersubjective validity*, which requires that scientific statements (as also those of philosophy) be validated through a procedure of argumentative discourse. Still less did he appreciate the circumstance that that objectivity which makes the world available to science does not have to lead to a scientizing conception of the world as absolute – a 'making available' in the sense of an 'enframing' – quite simply because the making-available of the world in the sense of the subject–object relation 'always already' presupposes that complementary communicative-understanding of one's co-subjects which proceeds from the existence of a discursive community. That through this complementarity a definitive success, i.e. an absolutization of methodologically reductive scientism is excluded a priori is even today hardly recognized.

Instead, late Heidegger will conceive of the objectivity of science (and the claim of philosophy itself to the intersubjective validity of its statements) as a merely contingent pre-condition of world-understanding, a pre-condition which is grounded in the 'thrown projection' of being-in-the-world – and, after the *Kehre*, this means in a world-establishing, epochal event in the history of being. I will come back later to this question of the threat represented by the above to the validation of philosophical statements, as also to Heidegger's statements about the historical conditions of the possibility (and validity) of Western science and philosophy. But first I would like to maintain that a peculiar reflective deficiency with regard to the constitution of objectivity (and connected therewith to the intersubjective criteria of validity for a scientific experience – as Kant had shown) attaches to the genial analysis of the pre-theoretical relational-world in *Being and Time*. Already in *Being and Time* Heidegger had only the following to say about the meaning of the Kantian idealization of the epistemological subject in the sense of a 'pure ego' or a 'consciousness in general':

> Is not such a subject a *fanciful idealization*? With such a conception have we not missed precisely the *a priori* character of that merely 'factual' subject Dasein? Is it not an attribute of the *a priori* character of the factical subject (that is, an attribute of Dasein's facticity) that it is in the truth and in untruth equi-primordially?[26]

After the turn introduced by Heidegger's 'hermeneutical revolution' no philosopher is going to deny that the world-understanding which comes before the truth of science and which makes it possible has the character of 'revealing-concealing'. But surely the possibility of the simple intersubjective validity – and of absolute truth in this sense – of the findings of science must therewith also become a questionable issue. Heidegger's answer to this question in *Being and Time* can be found in the following passage:

> There is truth only in so far as Dasein is and as long as Dasein is. Entities are uncovered only when Dasein is; and only as long as Dasein is, are they disclosed. . . . To say that before Newton his laws were neither true nor false, cannot signify that before him there were no such entities as have been uncovered and pointed out by those laws. Through Newton the laws became true; and with them, entities became accessible in themselves to Dasein. . . . That there are 'eternal truths' will not be adequately proved until someone has succeeded in demonstrating that Dasein has been and will be for all eternity. . . . Even the 'universal validity' of truth is rooted solely in the fact that Dasein can uncover entities in themselves and free them. . . . Why must we presuppose that there is truth? What is 'presupposing'? What do we have in mind with the 'must' and the 'we'? . . . 'We' presuppose truth because 'we', being in the kind of being which Dasein possesses, are 'in the truth'.[27]

But even this answer to the question posed by us with regard to the possibility of a strictly *intersubjective validity* remains ambiguous. That the truth of 'propositions' can no longer – as Thomas Aquinas and even Bolzano held – be regarded as independent of human knowledge on the ground of the creative knowledge of an 'intellectus divinus' can be accepted as following from Heidegger's 'methodological atheism'. But that the validity of true statements for any 'epistemological subject in general' has to be regarded as relative to the temporal duration of a world-disclosure which belongs to human Dasein, is already problematic. In his first Kant book Heidegger tried to align his thesis with regard to the dependence of truth in general upon the world-understanding of human Dasein with Kant's transcendental philosophy, more specifically, with the first edition of the *Critique of Pure Reason* and not with the second.[28] But after the historico-ontological 'Turn' of his interpretation of human Dasein and its 'disclosiveness' as that of 'thrown-projection', Heidegger radicalized the thesis about the relativity of the truth as the unhiddenness of the world with regard to the temporal-historical Dasein of human being in this sense, that even this relativity can be understood as relative to a specific epoch in ontological history, for example, as the relativity of the concept of the universal validity of scientific and philosophical truth with regard to the epoch of metaphysics which began in Greece and which is coming to an end today. At this point, a difficulty inherent to Heidegger's philosophy can, I suggest, be noted, a difficulty to which we shall have to come back, namely, the *pragmatic contradiction* between the relativity thesis and its own claim to universal validity. For the historico-ontological relativization of the universal validity of truth will itself have to be true, that is universally valid, as an insight into the necessity of this very relativization, and this in a sense which cannot itself be relativized – and that means for any possible epistemological subject in the context of an ideal dialogical community of human beings as potentially rational beings.

Here we see that even the much vaunted *pragmatism* of the Dasein's analyses undertaken in *Being and Time* is ambiguous. It may well be that it displays – as Richard Rorty has suggested[29] – an affinity to William James' and John Dewey's reduction of scientific and philosophical truth to practically serviceable aims in the sense of the needs of (individual or . collectively individual) human beings who happen to exist in a given world. But it has nothing to do with Peirce's pragmatism, for instance, with what Peirce, in opposition to James and Dewey, later called 'pragmaticism'. To be sure, the latter also interpreted the meaning of any possible true or false statement in terms of a possible life-*praxis*. But he also distinguished the intersubjective validity of experimental procedures and the dialogical *praxis* of an 'unlimited community of scientists' as the only possible regulative context for the pursuit of truth in practice. In distinction from Heidegger, he did not attempt to found the ultimate validity of truth upon the 'factical apriori' of being-in-the-world, but upon the ability of the truth to establish a consensus for all rational human beings, a consensus which is counterfactually anticipated in advance.[30]

So much for Heidegger's 'destruction' of world-understanding and for that idea of truth to which Western philosophy and science subscribe. With regard to what has already been said, where are we to locate the correspondence between Wittgenstein's critique of language and meaning and Heidegger's ambition to undertake a comprehensive philosophical destruction?

In the first place, a positive correspondence between language-game analysis and the pragmatically-oriented existential-hermeneutical analysis of the relational-world, together with the transition from world-understanding to the deficient mode of de-worlding (simply staring at what is present-at-hand) can very easily be found. It is to be sought in this, that the privileging of the denominative language game (taken for granted since the founding of ontological philosophy in Greece), a strategy pushed to the limit by Wittgenstein himself in the *Tractatus* through his characterization of objects and states of affairs, is radically called in question in his later language-game analysis. But it is not so much a matter of Wittgenstein completely giving up his earlier conception of name-giving and ostensive definition later on. Rather, he made it clear that a quite special language game operated here, one which always presupposed other language games which for their part were intimately bound up with the practice of a given life-form. The following passages from *Philosophical Investigations* will suffice to bring out these presuppositions.

> The ostensive definition explains the use – the meaning – of the word when the overall role of the word in language is clear. . . . One has already to know (or to be able to do) something in order to be capable of asking a thing's name.
>
> (*P.U.*, I, §30)

And:

> When one shows someone the king in chess and says: 'This is the king', this does not tell him the use of this piece – unless he already knows the rules of the game up to this last point: the shape of the king. . . . Only someone who already knows how to do something with it can significantly ask a name.
>
> (*P.U.*, I, §31)

A remark by Wittgenstein should also be seen in this connection, a remark which, so to speak, marks the semiotic equivalence with Heidegger's theory of 'de-worlding'. It shows how a self-sufficient theory of meaning-constitution through name-giving, taken out of the pragmatic context of language games bound up with life-forms, exactly corresponds to the transition described by Heidegger from contextual world-understanding over to the deficient mode of simply staring at the present-at-hand. Wittgenstein formulates this as follows:

Naming appears as a queer connexion of a word with an object – And you really get such a *queer* connexion when the philosopher tries to bring out *the* relation between name and thing by staring at an object in front of him and repeating a name or even the word 'this' innumerable times. For philosophical problems arise when language *goes on holiday*. And *here* we may indeed fancy naming to be some remarkable act of mind, as it were a baptism of an object.

(*P.U.*, I, §38)

To the Heideggerian limiting case of 'de-worlding' (in which what is present-at-hand is simply stared at and so can have no more 'meaning' for us), there corresponds, with Wittgenstein, the limiting case in which language 'goes on holiday', that is, is no longer bound up with its use in a given life-*praxis*. In this limiting case, it is indeed only possible to substitute a name for the 'this-there', a name which no longer carries with it any intelligible meaning. And this naturally implies that under these conditions the constitution of the meaning of linguistic predicates cannot be rendered intelligible.

It is therefore quite impossible to found a universally valid theory of linguistic meaning by the co-ordination of pure 'sensations' with 'logically proper names' as the elements out of which a given world can be constructed, as Russell, for example, wanted to do. Rather, the naming language game – or even the question concerning the correct way of naming some given entity – already presupposes those very language games in and through which the context of a life-*praxis* determines the possible role of words in the language game and so also, to this extent, their meaning.

We are now in a position to pull together the philosophical achievements of Wittgenstein and Heidegger. I would like to appeal here to the concept of the 'life-world' employed by late Husserl and advance the thesis that Wittgenstein and Heidegger each discovered the life-world in their own way and, moreover, that they were able to work out this concept (in opposition to the world-conception of the philosophical tradition) in a much more radical way than Husserl was able to do in *Crisis*.[31] To be sure, Husserl had seen that the abstract idealizing objectification of European science presupposed the emergence of meaning out of the life-world (and so had to be understood philosophically out of the latter). But, as the last classical representative of the post-Cartesian philosophy of consciousness, he assumed that even the meaning-constitution of the life-world and its intersubjective validity *could* be traced back to the intentional operations of a solipsistically transcendental consciousness, an 'I think' and, in the last analysis, *had to be* so understood. That the meaning-constitution of the life-world, as publicly valid, was always dependent upon language and that, to this extent, it was always dependent upon a historical and socio-culturally determined life-form, was something he did not appreciate.

While with Husserl the pre-linguistic intentional operation of an Ego consciousness is supposed to found the meaning-constitution of the life-world, it is this very life-world which, with Heidegger and Wittgenstein, assumes the role of the ultimate bedrock: with Heidegger, in the form of a historically determined 'thrown projection' of 'being-in-the-world' and, with Wittgenstein, in the form of the 'life-forms' which make up the background of those very 'language games' which have already been taken account of. In fact, bound up with the latter we find insights into the quasi-transcendental conditioning of our world and self-understanding, beyond which, at the present time, philosophy cannot go back. Belonging thereto we find, on the one hand, the insights mentioned by me concerning a critique of the meanings involved in metaphysical pseudo-problems, meanings which rest upon the non-reflection upon the linguistic a priori of language games and, on the other side, the corresponding existential-hermeneutical insights into the dependence of our positive understanding of worldly significance upon human being-in-the-world and, in connection therewith, upon the worldly disclosiveness of historical language(s).

With reference to this linguistically and historically conditioned pre-understanding of the life-world, we are no longer able to go back to a null-point of presuppositionless thinking about whatever is present, for example, to the self-givenness of phenomena. This can today be regarded as generally accepted by a philosophizing which has gone through the linguistically pragmatic and hermeneutically-oriented turn introduced by Wittgenstein and Heidegger. That things are like this can also be shown through a complementary turn in the philosophy of science which, since Thomas Kuhn's analysis in *The Structure of Scientific Revolutions*, has also brought out the dependence of scientific thinking and its possible development upon a historically conditioned agreement between a community of scientists.[32]

This reference to Kuhn's philosophy of science, in which Wittgensteinian motifs join together with motifs drawn from the hermeneutical philosophy inspired by Heidegger (and Gadamer) is intended to point to the questionable suggestions inherent in Wittgenstein's and Heidegger's thinking: the absolutization of the contingently a priori, the historically conditioned life-world, which does not lend itself to the forming of a consensus because it calls in question the conditions of the possibility of a universal philosophical consensus. I am here deliberately harping upon the pragmatic requirement of philosophical consistency, that is, upon the requirement of avoiding any *performative contradiction* in the argumentation. And I am drawing attention to the fact that, in his *reductio ad absurdum* of the Cartesian dream argument in *On Certainty*, Wittgenstein himself offered an example of the very self-suspension of a philosophical language game which has to be avoided.

With reference to Heidegger I have already had occasion to point to the danger which results from the inconsistency inherent in his destruction of that idea of truth which underlies Western metaphysics. Let us now take a closer look with reference to Wittgenstein. Consider Wittgenstein's radical critique of the vacuity or the 'disease' of language games. As is well known, in his *Philosophical Investigations* Wittgenstein did not really take back the dictum of 'non-sensicality' expressed in the *Tractatus*, a dictum directed against the propositions of philosophy in general – including those of the *Tractatus* itself – at least, not in the form indicated there. For he did not answer the question of how that critical language game of philosophy, the language game in which one talks about language games in general (their function and dis-function) and so is able to 'show the fly the way out of the fly-bottle', is itself possible and valid. To these questions, he seems only to have given critically therapeutic answers which apply equally to the language game needed to cure the disease and which, at the very least, seem not to recognize that the legitimacy of his characterization of philosophical problems in general as a linguistic disease itself rests upon a specifically philosophical insight which lays claim to universal validity (cf. especially *Philosophical Investigations* (*P.I.*), I, §§133, 255, 309).

If, as has been shown, the proof of the self-suspension of the philosophical language game through the performative self-contradiction involved turns out to be the most radical form of the critique of language and meaning, it then becomes possible to think with Wittgenstein against Wittgenstein and to conclude that the recommended programme of a *total self-therapy of philosophy as a disease* proves to be defective. It then becomes possible to counter the exaggerated emphasis laid upon the contingently a priori character of the many life-forms, for instance, that of the historically-determined own life-world, with one argument which, in the final analysis, so far from reclaiming a metaphysical standpoint beyond language and the world, simply recognizes the impossibility of getting behind that language game which is philosophy as the legitimate form of reflection with regard to all thinkable language games and life-forms and, to this extent, of any historically conditioned life-world.

And so I come to the second part of my comparison between Wittgenstein and Heidegger.

III Philosophy: self-criticism or self-suspension?

Thomas Kuhn's theory of the 'paradigms' of the history of science can with good reason be taken up as a particularly instructive example for the convergence of the historical efficiency of the thinking of Wittgenstein and Heidegger. For the concept of a paradigm, a concept which is introduced by Kuhn in the double role of the positive condition of the possibility and of the historical relativization of scientific progress,[33] this central and multi-faceted concept can be elucidated both out of the perspective of Wittgenstein's language games and their paradigms of 'certainty' and out of the perspective of the epochal revealing-concealing establishment of the world in Heidegger's history of being.

Seen from a Wittgensteinian perspective, Kuhn's 'incommensurable' paradigms of science and their possible development appear as illustrations of the idea that language games, as parts of 'life-forms', are 'bound up' with 'activities' and grammatically conditioned a priori valid forms of world-interpretation. To this extent they function as 'norms' for language usage, experimental *praxis* and for any acceptable research findings which can be expected to yield true or false conclusions and which for this reason cannot be called in question by empirical science since they have to be known a priori as conditions of the possibility of the functioning of the scientific language game and the *praxis* which belongs to it. The provocative point of the Kuhnian paradigm concept (both for the traditional linear representation of progress and for the unitary rationality of science) is to be sought along the lines of Wittgenstein's suggestion that one cannot go behind the multiplicity and the variety of language games and the life-forms which support them, that the multiplicity of life-forms, functioning as they do as the background for the different language games, can even make comprehension through the medium of language impossible. Lions, for example, could not be understood by us humans even if they could talk;[34] more pertinently, a similar limitation of our understanding must perhaps be assumed for the understanding of foreign human life-forms, i.e., so-called primitive cultures.[35]

To this primarily synchronous relativism of the Wittgensteinian perspective there now largely corresponds the primarily diachronic relativism of epochal world-clearing which (as has been shown above) with Heidegger emerges out of the historical transformation of a Dasein-related concept of truth as 'disclosure'. Above all it is the following intellectual configuration which seems to correspond to the function of Kuhn's concept of a paradigm. In a later statement in *Zur Sache des Denkens*[36] Heidegger conceded on the one hand that it would be 'inappropriate' to interpret his concept of world-clearing (for example, revealing-concealing or *a-lethia*) as the 'original concept of truth'. For the element of correctness, in the sense of a correspondence with something pre-given, is lacking. On the other hand, he emphasized once again that, with the concept of 'lighting', a dimension had been opened up which systematically preceded the traditional concept of truth. For in this instance it

was a question of the condition of the possibility of true or false judgments, i.e., statements about beings.

The connection of this intellectual configuration with the function of
the Kuhnian paradigm is clearly to be found in this, that in both cases
in which the possibility of an advance in knowledge is in question –
including the process of verification and falsification – the latter is, in a
one-sided manner, made to appear dependent upon a preceding condition. To Kuhn's normative paradigm there corresponds Heidegger's
clearing, a clearing which, as linguistically world-disclosive, first opens
up the meaning-horizon for possible scientific questions. And true or
false judgments must, as Gadamer has shown, be understood as answers
to actual, or at least to possible, questions.[37] To this extent it would be
true to conclude that the findings of Western science in general are
dependent upon paradigmatic meaning or interrogative horizons, horizons which could not be opened up at all in cultures with different
linguistic modes of world-disclosure – for example the Hopi Indians
of New Mexico.[38] At this point the convergence between Heidegger's
hermeneutical understanding of language and Wittgenstein's analytical
understanding of language games becomes even clearer.

One difference between Heidegger and Kuhn or Wittgenstein seems
to consist in this, that the uncovering-covering, meaning-clearing inherent
in Heidegger's understanding of Western world history is as a whole
quite explicitly characterized by the 'event' of the founding of philosophy
as metaphysics by the Greeks. To this extent, the different scientific
paradigms which follow therefrom can obviously not be regarded by
Heidegger as 'incommensurable' in every respect since they have to be
understood as consequences of the founding of metaphysics. The point
of Heidegger's supposition is to be found in the thesis that already in
the metaphysical uncovering of the meaning of being with Plato – that
is, in the so-called 'theory of Ideas' – the mode of uncovering of the
world assumes the form of the subject–object relation and therewith also
of an 'enframing' of scientific technology, that is, of the technological
science of modern Europe.

By comparison with this Heideggerian vision (which corresponds to
his life-long attempt at a reconstruction and destruction of Western
metaphysics) the Wittgensteinian representation of infinitely many language games and life-forms is, on the one hand, and as we have already
noted, marked by an a-historical intellectual model – especially in the
transitional period between the *Tractatus* and the *Philosophical Investigations*. On the other hand, it is illustrated in late Wittgenstein along
the lines of ethnological examples and, globally, with reference to the
idea of a 'natural history'.

These differences do not however make it impossible for us – as the
example of Kuhn has already shown – to establish a convergence of the

Heideggerian and the Wittgensteinian perspectives, in the sense, too, of a relativistic and historicalistic orientation of Western philosophy in general. Frequently these very characteristics are rejected as a misunderstanding – as the consequence of a way of thinking which is itself metaphysical and which has not learnt how to assimilate the new standpoint 'beyond relativism and objectivism'. At the end of my paper, I would like to resist precisely this suggestion.

To this end, I would like first to set out what, in my opinion, constitutes the most important philosophical results of the historically effective convergence of the intellectual claims of Wittgenstein and Heidegger. With Heidegger the most important claim consists in this, that meaning-clearing and the truth which, in the final analysis, is dependent upon it, must be thought as a meaning- (or truth-) *event*, that is, in its most radical accentuation. Even the insight – opened up with the philosophical truth claim – that our ability to pose questions is genetically dependent upon the clearing-event of the history of being is clearly, according to Heidegger, itself dependent upon the temporal occurrence of the history of being for its validity. The *logos* of our thinking (for instance, our argumentative procedures) which was above all taken to be independent of time by the Greek founders of philosophy now has to be regarded as dependent upon the 'other of reason' – the temporality of being. Nevertheless, it should be possible to frame this insight in the form of a universally valid philosophical thesis about the history of being. Is this claim, a claim which has been carried over from Heidegger into philosophical postmodernism, tenable from the standpoint of a critique of meaning? Or does it not rather lead to a self-suspension of the language game of philosophy?

With a view to answering these questions, we shall have recourse to Wittgenstein's critique of language and meaning. However, it must be said that Wittgenstein and the Wittgensteinians do not offer much in the way of helpful objections but rather tend to complete and to strengthen the Heideggerian claims. To be sure, Wittgenstein tirelessly traced the disease of seemingly unsolvable philosophical problems back to a misunderstanding of the function of language. And in this sense he did indeed – as shown above – take into consideration the phenomenon of the self-suspension of the philosophical language game. But he never applied these kinds of analyses in a strictly reflective manner to his own, suggestive statements about philosophy as a disease resulting from a misuse of language. Above all (and particularly after the paradoxical self-suspension of the philosophical language game in the *Tractatus*) he never again posed the reflective question concerning the linguistic conditions of the possibility of one's own language game, that is, the question concerning the presuppositions not of the pseudo-language games of metaphysics which were to be critically resolved by him, but about the language game involved in his own critically therapeutic philosophy which, clearly, could only 'show the fly the way out of the fly bottle' and cure the sickness through linguistically formulated insights, and not through the dispensing of medicaments.

At this point, we have to take account of the following circumstance. The well-known statements by Wittgenstein on the method of philosophy as, for example, 'we may not advance any kind of theory. . . . We must do away with all explanation, and description alone must take its place' (*P.I.*, I, §109) or 'Philosophy simply put everything before us and neither explains nor deduces anything. Since everything lies open to view there is nothing to explain. For what is hidden, for example, is of no interest to us' (*P.I.*, I, §126). Statements of this kind certainly attest to the originality of his method. But they do not make it clear to what extent they make it possible for Wittgenstein to communicate, through the summoning-up of examples, those insights into the 'workings of our language' (ibid., §109) which should help us to get things 'straight' and which are so complete 'that philosophical problems should completely disappear' (ibid., §133). It is just not enough to simply set out, or to describe, the everyday language games on the one hand and, on the other, the empty language games of philosophy. Rather, it is necessary to at least point out the reasons – that is, the universally valid insights of philosophy – which make it possible to play off the one language game against the others. These reasons are at least suggested by Wittgenstein in his ever-renewed intimations toward philosophical theory-building at the level of a specific philosophical languge game in which he, as much as any other philosopher, was obliged to participate.

Here we run up against a *reflective deficiency* which is bound up with his – in many instances helpful – predisposition for the 'pure describing' of examples. Certainly it is possible – as Wittgenstein's work demonstrates – to correct the a priori assumptions and over-hasty generalizations of systematic philosophy with the analysis of examples. But one cannot hope to render intelligible in this way the specific claims to validity of all philosophical statements – even those statements which bear the brunt of the critique of language and meaning. To put it otherwise; one cannot render intelligible the actual function of philosophical language games through language-game analysis in this way; that one presents this language game as just one language game among others or alongside others, which means, embedded in a particular form of life with particular 'conventions', 'uses', or 'customary practices'. For the claim that is raised by the philosophical language games practised by Wittgenstein in the descriptive presentation of particular 'conventions' has to rise above the embedding of all language games in particular life-forms and, to this extent, above the facticity and contingency of all language games and life-forms and so express something that is universally valid. This unavoidable claim to universality can only be rendered intelligible in the following way, that one seeks to analyse the function of the philosophical language game in strict reflection[39] upon what one does and presupposes as a philosopher, with the description of particular language games and life-forms. Such a methodological claim would however, at least for the post-*Tractatus* Wittgenstein, be taboo – as though, for the pragmatic language-game analysis, the view oriented toward the semantics of the statement were still true, the view namely, that any actual reflection upon language has to lead to semantic antinomies.[40]

A radically pragmatic questioning of the semantic paradigm, of the kind introduced by Wittgenstein in his language-game theory, leads however to the conclusion that the pragmatic function of language games must also be analysed, which means suspending the semantically-oriented prohibition against the self-reference of the speech act. Only in this way does one find oneself in a position to recognize the denial of the specifically philosophical claim to universality as a performative contradiction and, to this extent, as the self-suspension of the philosophical language game.[41]

As things stand today, Wittgenstein's one-sided and unsatisfactory thematization of the philosophical language game – just like Heidegger's one-sided (forgetfulness of the *logos*) analysis of the facticity of being-in-the-world (as a historically 'thrown projection') has tended to promote a very general confusion concerning the self-understanding of philosophy and to provoke an era of pragmatically inconsistent philosophical statements. I would like to support this with reference to two famous Wittgensteinian theses: the argument against the possibility of a 'private language' and the argument against the possibility of universal doubt in *Uber Gewißheit*.

In both cases I am deeply indebted to Wittgenstein's theses. And I would here like to interpret these theses in a transcendentally pragmatic fashion – as I have attempted to do elsewhere.[42] What does this mean?

In the case of the argument against the possibility of a private language, the emphasis should be placed on two points:

(1) It is not possible to talk meaningfully about a person S following a rule – for example, speaking a language – if it is not in principle possible for other subjects – for a community – to control the following of the rule on the basis of public criteria which make it possible for them too to follow the rule, for instance, to enter into communicative relations with the person S.

(2) In addition, the following must also be emphasized. The person S – e.g., the speaker S – must link up with an already existing procedure for rule-following – e.g., an actual language usage. To this extent, one might say, he is in fact subjected to a *factical apriori* and to *historicality*.

These two requirements can be grounded in a pragmatically transcendental manner. Their rejection through arguments which must be capable of eliciting acceptance must lead to a performative contradiction in the argumentative procedure. The latter could not of itself avoid the objection of having, in the course of his argumentative procedure, followed a rule which is in principle private. For in that case he would have suspended the language game of arguing – rather like the one who says (or thinks): 'Perhaps I am always dreaming.'

So far, so good. But the difficulties with Wittgenstein's argumentative procedures begin when one asks with him the question who – on the basis of what criterion – decides whether a rule – e.g., addition in arithmetic – has been followed correctly. Two possible answers for Wittgenstein can be distinguished here, even though both will have to be rejected in the end.

(1) The possibility of recurring to the remembered rule-following intentions of individual subjects as the actual states of a possible inner experience. Here Wittgenstein can quite appropriately object that in inner experience no distinction can be established between following the rule correctly and thinking that one has followed the rule correctly. The last of these alternatives can only be subjective, as I have already pointed out earlier.

(2) For Wittgenstein the possibility is also excluded of positing the criterion of validity for following rules with Plato or Frege – or with Karl Popper – as the ideal content of a third world (beyond the material outer world and the subjective world of inner experience). Wittgenstein is always able to object to such a rule-determining Platonism[43] that it is by no means clear how the individual subjects of the role-following procedure are going to relate, or be referred to this ideal criterion without once again recurring to the purely subjective evidence of their inner experience. They cannot have recourse to the ideal rule-following criterion in the same way that one has recourse to a public timetable.

If things are like this however, then what remains of the possible criterion for correct rule-following? Painfully tedious passages in the *Philosophical Investigations* and in the *Remarks on the Foundations of Mathematics* are devoted to thought-experiments which show, over and over again, that a rule – e.g., addition – could be followed quite differently from the way that is normally supposed and that these discrepant rule-following procedures cannot be excluded on the grounds that we would be referred to a mental fact pertaining to the intention to follow a rule. How then is it going to be possible to distinguish between 'right' and 'wrong'?

Wolfgang Stegmüller has characterized the calling in question of 'rule Platonism' by Wittgenstein as follows: Wittgenstein rejects even that objectivity which is recognized by mathematical intuitionism. In Wittgenstein's sense one could say:

> that, in so far as we have explained the meaning of a logical expression by means of a convention, we should think that such and such must now be recognized as a logical truth or as a logical inference – *this* is once again simply a new form of the platonic myth. . . . It is the belief in a logical 'must', in a logical necessity which forces us even if only in the form of the binding consequences of specific assertions.[44]

If however we are serious about letting go of these presuppositions what possible meaning can it then have to raise questions about the problem of 'rule Platonism' on the plane of philosophical discourse? Surely, at least on this plane, are we not assuming the 'unconstrained constraint' (Habermas) of arguments as an irradicable element?

As a matter of fact, it seems to me that Wittgenstein's point does not consist in saying that I can decide *ad hoc* that 'this sentence or that relation has to be regarded as irrefutable, so that nothing could count as an objection' (Stegmüller), even though it must be conceded that the non-necessity of the criteria of rule-following can be rendered intelligible in the light of 'rule Platonism' in the sense of decisionism. But then in what, according to Wittgenstein, is the *non-arbitrary* basis of the 'criterion' of rule following – e.g., linguistic usage – supposed to consist?

It seems to me that no other answer can be found in Wittgenstein's work than a reference to actual rule-following customs in actual situations in an actual rule-following community – in the same way as his theory of meaning relies, in the final analysis, upon actual linguistic usages under pragmatically determined circumstances. This is, or so it seems, the sense in which such typically obstinate expressions of later Wittgenstein are to be understood: 'this language game is played' (*P.I.*, I, §654); 'this is simply what I do'; or more explicitly: 'If I have exhausted the justifications I have reached the bedrock, and my spade is turned. Then I am inclined to say: "This is simply what I do." ' (*P.I.*, I, §217). And finally: 'What has to be accepted, the given is – so one could say – forms of life' (*P.I.*, II, p. 226).

If one takes these communications as ultimate answers a whole series of difficult questions immediately arises. What happens with innovations in the rule-following procedure – in the context of scientific progress for instance, or in an ethical or political context? Is it its correspondence with the actually existing usages of a community which provides the criterion for establishing a consensus over the right way to follow a rule or even over which rule or norm should be followed? Charles Peirce called this the 'method of authority', a method which is superseded by philosophy and science.[45] Or should the answer to our question even lie in Wittgenstein's talk about learning through a 'training' (or drill) by way of a 'blind' following of rules? It seems to me that this affirmation of Wittgenstein's can only mean that the learning of rules by children cannot begin with an interpretation (and the equivocation which belongs thereto) since the field for possible rule-interpretations is in principle unlimited and therefore does not lend itself to 'usages' which could be adopted along these lines. In my opinion, on the Wittgensteinian assumption of a learning through 'training', it is in turn not explicable how human children, in distinction from animals, are able to develop a capacity for interpreting and reflecting upon rules which manifests itself in a communicative competence that is not tied down to the linguistic competence of using one's mother language, but consists, for example, in an ability to translate out of one language into another.

The following question, a question which moves beyond the conception of the learning of rule-following, in the sense of the following of an already-existing usage, seems to me to be decisive: is it possible for Wittgenstein to argue that an individual (for example, a scientist or a philosopher or a reformer of customary practices) might be right against everyone else and might be capable of convincing them that his own conception of rule-following is the right one in cases where a dispute arises concerning the right way of following a rule or even concerning the right rule? Unless one is going to observe and describe language games behaviouristically from the outside rather than as intelligible components of a cultural reality in which the describer must be capable of participating, the latter must be possible. And then it is going to be necessary to allow for a relation of reciprocity between a rule-following community and an innovator of new rule-following procedures or between the former and the philosopher who describes language games and life-forms. In which case the same problem arises anew: on the basis of what criterion can one or should one arrive at a consensus over the right rule-following procedure?

Faced with this situation I have, with Charles Peirce, J. Royce and G. H. Mead, fallen back upon the normative conception of an ideal consensus to be established within an ideal and unlimited communicative community, that is, upon the conception of a regulative idea regarding the building up of a consensus over rule-following. In this connection the latter also leads to a regulative Idea regarding the normatively correct meaning of concepts (as for example over the simultaneity of two events or over justice or truth) which, in accordance with the 'pragmatic maxim' of Peirce, has to be tried out first in thought-experiments and therefore does not have to be reducible to actually existing linguistic usage even though it has to stand in relation to the latter. So it has to be emphasized that there would also have to be publicly accessible criteria for the establishment of a consensus in any post-conventional situation in which a consensus had to be established (experimental evidence, logical coherence and incoherence or even requirements or interests which could be transformed into morally valid claims) and this whether we are talking about scientific language-rulings or extensions of knowledge or a matter of the practical founding or application of norms. Such criteria would never be sufficient in themselves to build up a consensus. However, in the context of an experience which could be brought under the regulative principle of an ideal consensus, they could furnish the basis for a preliminary consensus, as also for a calling in question of any actual consensus with a view to arriving at a better solution to relevant problems.[46]

But this transcendentally pragmatic way out seems in the end not to be reconcilable with Wittgenstein's suggestions. In any case, this is the impression one gets when one tries to understand the convergence between the historical efficacy of Wittgenstein's thinking and the American neo-pragmatism of our times. Richard Rorty has done us the service of openly drawing all those radically relativistic and historically bound consequences of the thinking of Wittgenstein and Heidegger, which consequences are ordinarily only drawn in a marginal way. I mean such consequences as the denial of all universal (and if possible also transcendentally founded) criteria of philosophical discourse and also the ethically relevant thesis with regard to the necessity of falling back upon the only available basis for a consensus, namely, that of a contingent life-form, for example the political and cultural tradition of America.[47] Fortunately, it is a matter here of a tradition which, in distinction from the politico-cultural tradition of the Nazis in Germany, itself goes back to an institutional foundation which has not betrayed its philosophical legitimation with reference to universally valid principles, those of the rights of man. In this way Rorty is able to avoid the philosophical call to universal criteria of rectitude with reference to a political allegiance to rights already institutionalized in the American constitution; with the result that only the pragmatic inconsistency of the philosophical thesis – itself obviously claiming universal validity – that in a philosophical discussion one can only fall back upon a contingent basis for establishing a consensus remains indicative of the paradox inherent in this understanding of Wittgenstein.

The paradox of an understanding of Wittgenstein which relies upon an actual 'usage', for example a 'life-form', which is even more crass than that of Rorty is to be found in the Norwegian philosopher Viggo Rossvaer. For the latter has advanced the thesis that one can see – in so far as one has been taught to see by Wittgenstein – that in a certain sense even the SS in Auschwitz could have been observing the 'categorical imperative'.[48] This argument is supported by the claim that Wittgenstein has shown that the concept of a rule only becomes meaningful in conjunction with the appropriate application within the context of an actual life-form; to elaborate: the meaning of a rule is not given in a *counter-factual anticipation of a possible practice* which can be represented as the correct application of the rule in Peirce's sense.

It is perfectly obvious that the understanding of Wittgenstein illustrated above actually operates a suspension of the good sense of anything that might be called a rule – and especially any meaningful moral norm. For the latter are clearly only there – at least upon the plane of a *post-conventional* human culture – to provide a point of orientation for the practice, and that means: calling forth in advance and legitimizing a comportment in conformity with the rule through an application appropriate to the situation. One often has the impression with Wittgenstein that the post-conventional function of rules and norms has to be traced back to just such conventions and usages which always already preclude any possible explication and justification of the normative meaning of rules. And this fits in well with the conservative and populist tendency (inherent in the idea of a therapeutic philosophy) to suppose that in the life-world prior to philosophical clarification and its artificially constructed and so irresolvable pseudo-problems everything is already in order, both with respect to. language usages which are intricately bound up with a life-*praxis* as also with respect to what Hegel would have called 'naively substantialized moral conventions'.[49]

It is admittedly – perhaps – possible to interpret the ultimacy Wittgenstein attributes to language games (or the practice of a life-form which upholds them) in another sense. And this second interpretation can, in particular, be supported by the last writings *On Certainty* where statements can be found such as the following:

> Any proof, any validation or invalidation of a claim already takes place within a system. This system is not a more or less arbitrary and dubious starting point for all our reasonings. Rather it belongs to the very essence of what we call an argument. The system is not so much the point of departure as rather the vital element of the argument.
>
> (Aphorism 105)

Here it is once again pertinent to think about a transcendental-pragmatic interpretation of the impossibility of going beyond or behind the language games constitutive of *philosophical argumentation*, and in particular: the paradigmatic certainty of those presuppositions whose denial inevitably leads to the suspension of the philosophical language game. As a matter of fact, interpretations are to be found which do adhere to such a conception.[50] However, it seems to me today that they cannot be presented as Wittgensteinian interpretations, for the simple reason that Wittgenstein never reflected upon (and indeed never noticed) the difference in principle between those life-forms which are always presented in the plural and so as already contingently relativized and the discursive language game of philosophy itself in which a relativization of the many contingent life-forms, together with that paradigmatic certainty which belongs to them, can be carried through. It is therefore more plausible to conclude with Peter Strawson that Wittgenstein's argumentative procedure in *On Certainty* is to be understood as 'soft naturalism' and, to this extent, as the de-transcendentalized substitute for the foundational claims of transcendental argumentation.[51] The point would then be the following, that in place of the foundational claims of transcendental philosophy it would become apparent that it is simply unavoidable that certain presuppositions of the argumentative procedure (together with the life-*praxis* that goes along with them) should be presented as certain.

Many people today would be pleased with this. They would like to see an alternative to a transcendentally pragmatic foundation for philosophy – even for Ethics. However it does seem to me that, with Strawson (who has given his assent to this view), the decisive objection against such a substitution thesis has been voiced. For any philosophy which adopts a practical standpoint the task remains of distinguishing between the universally valid presuppositions of its critically reflective language game – the argumentative discourse – and the purely contingent, historically conditioned presuppositions which make up the background of the life-world, that is, of the many and various life-forms.

But for those who in a certain sense belong to a given life-form (e.g., a given language game) the latter would also furnish an *ultimate bedrock*. To be sure, it is only in a historically factual sense (in Collingwood's sense) that they are ultimate. On the other hand, since the philosophical enlightenment in Greece and again in modern times, they are already relativized by philosophical discourse as non-ultimate. Only those presuppositions – presuppositions of the entire argumentative procedure – are in a strict and methodologically relevant sense ultimate which function in the self-reflective language game of philosophy as conditions of the possibility of the relativization of all specific life-forms and which, in so far as they must still be presupposed cannot be challenged along with the condemnation of the performative contradiction involved in philosophical argumentation; as, for example, the presupposition that in any argumentative discourse a whole series of claims to validity are always going to make themselves known, and amongst these are the universal claims to validity and consensual legitimacy of certain basic moral norms.[52]

It is easy to see today that it is no longer possible to found a concrete life-form (e.g., some form of customary morality in Hegel's sense or even any recommendation for the individual realization of the good life) on the basis of such universally valid presuppositions of philosophical discourse alone. The only ultimately founded and universally valid discursive principles are those which are formal and procedural, which, as such, moreover establish limiting conditions for the complementary task of realizing the good life with respect to concrete, historically-evolved life-forms. On the basis of this complementarity thesis, a tendency inspired by Wittgenstein and/or Heidegger, a tendency shared by so many contemporary philosophers such as P. Winch, late Rawls, Rorty, Williams and MacIntyre, a tendency which consists in understanding moral norms simply as the reflective convictions of a historically contingent life-form, this tendency not merely becomes intelligible but begins to betray its limitations.

What seems to me to be decisive here is the assumption of the unavoidable complementarity of the ultimate presuppositions of philosophical discourse, on the one hand, and the contingent presuppositions which lie at the root of concrete life-forms, on the other. From the standpoint of the philosophical presuppositions of Wittgenstein and Heidegger such an assumption does not seem to me to be possible. In both cases it is obstructed by a certain forgetfulness of the *logos*, that is, a reflective deficiency with regard to their own intellectual and argumentative presuppositions. With Wittgenstein this leads quite obviously to a tendency to confuse his own philosophical language game with the descriptively objectifiable and, at the same time, contingently relativized language games – together with the concrete life-forms which underlie them. With Heidegger it leads to a deliberate overstepping of the philosophically universal validation of his own claims in favour of a hermeneutics of the facticity of understanding being-in-the-world; and this means in *Being and Time*: the temporality and historicality of 'thrown projection'. In the late work it goes even further in the direction of a total historicism, a reduction of the philosophical *logos* itself to an epochal event in the history of being. As was mentioned earlier, so-called post-modernism latches on at this point to a thinking which starts out from the standpoint of an 'alternative to reason'.

I hardly need to emphasize that I find in this outcome of the historical impact of two outstanding thinkers of this century the signs of a dangerous crisis in philosophy. Instead of moving towards a critique of meaning and a hermeneutical clarification of the presuppositions of philosophical and scientific thinking that would deepen and complete the previous phases of philosophical enlightenment and critical thinking, we seem to be moving towards a paralysis of post-conventional reason. The reflective concern for the rationality of argumentative discourse, a concern which lies at the root of both philosophy and science and which even today still links them together, this concern is (to the extent that there is any awareness of it left at all) understood to be just a reflex reaction left over from a contingent 'usage' or a hangover from a 'metaphysical' epoch in the history of being. 'What people accept as a justification – is shewn by how they think and live' (*P.I.*, I, §325). Indeed!

Translated by Christopher Macann

Notes

1 Cf. K.-O. Apel, *Transformation der Philosophie* (Frankfurt: Suhrkamp, 1973), Bd. I, Part II.

2 Cf., ibid., SS. 247ff., 269f., 272ff.

3 Cf. here also K.-O. Apel, 'Die Herausforderung der totalen Vernunftkritik und das Programm einer philosophischen Theorie der Rationalitätstypen', in *Concordia*, 11 (1987), pp. 2–23.

4 Cf. Ludwig Wittgenstein, *Philosophical Investigations*, tr. Anscombe (Oxford: Basil Blackwell, 1958), I, §§138–242, also §§243–363.

5 ibid., §265.

6 ibid., §202.

7 Peter F. Strawson, *The Bounds of Sense* (London: Methuen, 1966), pp. 125ff.

8 ibid., pp. 247ff.

9 Cf. E. K. Specht, *Der Analogiebegriff bei Kant und Hegel* (Köln, 1952) (Kantstudien, Erg.-Hefte, Vol. 55).

10 Martin Heidegger, *Sein und Zeit* (Halle: Niemeyer), tr. John Macquarrie and Edward Robinson as *Being and Time* (New York: Harper & Row, 1962), p. 213 (H. 169).

11 ibid., p. 207 (H. 163).

12 ibid., §26.

13 ibid., p. 248 (H. 204ff.).

14 See I. Kant, *Kritik der reinen Vernunft*, tr. Norman Kemp-Smith as *The Critique of Pure Reason* (London: Macmillan, 1929), B 275, p. 244.

15 Heidegger, *Being and Time*, p. 249 (H. 205).

16 ibid., p. 160 (H. 123).

17 ibid., p. 162 (H. 125).

18 Heidegger, *Being and Time*, p. 119 (H. 86).

19 ibid., p. 201 (H. 158).

20 Cf. Wittgenstein, *Philosophical Investigations*, I, §§1–60.

21 Cf. Heidegger, *Being and Time*, p. 105 (H. 75), p. 147 (H. 112), p. 190 (H. 149).

22 Cf. here Erich Rothacker's book *Zur Genealogie des menschlichen Bewußtseins* (Bonn: Bouvier, 1966).

23 Cf. G. Böhme (ed.), *Protophysik* (Frankfurt: Suhrkamp, 1976).

24 Cf. G. H. von Wright, *Explanation and Understanding* (Ithaca, NY: Cornell University Press, 1971), chap. II; also K.-O. Apel, *Die Erklären: Verstehen-Kontroverse in transzendental-pragmatischer Sicht*, tr. G. Harnke as *Understanding and Explanation: A Transcendental-Pragmatic Perspective* (Cambridge, Mass.: MIT Press, 1984), pp. 57ff. and pp. 83ff.

25 Cf. M. Heidegger, 'Die Frage nach der Technik', in *Vorträge und Aufsätze* (Pfullingen, 1954).

26 Heidegger, *Being and Time*, p. 272 (H. 229).

27 ibid., p. 269 (H. 226).

28 Cf. here K.-O. Apel, 'Sinnkonstitution und Geltungsrechtfertigung. Heidegger und das Problem der Transzendentalphilosophie', in Forum für Philosophie Bad Homburg (eds), *Martin Heidegger: Innen und Außensichten* (Frankfurt: Suhrkamp, 1989), pp. 131–75.

29 Cf. R. Rorty, *Consequences of Pragmatism* (Brighton: Harvester Press, 1982).

30 Cf. K.-O. Apel, *Der Denkweg von Charles S. Peirce, Eine Einführung in den amerikanischen Pragmatismus* (Frankfurt: Suhrkamp, 1975), tr. J. Krois as *Charles S. Peirce: From Pramatism to Pragmaticism* (Amherst, Mass.: University of Massachusetts Press, 1981).

31 Cf. E. Husserl, *Die Krisis der europäischen Wissenschaften und die transzendentale Phänomenologie*, tr. David Carr as *The Crisis of European Sciences and Transcendental Phenomenology* (Evanston: Northwestern University Press, 1970).

32 Cf. Thomas Kuhn, *The Structure of Scientific Revolutions* (Chicago: University of Chicago Press, 1962).

33 Cf. here M. Masterman, 'The nature of paradigm' in I. Lakatos and A. Musgrave (eds), *Criticism and the Growth of Knowledge* (Cambridge: Cambridge University Press, 1970), pp. 59–89.

34 Cf. L. Wittgenstein, *Schriften* (Frankfurt: Suhrkamp, 1960ff.), Bd. I, p. 536.

35 This is the sense in which Peter Winch first interpreted Wittgenstein's philosophy. See *The Idea of a Social Science and its Relation to Philosophy* (London: Routledge & Kegan Paul, 1958).

36 Cf. M. Heidegger, *Zur Sache des Denkens* (Tübingen, 1969), pp. 76ff.

37 H.-G. Gadamer, *Wahrheit und Methode* (Tübingen: Mohr, 1960), pp. 344ff.

38 Cf. B. L. Whorf, *Sprache, Denken, Wirklichkeit* (Reinbeck: Rowohlt, 1963). Also H. Gipper, *Gibt es ein sprachliches Relativitätsprinzip?* (Frankfurt: Fischer, 1972).

39 Cf. here W. Kuhlmann, 'Reflexive Letzbegründung. Zur These von der Unhintergehbarkeit der Argumentationssituation', in *Ztschr. f. Philosoph. Forschung*, 35 (1981), pp. 2–26.

40 It should not be overlooked that the penetrating distinction made in the *Tractatus* between what can be said and what can only be shown – the logical form of language and of the world – relies upon a transcendental and mystico-metaphysical transformation of Russell's theory of types. In the paradox of the self-suspension of the *Tractatus* only the pragmatic inconsistency – the performative self-contradiction – of the theory of types is reproduced, an inconsistency which can now be reformulated in a meta-language which could not have been foreseen and which holds for all signs.

41 Cf. here K.-O. Apel, 'Fallibilismus, Konsenstheorie der Wahrheit und Letztbegründung', in *Philosophie und Begründung*, ed. Forum für Philosophie Bad Homburg (Frankfurt: Suhrkamp, 1987), pp. 116–211, 130ff., 174ff.

42 Cf. here K.-O. Apel, 'Das Problem der philosophischen Letztbegründung im Lichte einer transzendentalen Sprachpragmatik', in B. Kanitscheider (ed.), *Sprache und Erkenntnis* (Innsbruck, 1976), pp. 55–82; tr. as 'The problem of philosophical transcendental grounding in the light of a transcendental pragmatics of language' in *Man and World*, 8 (1975), pp. 239–75, reproduced in K. Baynes *et al.* (eds), *After Philosophy: End or Transformation?* (Cambridge, Mass: MIT Press, 1987), pp. 250–90.

43 Cf. here W. Stegmüller's reconstruction of Wittgenstein's 'Philosophy of logic and mathematics', in *Hauptströmungen der Gegenwartsphilosophie* (Stuttgart: Kröner, 1969), pp. 673ff.

44 ibid., 685ff.

45 Charles S. Peirce, 'The function of belief', collected papers, ed. C. Hartshorne and R. Heiss (Cambridge, Mass.: Harvard University Press, 1931–5), vol. V, §§58–387.

46 Cf. here my work cited under note 41; also 'Linguistic meaning and intentionality', in G. Deledalle (ed.), *Semiotics and Pragmatics* (Amsterdam/Philadelphia: John Benjamin PC, 1989), pp. 19–70.

47 Cf. finally R. Rorty. 'The priority of democracy to philosophy', in M. Peterson and R. Vaughan (eds), *The Virginia Statute of Religious Freedom* (Cambridge, Mass.: MIT Press, 1987), and *idem*, 'Pragmatism and philosophy', in K. Baynes *et al.* (eds), *After Philosophy: End or Transformation?*, pp. 26–66. Cf. also my argument with Rorty in K.-O. Apel, *Diskurs und Verantwortung* (Frankfurt: Surhkamp, 1988) pp. 394ff.

48 Cf. V. Rossvaer, 'Transzendentalpragmatik, transzendentale Hermeneutik und die Möglichkeit, Auschwitz zu verstehen', in D. Böhler, T. Nordenstam and G. Skirbekk (eds), *Die pragmatische Wende* (Frankfurt: Suhrkamp, 1986), pp. 187–201.

49 In my paper 'Wittgenstein und das Problem des hermeneutischen Verstehens' (1966), reprinted in *Towards a Transformation of Philosophy* (London: Routledge & Kegan Paul, 1980), I have already advanced the thesis that late Dilthey's distinction between 'pragmatic' and 'methodological-hermeneutical understanding' opened the way for an important critical re-evaluation of Wittgenstein's contribution to the theory of understanding. Today I would want to give this point even greater emphasis, as follows: Wittgensein's clarification of understanding seems to reach just as far as Dilthey's concept of 'pragmatic understanding', for which Dilthey, just like Wittgenstein, adopted as his criterion of validation factical agreement in a comportmental *praxis* (e.g., in a 'common sphere' of work). According to Dilthey however, the conditions of the possibility and the criteria of validity are precisely not made available in this way for a – I would like to say: post-conventional, e.g., post-traditionalist – 'methodological understanding' of 'hermeneutics', for instance, for the understanding of foreign cultures or documents stemming from one's own culture from which one has become estranged. Here, where the hermeneutical reflection upon post-Enlightenment culture took its start, it is not possible to adopt the factical agreement in comportmental *praxis* as a sufficient criterion for reciprocal understanding (otherwise, it would have to be admitted that the members of a particular community understood each other better in every respect than any researcher could ever possibly do). Worse, it cannot even be assumed that the methodologico-hermeneutical understanding of a foreign life-form (at the limit, the quasi-hermeneutical understanding of the behaviour of a pride of lions which does not even assume that the lions are capable of language!) suffices for a clear recognition of any such factical agreement with the comportmental *praxis* of the life-form in question (this would exclude a critical understanding from the very outset). In any case, this post-conventional, critically hermeneutical understanding would have to recognize a counter-factual ideal for the communicative understanding of differing forms of *praxis* in an ideal 'interpretative community' (J. Royce). Moreover, in the course of a hermeneutical discussion with the representatives of other life-forms, it would also have to be assumed that there existed sufficient agreement with regard to the normative conditions for an understanding of the differences implicit in the life-form. Cf. here also K.-O. Apel: 'Szientismus oder transzendental Hermeneutik?', in *Transformation der Philosophie*, Bd. II, pp. 178–219. Also in *Towards a Transformation of Philosophy*.

50 Cf. for example my paper cited under note 42.

51 Cf. Peter Strawson, *Scepticism and Naturalism: Some Varieties* (London: Methuen, 1985); also the excellent work of M. Niquet, *Transzendentale Sinnkritik. Untersuchungen zum Problem transzendentaler Argumente* (Frankfurt University: Ph.D. dissertation, 1989, forthcoming with Suhrkamp).

52 Cf. J. Habermas, *Theorie des kommunikativen Handelns* (Frankfurt: Suhrkamp, 1981), Bd. I–III, and also *Moralbewußtsein und kommunkatives Handeln* (Frankfurt: Suhrkamp, 1983). I have to admit I am bothered by the proposal (inspired by Wittgenstein) for a solution to the problem on page 108 of the last-mentioned work. Cf. here K.-O. Apel: 'Normative Begründung der "Kritischen Theorie" durch Rekurs auf lebensweltliche Sittlichkeit? Ein transzendental pragmatisch orientierte Versuch, mit Habermas gegen Habermas zu denken', in A. Honeth (ed.), *Zwischenbetrachtungen. Festschrift für J. Habermas* (Frankfurt: Suhrkamp, 1989), pp. 15–65 (English tr. forthcoming with Cambridge Mass.: MIT Press).

Name Index

Aeschylus 222
Anscombe 2
Antigone 211
Apel, K.-O. 241–71
Aquinas, T. 253
Aristotle 8–10, 15, 22, 67, 69, 81; being
    128; end of philosophy 194;
    Heideggerian assimilation 27–60;
    language 250; logic 118; metaphysics
    208; Nietzschean critique 122;
    practical philosophy 139; space 138,
    145; time 97–8; truth 232
Aubenque, P. 117
Austin 1–2
Ayer, A.J. 1

Becker, O. 206–7
Bergson, H. 1, 136
Berkeley, G. 110
Bloch, E. 212
Bolzano 253
Bradley 3
Brentano, F. 23, 27, 30, 208

Cassirer 107, 117
Celan, P. 7, 207, 222
Cézanne, P. 206, 219–20
Char, R. 216
Collingwood 269

Dastur, F. 158–67
Derrida, J. 203, 242
Descartes, R. 28, 38, 67–95, 97–8, 126,
    208; dream argument 245–6, 248,
257; end of philosophy 194, 195, 196,
    202; language 244, 245, 248;
    objectivity 251; space 139–40
Dewey, J. 254
Dingler, H. 251

Euclid 138–9

Fichte, J.G. 69
Franck, D. 135
Frege 264

Gadamer, H.-G. 55, 257
Galileo 139, 145
Goethe, J.W. von 153, 219, 221
Gogh, V. Van 147

Habermas, J. 265
Hampshire, S. 2
Hegel, G.W.F. 28–9, 69, 74, 83, 118;
    Beginning 122; end of philosophy
    191–4, 198, 202–4; metaphysics 208;
    morality 269; Nietzschean critique
    126; subjectivity 130; time 121
Heidegger, M.: Aristotelian influence
    27–60; Cartesian critique 67–95; end
    of philosophy 191–204; introduction
    to 1–6; Kantian critique 97–118; last
    paths 206–22; Nietzsche critique
    121–33; periods of development
    8–23, 28–9; truth 227–40; turning
    points 17, 20–3; Wittgenstein
    critique 241–71
Heisenberg, W. 214–15, 222

Subject Index

abstraction 251
action, Aristotelian 54
Aesthetic, Transcendental 105, 106, 137
Africa 4
Analytic, Transcendental 105
analytic epistemology 112
Analytic Judgements 112
Analytic of Principles 98
analytical philosophy 1–3, 5–6, 241
Ancient Greeks *see* Aristotle; Greek
  philosophy; Plato; pre-Socratics
anthropocentrism 123
anthropology 49–50, 108
anthropomorphism 129
antiquarian culture 121
anxiety, concept of 108
appearance 105, 113–14, 139
apperception 107, 113, 116
apprehension 107
architectonic 104
architecture 151–3, 200
art 145–7, 150–2, 154, 207–10; classical
  131; determination of thinking
  211–13; saving power 218–22; Will to
  Power 124, 125
assertion, analysis of 100
astronautics 215
atheism 253
Aztecs 4

beauty 129
Bedeutsamkeit 101
Befindlichkeit 43, 51–5
Beginning 122

Being: Cartesian critique 82; character
  of 128; destiny of 204; difference 16;
  finitude of 108; Greek philosophy 8,
  11–12, 21–2; history of 94, 123,
  171–89; horizon 158; Kantian
  critique 97, 108; man 137; *praxis*
  27–60; science of 215; *Sein und Zeit*
  100; sense of 208; Shepherd of 130,
  132; space 134–44; time 36–7; truth
  138, 228; Will to Power 124
Being and Time: Kantian critique 97;
  see also Sein und Zeit
belief 127–8
biology 215
body 136, 145
bridge 151
building 149–50, 151
Bultmann school 206

calculations 125, 126–7
care 136, 144, 209; concept of 108;
  temporality 159
Cartesian ontology 139, 146
chaos 126, 128, 129
child psychology 112
China 216
Christianity 201
circle 128, 186–9
cogito 69, 71, 75–8, 83–95, 97
Cold War 4
commencement of thinking 203–4
communication 132
communism 4
computer science 191, 196